*Guide to Research*
*in*
# CLASSICAL
# ART
*and*
# MYTHOLOGY

Guide to Research
in
# CLASSICAL
# ART
and
# MYTHOLOGY

Frances Van Keuren

American Library Association
CHICAGO AND LONDON
1991

Cover and text designed by Harriett Banner

Composed by WordWorks, Inc. in Palatino
on Xyvision/Cg8600

Printed on 50-pound Glatfelter, a pH-neutral stock,
and bound in B-grade Holliston linen cloth by
Edwards Brothers, Inc.

The paper used in this publication meets the mini-
mum requirements of American National Standard
for Information Sciences—Permanence of Paper for
Printed Library Materials, ANSI Z39.48–1984. ∞

**Library of Congress Cataloging-in-Publication Data**

Van Keuren, Frances Dodds, 1946–
    Guide to research in classical art and mythology
/ by Frances Van Keuren.
        p.    cm.
    Includes bibliographical references and index.
    ISBN 0-8389-0564-1
    1. Mythology, Classical, in art. 2. Art, Classical.
I. Title.
N7760.V3   1991
709′.38—dc20                                         91-11122
                                                          CIP

Printed in the United States of America.

95  94  93  92  91        5  4  3  2  1

*To my husband David, in appreciation
for his patience and support.*

# CONTENTS

# ACKNOWLEDGMENTS

GUIDE TO RESEARCH IN CLASSICAL ART AND MYTHOLOGY has been written over a number of years. It would never have been completed without the generous assistance of many people and institutions. First, I would like to thank three graduate students in a seminar at the University of Georgia who wrote, under my direction, first drafts of several entries from Part Three: Melissa Loring Bryan, who wrote a draft of the entry "Athenian Vases"; Edward Alan Ford, who wrote drafts of the entries "Greek Coins," "Roman Republican Coins," "Etruscan Mirrors," and part of the entry "Roman Imperial Coins"; and Steven David Wright, who wrote a draft of part of the entry "Greek Sculpture." Herbert Bloom, senior editor, ALA Books, was a constant inspiration in his astute suggestions regarding the format of the entries and in his friendly support. Susan Brandehoff copyedited the manuscript and smoothed the rough edges of my prose. William R. Clayton from the University of Georgia Library was also a helpful adviser regarding the format of the entries, and he kindly ordered many of the books which are included in the GUIDE.

Professor R. Ross and Nancy Holloway from Brown University read all the entries and offered many useful suggestions on their content. They also graciously provided hospitality during the two and a half months when I was working on the GUIDE at Brown University. These additional scholars read entries and suggested changes: Professor Timothy N. Gantz from the University of Georgia; Professor A. D. Trendall from La Trobe University; Professor Rolf Winkes from Brown University; Carmen Arnold-Biucchi and William E. Metcalf from the American Numismatic Society; Francis D. Campbell from the library of the American Numismatic Society; and Judith J. Kelly from the University of Georgia Library, who also introduced me to many references dealing with postclassical art.

I would also like to extend my deep-felt appreciation to the staffs from these libraries, where I conducted research for the GUIDE: the University of Georgia Library, whose Fine Arts, Interlibrary Loan, and Reference Departments were particularly helpful; the Brown University Library; the Avery Library at Columbia University; and the library of the American Numismatic Society.

Research for the GUIDE was made possible through a Faculty Research Grant from the University of Georgia for summer 1984; a Departmental Summer Research Grant from the Department of Art at the University of Georgia for summer 1985; a research quarter funded by the Department of Art at the University of Georgia for spring 1989; a year's research leave funded by one-third salary from the University of Georgia for 1989/90; and a stipend from Brown University for fall 1989 for serving as Parker Visiting Scholar.

Last, I would like to thank my husband, David Gordon, who never stopped supporting me through all the ups and downs of preparing the manuscript. This book is dedicated to him.

# INTRODUCTION

Like librarians, classical archaeologists are classifiers. Both classify in order to determine the basic characteristics of the objects in their charge. Archaeological classification relates artifacts with the same or similar characteristics to one another. Even at its most elementary level, the task of classification involves the interpretation of many aspects of an object: its decoration, original function, date and place of manufacture, and artist. The difficulty of achieving such classification cannot be underestimated, and lively scholarly debate often prevents universal acceptance of a single possible classification. This difficulty is brought about by the fact that only a small percentage of ancient artifacts has survived, and the examples that do survive are often in a fragmentary or battered state and must be restored. The problem is frequently compounded by a lack of knowledge about the situations of the antiquities upon their discovery. Many surviving antiquities were not uncovered in formal excavations, but were chance finds whose original placement and associated objects were not recorded. Furthermore, most of ancient literature, which would allow us to perceive artifacts from the viewpoint of the ancient mentality, has been lost. In spite of these difficulties, dedicated archaeologists from this century and the last have labored to accomplish the classification of many thousands of antiquities. Achieving the classification of an object makes possible further study by art historians.

# PURPOSE OF THE WORK

Classification is the foundation of archaeology, and it would seem that the classified antiquities would be immediately accessible to scholars and students wishing to investigate other important aspects of the objects, such as their possible influence on the iconographic or stylistic content of contemporary or later art. Iconography, the study of the thematic content of art, is a very important aspect of art history. The representation of mythological figures in the art of different ancient periods and places and in postclassical times yields important clues about changing attitudes towards life and religion. Mythology in art must be investigated along with mythology in literature. In cases when both the literature and art from a period survive, reflections of the literary tradition and deviations from it can be traced in the art. In other cases where only the art survives, the lost literary tradition can be tentatively reconstructed on the basis of the art.

Unfortunately, the major publications containing classifications of antiquities have not provided easy access to the material. These authoritative classifications, written in several languages, list large numbers of antiquities but present them in complex organizational schemes; an intricate terminology of classification has arisen that refers to the types and aspects of objects. Nonetheless, the use of these complicated compilations of antiquities is essential for valid research on the countless specific problems of the field. Yet learning to use the research tools is a formidable task requiring assistance of several kinds.

GUIDE TO RESEARCH IN CLASSICAL ART AND MYTHOLOGY enables students and scholars to use these reference tools, and thereby encourages excellence in research techniques. This purpose is enfolded in a larger one of guiding researchers in their investigations. After a major reference is presented, related reference books, handbooks, and specialized studies are successively identified. They are arranged in categories that correspond to steps in the research process. The resultant arrangements suggest patterns in the use of all the types of research tools. By following these patterns, researchers should be able to acquire enough information on the art itself and sufficient familiarity with previous research approaches to undertake original research.

The procedures recommended in the GUIDE represent the library research process, as opposed to research in the field. The reference books are described in a way intended to direct students and scholars to the monographs and articles that deal with specific research topics. The latter will inform users of aspects that have already been discussed and suggest possible new areas of investigation. For those who wish to publish their studies, on-site examination of the objects is essential. Nonetheless, the collocation of reference sources and specialized studies in this guide facilitates the accomplishment of valid exercises for students and preliminary research for scholars within the walls of the library.

## FORM OF THE WORK

The entries in the GUIDE are presented in three parts. Part One includes the most general references on Greek, Etruscan, and Roman art and architecture; Part Two describes references dealing with mythology in the art and literature of antiquity and postclassical times; and Part Three concentrates on references that consider particular media of ancient art. These media are particularly rich in mythological content. Other media, such as Etruscan painting and Roman sculpture, are reviewed under the general entries in Part One.

Every entry includes four types of reference—a major reference, whose title appears at the beginning of the entry and whose contents and arrangement are thoroughly described in the entry; complementary references, which are to be used along with the major reference and are more summarily described; handbooks, which are briefly cited as sources for background information; and supplementary sources, which are presented as examples of particular research focuses. Major references are corpora that bring together significant numbers of antiquities and present them according to category, in lists or straightforward descriptions without subjective conclusions. The major references were selected on the basis of their pertinent contents, reliability and completeness, date of publication (the most up-to-date reference of its kind was selected), and consistency of format. A major reference can be a strictly factual compilation, a comprehensive handbook, or an encyclopedia. A complementary reference can assume the same forms as a major reference, or it can also be a dictionary or a bibliography. It contains a significant body of information that adds to the material contained in the major reference. A handbook is a relatively recent and reliable general account of the art form being considered. Finally, a supplementary source is a scholarly monograph or article that discusses a particular aspect of the art form with a specific art-historical research focus. Since the use of research tools is interrelated, the same work can function as a major reference in one entry and as a complementary reference or a handbook in other entries. Works in English, French, German, Italian, and modern Greek have been included, with a preference given to English titles when there was no superior reference in another language. Translations of non-English titles appear in parentheses after the actual titles.

The entry for each major reference is broken down into the following parts: *Art Form*, in which the object type encompassed by the major reference is introduced through a description of its basic appearance and use and its art historical significance; *Research Use,* in which the types of research that the reference permits are elucidated; *Organization,* in which the arrangement of the major reference is thoroughly explained, along with its potentially confusing aspects; *Complementary References,* in which the research tools that should be used with the major reference are outlined; *Handbooks,* in which the factual contents of reliable and up-to-date general accounts of the art form are characterized; *Supplementary Sources,* in which the hypotheses and the research methods of important monographs and articles related in subject matter to the major reference are briefly stated; and *Additional Supplementary Sources,* in which monographs and articles that deal with a less significant body of pertinent material are listed. Throughout the presentation of the categories of supplemental research tools, the relationship of their contents to that of the major reference is made clear.

## USE OF THE WORK

For the student or nonclassicist who desires guidance in the research process, the following procedures are recommended. Begin with the major reference and read the Art Form portion of the entry carefully. If further explanation of the art form is desired, consult the handbooks cited in the fifth part of the entry. Then proceed to Research Use, the second portion of the entry. Please keep in mind that other types of research are possible besides the suggestions that are provided as initial stimuli. The next portion of the entry, Organization, can be used in two ways. If the reference is at hand, read this portion of the entry and confirm all the specifics about the reference's arrangement by an examination of the book itself. If the reference is not immediately available, use the entry's description to help determine whether or not the reference is necessary for your research. Should you decide that you need the reference, find out from your library staff if the book can be ordered through interlibrary loan or consulted at a library in the vicinity.

Once you comprehend the type of information contained in the major reference and the presentation format, turn to the parts of the major reference that relate to your research topic. When all pertinent data in the major reference have been gathered, consult the Complementary References (the books most frequently cited in the major reference and important subsequent literature) and other materials that are mentioned in the major reference. The relevant data from these further references should be collected along with citations of additional bibliographic sources. The latter should be consulted as well.

It is also necessary to consult the Handbooks and the Supplementary Sources sections. The handbooks provide a general overview of the art genre and often present the most commonly accepted theories on famous but problematic pieces. They are also a good source for additional bibliography. Supplementary sources, written by leading scholars, present more controversial hypotheses about major pieces and general trends. These hypotheses need to be given serious consideration because the scholars who have proposed them have a broad knowledge of the art of the period. The footnotes and general bibliographies of the supplementary sources should be reviewed for further bibliography.

In short, the research process is successive. First, the major reference and the complementary references should be used. The data from these references can be more easily understood after consulting the handbooks for general discussions of the art form and major pieces. In the supplementary sources, researchers will be introduced to hypotheses on narrower topics regarding either particular examples or one facet of a group of examples. Through a critical evaluation of the arguments in the supplementary sources and additional monographs and articles, students and scholars will acquire both a familiarity with previously accomplished research and a comprehension of the research methods that were utilized. With this knowledge and critical skill, they can rework flawed arguments or formulate entirely new approaches.

When reading scholarly argumentation or conclusions intended to resolve problems, the researcher should be certain that he or she completely understands what preserved features of the artistic representations have been used as evidence in formulating hypotheses. By so doing, the researcher will be able to discern any weaknesses in arguments that lack secure support in the objects themselves and to suggest new possible solutions for problematic aspects.

I hope that the GUIDE will enable students and scholars to carry out thoughtful research in ancient art with a special regard to its mythological content. There are many ways in which antiquities still need to be studied, and this basic instructional tool can delineate models, particularly in the realm of iconography. These points of departure will nurture deeper insight into the wealth of antiquities that have survived, the literary inspiration that they embodied, and their influence on post-classical art.

*Part One*

# GENERAL
# RESEARCH

# ‹1›

# Greek Art and Architecture

Robertson, Martin. *A History of Greek Art.* 2 vols. New York: Cambridge Univ. Press, 1975.

## ART FORM

In *The Life of Pericles*, Plutarch made these observations regarding the construction of the Periclean buildings on the Athenian Acropolis (translation by J. J. Pollitt):

> As the works rose, shining with grandeur and possessing an inimitable grace of form, and as the artisans strove to surpass one another in the beauty of their workmanship, the rapidity with which the structures were executed was marvellous. . . . There is a certain bloom of newness in each work and an appearance of being untouched by the wear of time. It is as if some ever-flowering life and unaging spirit had been infused into the creation of them.

The "grace of form" and "bloom of newness" which Plutarch ascribed to the Periclean temples are qualities that are also apparent in Greek art in general. They were the natural products of the fact that the public art of the Greeks was intended to exemplify the civic ideals of aesthetic and moral harmony. Public art took the form of sacred and

9

secular buildings that were used by the Greek community; the sculptures, paintings, and mosaics that decorated the exterior and interior entablatures, walls, and floors of these structures; and freestanding sculptures of monumental to miniature scale that were placed inside or outside these buildings. Another category of public art was memorials in cemeteries, which could be as modest as a painted vase or as colossal as the Mausoleum at Halicarnassus. Greek coins, many of which circulated outside the city-states that minted them, constituted a further type of public art. All these classes of monuments were intended to be viewed by the public, and the ideal composure of the contemporary and mythological characters whose stories formed their decoration was to be emulated.

The private art of the Greeks tended to be less formal and serious. It consisted of such objects as painted vases of the household, gems, metalware pieces such as mirrors, statuettes made of various materials, and wall paintings and mosaics. In this art there is a greater variety of thematic content, particularly in the realm of genre scenes, and the emphasis on ideal conduct is not so relentless. Nonetheless, the beauty and idealization of individual figures and the balance of compositions involving more than one figure are traits which are shared with public art.

Unlike the more changeless art of powerful states such as Egypt, Greek art underwent a rapid succession of developments that led to the achievement of a human figure that was convincingly naturalistic when depicted both at rest and in motion. No one is certain why Greek artists were able to achieve such a rapid mastery of the human figure. Perhaps this accomplishment was made possible in part by the Greek love of athletics and the ample opportunities that competitions provided for the observation of nude athletes in action. In any case, there is a discernible progression of ever more naturalistic styles of Greek art—Geometric, Orientalizing, Archaic, Classical, and Hellenistic, each of which has distinct and unique characteristics. Yet at the same time there are traits that are common to all the styles. In particular, a sense of calm and control and a distinct articulation of individual components are overriding tendencies that persist throughout all periods of Greek art. Surely it can be said that these qualities reflect the unchanging and acute mental attitudes of the ancient Greeks.

# RESEARCH USE

A History of Greek Art, by Martin Robertson, is the only lengthy discussion in English of the developments of all the media in Greek art, including architectural sculpture but excluding architecture. Written in an interesting style which presents both accepted facts and the author's conclusions regarding controversial issues, Robertson's account is comprehensible for "anyone who is interested" in Greek art. The standard periods of Greek art from the Geometric to the Hellenistic receive attention in separate chapters. In addition, a prologue outlines aspects of continuity between prehistoric products and the Iron-Age art that forms the main focus of discussion, while an epilogue surveys Greek influence on Etruscan and Roman art. Authoritative publications of all art works mentioned in the text are cited in the notes and many works are illustrated. General and museum indexes provide quick access to discussions in the text and notes on particular artists, media, places, themes, and objects.

Because of its length of more than seven hundred pages of text and notes, this is not a book that can be used as required reading for a class on Greek art. For that purpose, *A Shorter History of Greek Art*, by the same author, is recommended (see Complementary References below). But this work can be dipped into at any point for a fascinating overview of the significance, beauty, and scholarly problems that accompany the study of all the major monuments of Greek sculpture and painting—those that survive, those that are known from Roman copies, and those that are lost but described in ancient literature. Robertson's reference also devotes attention to typical or important examples of the minor arts. In addition, *A History of Greek Art* elucidates the historical circumstances that helped shape the character of works from different periods and places, and it points out both the interrelationships between media and the impact of important art centers on products from other cities. The views presented throughout are unique to Robertson rather than being a pastiche of other scholars' opinions. This lends a coherence to the account, as well as a freshness, in the sense that each monument has clearly been looked at anew from the standpoint of its place within the whole development of Greek art. In short, Robertson's study provides a wealth of ideas in areas such as aesthetics, iconography, chronology, and stylistic development; the relative stature and functions of different media; and the influential positions of certain ancient centers. It can be read simply for its information on individual works and their aesthetic and cultural contexts, or it can be consulted as a useful source for research questions and possible directions that can be taken to shed new light on these questions.

## ORGANIZATION

*A History of Greek Art* is a two-volume work. Volume 1 contains all the text and volume 2 the notes, bibliography, plates, and indexes. Both volumes have tables of contents at the front—volume 1 for the contents of both

volumes and volume 2 only for its contents. The text of volume 1 contains eight chapters in addition to the prologue and epilogue described
above: one chapter on Geometric and Orientalizing art, two on Archaic
art, one on Late Archaic and Early Classical art, one on High Classical
art, two on Late Classical art, and one on Hellenistic art. With the exception of chapter 1, each chapter is broken down into subheadings that
deal with specific media, and often with regional styles within media.
Robertson explains his organization of the chapters thus: "In my book
the main chapter-divisions are chronological, and an attempt is made to
present the changes in the different branches of representational art as
aspects of a single historical development." But the author also cautions:
"I mention any work at any point where it comes conveniently into my
argument, which may be a long way out of its chronological context."
The reader should therefore always make use of the general index or the
museum index at the back of volume 2 when searching for all mentions
of a particular monument.

The notes that accompany the text in volume 1 can be found at the
beginning of volume 2. They are numbered separately for each chapter.
The relevant page numbers from the text are found at the top of each
right-hand page of the notes, a feature which enables the researcher to
speedily locate any note he or she is interested in. The notes make use
of bibliographic abbreviations that are explained in the "Abbreviations
and Bibliography" which follow the notes. Here full bibliographic entries
and abbreviations are listed together in a strictly alphabetical order. Four
additional references are named in the addenda on the last page of the
"Abbreviations and Bibliography." Robertson states: "The bibliography,
combined with a list of abbreviations, includes all works mentioned in
the notes."

After the "Abbreviations and Bibliography" in volume 2 is the "List
of Illustrations," which provides information on the figures and plates
that follow. As the researcher will soon discover, the labels in this list
are less complete than the captions which appear under the illustrations themselves, but they do name the sources for the illustrations—
information which is not repeated in the captions. The illustrations
consist of a map of Italy, Greece, and Western Turkey; three plates of
drawings; and 192 plates of black-and-white photographs, unfortunately
of mediocre quality. (According to Cambridge University Press, a reprint
with improved plates will soon be available.) The captions for the
photographs include the following information: the medium of the
work; its provenance, current location, and museum inventory number;
date; height; and the page in the text where it is discussed. Strangely,
the mythological and nonmythological themes of works are not identified in the captions and artists are named only for works that bear artists'
signatures.

At the end of volume 2 are the two indexes—"General" and "Museums and Collections." Both are comprehensive in their references to the contents of the text in volume 1, but they only refer to something found in the notes in volume 2 if it has not been mentioned in the text, or (in the case of objects) if additional information can be found in the notes. Objects and monuments are listed in the general index under their provenances and artists, while they are listed in the museum index under their current locations, media, and inventory numbers. The general index also provides access to discussions of particular themes and mythological characters in Greek art, as well as art forms, media, and historical personages and places.

## COMPLEMENTARY REFERENCES

In *A History of Greek Art*, Robertson does not repeat bibliography on Archaic statues and Athenian vases that can be found in five other references: Richter's *Kouroi* and *Korai* (see chapter 9, "Greek Sculpture," under Supplementary Sources); and Beazley's *Attic Black-figure Vase-painters*, *Attic Red-figure Vase-painters*, and *Paralipomena* (see the beginning of chapter 10, "Athenian Vases").

After finishing *A History of Greek Art*, Martin Robertson went on to write *A Shorter History of Greek Art*, whose text and notes of slightly more than two hundred pages make it a suitable book for classroom use. Although fewer works are discussed in *A Shorter History of Greek Art*, illustrations are conveniently interspersed with text and they are darker and more legible than those in volume 2 of *A History of Greek Art*. Bibliography published after Robertson's longer study is cited in the "Notes" and marked with asterisks in the "Abbreviations and Bibliography" of *A Shorter History of Greek Art*.

General books on Greek art as a whole or on the different media that have been published after *A Shorter History of Greek Art* are cited in the "Selected Bibliography" of the new revised edition of *Greek Art*, by John Boardman. Unlike Robertson's books, which deal with all preserved evidence relating to Greek art, Boardman's summary of the stylistic and thematic developments in the different media of Greek art concentrates on surviving originals. It includes recently discovered original works, such as the bronze warriors from Riace, which Robertson's books do not discuss. Boardman's handbook can also be used to advantage along with Robertson's references as a good source of color photographs. *The Art of Greece*, by Kostas Papaioannou, is another source of excellent color photographs. This reference is also useful for its complete record in black-and-white photographs of sequences of architectural sculptures such as the Parthenon frieze. For recently published literature on Greek sculpture and for recently discovered masterpieces, the reader is urged to consult the bibliography at the end of volume 1 and the text and plates of Andrew Stewart's comprehensive new study, *Greek Sculpture: An Exploration* (see chapter 9, "Greek Sculpture," under Complementary References). For new and in-print surveys of Greek art, the reader should look at the latest edition of the *Subject Guide to Books in Print* under "Art, Greco-Roman" and "Art, Greek."

*The Art of Greece 1400–31 B.C.: Sources and Documents,* by J. J. Pollitt, collects and translates many of the Greek and Latin passages on Greek art which Robertson refers to but often does not translate himself. Translations of passages from different authors that describe works by particular artists can be quickly located by using Pollitt's "Index of Artists." These passages can then be matched up with the authors, books, and chapter numbers that are cited in Robertson's notes.

An excellent companion volume for *A History of Greek Art* is *The Art and Architecture of Ancient Greece,* by John Boardman, José Dörig, Werner Fuchs, and Max Hirmer. While this survey avoids the scholarly problems of interpretation and reconstruction that Robertson's book delves into, it provides many possible insights into the ancient view of Greek art through its consistent emphasis on the aesthetic qualities of each work discussed. Furthermore, its splendid black-and-white and color photographs by Max Hirmer give a truer impression of the appearance of major works than the often pale photos in Robertson's reference, and the descriptions, plans, and reconstructions of monuments with architectural sculptures in this book can be consulted as supplements to Robertson's treatments of the sculpture from the same buildings.

*Greek Architecture,* by A. W. Lawrence, provides additional explanations of the architectural aspects of important buildings with architectural sculptures, such as the Parthenon. Lawrence makes clear in his text and illustrations where the sculptures were positioned on these buildings, and he notes aesthetic refinements in the execution both of the architectural members and the sculptures. Besides the seventeen chapters covering Greek architecture of the historic periods, Lawrence's book contains six chapters on Greek architecture of the Neolithic period and the Bronze Age. Thus it is valuable for those interested in the architectural context of wall paintings from the Greek Bronze-Age palaces. Publications on particular buildings are cited both in the volume's notes and in the lengthy bibliography that follows the notes. The bibliography is broken down by the references pertinent to each chapter.

For summaries of the urban development and physical remains (particularly monuments with and without architectural sculptures) of ancient Greek cities in existence from circa 750 B.C. and onward, the reader should consult *The Princeton Encyclopedia of Classical Sites.* This exhaustive reference lists cities alphabetically by the names the sites had in antiquity; modern names that are different from ancient names are listed, with cross-references made to the correct ancient names. The locations of all the sites included are shown on twenty-four maps at the back of the volume; each encyclopedia entry refers the reader to the proper map. While this volume has no illustrations other than the maps, the bibliography at the end of each entry has superscript letters after the references which contain illustrations of different types: [M] means the reference cited includes maps; [P] denotes plans; and [I] illustrations. Another excellent source for summaries of archaeological remains from major Greek cities is *The Oxford Classical Dictionary*, edited by N. G. L. Hammond and H. H. Scullard. Like *The Princeton Encyclopedia of Classical Sites*, this reference is not illustrated but mentions other publications with plans and plates. Unlike *The Princeton Encyclopedia*, it places emphasis on the roles of Greek cities in promoting literature, and it includes information on the Bronze Age in entries for specific mainland Greek cities and in general entries entitled "Mycenaean Civilization" and "Minoan Civilization." Besides entries on Greek cities, *The Oxford Classical Dictionary* has entries on some regions of Greece; on major artists; on art forms, such as "Sculpture, Greek"; and on disciplines, such as "Archaeology, Classical."

In addition to the above references, two illustrated encyclopedias contain much useful information on Greek art and architecture as well as extensive citations of scholarly publications of all kinds. One of these references, *Encyclopedia of World Art*, has a general entry on "Greek Art" and the following entries on periods of Greek art: "Cretan-Mycenaean Art"; "Geometric Style"; "Orientalizing Style"; "Archaic Art"; "Classic Art"; "Hellenistic Art"; and "Hellenistic-Roman Art." In addition, the surviving architectural remains of many Greek sites are described in the long articles entitled "Greece" and "Italy." A discussion of a particular Greek site in one of these countries or elsewhere can be located quickly through the use of volume 15, the *Index*. General articles on media in art, such as the entry "Ceramics," often include sections on Greek products. The same holds true for articles on art forms, such as "Portraiture," and on themes in art, such as "Myth and Fable." The researcher can also find summaries of regional styles of Greek art, such as the entry "Attic and Boeotian Art," and there are articles on the most important Greek artists (less important ones who receive mention, but not whole articles, are cited in the *Index*). In the *Supplement* volume, pages 69–82, new finds of Greek art and architecture are summarized and illustrated, new research methods are explicated, and recent publications are named.

*Enciclopedia dell'arte antica, classica e orientale* (Encyclopedia of Ancient Art: Classical and Oriental) also has both general and specific articles. The most general article on Greek art can be found under "Greca, Arte" (Greek Art); articles on periods of Greek art appear under such titles as

"Orientalizzante, Arte" (Orientalizing Art). There are entries for categories of art, such as "Attici, Vasi" (Attic Vases); for specific topics, such as "Apoteosi" (Apotheosis); and for names of mythological characters, such as "Eracle" (Heracles). Furthermore, there are separate entries for building types, such as "Teatro e Odeon" (Theater and Odeum); archaeological sites, such as "Olimpia" (Olympia); and noted archaeologists, such as "Schliemann, Heinrich." The most famous and the most obscure Greek artists, for example, "Policleto" (Polycleitus), also have entries. The *Supplemento* volume adds new articles and updates articles in the original *Enciclopedia*, particularly those on sites, artists, and media; and the *Atlante dei complessi figurati* (Atlas of Figured Monuments) provides drawings of the entire narrative decoration of major monuments and of capitals from the columns of important structures. The *Enciclopedia* has no index, so the researcher must remember to look up names in their Italian forms (see the Italian renderings of names cited above).

The latest volumes of *L'Année philologique* (Philological Year), a comprehensive annual annotated bibliography of all types of publications on the classical world, can be consulted for the most recent scholarly literature on Greek art and archaeology. The researcher can consult the section in the bibliography entitled "Archéologie grecque" (Greek Archaeology) for publications on monuments from historic periods from the Greek mainland. For Bronze-Age Greek art and art of historic periods from the Greek colonies, the section entitled "Archéologie préclassique et périphérique" (Preclassical and Peripheral Archaeology) should be reviewed. The reader should note that literature on Greek coins is listed separately under the heading "Numismatique" (Numismatics). For those interested in mythology in Greek art, the section entitled "Religion et mythologie grecque et mycénienne" (Greek and Mycenaean Religion and Mythology) is recommended. Literature on Greek artists whose ancient names are known and on historical and mythological personages portrayed in Greek art can be located quickly through the use of each volume's "Index Nominum Antiquorum" (Index of Ancient Names). Publications on geographical sites are listed under the name of each location in the "Index Geographicus" (Geographical Index). Entries in *L'Année philologique* are numbered sequentially; these are the numbers that are cited in the two indexes.

*Art Index*, a quarterly compilation of citations from major journals, provides easy access to the most recent and significant periodical literature. Besides listing articles under the names of the authors, *Art Index* repeats citations under various subject headings. For example, the researcher can find general literature under the headings "Art, Greek" and "Architecture, Greek." Additional headings for media, such as "Pottery, Greek" and "Vases, Greek," and for Greek mythology, such as

"Iconography, Classical," provide access to articles of a more limited scope. More specific literature can be found under the names of Greek artists, historical and mythological characters, sites, major monuments, and monument types. *Art Index* can be searched by computer on the Wilsonline online vendor service for the period from September 1984 onwards.

## Bibliographic Entries for Complementary References

*L'Année philologique: Bibliographie critique et analytique de l'antiquité gréco-latine.* Paris: Société d'édition "Les Belles Lettres," 1928- .

*Art Index: A Cumulative Author and Subject Index to a Selected List of Fine Arts Periodicals and Museum Bulletins.* New York: H. W. Wilson, 1929/30- .

Boardman, John. *Greek Art.* New rev. ed. World of Art. London: Thames & Hudson, 1985.

Boardman, John, José Dörig, Werner Fuchs, and Max Hirmer. *The Art and Architecture of Ancient Greece.* London: Thames & Hudson, 1967.

*Enciclopedia dell'arte antica, classica e orientale.* Edited by Ranuccio Bianchi Bandinelli. 7 vols., *Supplemento,* and *Atlante dei complessi figurati.* Rome: Istituto della Enciclopedia Italiana, 1958–73.

*Encyclopedia of World Art.* Translation of *Enciclopedia universale dell'arte.* 14 vols. New York: McGraw-Hill, 1959–67. Vol. 15, *Index.* New York: McGraw-Hill, 1968. Vol. 16, *Supplement: World Art in Our Time.* Edited by Bernard S. Myers. New York: McGraw-Hill and Publishers Guild, 1983.

Hammond, N. G. L., and H. H. Scullard, eds. *The Oxford Classical Dictionary.* 2d ed. Oxford: Clarendon Press, 1970.

Lawrence, A. W. *Greek Architecture.* 4th ed. Revised with additions by R. A. Tomlinson. The Pelican History of Art. New York: Penguin, 1983.

Papaioannou, Kostas. *The Art of Greece.* Translated by Mark Paris. New York: Abrams, 1989.

Pollitt, J. J. *The Art of Greece 1400–31 B.C.: Sources and Documents.* Sources and Documents in the History of Art Series, edited by H. W. Janson. Englewood Cliffs, N.J.: Prentice-Hall, 1965.

*The Princeton Encyclopedia of Classical Sites.* Edited by Richard Stillwell, William L. MacDonald, and Marian Holland McAllister. Princeton: Princeton Univ. Press, 1976.

Robertson, Martin. *A Shorter History of Greek Art.* New York: Cambridge Univ. Press, 1981.

Stewart, Andrew. *Greek Sculpture: An Exploration.* 2 vols. New Haven and London: Yale Univ. Press, 1990.

*Subject Guide to Books in Print.* New York: R. R. Bowker, 1990- .

# HANDBOOKS

*The New Century Handbook of Greek Art and Architecture,* edited by Catherine B. Avery, is recommended for the reader who wishes to find a quick summary of the output of a particular Greek artist or of the surviving ancient buildings at an important Greek site. The reference also contains explanations of artistic and architectural terms. Further entries are included on famous Greek sculptures and on Roman copies of Greek masterpieces; they can be found under the names by which the sculptures are commonly known, such as "Elgin Marbles" and "Farnese Bull." This reference is conveniently arranged with entries in alphabetical order and is written in a pleasantly nontechnical style. It is illustrated by both line drawings and photographs. No general or specific bibliography is provided.

*A Handbook of Greek Art,* by Gisela M. A. Richter, provides well-illustrated and reliable surveys of all media of Greek art; ancient literary sources are frequently referred to or quoted. This comprehensive handbook contains separate chapters on architecture, large sculptures (free-standing and architectural), statuettes of all materials except terra-cotta, metalware vessels and other objects, terra-cotta statuettes and reliefs, gems, coins, jewelry, paintings and mosaics, pottery, furniture, textiles, glassware and glazes, ornamental motifs such as palmettes, and inscriptions. At the back of the volume is a chronologically arranged list of important works of Greek sculpture, with page numbers of textual discussions and bibliographic citations. Additional publications are mentioned in the notes and listed in the bibliography, where references are arranged by chapter. The last page of the bibliography of the eighth and ninth editions of Richter's *Handbook* has addenda consisting of recent general publications in English and publications in different languages on recent finds.

For the reader who wishes to investigate the stylistic and technical development of each medium, R. M. Cook's *Greek Art: Its Development, Character and Influence* is recommended. Like Richter, Cook surveys each medium, including architecture, in a separate chapter. Unlike Richter, he provides detailed discussions of the steps in the mastery of such complexities as truly three-dimensional postures of human figures in statuary. Also unlike Richter, he stresses problems in dating works in each medium and relates what has survived to what seems to have once existed. An unfortunate feature in Cook's handbook is his tendency to make frequent reference to works which he does not illustrate and for which he provides no literature either in his "Notes on Museums" or in his bibliography.

An old handbook, but one which is still useful, is *Greek Sculpture and Painting to the End of the Hellenistic Period,* by the eminent scholars J. D. Beazley and Bernard Ashmole. This thin volume contains concise and eloquent surveys of the stylistic development of sculptures and paintings (especially vase-paintings) from the major regional schools in Greece. Additions to the text of the 1932 edition are found after the text and before the updated bibliography in the 1966 reprint. Bernard Ashmole is also the author of two parts of the handsome volume, *Art of the Ancient World: Painting, Pottery, Sculpture, Architecture from Egypt, Mesopotamia, Greece, and Rome*. One of these parts is a lengthy discussion of Iron-Age Greek art and the other part presents briefer surveys of Cypriote art, Etruscan art, and Roman art. Each of Ashmole's chapters on Greek art reviews all the art forms from a single period or subdivision of a period; pottery and painting are examined first, then architecture and sculpture. The author confines his sensitive and informative commentary to works and buildings which are illustrated in the numerous black-and-white and color photos and line drawings. Thus his arguments on the stylistic developments of the different media of Greek art are easy to follow and remember. Specific and general studies of Greek art are identified in the notes and the bibliography at the back of the volume. This reference also contains a brief but illuminating survey by Henriette Antonia Groenewegen-Frankfort of significant aspects of Greek Bronze-Age art from Crete and the mainland.

*Arts of the Ancient Greeks*, by Richard Brilliant, presents an interesting overview of the stylistic and intellectual development of Greek art from the era of the Bronze-Age Mycenaeans to the end of the Hellenistic period. Brilliant achieves this difficult goal by juxtaposing sensitive stylistic analyses with pertinent ancient texts on the art works themselves and on prevailing cultural attitudes. *Arts of the Ancient Greeks* has numerous black-and-white and color photographs, drawings, and reconstructions, which are placed alongside the text. A useful bibliography follows each chapter. An especially valuable feature of the book is its introductory essay on the history of research methods used in the study of Greek and Roman art, archaeology, and architecture. The volume's only flaw is an occasional error in fact and identification.

*Greek Art*, by Walter-Herwig Schuchhardt, lucidly demonstrates how style, composition, and thematic content are combined in Greek monuments from different periods and by different artists, with varying intended impacts. Schuchhardt illustrates every work he discusses, some with color photos, and also provides detailed labels for the reproductions that furnish additional information; for example, surviving paint traces on marble sculptures are noted. Particularly helpful for the comprehension of buildings with architectural sculptures are several reconstruction drawings in the portion of the volume devoted to architecture. A brief but useful bibliography can be found immediately before the index.

A trilogy of beautifully illustrated books by Jean Charbonneaux, Roland Martin, and François Villard presents eloquent summaries of the formal and narrative development of Greek painting and pottery, sculpture, and architecture. These volumes are entitled *Archaic Greek Art (620–480 B.C.); Classical Greek Art (480–330 B.C.);* and *Hellenistic Art*

*(330–50 B.C.)*. Most of the art works discussed are illustrated with adjacent black-and-white and color photographs; plans and reconstructions of buildings and sites appear at the back of all three volumes. Beyond these architectural drawings in each book are a chronological chart of historical events and major art works; a list of abbreviations and a lengthy bibliography broken down by medium and by general and specific studies; a list of illustrations with more information (such as dates and materials) than the labels on the photos and drawings themselves; a glossary-index which explains real and mythological names and technical terms and refers the reader to textual discussions and illustrations; and maps which have alphabetical indexes of places.

*The Art of Ancient Greece and Rome from the Rise of Greece to the Fall of Rome*, by the renowned Italian scholar Giovanni Becatti, is a sophisticated study of the religious and secular functions and aesthetic qualities of Greek, Etruscan, and Roman art. Becatti's discussions of the different periods of Greek art distinguish among the various regional styles and do not neglect the dynamic products of the Greek colonies of South Italy and Sicily, as is so often the case in surveys. The author constantly emphasizes evidence for interaction between contemporary ancient cultures, and he takes special care to elucidate the impacts of Greek art and artists on Etruscan and Roman art. Becatti's study is accompanied by many high-quality black-and-white and color photos, and a lengthy glossary and a bibliography, arranged by medium, appear at the back.

*The Architecture of Ancient Greece*, by William Bell Dinsmoor, is a comprehensive illustrated handbook that describes important examples of Greek architecture from the Neolithic period and the Bronze Age, the historic Greek periods, and the Roman Empire. Religious and secular buildings from these periods are presented as part of the general development of Greek architecture, whose high point is considered to be the era of the Periclean embellishment of Athens. When each structure is discussed, both major and minor design features are described, and any similarities with other buildings are noted; architectural sculptures are also mentioned. Footnotes that elaborate on some of Dinsmoor's observations appear at the bottom of many pages, while a lengthy bibliography broken down by topics and archaeological sites is located at the back of the volume. This is followed by a list of abbreviations for journals that are cited in the bibliography. Next is a detailed glossary of architectural terms. The "Index to Text and Illustrations," which is divided into three parts, refers the reader to textual discussions, notes, figures and plates, and bibliography. The 1975 reprint differs from the third revised edition only in the addition of a new preface, which mentions major discoveries after 1950, and in the printing of new photographs.

There are also handbooks devoted to different media of Greek art. *Greek Painted Pottery*, by R. M. Cook, provides a comprehensive introduction to this important art form (for further references on the painted vases of Athens and the Greek colonies in the West, see chapter 10, "Athenian Vases," and chapter 11, "South Italian and Sicilian Vases"). Cook reviews the products and interrelations of all the major Greek and Etruscan workshops and also explains shapes, methods of manufacture, inscriptions, dating, and the types of information that painted vases yield. For instance, when a deposit of painted pottery whose approximate date is known is found beneath the foundation of a building, we know that the structure must be later in date than the pottery. For handbooks on other media of Greek art, see chapter 9, "Greek Sculpture," chapter 13, "Ancient Engraved Gems," and chapter 14, "Greek Coins."

## Bibliographic Entries for Handbooks

Ashmole, Bernard, and Groenewegen-Frankfort, Henriette Antonia. *Art of the Ancient World: Painting, Pottery, Sculpture, Architecture from Egypt, Mesopotamia, Greece, and Rome.* Janson Art History Series. Englewood Cliffs, N. J.: Prentice-Hall, 1971.

Avery, Catherine B., ed. *The New Century Handbook of Greek Art and Architecture.* New York: Appleton, 1972.

Beazley, J. D., and Bernard Ashmole. *Greek Sculpture and Painting to the End of the Hellenistic Period.* 1932. Reprint with additions. New York: Cambridge Univ. Press, 1966.

Becatti, Giovanni. *The Art of Ancient Greece and Rome from the Rise of Greece to the Fall of Rome.* Translated by John Ross. New York: Abrams, 1967.

Brilliant, Richard. *Arts of the Ancient Greeks.* New York: McGraw-Hill, [1973].

Charbonneaux, Jean, Roland Martin, and François Villard. *Archaic Greek Art (620–480 B.C.).* Translated by James Emmons and Robert Allen. The Arts of Mankind. New York: Braziller, 1971.

———. *Classical Greek Art (480–330 B.C.).* Translated by James Emmons. The Arts of Mankind. New York: Braziller, 1972.

———. *Hellenistic Art (330–50 B.C.).* Translated by Peter Green. The Arts of Mankind. New York: Braziller, 1973.

Cook, R. M. *Greek Art: Its Development, Character and Influence.* New York: Farrar, 1973.

———. *Greek Painted Pottery.* 2d ed. London: Methuen, 1972.

Dinsmoor, William Bell. *The Architecture of Ancient Greece.* 3d ed. rev. 1950. Reprint with new preface and new photos. New York: Norton, 1975.

Richter, Gisela M. A. *A Handbook of Greek Art.* 9th ed. New York: Da Capo, 1987.

Schuchhardt, Walter-Herwig. *Greek Art.* Translated by Sabine MacCormack. New York: Universe, 1972.

# SUPPLEMENTARY SOURCES

To arrive at a full understanding of Greek art, the researcher must not only come to appreciate it for its mastery of such modern concepts as the "internal dynamics" of lines, but he or she must also make an attempt to comprehend the goals of Greek artists and the response of ancient viewers. The evidence for the latter type of inquiry consists of passages that are scattered among many ancient authors. Fortunately, this material has been brought together and synthesized by J. J. Pollitt in *The Ancient View of Greek Art: Criticism, History, and Terminology*. The bulk of Pollitt's volume is a long glossary consisting of two alphabetized lists of Greek and Latin terms used by ancient authors when making critical comments about Greek art. Each entry in the glossary is a chronologically arranged selection of passages from ancient authors, most of which are quoted and translated; interpretive commentary, in which Pollitt explains what the term seems to have signified, appears after each selection of passages. The glossary is preceded by a prologue with a summary of modern criticism of Greek art, and by chapters on the evolution of art criticism in antiquity and on the more formalized ancient discipline of art history.

Two excellent surveys investigate the instructive and aesthetic roles that Greek art had for the ancients. *A View of Greek Art*, by R. Ross Holloway, stresses how the style of Greek art from each period was shaped by the Greeks' changing responses to the questions "What is it to be a hero?" and "What is it to be a god?" By concentrating on major or important monuments from each period, Holloway convincingly demonstrates that the ideal for heroic representation changed from early "confidence," to Classical "humanity," to Hellenistic "fear and apprehension" (p. 193). Footnotes that make reference to important scholarly literature appear in the margins next to Holloway's textual discussion. It would have been helpful if these had been more complete and had cited publications of all the monuments that are mentioned but not illustrated. At the back of the volume is a selection of passages by fifth-century writers, in Greek and in translation, that refer to Greek art. A second appendix is a chronological chart that lays out the periods and dates for the phases of Greek art that are discussed in the book. A brief bibliography of general references follows this appendix.

For the researcher who is interested in discovering what seem to have been the aesthetic goals of Greek artists, Rhys Carpenter's *The Esthetic Basis of Greek Art of the Fifth and Fourth Centuries* is recommended. Carpenter presents a unified interpretation of extant ancient texts on aesthetic theory and of data derived from surviving monuments. For example, Carpenter demonstrates that the principle of harmonious, interrelating proportions that ancient authors ascribe to Polycleitus's sculptural Canon for the ideal male form was also utilized in Greek architecture; the demonstration consists of an examination of the inter-relating dimensions of different architectural elements in important Classical temples. Carpenter argues that the Greeks believed that ideal form could be achieved only if such numerical relationships determined the measurements of component parts. Yet he makes it clear that the most eminent artists and architects of the fifth century felt it was also necessary to enliven ideal form with enough irregularities to give works a sense of organic vitality. Carpenter elaborates on some of his points and cites supportive ancient and modern literature in his notes, which appear at the back of the volume before the three indexes. The revised edition of Carpenter's book differs from the first edition in a few textual changes and in the addition of eight plates and a useful bibliography.

Because our record of antiquity is incomplete, it is difficult to define the interrelationships between Greek art and literature. Thomas Bertram Lonsdale Webster attempts to determine parallel developments of these art forms and thereby to penetrate the intellectual context of visual art in five fascinating illustrated studies that cover Greek art from the Bronze Age through the Hellenistic period: *From Mycenae to Homer; Greek Art and Literature 700–530 B.C.: The Beginnings of Modern Civilization; Greek Art and Literature 530–400 B.C.; Art and Literature in Fourth Century Athens;* and *Hellenistic Poetry and Art.* For example, Webster suggests that the simple precision of Proto-Geometric and Geometric vases, with their limited repertoire of decorative motifs, may have been an expression of a new rational, "unmysterious" approach to existence that is also reflected in the "unromantic . . . view of the gods" in Homer's epics (*From Mycenae to Homer,* pp. 292–93). In *Greek Art and Literature 700–530 B.C.,* Webster concludes (pp. 98–99):

> The painters, sculptors, and poets of the seventh and early sixth century were in revolt against formalism, and vital individualism showed itself in many different ways—in the swagger of Archilochos, the great stormy figures of proto-Attic vases, the tremendous imagery of Solon, the Gorgon of Corfu, the widely different ecstasies of maenads and fat men.

Four dominant trends are discerned by Webster in *Greek Art and Literature 530–400 B.C.:* a "sensuous style of the ripe archaic period"; a "strong style" of the Early Classical period; a "new and suppler style" of the Parthenon period; and "a new court style" of the late fifth century (pp. 204–6). Webster traces three attitudes in *Art and Literature in Fourth Century Athens:* "seeing in contrasts, seeing the structure, and seeing the appearance" (p. 149). Finally, in *Hellenistic Poetry and Art,* Webster observes a "broad sequence of artistic styles—elegant, violent, new classical, Neo-Attic" (p. xvi). But since these Hellenistic styles do not seem to him to be based on "common ideals or ideas" that were shared by contemporary poets (as in previous periods), he organizes his discussions around the poetry and art that were produced in major centers and notes "cross-references both between the arts and between the centres" (p. xvii). *Hellenistic Poetry and Art* concludes with a chapter entitled "Italian Epilogue," in which Webster characterizes the Greek art and literature of Hellenistic South Italy and outlines Rome's reception of these art forms from the region and from mainland Greece.

In the modern era of architectural simplification, many students find it difficult to master the standard parts of the Greek architectural orders and the ground plans of popular Greek building types. As a result, they find it even more difficult to comprehend the fine points of the evolution of standard building types. More than any other study of Greek architecture, *Greek Temples, Theatres and Shrines* addresses this problem in its lucid outline of the development of important types of public monuments. Through the use of constant cross-references between buildings with respect to such aspects as changes in the proportions of columns, authors Helmut Berve and Gottfried Gruben provide detailed documentation for the changing Greek conception of what was aesthetically appropriate. Besides emphasizing architectural refinements, the authors explain the contributions made by architectural sculptures and statues to the narrative and spiritual impacts of buildings, particularly sacred structures. Furthermore, they outline the significant activities that took place in each complex of buildings, thereby enabling the reader to imagine the sanctuaries and theaters of antiquity peopled and in use. Numerous black-and-white and color photos by Max Hirmer, plans and reconstructions, and a glossary of architectural terms help clarify all the textual material. In addition, a bibliography with references on each ancient site appears before the glossary at the back of the volume.

*Die Griechen und ihre Nachbarn* (The Greeks and Their Neighbors), by Karl Schefold and other scholars, is a beautifully produced volume that attempts to explain Greece's importance in the ancient world as a whole. The bulk of the hefty volume consists of hundreds of black-and-white and color plates and reconstructions, with extensive commentary, of Greek art from the Proto-Geometric through the Hellenistic periods, and of the art of the neighbors of the Greeks. Among the peoples in the latter category are the Phrygians, Lydians, Scythians, Iranians, Phoenicians, Iberians, Sardinians, Etruscans, and Celts. Greek art receives the fullest treatment and is presented according to the media of sculpture, minor arts, painting (including vase-painting), and architecture. Ground plans and reconstruction drawings accompany the commentary on the architecture of the Greeks and their neighbors. The introductory observations that precede the commentary on the art of each peripheral culture stress any significant influence that Greek art had in shaping non-Greek products. The same issue and the opposite problem of influence from abroad on Greek art are taken up by Schefold in his essay at the front of the volume entitled "Die weltgeschichtliche Stellung der griechischen Kunst" (The International Position of Greek Art). This essay is followed by a second one, also by Schefold, in which the progression of styles of Greek art is elucidated; an "Übersicht der Perioden" (Summary of the Periods) on pages 335–36 outlines the main developments explained by Schefold in his second essay. Following the summary are a list of bibliographical abbrevations that are used in the commentary on the plates; a long bibliography; and a chronological chart of important events in the history and art of Greece and her neighbors.

A number of useful studies limit their consideration to one or more periods, but not the whole development, of Greek art and architecture. *The Arts in Prehistoric Greece*, by Sinclair Hood, is an illustrated account of the pottery, painting, sculpture, and the various minor arts that were produced in Greece during the Neolithic period and the Bronze Age. Hood summarizes the products of each art form in separate chapters, within which the material is arranged chronologically and by the three regional styles of Crete, the Cycladic islands, and the mainland. He emphasizes throughout this scholarly volume not only the distinctions between the regional styles, but also their common features, which provide evidence for extensive cultural exchange. The abbreviations and lengthy notes and bibliography located at the back of the reference cite further studies of both a general and specific nature.

*The Birth of Greek Art: From the Mycenaean to the Archaic Period*, by Roland Hampe and Erika Simon, explores the difficult issue of cultural continuity in Greek art from the Mycenaean Bronze Age to the end of the Orientalizing period (ca. 1600–600 B.C.). The authors cautiously review architecture and the different art forms and note features that seem to have persisted through Greece's Dark Ages, such as the technical aspects of manufacturing vases, and funerary and cult practices and beliefs. They also call attention to disruption in traditions, such as the cessation and revival, through contact with the East, of ivory carving. This reference is lavishly illustrated with line drawings and high-quality black-and-white and color photos. It also has a long bibliography that is keyed to the plates (whose numbers are cited in the margins) and a glossary of terms, object types, and styles.

Bernhard Schweitzer defines the different regional styles of vases, statuettes, bronze vessels and fibulae, gold bands, and architecture from the Geometric period in *Greek Geometric Art*. Pieces are gathered into regional groupings on the basis of both their provenances and their common stylistic and technical characteristics. In *The Art of Greece: Its Origins in the Mediterranean and Near East*, Ekrem Akurgal describes the principal traits of the styles of the most important Near Eastern civilizations between 1000 and 500 B.C. (Egypt is excluded from consideration.) The author then demonstrates the debt of Greek art and mythology to Near Eastern prototypes. Gisela M. A. Richter outlines the regional styles of three phases of Greek Archaic art in *Archaic Greek Art against Its*

*Historical Background.* Discussion of prominent examples from each region and phase is introduced by a summary of our knowledge of the contemporary history of the region; any characteristics of the examples that reflect the current historical situation are made clear.

The forms and evolutions of early Greek art are discussed in their cultural contexts by Jeffrey M. Hurwit in *The Art and Culture of Early Greece, 1100–480 B.C.* For example, Hurwit perceives the early Greek *kouros* (a standard statuary type of the Archaic period consisting of a standing male nude with one leg advanced) to be an expression of unchanging heroic excellence and the belief "as old as Homer: that immortal *kleos* (fame) is the only compensation for death and that fame can be conferred only by poetry or art" (p. 202). The latest examples of the same statuary type, created at the end of the Archaic period and exhibiting a new freedom of pose, are interpreted by Hurwit as expressions of "a new ideal, a new virtue: *sophrosyne*, moderation, the doctrine of self-knowledge and the knowledge of human limitations—the Classical doctrine par excellence" (p. 344).

In *Art and Experience in Classical Greece* and *Art in the Hellenistic Age*, Pollitt adopts an approach similar to Hurwit's—that is, he strives to "suggest some of the basic cultural experiences which the arts were used to express and to analyze how they were used to express them." Pollitt attempts to achieve this goal by an exploration of contemporary art, poetry, philosophy, and history, which are all perceived as reflections of the same attitudes formed as reactions to shared experiences. In the preface to *Art in the Hellenistic Age*, Pollitt expresses a second purpose for this book: "to present a selective history of the formal development of this art organized around those genres, schools, or styles which seem to me to have been of particular importance." Thus, unlike *Art and Experience in Classical Greece,* which is organized around changing attitudes, *Art in the Hellenistic Age* (apart from the lengthy introduction on the five Hellenistic "states of mind") presents art works in chapters on styles and regional centers. Particularly valuable in this volume is the incorporation into the argument of important recent finds, such as the painted tombs at Vergina in Macedonia. Both studies by Pollitt cite additional scholarship in the notes and bibliographies; the citations in *Art in the Hellenistic Age* are especially extensive.

### Bibliographic Entries for Supplementary Sources

Akurgal, Ekrem. *The Art of Greece: Its Origins in the Mediterranean and Near East.* Translated by Wayne Dynes. New York: Crown, 1968.

Berve, Helmut, and Gottfried Gruben. *Greek Temples, Theatres and Shrines.* New York: Abrams, [1963].

Carpenter, Rhys. *The Esthetic Basis of Greek Art of the Fifth and Fourth Centuries.* Rev. ed. Bloomington: Indiana Univ. Press, 1959.

Hampe, Roland, and Erika Simon. *The Birth of Greek Art: From the Mycenaean to the Archaic Period.* Foreword by John Boardman. New York: Oxford Univ. Press, 1981.

Holloway, R. Ross. *A View of Greek Art.* New York: Harper, 1974.

Hood, Sinclair. *The Arts in Prehistoric Greece.* The Pelican History of Art. New York: Penguin, 1978.

Hurwit, Jeffrey M. *The Art and Culture of Early Greece, 1100–480 B.C.* Ithaca and London: Cornell Univ. Press, 1985.

Pollitt, J. J. *The Ancient View of Greek Art: Criticism, History, and Terminology.* Yale Publications in the History of Art, no. 25. New Haven and London: Yale Univ. Press, 1974.

———. *Art and Experience in Classical Greece.* London: Cambridge Univ. Press, 1972.

———. *Art in the Hellenistic Age.* New York: Cambridge Univ. Press, 1986.

Richter, Gisela M. A. *Archaic Greek Art against Its Historical Background.* The Mary Flexner Lectures. New York: Oxford Univ. Press, 1949.

Schefold, Karl, et al. *Die Griechen und ihre Nachbarn.* Propyläen Kunstgeschichte 1. Berlin: Propyläen Verlag, 1967.

Schweitzer, Bernhard. *Greek Geometric Art.* Translated by Peter and Cornelia Usborne. London: Phaidon Press, 1971.

Webster, Thomas Bertram Lonsdale. *Art and Literature in Fourth Century Athens.* London: Univ. of London, Athlone Press, 1956.

———. *From Mycenae to Homer.* London: Methuen, 1958.

———. *Greek Art and Literature 530–400 B.C.* Oxford: Clarendon Press, 1939.

———. *Greek Art and Literature 700–530 B.C.: The Beginnings of Modern Civilization.* De Carle Lectures, 1959. London: Methuen, 1959.

———. *Hellenistic Poetry and Art.* New York: Barnes & Noble, 1964.

## Additional Supplementary Sources

Amyx, Darrell A. *Corinthian Vase-Painting of the Archaic Period.* Vol. 1, *Catalog.* Vol. 2, *Commentary.* Vol. 3, *Indexes, Concordances, and Plates.* California Studies in the History of Art, no. 25. Berkeley: Univ. of California Press, 1988.

Andrén, Arvid. *Deeds and Misdeeds in Classical Art and Antiquities.* Studies in Mediterranean Archaeology, Pocket-book 36. Partille, Sweden: Paul Åström, 1986.

Boardman, John. *Pre-Classical.* Style and Civilization. 1967. Reprint with additions to bibliography. New York: Penguin, 1978.

Demargne, Pierre. *The Birth of Greek Art.* Translated by Stuart Gilbert and James Emmons. The Arts of Mankind. New York: Golden Press, 1964.

Havelock, Christine Mitchell. *Hellenistic Art: The Art of the Classical World from the Death of Alexander the Great to the Battle of Actium.* 2d ed. New York: Norton, 1981.

Higgins, Reynold Alleyne. *Minoan and Mycenaean Art.* Rev. ed. World of Art. New York: Thames & Hudson, 1985.

Hölscher, Tonio, *Griechische Historienhilder des 5. und 4. Jahrhunderts v. Chr.* Beiträge zur Archäologie. Würzburg: Konrad Triltsch, 1973.

Homann-Wedeking, E. *The Art of Archaic Greece.* Translated by J. R. Foster. Art of the World. New York: Crown, 1968.

Matz, Friedrich. *The Art of Crete and Early Greece: The Prelude to Greek Art.* Translated by Anne E. Keep. New York: Greystone, 1962.

Onians, John. *Art and Thought in The Hellenistic Age: The Greek World View 350–50 B.C.* London: Thames & Hudson, 1979.

Schefold, Karl. *The Art of Classical Greece.* Translated by J. R. Foster. Art of the World. New York: Crown, 1967.

Sweeney, Jane, Tam Curry, and Yannis Tzedakis, eds. *The Human Figure in Early Greek Art.* Translated by Nancy Winter, Evelyn Harrison, Myriam Caskey, and David Hardy. Catalog of an exhibition in the National Gallery of Art, Washington, D.C., January–June, 1988. Athens: Greek Ministry of Culture; Washington, D.C.: National Gallery of Art, 1988.

Vermeule, Cornelius C. *Greek Art: Socrates to Sulla, from the Peloponnesian Wars to the Rise of Julius Caesar.* Art of Antiquity 2.2. Cambridge and Everett, Mass.: CopyQuik Corp., 1980.

Vermeule, Emily. *Greece in the Bronze Age.* 5th printing, with updated preface. Chicago and London: Univ. of Chicago Press, 1972.

Webster, Thomas Bertram Lonsdale. *The Art of Greece: The Age of Hellenism.* Art of the World. New York: Crown, 1966.

# \2\

# Etruscan Art and Architecture

Brendel, Otto J. *Etruscan Art.* Prepared for press by Emeline Richardson. The Pelican History of Art. New York: Penguin, 1978.

## ART FORM

The Etruscans, the fascinating ancient inhabitants of the region in central Italy that was named Tuscany after them, produced an art which followed the development of Greek art in many respects, but which also had a distinct vitality and expressiveness all its own. Like Greek art, Etruscan art progressed through Geometric, Orientalizing, Archaic, Classical, and Hellenistic stylistic phases. The Etruscans further demonstrated their admiration for Greek art through their frequent adoption of Greek myths as the subject matter for their art. Yet often these depictions of Greek myths were not totally Greek in content, but included Etruscan characters alongside Greek ones. Other myths in Etruscan art were local stories that bore no relationship to Greek legends.

The Etruscans diverged from the Greeks in their early preference for the sculptural media of bronze and terra-cotta instead of marble and limestone, and they manipulated these media to achieve more decorative, less structural forms. Etruscan art is decorative, but at the same time it is also vital and expressive. Rather than seeking to achieve the dignified

29

and serene figures that constituted the ideal types of the Greeks, the Etruscans strove to capture dynamic postures whose expressive content was enhanced by lively gestures and figural interaction. In short, Etruscan art has a spontaneity that is entirely unlike the calculated grandeur of Greek art.

The richest finds in terms of intact objects (many of them Greek imports) and wall paintings come from Etruscan chamber tombs. At some places and times, for example, at Caere, these tombs were designed like Etruscan houses and were equipped with items that were apparently believed to be necessary in the afterlife, such as the handsome engraved Etruscan mirrors (see chapter 12). Additional finds consisting of architectural sculptures and votive offerings have been unearthed in Etruscan sanctuaries. Several habitation sites have been investigated as well, and have revealed house and possible palace remains, along with architectural terra-cottas and household items, such as Etruscan pottery and bone plaques, which were once ornaments for Etruscan furniture.

Etruscan art and the Etruscans themselves are less well understood than the art of the Greeks and the Romans. While we have extensive Greek and Roman literature and historical accounts, no comparable written works of the Etruscans survive. Most extant Etruscan inscriptions are simply labels for figures in Etruscan art and epitaphs in Etruscan tombs. A few incompletely understood documents that spell out details of Etruscan rituals also survive. Because of the absence of Etruscan literature and history, we lack explanations for basic questions, such as who the Etruscans were, and when they settled in central Italy. We do know, however, that their language was a non-Indo-European tongue. Evidence of the use of their language outside Italy has not been discovered. Perhaps in the future, longer, more significant texts that unravel some of the mysteries surrounding the Etruscans and permit the modern viewer to fully appreciate Etruscan art in its original cultural context may turn up in excavations or in chance finds.

# RESEARCH USE

*Etruscan Art*, by Otto J. Brendel, provides an excellent introduction to the major periods and forms of Etruscan art. By presenting detailed discussions of important and typical examples, which are illustrated beside the text, the author leads the reader through the stylistic and iconographic developments of the different media of Etruscan art. While tracing these developments, he explains instances of indebtedness to Greek prototypes as well as characteristics such as expressiveness and innovative iconography that seem to be Etruscan. Brendel also outlines the emergence of Roman art under the influence of Etruscan and then Greek artists. Notes located at the back of the volume suggest further reading on each art work discussed, and a lengthy bibliography appearing after the notes and arranged by topic and medium lists useful general references and articles.

In short, Brendel's study can be consulted for a general overview of trends in Etruscan art. Furthermore, the reference is invaluable for anyone interested in acquiring detailed information on particular monuments, which are always thoroughly discussed in terms of materials, thematic content, dating, possible place of manufacture, and possible original setting and function. The hypotheses that are suggested in *Etruscan Art* regarding uncertain aspects, such as stylistic traits of regional styles, can be tested by researchers in the future, particularly as new finds turn up with known provenances.

## ORGANIZATION

Brendel explains the guiding purpose of his book thus: ". . . our attention must focus on the formation and growth of an Italian, western art which by character and origin was, and for a long time remained, predominantly Etruscan. Only gradually did the Roman centre move into the limelight." The "formation and growth" of Etruscan art are traced in six parts of the volume: "The Villanovan and Orientalizing Periods"; "The Early and Middle Archaic Periods"; "The Late Archaic Period"; "The Classical Era: The Fifth Century"; "The Classical Era: The Fourth Century"; and "The Hellenistic Period: Last Manifestations and Legacy." These parts are divided into thirty-one chapters which are themselves broken down into headings and subheadings; an example of the latter is *The Chimaera of Arezzo*.

A single index at the back provides access to textual discussions and illustrations of art works by their themes, provenances, and current locations. The index also cites discussions of historical personages (including artists) and places, and other topics, such as "Attic art and influence." Before the index are a brief list of abbreviations; the notes, which make use of the abbreviations and cite textual page numbers in bold-faced type; and the long bibliography described above (see Research Use).

## COMPLEMENTARY REFERENCES

*The Etruscans: Their History, Art, and Architecture*, by Maja Sprenger and Gilda Bartoloni, forms an excellent companion volume to Brendel's *Etruscan Art*. For one thing, *The Etruscans* has nearly three hundred high-quality, full-page photographic plates, some in color, by Max and

Albert Hirmer. Many of these plates show the same pieces which Brendel discusses and illustrates with smaller black-and-white photos. The scholarly commentary that accompanies the Hirmers' plates, by Gilda Bartoloni, presents facts and sensitive stylistic observations, as well as bibliographic citations, that supplement the material in Brendel's study. *The Etruscans* furthermore, has valuable introductory chapters by Maja Sprenger on different facets of Etruscan history and culture, the phases of stylistic development of Etruscan art, and the evolution of different art forms, including architecture (which Brendel does not discuss). The architecture chapter, illustrated by ground plans and reconstructions, provides an overview of town planning and Etruscan temple, house, and tomb design. At the back of *The Etruscans* are a detailed table of important events in Etruscan history; a chart of classical divinities with their Greek, Roman, and Etruscan names; a chart of the twelve traditional Etruscan cities with their modern, Latin, and Etruscan names; a glossary of architectural and artistic terms and geographic regions; a bibliography containing items published after Brendel's book; and a good map of Etruria.

An additional and more complete source for recent publications on Etruscan art is *Etruscan Life and Afterlife: A Handbook of Etruscan Studies*, edited by Larissa Bonfante. This is a collection of essays by leading Etruscologists on various aspects of Etruscan culture and studies. Each article is followed by notes and/or a current bibliography, and there is also a general bibliography at the end of the volume. Particularly useful are the summaries of our current understanding of Etruscan art, architecture, coinage, and daily life and practices regarding the afterlife. The last article, by Larissa Bonfante, draws on Etruscan art as a primary source of evidence, and the article by Marie-Françoise Briguet specifically on art adopts the view that "Etruscan art is not a discipline, like Greek art" (p. 172). Another fascinating article by Nancy Thomson de Grummond, entitled "Rediscovery," is the first attempt to survey the study of Etruscan history, religion, and art by scholars and artists from the time of the Romans to the nineteenth century. *Etruscan Life and Afterlife* has nine maps at the front pertaining to the history of the Etruscans and the peoples who traded with them.

In 1985, there were several wonderful exhibitions in Italy of Etruscan artifacts, which comprised the "Progetto Etruschi" (Project Etruscans). The catalogs for these exhibitions, with many black-and-white and color photographs and up-to-date bibliographies, present important syntheses of aspects of Etruscan culture and art. The largest exhibit, at Florence, was called "Civiltà degli etruschi" (Civilization of the Etruscans). This was a chronologically arranged explanation of the social structure and physical remains from each period of the Etruscans' history. Special emphasis was laid on the relations of the Etruscans with other civilizations. "Santuari d'Etruria" (Sanctuaries of Etruria), the exhibit in Arezzo, focused on the physical remains of sacred buildings and on the votive offerings from sanctuaries, which sometimes consist of life-size statues or heads of worshippers. "Case e palazzi d'Etruria" (Houses and Palaces of Etruria), the exhibit in Siena, concentrated on the architectural terra-cottas and small finds from recently excavated Etruscan sites with domestic architecture. In all the catalogs for the exhibits in the "Progetto Etruschi," bibliography was provided for each piece; maps, views of sites, site plans, and ground plans and reconstructions of buildings also help the researcher to understand the original archaeological contexts of the pieces. The latter material is especially imporant in the case of the catalog, *Case e palazzi d'Etruria*, because Etruscan domestic architecture, only recently attested by excavated examples, is not discussed in most handbooks of Etruscan art.

Two illustrated encyclopedias—one in English and one in Italian—provide useful summaries of our knowledge of Etruscan art and architecture along with citations of scholarly publications of all kinds. The English reference, *Encyclopedia of World Art*, has the general entry, "Etrusco-Italic Art," and brief descriptions of Etruscan remains from different ancient sites under the entry "Italy." The exact page numbers of the latter can quickly be ascertained by looking up each city in the *Index*, which is volume 15 of the *Encyclopedia*. The *Index* can also be used to locate mentions in different articles of Etruscan artists. *Enciclopedia dell'arte antica, classica e orientale* (Encyclopedia of Ancient Art: Classical and Oriental) is the Italian reference. It contains a general entry, "Etrusca, Arte" (Etruscan Art); entries which deal with monument types (for example, "Sarcofago, 6. Etruria" [Sarcophagus, 6. Etruria]) and types of structures (such as "Tomba, 6. Etruria" [Tomb, 6. Etruria]); and separate entries on Etruscan cities and artists.

For summaries of the urban development and physical remains (particularly architecture) of Etruscan cities in existence from circa 750 B.C. onward, the reader should consult *The Princeton Encyclopedia of Classical Sites*. This exhaustive reference lists cities alphabetically by the names the sites had in antiquity; modern names that are different from ancient names are also listed, with cross-references made to the correct ancient names. While this volume has no illustrations except the maps at the back, the bibliography at the end of each entry cites references which contain reproductions. Another excellent source for summaries of archaeological remains from major Etruscan cities is *The Oxford Classical Dictionary*, edited by N. G. L. Hammond and H. H. Scullard. Like *The Princeton Encyclopedia of Classical Sites*, this reference is not illustrated, but mentions publications with plans and plates.

The latest volumes of *L'Année philologique* (Philological Year), an annual annotated bibliography of publications of all kinds on the classical world, list the most recent literature on Etruscan art and archaeology under the heading, "Régions italiques, Étrurie, Corse, Grande Grèce, Sicile" (Italic Regions, Etruria, Corsica, Magna Graecia, Sicily). Literature on specific Etruscan personages and cities can be located quickly by consulting the same reference's "Index Nominum Antiquorum" (Index of Ancient Names) and "Index Geographicus" (Geographical Index). The numbers cited in the indexes correspond to the numbers assigned to separate entries. *Art Index*, a quarterly compilation of citations of articles from major journals, cites articles on Etruscan art under the names of authors and under various subject headings. General articles are listed under "Art, Etruscan"; articles on mythology in Etruscan art can be found under "Iconography, Etruscan"; literature on different media is collected under such headings as "Mirrors, Etruscan"; and literature on different monument types is presented under such headings as "Tombs, Etruscan." *Art Index* can be searched by computer on the Wilsonline online vendor service for the period from September 1984 onwards.

## Bibliographic Entries for Complementary References

*L'Année philologique: Bibliographie critique et analytique de l'antiquité gréco-latine.* Paris: Société d'édition "Les Belles Lettres," 1928– .

*Art Index: A Cumulative Author and Subject Index to a Selected List of Fine Arts Periodicals and Museum Bulletins.* New York: H. W. Wilson, 1929/30– .

Bonfante, Larissa, ed. *Etruscan Life and Afterlife: A Handbook of Etruscan Studies.* Detroit: Wayne State Univ. Press, 1986.

*Enciclopedia dell'arte antica, classica e orientale.* Edited by Ranuccio Bianchi Bandinelli. 7 vols. *Supplemento,* and *Atlante dei complessi figurati.* Rome: Istituto della Enciclopedia Italiana, 1958–73.

*Encyclopedia of World Art.* Translation of *Enciclopedia universale dell'arte.* 14 vols. New York: McGraw-Hill, 1959–67. Vol. 15, *Index.* New York: McGraw-Hill, 1968. Vol. 16, *Supplement: World Art in Our Time.* Edited by Bernard S. Myers. New York: McGraw-Hill and Publishers Guild, 1983.

Hammond, N. G. L., and H. H. Scullard, eds. *The Oxford Classical Dictionary.* 2d ed. Oxford: Clarendon Press, 1970.

*The Princeton Encyclopedia of Classical Sites.* Edited by Richard Stillwell, William L. MacDonald, and Marian Holland McAllister. Princeton: Princeton Univ. Press, 1976.

Progetto Etruschi. *Case e palazzi d'Etruria.* Edited by Simonetta Stopponi. Catalog of an exhibition in the Spedale di Santa Maria della Scala, Siena, May–October, 1985. Milan: Electa; Regione Toscana, 1985.

———. *Civiltà degli etruschi.* Edited by Mauro Cristofani. Catalog of an exhibition in the Museo archeologico, Florence, May–October, 1985. Milan: Electa; Regione Toscana, 1985.

———. *Santuari d'Etruria.* Edited by Giovanni Colonna. Catalog of an exhibition in the Sottochiesa di San Francesco and the Museo archeologico C. Cilnio Mecenate, Arezzo, May–October, 1985. Milan: Electa; Regione Toscana, 1985. Sprenger, Maja, and Gilda Bartoloni. *The Etruscans: Their History, Art, and Architecture.* Translated by Robert Erich Wolf. New York: Abrams, 1983.

# HANDBOOKS

For the researcher who wishes to understand Etruscan art in the context of our current knowledge of Etruscan culture in general, *The Etruscans*, by the eminent Italian scholar Massimo Pallottino, is recommended. This is an English translation of the sixth edition of Pallottino's *Etruscologia* (Etruscology), of which a seventh edition in Italian appeared in 1984. The chapters from *The Etruscans* entitled "The Cities and Cemeteries of Etruria" and "Literature and the Arts" present a more positive view of Etruscan art than can be found in many other surveys. Here the expressive emphasis in Etruscan art is seen as a persistent and original trait, and one which was passed on to the Roman Imperial and medieval eras. The black-and-white plates in *The Etruscans* are accompanied by descriptive commentary with bibliography (see "Notes on the Plates"). Further literature is cited in the "Notes on the Text" and in the "Notes on Further Reading."

*L'arte degli Etruschi: Produzione e consumo* (Art of the Etruscans: Production and Use), by Mauro Cristofani (a student of Pallottino), is the most up-to-date survey of Etruscan art and architecture that has come to my attention. The recently excavated finds from Acquarossa and Poggio Civitate of what are believed to be palace complexes are discussed here along with better-known sites such as the Portonaccio sanctuary at Veii. Throughout his considerations of different periods and aspects of Etruscan art, Cristofani tries to reconstruct the activities and distinguishing traits of Etruscan workshops and the relationship of their products to art imported from Greek and Near Eastern centers. Notes at the ends of the chapters refer the reader to further scholarly literature.

For the point of view that much of the best Etruscan art was inspired by Greek models or actually made by Greek artists working in Etruria, the reader should consult the essay on Etruscan art by Vagn Poulsen in *Etruscan Culture, Land and People*, by Axel Boëthius and others. Besides the thought-provoking essay by Poulsen, this lavishly illustrated volume with many color photographs includes a lengthy scholarly essay on Etruscan political, social, and cultural history by Axel Boëthius; "The Etruscans and Rome in Archaic Times," by Einar Gjerstad; and an essay on Etruscan tombs and houses which were excavated at San Giovenale and environs by the Swedish Institute (by Krister Hanell and others). A useful bibliography subdivided into general references, studies of different media in Etruscan art, and references pertinent to the different essays, is located at the back of the volume.

*The Etruscans: Their Art and Civilization,* by Emeline Hill Richardson, is a chronologically arranged, straightforward introduction to the surviving works of art and architecture of the Etruscans and to significant aspects of Etruscan history and culture. Particularly valuable features of Richardson's handbook are its full descriptions of the literary and archaeological evidence available on controversial issues such as the origin and date of arrival of the Etruscans, and its clear explanations of the author's preferred interpretations of the evidence. At the back of the reference is a lengthy bibliography, with sections on general books, studies of particular sites, and material pertinent to specific chapters.

*The Art of Etruria and Early Rome,* by G. A. Mansuelli, is a sensitive stylistic history of Etruscan art which explains stylistic changes as reflections of parallel changes in imported art from Greek centers and elsewhere. Besides the chronologically arranged chapters devoted to different periods of Etruscan art of all media (including architecture), Mansuelli's handbook has a final chapter on the Etruscan elements in Roman Republican art. The book is illustrated with high-quality color plates and line drawings and has at the back a chronological table listing events and monuments of the Etruscans and the civilizations within their commercial sphere; an alphabetically arranged series of paragraphs summarizing the artistic developments of Etruscan cities; a map of Etruscan cities in Etruria and the colonized regions of Campania in South Italy and the Po Valley; a glossary with artistic and architectural terms and names of Etruscan divinities; and a bibliography arranged by general books and studies of periods and media.

*Les Étrusques et l'Italie avant Rome: De la Protohistoire à la guerre sociale* (The Etruscans and Italy before Rome: From Protohistory to the Social War), by Ranuccio Bianchi Bandinelli and Antonio Giuliano, examines the products of the major cultures in Italy before the Late Republic, especially those of the Greek colonists and the Etruscans. This type of investigation permits the authors to distinguish three classes of art works found in Etruria: imports from Greek and Near Eastern centers; local imitations of imports; and locally made products with an Etruscan expressiveness. *Les Étrusques et l'Italie avant Rome* is beautifully illustrated with sharp black-and-white and color photos and has a lengthy bibliography and dictionary/index at the back.

For new and in-print handbooks on Etruscan art, the researcher should consult the heading "Art, Etruscan" in the latest edition of the *Subject Guide to Books in Print.*

*Tarquinia and Etruscan Origins,* by Hugh Hencken, summarizes the archaeological evidence from the graves at Tarquinia of the people called the Villanovans. These people, who buried the cremated remains of their dead in biconical urns, preceded the Etruscans at many sites and may or may not have been the same as the Etruscans. Hencken examines the first two phases of the Villanovan period as well as the third, which coincides with the Orientalizing period, when the earliest Etruscan inscriptions are attested. For a fuller discussion of the same evidence from Tarquinia, the reader is advised to consult the same author's more scholarly publication, *Tarquinia, Villanovans and Early Etruscans*. Both publications by Hencken contain bibliographies, but the one in *Tarquinia, Villanovans and Early Etruscans* is more complete in its citation of early literature.

It has often been observed that Etruscan art is episodic. According to Mario Torelli, author of the Introduction to *Etruscan Cities*, this phenomenon can be explained by the conclusion on the part of archaeologists that "identifiable workshops were remarkably short-lived" (p. 25). Besides the insightful introduction, *Etruscan Cities*, by Francesca Boitani and others, contains useful summaries of the history and archaeological finds of all types from numerous Etruscan cities in Etruria proper and from the two areas colonized by the Etruscans—the Po Valley and Campania in South Italy. This reference also describes the provenances and classes of finds in Etruscan museums, including the Museo Archeologico in Florence and the Villa Giulia Museum in Rome. All the numerous photographs in the book are in color and many site plans and ground plans, also in color, are included. A bibliography at the back lists general books and publications on specific cities and museums. In addition, there is a table of historical events and a glossary of artistic and architectural terms.

*Etruscan and Early Roman Architecture*, by Axel Boëthius, surveys Italian prehistoric and Etruscan and Roman architecture from the Neolithic period to the end of the Roman Republic. Chapter 3, devoted to Etruscan architecture, reviews the development of Etruscan temples, urban planning, houses, and tombs; and chapter 4 summarizes our knowledge about the architecture of Rome from the period of the Etruscan kings (the late seventh to the late sixth century B.C.) to the city's destruction by the Gauls in 386 B.C. The second edition of *Etruscan and Early Roman Architecture* has an updated bibliography and notes that include important new material from recent excavations.

## Bibliographic Entries for Handbooks

Bianchi Bandinelli, Ranuccio, and Antonio Guiliano. *Les Étrusques et l'Italie avant Rome: De la Protohistoire à la guerre sociale*. Translated by Jean-Charles and Évelyne Picard. Vol. 1, *Le monde romain: 800 av.–410 ap. J.-C. L'univers des formes*. Paris: Gallimard, 1973.

Boëthius, Axel. *Etruscan and Early Roman Architecture*. 2d ed. Revised by Roger Ling and Tom Rasmussen. Pelican History of Art. New York: Penguin, 1978.

———, et al. *Etruscan Culture, Land and People: Archeological Research and Studies Conducted in San Giovenale and Its Environs by Members of the Swedish Institute in Rome*. New York: Columbia Univ. Press; Malmö, Sweden: Allhem, 1962.

Boitani, Francesca, Maria Cataldi, and Marinella Pasquinucci. *Etruscan Cities*. Introduction by Mario Torelli; translated by Catherine Atthill et al. London: Cassell, 1975.

Cristofani, Mauro. *L'arte degli Etruschi: Produzione e consumo*. Saggi 605. Torino: Einaudi, 1978.

Hencken, Hugh. *Tarquinia and Etruscan Origins*. Ancient People and Places, no. 62. New York and Washington: Praeger, 1968.

———. *Tarquinia, Villanovans and Early Etruscans*. 2 vols. American School of Prehistoric Research, Peabody Museum, Harvard University. Bulletin no. 23. Cambridge, Mass.: Peabody Museum, 1968.

Mansuelli, G. A. *The Art of Etruria and Early Rome*. Translated by C. E. Ellis. Art of the World. New York: Crown, 1965.

Pallottino, Massimo. *The Etruscans*. Rev. and enl. Translated by J. Cremona; edited by David Ridgway. [Harmondsworth, Middlesex]: Penguin, 1978.

Richardson, Emeline Hill. *The Etruscans: Their Art and Civilization*. 1964. Reprint with corrections. Chicago and London: Univ. of Chicago Press, 1976.

*Subject Guide to Books in Print*. New York: R. R. Bowker, 1990– .

## SUPPLEMENTARY SOURCES

The lion was an animal which most Etruscan artists never observed firsthand, yet it was frequently represented in Etruscan art of all media. The various Etruscan formulae for depicting the lion were clearly derived from artistic representations brought into Etruria from different regions of the Near Eastern and Greek worlds. Because of its usefulness in revealing sources, the lion in Etruscan art from the late eighth through the late third century B.C. is the focus of *The Etruscan Lion*, by W. Llewellyn Brown. Brown's stated purpose for this study is "to unravel the complicated nexus of influences and currents which go to make up the story of Etruscan art, especially in the archaic period." Particularly interesting aspects of Brown's investigations are his suggestions regarding the importation not only of foreign products but also of craftsmen, whose own work would be indistinguishable from the products of their homelands, but whose local apprentices' work would exhibit a more recognizably Etruscan style. Brown's study also sheds light on the dating and attribution to the Etruscans of such controversial works as the bronze chimaera from Arezzo, which many scholars formerly believed was a Greek masterpiece.

One of the most difficult problems one encounters in the study of Etruscan art is the dating of particular works. The problem is particularly acute for the Etruscan Classical period. During this period, unlike previous periods, the stream of Greek imports dwindled and many Etruscan artisans tended to echo Greek styles of earlier rather than contemporary times. Tobias Dohrn attempts to sort out Etruscan Classical sculpture into different, roughly dated trends in his study, *Die etruskische Kunst im Zeitalter der griechischen Klassik: Die Interimsperiode* (Etruscan Art in the Era of Greek Classical Art: The Interim Period). The first part of Dohrn's study is devoted to more or less progressive trends in fifth-century Etruscan sculpture, while the second part concentrates on Etruscan terra-cottas and bronzes from the fourth century, particularly the products attributed to the leading workshops at Orvieto. The discussion of each grouping of sculptures representing a trend is introduced by a catalog of examples with bibliography; a general bibliography that explains the abbreviations in the catalogs appears at the back.

Several categories of Etruscan art are attested by many surviving examples, but firm information about these examples, such as carefully documented provenances, is scanty. The study of these classes of art is further complicated by the fact that examples are scattered in museums throughout Italy and elsewhere. *Etruscan Votive Bronzes: Geometric, Orientalizing, Archaic*, a two-volume corpus by Emeline Hill Richardson, catalogs and arranges by period and type all surviving examples of one such category—Etruscan bronze statuettes that were produced during the period of circa 700 to 450 B.C. for placement as offerings in Etruscan sanctuaries. Through comparisons with stylistically similar decorative statuettes from dated Etruscan tombs, Richardson establishes some fixed points in the chronology of votive statuettes. Other dates are less precise and rely on comparisons with dated Greek art or on internal developments within established Etruscan statuette types. In some cases where substantial archaeological evidence supports her attributions, Richardson assigns particular statuettes to specific places of manufacture. The types of statuettes included in Richardson's exhaustive study include nude and draped men and women, warriors, athletes, gods, and heroes. Many of the statuettes in the catalogs of types are illustrated in excellent black-and-white photos showing more than one view. Earlier publications of the statuettes are cited in the catalog entries by bibliographic abbreviations which are explained in the list of abbreviations at the front of volume 1.

A possible companion volume for Richardson's *Etruscan Votive Bronzes* is *I bronzi degli Etruschi* (The Bronzes of the Etruscans), by Mauro Cristofani. Like Richardson's study, this survey concentrates on votive bronze statuettes. The examples for which provenances were reported are presented in groups according to where they reputedly were found ("find spots"); other votive statuettes of unknown provenance are arranged according to thematic categories. Animal statuettes, a category of votive offerings not presented by Richardson, are discussed along with human figures. A series of large bronzes from funerary, sacred, and public contexts is also described by Cristofani. Every statuette and statue in Cristofani's catalog, in the second part of the volume, is illustrated by one or more beautiful color photos. Many of these examples are discussed by Richardson, but Cristofani's catalog also includes bronzes from beyond the periods covered by Richardson, that is, from the Classical and Hellenistic periods. Besides the illustrated catalog with bibliographic citations of further literature, Cristofani's survey has introductory chapters on the evolution of the main statuary types and our knowledge of their original settings; attributions to workshops and regional styles and explanations of bronze-working techniques; and the histories of the Capitoline wolf, the chimaera from Arezzo, and the Arringatore (The Orator).

References on Etruscan engraved mirrors, one of the handsomest and best attested forms of bronze work, are discussed in chapter 12, "Etruscan Mirrors."

Other categories of Etruscan art, such as architectural terra-cottas, have better-known provenances and dates. In *Etruscan Types of Heads: A Revised Chronology of the Archaic and Classical Terracottas of Etruscan Campania and Central Italy,* P. J. Riis presents seven typological sequences of male and female Etruscan terra-cotta heads from Archaic and Classical architectural, votive, and funeral sculptures. By combining the typological approach with the knowledge gained from examples discovered in dated deposits of known provenance, Riis establishes a framework that can be used both to date and to suggest places of manufacture for future finds, especially those without known provenances. Each of the typological sequences is assigned to a particular Etruscan city and is explained through a catalog of examples, a discussion of the archaeological evidence, and a chronological chart with line drawings of the examples. Bibliographic abbreviations utilized in the catalogs of examples are explained in the "Abbreviations" at the front.

A particularly fascinating genre of Etruscan art is stone statuary from the Archaic period. This is the focus of *Recherches sur la statuaire en pierre étrusque archaïque* (Examinations of Etruscan Archaic Statuary in Stone), by Alain Hus. After cataloging all known examples according to provenances, Hus suggests a chronology for each city's stone statuary which is based on stylistic comparisons with dated Near Eastern and Greek statuary, and with Etruscan art of other materials. He then discusses some general issues, the most significant of which are found in the chapters, "Caractère funéraire de la statue en pierre archaïque" (Funerary Character of the Archaic Stone Statue), and "Statue en pierre et croyances funéraires" (The Stone Statue and Funerary Beliefs). On the basis of the funerary provenances and negative evidence with regard to other contexts, Hus concludes in the first chapter that these primitive sculptures fashioned out of locally available stones were intended for tombs. In the other chapter, the author suggests that the statues represented a goddess who protected and nourished the deceased in the afterlife, and her demonic attendants in the form of sphinxes, lions, and centaurs. Hus's conclusions are supported by the remarkable find of a stepped funerary altar and associated statuary from recent excavations at Cortona.

Etruscan tomb paintings, with their vivid depictions of activities such as banqueting and dancing, have fascinated scholars and laymen since the Renaissance. Significantly, the process of discovering these monuments continues today in the recent archaeological campaigns of the Lerici Foundation of Milan. Entering Etruscan tombs for firsthand viewing causes damage to the wall paintings; thus the visitor to tomb sites is only allowed to see a limited selection of examples. Under these circumstances, the first complete corpus of tomb paintings, *Etruscan Painting: Catalogue Raisonné of Etruscan Wall Paintings*, by Stephan Steingräber and others, provides a welcome means of access to the tombs' pictorial programs. According to Steingräber, this corpus "is an attempt . . . to illustrate all the more important tomb walls with painting in Etruria" (p. 257). The tombs are illustrated by black-and-white drawings and photos alongside the catalog entries, and by nearly two hundred color photos of the paintings themselves and of watercolors based on them. The catalog entry for each tomb includes a description of the tomb's plan, its decoration, date, archaeological contents (if known), and important features; bibliography for each tomb is also provided. Plans of individual tombs and of the whole cemetery at Tarquinia, by far the richest site in terms of finds, can be found on pages 384–87. After these plans is a useful index of the thematic motifs in the paintings. *Etruscan Painting* also has valuable introductory chapters, the most important of which is the discussion, broken down by period, in the chapter entitled "Style, Chronology, and Iconography." Some new suggestions are made here regarding possible interpretations of recurrent motifs. For example, it is proposed that the banquet, the grove, and the grove "peopled by a tipsy company" may "illustrate the Dionysian aspect of the Etruscan funerary cult and belief in the hereafter" (p. 48). Researchers should also be on the lookout for the future publication of a lengthier, more detailed corpus of Etruscan tomb paintings that is being planned by the Istituto di Studi Etruschi ed Italici at Florence.

On the first page of *Etruscan Vase-painting*, J. D. Beazley makes the following observations: "The Etruscans were gifted artists, but clay vases were not their forte. . . . Yet many of their clay vases have great interest of subject. In style, they imitate Greek models, but they have a characteristic flavour which is sometimes agreeably racy." While the corpus of examples in this study can be added to, Beazley's treatment of the history of Etruscan vase-painting is still the most insightful, especially in chapter 1, a survey of some of the vases with the most interesting subjects. These subjects are often Greek myths with new emphases, as in the case of plate 10.3, the only known depiction of Pasiphae nursing an infant Minotaur. The rest of Beazley's study consists of additions and corrections to earlier literature on Etruscan black-figure vases; and chapters of attribution lists and groups, with discussions, of Etruscan red-figure vases and of vases executed in other techniques such as "superposed colour." Beazley's discussions include digressions on Etruscan vase representations that have clearly been copied from works in other media or from Athenian vases. Addenda for each chapter are at the back of the volume. The reader familiar with the format of Beazley's corpora on Athenian vase-painting (see chapter 10, "Athenian Vases") will have no difficulty using *Etruscan Vase-painting*.

Ash urns in the form of small sarcophagi, with the deceased shown reclining on the lids, were produced in great numbers during the Etruscan Hellenistic period at three centers in northern Etruria—Volterra, Chiusi, and Perugia. The urns of Volterra are the subject of the study by Gabriele Cateni and Fabio Fiaschi, *Le urne di Volterra e l'artigianato artistico degli Etruschi* (The Urns of Volterra and the Workshop Practices of the Etruscans). This study is valuable in two ways: first, it has excellent color and black-and-white general views and details of the tufa and alabaster urns of Volterra, and second, it provides interesting hypotheses on important issues such as the significance and sources of the mythological reliefs that decorate the fronts of many of the urns. The authors suggest, for instance, that when females play heroic roles in mythological scenes on the urns, the deceased for whom the urns were intended were also females perceived as having possessed the same heroic qualities as their mythological prototypes. In a number of instances, the prominent roles for females do not correspond with the preserved Greek literary tradition, particularly the dramatic one. It seems, then, that the Etruscans either had their own separate literary tradition that only survives in artistic representations based on it, or that Etruscan artists modified the Greek tradition to fit the requirements of those commissioning the monuments. Footnotes at the bottoms of the pages refer the reader to previous scholarship.

Enough Etruscan words and linguistic constructions are understood, that with the help of *The Etruscan Language: An Introduction,* by Giuliano and Larissa Bonfante, the reader can decipher simple, formulaic Etruscan inscriptions. Particularly useful chapters for such endeavors are those entitled "Grammar"; the "Glossary" (a dictionary of known Etruscan words and names); "Mythological Figures" (names of mythological characters, with variants given, some of which are not included in the "Glossary"); "Sources: Sample inscriptions and texts" (many of these, which are illustrated by line drawings are from art works of different media); and "Archaeological Introduction" (chronologically arranged histories of the evidence regarding writing in different Etruscan cities). Frequent reference is made to other publications of the Etruscan inscriptions under discussion; these are referred to in abbreviated forms which are explained in the list of abbreviations located before the bibliography at the back of the volume.

## Bibliographic Entries for Supplementary Sources

Beazley, J. D. *Etruscan Vase-painting*. Oxford Monographs on Classical Archaeology. Oxford: Clarendon Press, 1947.

Bonfante, Giuliano, and Larissa Bonfante. *The Etruscan Language: An Introduction*. New York and London: New York Univ. Press, 1983.

Brown, W. Llewellyn. *The Etruscan Lion*. Oxford Monographs on Classical Archaeology. Oxford: Clarendon Press, 1960.

Cateni, Gabriele, and Fabio Fiaschi. *Le urne di Volterra e l'artigianato artistico degli Etruschi*. Florence: Sansoni, 1984.

Cristofani, Mauro. *I bronzi degli Etruschi*. Contributions by Edilberto Formigli and Maria Elisa Micheli. Novara: Istituto Geografico De Agostini, 1985.

Dohrn, Tobias. *Die etruskische Kunst im Zeitalter der griechischen Klassik: Die Interimsperiode*. Mainz am Rhein: P. von Zabern, 1982.

Hus, Alain. *Recherches sur la statuaire en pierre étrusque archaïque*. Vol. 198, *Bibliothèque des Écoles Françaises d'Athènes et de Rome*. Paris: E. de Boccard, 1961.

Richardson, Emeline Hill. *Etruscan Votive Bronzes: Geometric, Orientalizing, Archaic*. 2 vols. Mainz am Rhein: P. von Zabern, 1983.

Riis, P. J. *Etruscan Types of Heads: A Revised Chronology of the Archaic and Classical Terracottas of Etruscan Campania and Central Italy*. Vol. 9.5, *Det Kongelige Danske Videnskabernes Selskab*. *Historisk-filosofiske Skrifter*. Copenhagen: Munksgaard, 1981.

Steingräber, Stephan, and David and Francesca R. Ridgway, eds. *Etruscan Painting: Catalogue Raisonné of Etruscan Wall Paintings*. Translated by Mary Blair and Brian Phillips. New York: Johnson Reprint Corp. and Harcourt, 1986.

## Additional Supplementary Sources

Andreae, Bernard, Horst Blanck, Cornelia Weber-Lehmann, et al. *Pittura Etrusca: Disegni e documenti del XIX secolo dall'archivio dell'Istituto Archeologico Germanico*. Translated by Margarete Bambas Bernava. Studi di archeologia pubblicati dalla Soprintendenza Archeologica per l'Etruria Meridionale 2. Catalog of an exhibition in the Museo Nazionale, Tarquinia, April–September, 1986. Rome: De Luca, 1986.

Andrén, Arvid. *Architectural Terracottas from Etrusco-Italic Temples*. Lund: C. W. K. Gleerup; Leipzig: O. Harrassowitz, 1940.

———. *Deeds and Misdeeds in Classical Art and Antiquities*. Studies in Mediterranean Archaeology, Pocket-book 36. Partille, Sweden: Paul Åström, 1986.

Banti, Luisa. *Etruscan Cities and Their Culture*. Translated by Erika Bizzarri. Berkeley and Los Angeles: Univ. of California Press, 1973.

Bordenache Battaglia, Gabriella, Mario Moretti, Massimo Pallottino, and Giuseppe Proietti. *Il Museo Nazionale Etrusco di Villa Giulia*. Scientific direction by Massimo Pallottino; edited by Giuseppe Proietti. Rome: Edizioni Quasar, 1980.

Briguet, Marie-Françoise. *Le sarcophage des époux de Cerveteri du Musée du Louvre*. With the assistance of Pier Roberto Del Francia. Monumenti Etruschi 4. Leo S. Olschki, 1989.

Cristofani, Mauro. *Statue-cinerario chiusine di età classica*. Archaeologica 1. Rome: Giorgio Bretschneider, 1975.

Cristofani, Mauro, and Marina Martelli, eds. *L'oro degli etruschi*. Novara: Istituto Geografico De Agostini, 1985.

Del Chiaro, Mario. *Etruscan Red-Figured Vase-Painting at Caere*. Berkeley: Univ. of California Press, 1974.

Dennis, George. *The Cities and Cemeteries of Etruria*. Abridged ed. Edited and with new introduction and bibliography by Pamela Hemphill. Princeton: Princeton Univ. Press, 1985.

Galestin, Marjan C. *Etruscan and Italic Bronze Statuettes*. Warfhuizen: Rijksuniversiteit Groningen, 1987.

Grant, Michael. *The Etruscans*. New York: Scribner, 1981.

Haynes, Sybille. *Etruscan Bronzes*. London and New York: Sotheby's Publications, 1985.

Herbig, Reinhard. *Götter und Dämonen der Etrusker*. 2d ed. Edited and revised by Erika Simon. Mainz: P. von Zabern, 1965.

———. *Die jüngeretruskischen Steinsarkophage*. Vol. 7, *Die antiken Sarkophagreliefs*. Berlin: Gebr. Mann, 1952.

Jannot, Jean-René. *Les reliefs archaïques de Chiuṣi*. Collection de l'École Française de Rome 71. Rome: École Française de Rome, 1984.

Pallottino, Massimo. *Etruscan Painting*. Translated by M. E. Stanley and Stuart Gilbert. The Great Centuries of Painting. Geneva, Switzerland: Albert Skira, 1952.

Pallottino, Massimo, and H. and I. Jucker. *Art of the Etruscans*. London: Thames & Hudson, 1955.

Prayon, Friedhelm. *Frühetruskische Grab- und Hausarchitektur*. Mitteilungen des Deutschen Archäologischen Instituts. Römische Abteilung. Ergänzungsheft 22. Heidelberg: F. H. Kerle, 1975.

Rasmussen, Tom B. *Bucchero Pottery from Southern Etruria*. Cambridge Classical Studies. New York: Cambridge Univ. Press, 1979.

Riis, P. J. *Tyrrhenika: An Archaeological Study of the Etruscan Sculpture in the Archaic and Classical Periods*. Copenhagen: Munksgaard, 1941.

Scullard, H. H. *The Etruscan Cities and Rome*. Aspects of Greek and Roman Life. Ithaca, N.Y.: Cornell Univ. Press, 1967.

Sox, David. *Unmasking the Forger: The Dossena Deception*. New York: Universe, 1988.

Spivey, Nigel Jonathan. *The Micali Painter and his Followers*. Oxford Monographs on Classical Archaeology. Oxford: Clarendon Press, 1987.

Sprenger, Maja. *Die etruskische Plastik des V. Jahrhunderts v. Chr. und ihr Verhältnis zur griechischen Kunst*. Rome: "L'Erma" di Bretschneider, 1972.

Steingräber, Stephan. *Etrurien: Städte, Heiligtümer, Nekropolen*. Reise und Studium. Munich: Hirmer, 1981.

Torelli, Mario. *Etruria*. Guide archeologiche Laterza 3. Rome-Bari: Gius. Laterza & Figli, 1980.

# ۱3۱

# Roman Art and Architecture

Strong, Donald E. *Roman Art.* 2d ed. Preface by and prepared for press by Jocelyn M. C. Toynbee; revised by Roger Ling. Harmondsworth, Middlesex, and New York: Penguin, 1988.

## ART FORM

Roman art glorifies specific policies and accomplishments of the Roman state and its leaders, while Greek art gives expression to the more general ideals of Greek civilization as a whole. The specificity of Roman art manifests itself in realistic Roman portraits in statuary and on coins, in Roman historical reliefs such as the decoration on the column of Trajan, and in Imperial monuments such as the arch of Titus, where divinities like Victory are shown giving assistance to and approbation of the actions of the emperor. Besides supporting this public, propagandistic art, wealthy Romans spent vast sums on lavish decoration of their homes and villas. Handsome paintings, often with mythological content and apparently often derived from lost Greek originals, decorated the walls of these dwellings, while floors often bore ornate mosaic configurations. Statuary and statuettes—both Roman originals and copies of Greek masterpieces—graced interiors and garden courts, and small objects of precious and semiprecious materials, such as exquisitely executed gemstones, were the personal property of the Roman nobility. In short, the Imperial family and Roman aristocrats achieved a lifestyle whose luxury far surpassed the simpler, more community-based existence of the Greeks.

The Romans were also great master-builders. Having perfected construction in concrete, they erected huge amphitheaters that were supported by vaults, as well as enormous vaulted bathing establishments, market halls, and temples. The concrete vaults of these structures, with their various curved shapes, manipulated space in a completely new and free fashion in comparison to the post-and-lintel construction technique of the Greeks. The Roman structures were further beautified through the addition of stucco and marble veneering and handsome facades displaying columns in the Greek orders.

The magnificence of Roman architecture and the historical emphasis in her art forms can be said to be the traits that are uniquely Roman. The many Roman copies of Greek paintings and sculptures demonstrate another facet of Roman art—admiration for Greek masterpieces. The same tendency is also evident in the frequent intrusion of elements of Greek idealization into works that also exhibit aspects of Roman realism. The result of the mingling of Greek and Roman elements was an uneven stylistic development in Roman art, with sometimes a stronger Greek emphasis and sometimes a more marked Roman verism apparent. The exact nature of this blend in the art of each Republican statesman and each emperor of the Imperial period evidently depended on the propagandistic goals of the leader in question. An emperor such as Augustus who wanted to stress his noble ancestry tended to adopt a classicizing style, while one of humbler origins, such as Vespasian, utilized a straightforward, realistic style that projected a soldierly competence. Yet even in the most classicizing Roman art, the thread of Roman realism and purposefulness is always present.

Art of the Late Roman Empire took a new turn away from both classicism and realism; in their places Diocletian and his three co-rulers from the Tetrarchy established a "de-personalized formula—an imperial cult image achieved at the expense of personal identity" (Strong, *Roman Art*, p. 264). This new image was simplified and forceful, and was intended to reassure the inhabitants of the Empire that a politically stable government had replaced the brief and chaotic rules of the third-century Soldier-Emperors. The same type of unnaturalistic image persisted in the spiritualized art of the Early Byzantine period.

## RESEARCH USE

*Roman Art*, by Donald E. Strong, forms an excellent introduction to the manifold art forms, styles, and thematic emphases of Roman art of Italy and the provinces and their sources. According to Strong, the variety of modes of artistic expression within the Roman Empire arises from the imitation of art imported from other cultures, especially the admired Etruscan and Greek civilizations; from the commissioning of foreign artists; and from diverse propagandistic goals on the part of the patrons themselves. At least some of Strong's theories on the sources for particular styles and themes may need to be revised in the future as poorly represented periods and regions are better understood through the discovery and study of more examples. Nonetheless, Strong's reference work, by attempting to make sense of all the major artistic movements in the vast Roman Empire, provides an enormously useful foundation which can be refined in its specifics by future generations of scholars. The particular art works considered in *Roman Art* are presented as examples of developments of particular phases and are not described in exacting detail. In addition, the bases for accepting particular datings and other controversial aspects are not always explained. Thus the reader needs to use the notes in the second edition of *Roman Art* for further literature on specific works, or to turn to the lengthy, up-to-date bibliography of the second edition, which is arranged by general books and studies of media, for references of a broader scope. Furthermore, some of the books discussed in Complementary References below contain excellent detailed descriptions of major Roman monuments.

# ORGANIZATION

The table of contents, which lists both chapter titles and subheadings, appears at the front of *Roman Art*. The subheadings, which break the chapters down into discussions of media, are used for all but the first chapter. Each chapter surveys the Roman relief sculpture, portraiture, sarcophagi, interior decoration consisting of wall paintings and mosaics, and provincial art of a coherent stylistic phase; for example, chapter 10 is devoted to the art of the Severans from 193 to 235 A.D. Strong's textual discussion begins with the simple figures from graves of the Early Iron Age, traces the emergence of Roman art during the Republic, and continues throughout the Empire and beyond the reign of Constantine to the introduction of the Early Byzantine style. Major art forms including architectural sculpture are considered, along with the minor arts, but architecture is omitted. Two hundred sixty-three black-and-white photographs and drawings accompany the text. Also, preceding the first chapter are two maps showing the locations of Roman cities in the entire Roman Empire and in Italy alone.

Before the maps and after the table of contents are the "Editor's Foreword" and the prefaces to the two editions. A list of abbreviations and the notes (which make use of the abbreviations) appear after the fourteen chapters of text. The numbers in the notes that are in bold-faced type are the matching page numbers in the text. A useful glossary of technical terms in Latin, Greek, Italian, and English follows the notes, and the long bibliography (described above) is next. The labels that appear under the illustrations within the text identify the theme of each work, the medium (if other than marble), the provenance (if known), the date, and the current location. The list of illustrations, located before the index at the back of the volume, repeats this information and adds sources for the illustrations which were not provided by the museums or collections where the pieces are currently housed. The general index at the end of Strong's book provides access to textual mentions and illustrations of particular art works by their provenances, current locations, themes, and artists. Also, when a work is named only in a note, the page of the note is given, while the chapter number is cited in parentheses and the number of the note appears in superscript. The index also refers the reader to discussions of mythological and historical personages, regional styles, and categories of art, such as "Christian iconography."

## COMPLEMENTARY REFERENCES

*The Art of Rome,* by Bernard Andreae, forms a pictorial complement to Strong's *Roman Art.* It is furnished with 158 color photos and more than seven hundred black-and-white photos and architectural plans and reconstructions. This lavish selection of illustrations concentrates on portraiture, relief sculpture (with complete photographic records of a number of important Roman triumphal arches), wall painting and mosaics, and architecture; a limited selection of gems, metalware vessels, and coins is also illustrated. The goal of the textual discussion is to present "a step-by-step exposition of Roman art as the expression of a historical reality conditioned by political, social, economic, religious, and cultural factors. . ." (p. 9). Thus, the artistic programs of individual Roman emperors and of specific monuments erected in their honor are revealed to be calculated and effective propaganda tools that promoted their Imperial policies. The last part of Andreae's text consists of illustrated surveys of the urban development and significant surviving buildings from major Roman cities throughout the Empire. Here frequent references are made, in abbreviated forms, to publications that are more fully cited in the bibliography at the end of the volume.

For those who read German, *Das römische Weltreich* (The Roman Empire), by Theodor Kraus and others, forms another excellent companion-volume for Strong's *Roman Art.* It has over four hundred black-and-white and thirty-two color plates, all of excellent quality, and many of them the same monuments from Italy and the provinces which Strong discusses. The plates are arranged by medium; all media are illustrated, including architecture, which Strong omits. After the plates is extensive commentary consisting of introductions to each medium and detailed descriptions of the works illustrated, with bibliography. (For an explanation of the abbreviations used, see pp. 301–4.) The architectural commentary includes many ground plans and reconstructions. Preceding the plates are chronologically arranged chapters on the general development of Roman art from the Republican period through the Empire, and up to the beginning of the Byzantine period. An additional chapter considers Parthian art, which provided an important stylistic component of Byzantine art. Throughout the commentary, the introductions to the commentary, and the general chapters at the front of the book, an effort is made to define the Roman ideology that caused the reshaping of features derived from the art of other cultures, particularly the Greek, into a distinctly Roman style. Attempts are also made to define the propagandistic purposes of specific Roman monuments. At the end of the volume, after the list of abbreviations, is a lengthy bibliography first divided into several general categories and then arranged by medium. Following this is a chronological chart covering the time frame from 800 B.C. to 500 A.D. that correlates political events with architectural monuments, art works and styles, and literary and philosophical figures and compositions.

*Roman Art: A Modern Survey of the Art of Imperial Rome*, by George M. A. Hanfmann, provides detailed descriptions of a select number of masterpieces of Roman art and architecture, enlivened with pertinent texts from ancient literary sources. After five brief introductory chapters that define the character of the major phases of Roman art, a chronological table, and a general bibliography, Hanfmann's handbook presents two sets of plates accompanied by detailed commentary and bibliography. In the hardback edition of 1964, the first set of plates consists of black-and-white photographs, drawings, and reconstructions of architecture, portraits, and relief sculptures. The second set, all color photographs, consists of wall paintings and mosaics. The paperback edition of 1975 has all black-and-white reproductions but incorporates many additions to both the general bibliography and the bibliographic citations for individual illustrations (see the addenda at the back of the book).

Two corpora bring together translated passages from works in Latin and Greek on ancient Roman art and architecture. *The Art of Rome c. 753 B.C.–337 A.D.*, by J. J. Pollitt, presents the ancient sources in chapters on the art of the different phases of the Roman Republic and the reigns of the Roman emperors; each chapter is divided into groups of passages that deal with particular media. Pollitt's corpus can enliven textual discussions in Strong's book with eyewitness accounts of particular monuments (see the "Geographical Index") or Roman artists (see the "Index of Artists"), and it can help the reader achieve a sense of the whole artistic climate during a particular period or emperor's reign (see the pertinent chapter). The second book is *Urbs Roma: A Source Book of Classical Texts on the City and Its Monuments*, by Donald R. Dudley. While Pollitt's collection of literary sources covers the art and architecture of the entire Roman Empire, in Dudley's work all literary sources deal exclusively with the architecture of Rome. The sources on a particular ancient building in Rome are presented as a unit; these units are grouped according to the regions in the city where the buildings are or were located. The volume also contains an introductory chapter which includes literary sources that describe general trends in the urban development of Rome. At the back of Dudley's reference are black-and-white photographs showing preserved monuments and their commemorative inscriptions, coins that record lost details of buildings, and views of the model of ancient Rome at the Museo della Civiltà Romana outside Rome. Descriptive captions beneath these plates include references to textual discussions. Notes preceding the plates provide citations of scholarly literature on specific buildings.

Two illustrated encyclopedias provide extensive information on Roman art and architecture along with citations of scholarly literature of all types. One of these references, *Encyclopedia of World Art*, has two general entries, entitled "Hellenistic-Roman Art" and "Roman Imperial Art," and several entries on regional styles, such as "Roman Art of the Eastern Empire." In addition, the ruins of Roman cities are concisely described in lengthy articles on the architecture of entire countries, such as "Italy." The researcher can quickly locate the volume and page number where a particular Roman city is discussed by looking the city up in the *Index*, which is volume 15 of the *Encyclopedia*. Articles on media, such as "Ceramics," on art forms, such as "Portraiture," and on other topics, such as "Historical Subjects," contain portions on Roman art. Furthermore, whole entries are devoted to famous Roman artists and architects, for example, "Apollodoros of Damascus." Mentions of less eminent Roman artists in general articles can be located in the *Index* volume. The illustrated *Supplement*, volume 16 of the *Encyclopedia*, contains a section on pages 83–87 that describes new Roman finds, current research methods, and recent publications. The second comprehensive reference is the Italian *Enciclopedia dell'arte antica, classica e orientale* (Encyclopedia of Ancient Art: Classical and Oriental). This has a general entry entitled "Romana, Arte" (Roman Art) and entries on Roman monument types (such as "Sarcofago, 7. Roma" [Sarcophagus, 7. Rome]), structural types (such as "Arco onorario e trionfale" [Honorary and triumphal arches]), themes, sites, and artists.

For summaries of the urban development and physical remains (particularly architecture) of pagan Roman cities in existence up to the early sixth century A.D., the reader should consult *The Princeton Encyclopedia of Classical Sites*. This exhaustive reference lists cities alphabetically by the names the sites had in antiquity; modern names that are different from ancient names are also listed with cross-references to the correct ancient names. The locations of all the sites included are shown on twenty-four maps at the back of the volume; each entry for a site refers the reader to the proper map. While this volume has no illustrations other than the maps, the bibliography at the end of each entry has superscript letters after references which contain illustrations of different types: [M] means the reference cited includes maps, [P] denotes plans, and [I] illustrations. Another excellent source for summaries of archaeological remains from major Roman cities is *The Oxford Classical Dictionary*, edited by N. G. L. Hammond and H. H. Scullard. Like *The Princeton Encyclopedia of Classical Sites*, this reference is not illustrated but mentions other publications with plans and plates. Unlike *The Princeton Encyclopedia*, it emphasizes the roles of Roman cities as cultural centers. Besides entries on Roman cities, *The Oxford Classical Dictionary* contains entries on major Roman artists and architects and on art forms, for example, "Sculpture, Roman."

*The Pictorial Dictionary of Ancient Rome*, by Ernest Nash, is an excellent source for photographs of all the surviving monuments of ancient Rome, including many details of sculptured and painted decoration. When a building's appearance was recorded before it suffered damage or destruction, Nash reproduces ancient coin illustrations or early prints of the building. Except for temples, the monuments are arranged alphabetically according to the Latin name for the building type; for example, the Golden House of Nero can be found under "Domus Aurea." Temples, however, are listed under the names of the divinities worshipped in them; for example, the Capitoline temple of Jupiter is found under "Iuppiter Optimus Maximus Capitolinus." For help in locating entries for specific buildings, see the index at the back of volume 2. Besides the photographs, each entry in *The Pictorial Dictionary* includes a brief account of the building from antiquity to the twentieth century, including mentions of modern excavations, as well as extensive bibliographic citations whose abbreviations are explained at the front of each volume.

The latest volumes of *L'Année philologique* (Philological Year), an annual annotated bibliography of publications of all kinds on the classical world, can be consulted for recent scholarship on Roman art and archaeology. For Roman material from Italy, the researcher can review the listings under the heading "Archéologie romaine" (Roman Archaeology). For Roman works from outside Italy, the researcher should consult the pertinent sections under "Archéologie préclassique et périphérique" (Preclassical and Peripheral Archaeology). Literature on the Roman remains from the British Isles, for example, is listed under the heading "Grande-Bretagne et Irlande (Great Britain and Ireland). If the researcher wishes to quickly locate literature on a particular Roman site, he or she can look up the site in the "Index Geographicus" (Geographical Index). Literature on a particular Roman artist, leader, or mythological character can be found by consulting another index, the "Index Nominum Antiquorum" (Index of Ancient Names). The numbers cited in both indexes are those that introduce each entry. The reader should note that literature on Roman coins is listed separately under the heading "Numismatique" (Numismatics). For those interested in mythology in Roman art, the section entitled "Religion et mythologie romaine et italique" (Roman and Italic Religion and Mythology) is recommended.

*Art Index,* a quarterly compilation of citations of articles from major journals, also provides access to literature on Roman art and architecture. Besides listing articles under the names of the authors, *Art Index* repeats citations under various subject headings. General articles are brought together under the headings "Art, Roman," and "Architecture, Roman." Articles on the thematic content of Roman art can be found in "Iconography, Roman." Additional literature is listed under headings for building types, such as "Arches, Triumphal," for media, such as "Pottery, Roman," and for the names of specific buildings, artists, and eminent historical personages. *Art Index* can be searched by computer on the Wilsonline online vendor service for the period from September 1984 onwards.

A comprehensive listing of the literature on Imperial state reliefs in Rome appears in Gerhard Koeppel's "Official State Reliefs of the City of Rome in the Imperial Age. A Bibliography." This bibliography provides exhaustive citations of the literature on major monuments in journals, monographs, and dictionaries. In addition, general books on Roman art, historical reliefs, and specific periods of Roman art are listed.

## Bibliographic Entries for Complementary References

Andreae, Bernard. *The Art of Rome.* Translated by Robert Erich Wolf. New York: Abrams, 1977.

*L'Année philologique: Bibliographie critique et analytique de l'antiquité gréco-latine.* Paris: Société d'édition "Les Belles Lettres," 1928– .

*Art Index: A Cumulative Author and Subject Index to a Selected List of Fine Arts Periodicals and Museum Bulletins.* New York: H. W. Wilson, 1929/30– .

Dudley, Donald R. *Urbs Roma: A Source Book of Classical Texts on the City and Its Monuments Selected and Translated with Commentary.* London: Phaidon Press, 1967.

*Enciclopedia dell'arte antica, classica e orientale.* Edited by Ranuccio Bianchi Bandinelli. 7 vols., *Supplemento,* and *Atlante dei complessi figurati.* Rome: Istituto della Enciclopedia Italiana, 1958–73.

*Encyclopedia of World Art.* Translation of *Enciclopedia universale dell'arte.* 14 vols. New York: McGraw-Hill, 1959–67. Vol. 15, *Index.* New York: McGraw-Hill, 1968. Vol. 16, *Supplement: World Art in Our Time.* Edited by Bernard S. Myers. New York: McGraw-Hill and Publishers Guild, 1983.

Hammond, N. G. L., and H. H. Scullard, eds. *The Oxford Classical Dictionary.* 2d ed. Oxford: Clarendon Press, 1970.

Hanfmann, George M. A. *Roman Art: A Modern Survey of the Art of Imperial Rome.* Greenwich, Conn.: New York Graphic, 1964. Paperback ed., with bibliographic additions. New York: Norton, 1975.

Koeppel, Gerhard. "Official State Reliefs of the City of Rome in the Imperial Age. A Bibliography." In *Aufstieg und Niedergang der römischen Welt: Geschichte und Kultur Roms im Spiegel der neureren Forschung 2, Principat 12.1,* pp. 477–506. Berlin and New York: Walter de Gruyter, 1982.

Kraus, Theodor, et al. *Das römische Weltreich.* Propyläen Kunstgeschichte 2. Berlin: Propyläen Verlag, 1967.

Nash, Ernest. *Pictorial Dictionary of Ancient Rome.* 2d ed. 2 vols. New York and Washington: Praeger, 1968.

Pollitt, J. J. *The Art of Rome c. 753 B.C.–337 A.D.: Sources and Documents.* Sources & Documents in the History of Art Series, edited by H. W. Janson. Englewood Cliffs, N.J.: Prentice-Hall, 1966. Reprint. New York: Cambridge Univ. Press, 1983.

*The Princeton Encyclopedia of Classical Sites.* Edited by Richard Stillwell, William L. MacDonald, and Marian Holland McAllister. Princeton: Princeton Univ. Press, 1976.

# HANDBOOKS

*A Handbook of Roman Art: A Comprehensive Survey of All the Arts of the Roman World,* by Martin Henig and others, is a reliable, well-documented, up-to-date and comprehensive survey of Roman art. After an introduction by Henig that characterizes the diversity of Roman art, there is a chapter called "Early Roman Art," by Tom Rasmussen, which describes the development of Roman Republican art under the influence of Etruscan and Greek art. Following this are chapters by different authors devoted to the separate media of architecture, sculpture, wall painting, mosaics, metalwork and jewelry, coins, pottery, products made from terra-cotta, glassware, and inscriptions. Finally, a chapter by Richard Reece entitled "Art in Late Antiquity" investigates the "clear change in direction from representation of individuals to symbolic types" (p. 234). The text is illustrated by black-and-white photos, plans, and reconstructions, and by some color photos, primarily of paintings and mosaics. At the end of the handbook are abbreviations, a chart of labeled drawings showing Roman vessel shapes, a glossary of technical terms, a map of the Roman Empire, notes for the different chapters of text, and a lengthy bibliography divided into general books and those on particular media.

*Roman Art, Romulus to Constantine*, by Nancy H. and Andrew Ramage, is a clear and concise handbook which is particularly valuable for instructing students with no previous exposure to Roman art. After two chapters on Etruscan prototypes and Roman Republican art, the text is arranged chronologically according to the periods of rule of major emperors or families of emperors. These chapters on different phases of Roman Imperial art are broken down into lucid discussions of different media such as architecture, portraiture, relief sculpture, and wall paintings. The text is accompanied by architectural drawings and black-and-white and color photographs. A chronological table of the Roman emperors, a glossary, and a general bibliography are at the back of this handbook.

*Roman Art: Early Republic to Late Empire*, by Cornelius Vermeule, is an exceptionally learned stylistic history of Roman art and architecture. Through a careful consideration of selected monuments from all the different periods in the development of Roman art, Vermeule distinguishes characteristics which seem to be the result of conscious emulation of different phases of Greek art from those traits which he defines as Roman. Works of all the different media and from every part of the Empire are discussed, with special emphasis given to pieces in Boston's Museum of Fine Arts. At the beginning of the volume, after a chart of significant events in the history of Greece, the Eastern Mediterranean, and Italy, Vermeule presents a concise summary of the main stylistic trends in Roman art. Following this is the main text, divided into chronologically arranged discussions of selected genres of Roman art and architecture and of specific monuments, which are illustrated at the back. Preceding these black-and-white illustrations is a list of captions which includes information on the pieces illustrated and bibliography; also, there are bibliographical notes for the text in the "Additions."

*The Art of the Romans*, by Jocelyn M. C. Toynbee—one of the great scholars of Roman art—is a lucid and very readable survey of Roman art of the entire Empire. After an introductory chapter on all media of Republican art from the sixth through the second centuries B.C., Toynbee devotes separate chapters to the characteristic Roman art forms that are the focus of her handbook: sculpture, painting, and mosaics. One chapter, for instance, is entitled "Portrait Sculpture in the Round and in High Relief," while another is called "Historical Reliefs in Stone and Marble." Toynbee's black-and-white plates, besides being discussed in the text, are described in "Notes on the Plates," where bibliography is also frequently provided. Publications featuring art works that Toynbee mentions in the text but does not illustrate are named in the notes, which are followed by a useful "Select Bibliography," located immediately before Toynbee's plates. In *Some Notes on Artists in the Roman World*, the same author combines information from ancient literary sources with evidence from signed and unsigned, but stylistically distinctive, art works to offer "a sketch for a general picture of artists *qua* persons in Roman-age life and society, whether they were architects, sculptors, painters, mosaicists, metal-workers, gem-engravers, or medallists" (p. 7). The conclusions which Toynbee arrives at, for example, regarding the influence of the sculptural school of Turkish Aphrodisias on the relief sculptures of Northern Africa and Rome, establish artistic connections between cities in different regions of the Empire that suggest explanations for innovations in areas such as thematic content, figural composition, and methods of execution. This slender but useful study has no illustrations, but includes notes that refer the reader to the ancient literary sources and to modern scholarship.

*The Art of Rome and Her Empire* is by another eminent authority on Roman art, Heinz Kähler. After devoting a long chapter to the topic, "Fundamental Characteristics of Roman Art," Kähler presents a chronologically arranged survey of the artistic goals and monuments of Roman emperors from Augustus to Constantine. Changes during the Empire in the designs of public and private buildings, and in the styles of relief sculptures, portraits, and wall paintings, are verbally elucidated and illustrated with plans, reconstructions, and color and black-and-white photographs. At the back of the volume is a map of the provinces of the Roman Empire at the time of its greatest extent under Trajan; a bibliography, with literature cited for monuments discussed in the text; and two tables chronicling parallel events in history and the arts.

*Rome: The Center of Power 500 B.C. to A.D. 200*, by Ranuccio Bianchi Bandinelli, is a lavishly illustrated examination of the art of Rome during the period of the Republic and the first two hundred years of the Empire. In this chronologically arranged consideration, Bianchi Bandinelli traces two stylistic threads—a formal and idealizing approach inherited from the Greeks, and a simple and straightforward "mid-Italic" or "plebeian" trend that was native to the region of Rome. The author discerns a successful fusion of these two styles by the time of Trajan, and the creation of an art with a grandeur and historical content appropriate for the propagandistic goals of the Roman emperors. After the textual discussion, with black-and-white and color photos of all media of Roman art placed alongside it, *Rome: The Center of Power* offers the following research aids at the back: some architectural plans and reconstructions; a lengthy chart tracing contemporary historical and artistic events; a bibliography listing general books and studies of different periods of art and of architecture; "Notes on the Illustrations"; a useful "Glossary-Index" with names and terms; two maps showing Rome's Imperial expansion; and a plan showing the locations of Rome's principal monuments.

Rome: The Late Empire, Roman Art A.D. 200–400, also by Bianchi Bandinelli, is the sequel volume to Rome: The Center of Power. Unlike the previous study, which concentrates on the art of the capital city of Rome, this work examines the art of the entire Empire, including the West and the East. The author attempts to demonstrate that the "plebeian" style of the earlier Empire was the predecessor for the emotionally charged but unnaturalistic local modes of expression of the Late Empire. These expressive styles in turn led to Medieval art in Europe and Byzantine art in the East. Rome: The Late Empire has the same format of text alongside handsome illustrations as Rome: The Center of Power; and the research aids at the end of the volume are also similar.

In Roman Art from the Republic to Constantine, Richard Brilliant combines studies of particular media in Roman art with general histories of its styles. After an introduction that summarizes the varied approaches that have been applied to the study of Roman art history, Brilliant devotes four chapters to different classes of Roman architecture and art; two final chapters then examine "Non-Periodic Styles" (such as plebeian art) and "Periodic Styles" (such as Julio-Claudian classicizing art). At the end of the survey is a bibliography arranged by references pertinent to chapters in the text, and an historical table covering major events and personages of cultural eminence from Rome's foundation to the end of the Empire.

Ancient Italy: A Study of the Interrelations of Its Peoples as Shown in Their Arts, by Gisela M. A. Richter, provides an excellent summary of evidence pertaining to the roles Greek art and artists played in shaping Roman art. After two chapters on the major regional styles in Italy in the Archaic, Classical, and Hellenistic periods, Richter's fascinating study continues with three chapters on copies and adaptations of Greek art of different media for Roman patrons. The final chapter, "Original Contributions of the Roman Age," focuses on Roman portraits, funerary monuments, and historical reliefs. Richter demonstrates that even in the art forms where Roman content and style are very apparent, Greek figure types and stylistic devices are intermingled with Roman elements. Following this chapter are appendixes on the modern and ancient painting process and on the Greek sculptors called "the Pasiteleans." Ancient Italy contains footnotes below the text; a list of abbreviations and a bibliography at the front; and black-and-white photographs at the back.

H. P. L'Orange discerns parallel developments in Roman art and government in Art Forms and Civic Life in the Late Roman Empire. In this concise and insightful consideration, the author demonstrates how, circa

300 A.D., "the new 'block-style' in art emerged contemporary with the formation of massive structures in the state and community" (p. 126). According to L'Orange, the similarities in the structure of art and the organization of the Late Imperial state were expressions of the same spiritual desire for stability in all aspects of life. The art forms that L'Orange focuses on in his illustrated study are architecture, relief sculpture, and portrait sculpture. Footnotes at the bottoms of the pages direct the reader to further scholarly discussions.

*Roman Crafts*, edited by Donald E. Strong and David Brown, utilizes different types of evidence to reconstruct the processes by which the various Roman art forms were manufactured. The art forms considered encompass the minor arts, such as pottery and glassware, and the monumental arts, such as marble sculpture and wall painting. The discussion of each artistic process is accompanied by reconstruction drawings of tools and stages of production, and by color and black-and-white photos of Roman artifacts and any surviving materials from Roman workshops. At the end of each chapter is a useful bibliography on the process under consideration.

In *Roman Art and Architecture*, Mortimer Wheeler achieves a nice balance between an emphasis on the creative aspects of Roman architecture and art and clarification of the debt of Roman art to earlier Greek styles, particularly those of the Hellenistic period. According to Wheeler, the greatest Roman contributions were in the realms of the grandeur of architecture, with its new concern for shaping vast interior spaces; individual characterization in portraiture; the narrative vigor and scope of historical reliefs; and the thematic and stylistic variation in landscape paintings and in paintings of smaller aspects of daily life. The main chapters in Wheeler's interesting survey deal with Roman town planning in Italy and the provinces; major Roman building types throughout the Empire; and Roman contributions in sculpture and painting. Accompanying the textual discussion are plans, reconstructions, and black-and-white and color photos. At the back of the volume are bibliographic notes for the text and a brief general bibliography.

For new and in-print handbooks on Roman art, the researcher should consult the headings "Art, Greco-Roman" and "Art, Roman" in the latest edition of the *Subject Guide to Books in Print.*

There are two excellent handbooks in the Pelican History of Art series that discuss the entire history of Roman architecture. In the first edition, the text of these two books appeared together in a single volume entitled *Etruscan and Roman Architecture.* The second editions of these handbooks, however, were published as two separate volumes: *Etruscan and Early Roman Architecture,* by Axel Boëthius, and *Roman Imperial Architecture,* by J. B. Ward-Perkins. (The Etruscan sections of *Etruscan and Early Roman Architecture* are described in chapter 2, "Etruscan Art and

Architecture," under Handbooks.) After the chapter, "Etruscan Rome," in *Etruscan and Early Roman Architecture*, are the chapters, "Rome during the Struggle for Supremacy in Italy (386–about 200 B.C.)" and "Hellenized Rome 'Consuetudo Italica.'" In the last-named chapter, Boëthius stresses that "the amalgamation of Roman architectural patterns with hellenistic taste created something new" (p. 137). This chapter on the last two centuries of Roman Republican architecture traces the use of new materials and construction techniques in public and private buildings and the introduction of various Roman building types and regular town planning.

*Etruscan and Early Roman Architecture* discusses the pre-Imperial architecture òf the region of central Italy only, while *Roman Imperial Architecture* studies Imperial Roman architecture from the entire Roman Empire. In the latter survey, Ward-Perkins traces the development of architecture in the capital city of Rome and demonstrates how the architecture of each region outside Rome had its own unique character, in which diverse local traditions were combined with those from Rome. The author's goal is "the presentation of a reasonably coherent picture of some of the forces that were at work shaping the larger scene. . ." (p. 10). Within this framework specific building programs and monuments are discussed. The text is divided into three parts: "Architecture in Rome and Italy from Augustus to the Mid Third Century"; "The Architecture of the Roman Provinces"; and "Late Pagan Architecture in Rome and in the Provinces." These broad divisions are broken down into chapters and subheadings within chapters. *Etruscan and Early Roman Architecture* and *Roman Imperial Architecture* both have maps at the front; alongside the text illustrations consisting of plans, reconstructions, and black-and-white photos; a list of abbreviations; notes for the text, with many bibliographic citations; a glossary of architectural terms; and a bibliography with general references and references pertinent to particular chapters.

## Bibliographic Entries for Handbooks

Bianchi Bandinelli, Ranuccio. *Rome: The Center of Power 500 B.C. to A.D. 200.* Translated by Peter Green. The Arts of Mankind. New York: Braziller, 1970.
———. *Rome: The Late Empire, Roman Art A.D. 200–400.* Translated by Peter Green. The Arts of Mankind. New York: Braziller, 1971.
Boëthius, Axel. *Etruscan and Early Roman Architecture.* 2d ed. Revised by Roger Ling and Tom Rasmussen. Pelican History of Art. New York: Penguin, 1978.
Brilliant, Richard. *Roman Art from the Republic to Constantine.* London: Phaidon Press, 1974.
Henig, Martin, ed. *A Handbook of Roman Art: A Comprehensive Survey of All the Arts of the Roman World.* Ithaca, N.Y.: Cornell Univ. Press, 1983.
Kähler, Heinz. *The Art of Rome and Her Empire.* Rev. ed. Translated by J. R. Foster. Art of the World. New York: Greystone, 1965.

L'Orange, H. P. *Art Forms and Civic Life in the Late Roman Empire.* Translated by Knut Berg. Princeton: Princeton Univ. Press, 1965.

Ramage, Nancy H. and Andrew Ramage. *Roman Art, Romulus to Constantine.* Englewood Cliffs, N.J.: Prentice-Hall, 1991.

Richter, Gisela M. A. *Ancient Italy: A Study of the Interrelations of Its Peoples as Shown in Their Arts.* Jermone Lectures, Fourth Series. Ann Arbor, Mich.: Univ. of Michigan Press, 1955.

Strong, Donald E., and David Brown, eds. *Roman Crafts.* New York: New York Univ. Press, 1976.

*Subject Guide to Books in Print.* New York: R. R. Bowker, 1990– .

Toynbee, Jocelyn M. C. *The Art of the Romans.* Ancient People and Places, no. 43. New York and Washington: Praeger, 1965.

———. *Some Notes on Artists in the Roman World.* Collection Latomus 6. Brussels: Latomus, 1951.

Vermeule, Cornelius C. *Roman Art: Early Republic to Late Empire.* Art of Antiquity no. 3. Boston: Museum of Fine Arts, 1979.

Ward-Perkins, J. B. *Roman Imperial Architecture.* 2d ed. Pelican History of Art. New York: Penguin, 1981.

Wheeler, Mortimer. *Roman Art and Architecture.* World of Art Library. History of Art. London: Thames & Hudson, 1964. Reprint. New York: Thames & Hudson, 1985.

## SUPPLEMENTARY SOURCES

One of our greatest problems in understanding Roman art is our ignorance of the messages it was supposed to impart to the Roman people. In *Roman Art and Imperial Policy,* Niels Hannestad makes convincing suggestions about these messages in the course of his investigation of the propaganda content and the methods of presenting this content for a selection of Roman state monuments of all classes. Since Hannestad's study of the late Republican and Imperial periods is arranged chronologically, with different types of monuments from the same emperor's reign discussed as a unit, a general picture of each ruler's use of art as a propaganda tool emerges. In the epilogue, the author summarizes his goals: "it has been my intention to demonstrate, on the basis of . . . the monuments, that the emperor could rule actively, and that many emperors stood for a distinctive policy which they were actually able to carry through" (p. 347). Hannestad's thorough study has black-and-white photographs and drawings alongside the text, and extensive notes at the back of the volume. The notes refer to the numbers which appear next to references in the bibliography that follows the notes.

Another problem confronting scholars of Roman art is determining distinctions between Roman monuments of Italy and those in the provinces. An important contribution to this type of investigation is Cornelius C. Vermeule's *Roman Imperial Art in Greece and Asia Minor,* in which the author attempts to define the basic characteristics of Roman state art that was produced at Greek cities. Vermeule concludes that "this art is Roman in the sense that subjects and motivations are Roman, but it is Greek in design, style and execution" (p. 13). After the general introductory chapter containing this quote, Vermeule's book includes chapters on the following official Roman art forms from the Greek world: architecture, sculpture, inscriptions on different types of monuments, significant monuments (with special emphasis given to the Antonine altar from Ephesus), metalwork, and coins. Additional chapters adopt a chronological approach and summarize Roman art from the same region according to the reigns of the major Roman emperors. Black-and-white photos and drawings appear alongside the text. Bibliographic abbreviations and notes for the text precede and succeed the appendixes; the latter include annotated lists of portraits from Greek cities of Roman emperors and their family members, and lists of Roman monuments and inscriptions from monuments, arranged by their Greek provenances.

Three general studies in English investigate aspects of Roman sculpture. The Roman portion of A. W. Lawrence's *Greek and Roman Sculpture* provides discussions of selected Roman monuments and monument types of freestanding and relief sculpture whose Greek characteristics are highlighted. At the back of the volume are useful notes that cite bibliography on monuments described in the text; preceding these are a brief general bibliography and a list of abbreviations. Immediately after the last chapter of text is an appendix, "Deities, Their Attributes and Types." The 1969 reprint of the 1907 book by Eugénie Sellers Strong, *Roman Sculpture from Augustus to Constantine,* while outdated in its bibliographic citations, still provides very useful detailed descriptions of major Roman monuments of freestanding and relief sculpture. In addition, Strong's fascinating introduction summarizes scholarship on and attitudes to Roman art from the Renaissance to the early twentieth century. Unlike Lawrence, Strong stresses the continuing process of "Romanization" of Roman sculpture. Also, in the course of her discussions of particular sculptured monuments, she provides numerous quotations from ancient authors, thereby demonstrating that the concepts expressed in contemporary literature and art were similar. The history of primarily architectural Roman relief sculpture is presented in a more recent study by Donald E. Strong, *Roman Imperial Sculpture.* Major monuments from the Late Republic through the Empire are described, both in the chapters of text and in the commentary on the black-and-white plates. Strong stresses the ideological content of public relief sculptures, as well as stylistic changes and their possible sources in phenomena such as new importations of sculptors from different regions of the Greek world. Bibliographic citations are supplied both within the commentary for the plates and in a separate bibliography preceding the commentary.

One of the most fascinating but difficult branches of study in Roman sculpture is portraiture. Roman portrait statues and busts often have inadequately recorded or completely unknown provenances. In addition, since inscriptions are usually lacking, tentative identifications of portraits of eminent Roman statesmen and of Roman emperors and their family members have often been made on the basis of comparisons with inscribed miniature portraits on coins. A recent catalog by Maxwell L. Anderson and Leila Nista for an exhibition at Emory University, *Roman Portraits in Context: Imperial and Private Likenesses from the Museo Nazionale Romano*, discusses the different types of settings for Roman portraits and describes one or more examples from each setting. According to our current archaeological knowledge, Roman portraits were placed in homes, private villas, Imperial palaces and estates, marketplaces or fora, sanctuaries, and tombs. In *Roman Historical Portraits*, Jocelyn M. C. Toynbee demonstrates the methodology of identifying uninscribed sculptured portraits using inscribed coin portraits. This study examines portraits of Roman Republican statesmen to the beginning of Augustus's reign and of rulers in the provinces during the Republican and Imperial ages. Portraits of an individual statesman on coins, gems, reliefs, and freestanding sculptures are discussed as a unit, with frequent reference made to "ancient writers' comments, where such exist, on the characters' physique"; stylistic similarities between the coin portraits and portraits in other media are elucidated. Bibliography is provided for each portrait mentioned, whether it is illustrated or not, and bibliographic abbreviations are explained at the front of the volume.

Other investigations explore additional aspects of Roman portraits, such as expressive content, portrait types, and important collections of portraits. In the exhibition catalog, *Roman Portraits: Aspects of Self and Society*, K. Patricia Erhart and other scholars describe a selection of Republican and Imperial portraits from the Getty Museum. Emphasis is given to the way in which stylistic traits are manipulated to produce statements about the characters of the personages represented. Three of the four authors of the commentary on the portraits also provide useful general introductions to contextual and interpretive aspects of Roman portraits. *Studien zur statuarischen Darstellung der römischen Kaiser* (Studies on the Statuary Representation of the Roman Emperors), by Hans Georg Niemeyer, examines portraits of Roman emperors from the standpoints of the information gleaned from ancient literature, the different settings in which they were displayed, and the different costumes and roles the emperor assumes in them. An illustrated catalog of examples follows these general discussions. *Les portraits romains* (Roman Portraits), by Vagn Poulsen, is a two-volume catalog of the fine collection of Republican and Imperial Roman portraits in the Glyptotek Ny Carlsberg in Copenhagen. Each volume begins with a useful stylistic overview. The catalog entries, with extensive bibliographic citations, discuss not only the portraits in Copenhagen, but also uncontested and contested portraits of the same personages at other locations. Each portrait in Copenhagen is illustrated with at least one black-and-white photograph.

The Roman portraits in all the public museums in Rome are being lavishly published in the ongoing *Katalog der römischen porträts in den Capitolinischen Museen und den anderen kommunalen Sammlungen der Stadt Rom* (Catalog of the Roman Portraits in the Capitoline Museums and the Other Municipal Collections in the City of Rome). The volumes that have appeared, both of them by Klaus Fittschen and Paul Zanker, are *Kaiser- und Prinzenbildnisse* (Portraits of Emperors and Princes, vol. 1), and *Kaiserinnen- und Prinzessinnenbildnisse, Frauenporträts* (Portraits of Empresses, Princesses and Women, vol. 3). The catalog entries give full descriptions of each portrait, frequently referring to inscribed coins that support identifications and datings; other sculptured portraits of the same personages are also referred to. Citations of the scholarly literature are supplied both at the beginning of each entry and in notes. Multiple high-quality black-and-white photographs illustrate each portrait in Rome, and additional photographs are provided of portraits at other locations mentioned in the catalog entries.

Another important class of Roman statues is cult images. Evidence for these images from temples and for other representations of divinities in the city of Rome is brought together by Cornelius C. Vermeule in the illustrated study *The Cult Images of Imperial Rome*. A few actual images and fragments of images survive, and others were reproduced in large marble copies, but most are known only through miniature copies on coins, medallions, and statuettes. Vermeule discusses the different types of images of divinities as well as their often eclectic sources in Greek cult statues and other genres of Greek sculpture. Footnotes at the bottoms of the pages refer the reader to further scholarly literature.

Like Roman sculptures from other contexts, most statues from Roman villas have been separated from their original settings. Thus it requires effort and imagination to visualize the stunning effects these statues must have once created against the backdrops of the villas' architecture. Furthermore, it is difficult to reconstruct the complexes of sculptures that once decorated different areas of Roman villas and to determine their significance. *Die Skulpturen-Ausstattung römischer Villen in Italien* (The Sculptural Decoration of Roman Villas in Italy), by Richard Neudecker, begins to address these research questions in an examination of the classes of sculptures that were placed in Roman villas in Italy during the Republic and the Empire. Two chapters on the different statuary types (such as gods and athletes) from Republican and Imperial villas bring together and compare information from ancient literature and archaeological finds, and another chapter reviews the well-documented sculptural decoration of the Villa of the Papyri at Hercula-neum. There is also a summary chapter on the purposes of unified sculptural programs with particular thematic emphases. Following these chapters is an illustrated and annotated catalog that presents the archaeological history and sculptural finds from seventy-eight Italian villas; extensive bibliographical citations are provided to guide the reader to additional publications on the sculptures themselves and the villas where they were discovered.

Different categories of Roman relief sculpture have also been dis-cussed in scholarly studies. One of the most characteristically Roman forms of relief sculpture is state reliefs on public monuments. These reliefs are difficult for the modern observer to interpret, since they appear to be strictly realistic reproductions of actual events. However, a closer examination reveals that even the seemingly most accurate relief representations on monuments such as the column of Trajan include elements that have a symbolic value. Mario Torelli's *Typology and Structure of Roman Historical Reliefs* defines the distinctive characteristics and parallel literary forms for two major types of state reliefs: the " 'narrative,' meaning to describe well-determined historical events in a narrative form," and the relief which "aims at representing a status or a function and, eventually, moral qualities that are inherent to such status" (p. 119). Through a careful examination of Roman coins, state reliefs, and sarcophagi, Per Gustaf Hamberg, in *Studies in Roman Imperial Art with Special Reference to the State Reliefs of the Second Century,* draws a similar distinction between "the presentation of *res gestae* in a narrative over-flowing with analytical and concrete details" and "the synthetic and visionary attitude towards history" (p. 190). There are also monographs devoted to the study of individual monuments with state reliefs in Rome and in other cities within the Empire. Recent studies of such monuments include: *Der Titusbogen* (The Arch of Titus), by Michael Pfanner, which investigates both the architectural form and the sculptural decoration of the arch of Titus in Rome; and *La Colonna Traiana* (The Column of Trajan), by Salvatore Settis and others, which discusses the significance and artistic conventions of the reliefs from the column of Trajan in Rome and presents color photographs of all the scenes, taken from the column itself.

Besides buildings, another type of Roman monument with a rich and varied sculptural decoration is sarcophagi. These stone coffins bear sculptured reliefs on their sides and often on their lids. They have dif-ferent forms depending on the burial customs of the region where they were produced, and their reliefs represent aspects of the lives of the de-ceased as well as mythological scenes that seem to have been relevant to the earthly accomplishments of the deceased or to his or her aspirations regarding the afterlife. *Römische Sarkophage* (Roman Sarcophagi), by

Guntram Koch and Hellmut Sichtermann, provides a comprehensive scholarly introduction to Roman Imperial sarcophagi from Rome and all regions of the Empire. This illustrated reference reviews the forms of sarcophagi, their methods of manufacture, and their thematic content. Citations of further literature in the text and notes are abundant.

As Frank Sear observes in the preface to *Roman Architecture*, the history of Roman architecture always proves more difficult for students to understand than that of Greek architecture. This difficulty apparently arises out of the Romans' more complicated construction methods, which made frequent use of concrete cores with facings of various materials; the Roman preference for more ambitious and spatially and symbolically more sophisticated architectural complexes; and the tendency, especially during the late Empire, for the architecture of the provinces to have a transforming impact on the architecture of Rome and Italy. For the reader who wishes to have at his or her disposal a comprehensible introduction to the technical aspects of Roman architecture as well as to its cultural significance and diversity, Sear's illustrated survey is recommended. Besides the chronologically arranged chapters on the development of Republican and Imperial architecture, there are chapters entitled "Roman Building Types," and "Roman Architects, Building Techniques and Materials," and chapters on the architecture of both Roman towns in Italy and Roman cities in the provinces. Sear provides some bibliography at the front of the volume and in notes at the back.

*The Ancient Roman City*, by John E. Stambaugh, presents a fascinating overview of urban planning and daily life in Rome, Italy, and the provinces. By skillfully combining evidence from ancient accounts of city life with information from physical remains, Stambaugh defines both the architectural forms in the different phases of Rome's history and the types of activities that took place in them. The urban developments of Cosa, Pompeii, Ostia, Arles, and Timgad are more briefly outlined. City plans accompany the textual discussion and photographs and reconstructions appear at the back. Detailed notes following the plates cite many further studies of the topography of Roman cities and aspects of their civic life.

In addition to general reviews of Roman urban planning, such as Stambaugh's book, there are many monographs devoted to the architecture of individual Roman cities. An excellent example of such a study is the recent book by L. Richardson, *Pompeii: An Architectural History*. This scholarly consideration of the evolution of different building types at Pompeii cites material from the latest excavations in the city as evidence for new conclusions regarding the city's retarded urban development but subsequent architectural sophistication. It now appears that until Pompeii experienced a financial boom during the first two Punic Wars of the third century B.C., the site was a small village without a coherent city plan. Only in the mid-third century, between the wars, was Pompeii protected with fortifications and given a regular layout for its streets. After this point, Pompeii seems to have been a thriving agricultural and commercial center "in constant contact with Rome and responsive to Roman changes in style and developments in engineering and the uses of space" (p. xvi). Thus, contrary to most current opinion, Pompeii's late Republican and early Imperial architecture should be viewed as mainstream rather than provincial; Richardson implies that it can be safely utilized to reconstruct gaps in the urban history of Rome.

Finally, particular building types have been the focus of scholarly investigations. One of the best studies of this kind is *Houses, Villas and Palaces in the Roman World*, by A. G. McKay. Here the surviving remains and ancient representations of domestic architecture of the Etruscans, the Romans in Republican Italy, and the Romans throughout the Empire are reviewed, with frequent citations made to ancient sources which allow us to imagine ancient Roman houses in use.

For a discussion of wall painting, another important Roman art form, the reader should consult chapter 17, "Greek and Roman Interior Decoration."

## Bibliographic Entries for Supplementary Sources

Anderson, Maxwell L., and Leila Nista. *Roman Portraits in Context: Imperial and Private Likenesses from the Museo Nazionale Romano*. Catalog of an exhibition at the Emory University Museum of Art and Archaeology, Atlanta, July 1988–January 1989. Rome: De Luca Edizioni d'Arte, 1988.

Erhart, K. Patricia, et al. *Roman Portraits: Aspects of Self and Society, First Century B.C.–Third Century A.D.*, a Loan Exhibition. Catalog of an exhibition at the University of California at Santa Cruz and Loyola Marymount University, Los Angeles, February–November, 1980. Regents of the Univ. of California, Loyola Marymount Univ., and J. Paul Getty Museum, 1980.

Fittschen, Klaus, and Paul Zanker. *Katalog der römischen Porträts in den Capitolinischen Museen und den anderen kommunalen Sammlungen der Stadt Rom*. Vol. 1, *Kaiser- und Prinzenbildnisse*. Beiträge zur Erschließung hellenistischer und kaiserzeitlicher Skulptur und Architektur 3. Mainz am Rhein: P. von Zabern, 1985. Vol. 3, *Kaiserinnen- und Prinzessinnenbildnisse, Frauenporträts*. Beiträge zur Erschließung hellenistischer und kaiserzeitlicher Skulptur und Architektur 5. Mainz am Rhein: P. von Zabern, 1983.

Hamberg, Per Gustaf. *Studies in Roman Imperial Art with Special Reference to the State Reliefs of the Second Century*. 1945. Reprint. Rome: "L'Erma" di Bretschneider, 1968.

Hannestad, Niels. *Roman Art and Imperial Policy*. Translated by P. J. Crabb. Aarhus: Aarhus Univ. Press, 1988.

Koch, Guntram, and Hellmut Sichtermann. *Römische Sarkophage*. Handbuch der Archäologie. Munich: C. H. Beck, 1982.

Lawrence, A. W. *Greek and Roman Sculpture*. New York: Harper, 1972.

McKay, A. G. *Houses, Villas and Palaces in the Roman World*. Aspects of Greek and Roman Life. Ithaca, N.Y.: Cornell Univ. Press, 1975.

Neudecker, Richard. *Die Skulpturen-Ausstattung römischer Villen in Italien*. Beiträge zur Erschließung hellenistischer und kaiserzeitlicher Skulptur und Architektur 9. Mainz am Rhein: P. von Zabern, 1988.

Niemeyer, Hans Georg. *Studien zur statuarischen Darstellung der römischen Kaiser*. Monumenta Artis Romanae 7. Berlin: Gebr. Mann, 1968.

Pfanner, Michael. *Der Titusbogen*. Beiträge zur Erschließung hellenistischer und kaiserzeitlicher Skulptur und Architektur 2. Mainz am Rhein: P. von Zabern, 1983.

Poulsen, Vagn. *Les portraits romains*. Vol. 1, *République et Dynastie Julienne*. Translated by Hélène Laurent-Lund. Vol. 2, *De Vespasien à la Basse-Antiquité*. Translated by Ghani Merad. Publications de la Glyptothèque Ny Carlsberg, 7–8. Copenhagen: Glyptothèque Ny Carlsberg, 1973–74.

Richardson, L. *Pompeii: An Architectural History*. Baltimore and London: Johns Hopkins Univ. Press, 1988.

Sear, Frank. *Roman Architecture*. Ithaca, N.Y.: Cornell Univ. Press, 1982.

Settis, Salvatore, et al. *La Colonna Traiana*. Edited by Salvatore Settis. Saggi 716. Torino: Giulio Einaudi, 1988.

Stambaugh, John E. *The Ancient Roman City*. Baltimore and London: Johns Hopkins Univ. Press, 1988.

Strong, Donald E. *Roman Imperial Sculpture: An Introduction to the Commemorative and Decorative Sculpture of the Roman Empire down to the Death of Constantine*, London: Alec Tiranti, 1961.

Strong, Eugénie Sellers. *Roman Sculpture from Augustus to Constantine*. London: Duckworth; New York: Scribner, 1907. Reprint. New York: Arno, 1969.

Torelli, Mario. *Typology and Structure of Roman Historical Reliefs*. Jerome Lectures, Fourteenth Series. Ann Arbor: Univ. of Michigan Press, 1982.

Toynbee, Jocelyn M. C. *Roman Historical Portraits*. Aspects of Greek and Roman Life. Ithaca, N.Y.: Cornell Univ. Press, 1978.

Vermeule, Cornelius C. *The Cult Images of Imperial Rome*. Archaeologica 71. Rome: Giorgio Bretschneider, 1987.

———. *Roman Imperial Art in Greece and Asia Minor*, Cambridge, Mass.: Belknap Press of Harvard Univ. Press, 1968.

## Additional Supplementary Sources

Andrén, Arvid. *Deeds and Misdeeds in Classical Art and Antiquities*. Studies in Mediterranean Archaeology, Pocket-book 36. Partille, Sweden: Paul Åström, 1986.

Bonanno, Anthony. *Portraits and Other Heads on Roman Historical Relief up to the Age of Septimius Severus*. British Archaeological Reports, Supplementary Series, no. 6. Oxford: British Archaeological Reports, 1976.

Brilliant, Richard. *Gesture and Rank in Roman Art: The Use of Gestures to Denote Status in Roman Sculpture and Coinage*. Memoirs of the Connecticut Academy of Arts & Sciences, no. 14 (February 1963). New Haven, Conn.: Connecticut Academy of Arts & Sciences, 1963.

Cichorius, Conrad. *Trajan's Column: A New Edition of the Cichorius Plates.* Introduction, commentary, and notes by Frank Lepper and Sheppard Frere. Wolfboro, N. H.: Alan Sutton, 1988.

Dwyer, Eugene J. *Pompeian Domestic Sculpture: A Study of Five Pompeian Houses and Their Contents.* Archaeologica 28. Rome: Giorgio Bretschneider, 1982.

Heintze, Helga von, ed. *Römische Porträts.* Wege der Forschung 348. Darmstadt: Wissenschaftliche Buchgesellschaft, 1974.

Kleiner, Diana E. E. *Roman Imperial Funerary Altars with Portraits.* Archaeologica 62. Rome: Giorgio Bretschneider, 1987.

L'Orange, Hans Peter, and Reingart Unger. *Das spätantike Herrscherbild von Diokletian bis zu den Konstantin-Söhnen 284–361 n. Chr.* With supplement by Max Wegner, *Die Bildnisse der Frauen und des Julian. Das römische Herrscherbild,* Abteilung 3, Band 4. Berlin: Gebr. Mann, 1984.

MacDonald, William L. *The Architecture of the Roman Empire.* Vol. 1, *An Introductory Study.* Rev. ed. Yale Publications in the History of Art, no. 17. New Haven and London: Yale Univ. Press, 1982. Vol. 2, *An Urban Appraisal.* Yale Publications in the History of Art, no. 35. New Haven and London: Yale Univ. Press, 1986.

Oppermann, Manfred. *Römische Kaiserreliefs.* Seemann-Beiträge zur Kunstwissenschaft. Leipzig: VEB E. A. Seemann, 1985.

Poulsen, Frederick. *Glimpses of Roman Culture.* Translated by J. Dahlmann-Hansen. Leiden: E. J. Brill, 1950.

Riegl, Alois. *Late Roman Art Industry.* Translated with foreword, annotations from an 1898 lecture, bibliography, and glossary by Rolf Winkes. Archaeologica 36. Rome: Giorgio Bretschneider, 1985.

Robinson, Henry S. *Pottery of the Roman Period: Chronology.* Vol. 5, *The Athenian Agora: Results of Excavations Conducted by the American School of Classical Studies at Athens.* Princeton, N.J.: American School of Classical Studies at Athens, 1959.

Stemmer, Klaus. *Untersuchungen zur Typologie, Chronologie und Ikonographie der Panzerstatuen.* Berlin: Gebr. Mann, 1978.

Strong, Eugénie Sellers. *Art in Ancient Rome.* Vol. 1, *From the Earliest Times to the Principate of Nero.* Vol. 2, *From the Flavian Dynasty to Justinian, with Chapters on Painting and the Minor Arts in the First Century, A.D.* Ars Una. London: William Heinemann, 1928.

Vitruvius. *The Ten Books on Architecture.* Translated by Morris Hicky Morgan. Illustrations and original designs prepared under the direction of Herbert Langford Warren. 1914. Reprint. New York: Dover, 1960.

Walker, Susan. *Memorials to the Roman Dead.* London: British Museum Publications, 1985.

Walters, H. B. *The Art of the Romans.* London: Methuen, 1911.

Ward-Perkins, John B. *Roman Architecture.* New York: Abrams, 1977. Redesigned paperback ed. History of World Architecture. New York: Electa/Rizzoli, 1988.

Wickhoff, Franz. *Roman Art: Some of Its Principles and Their Application to Early Christian Painting.* Translated and edited by Eugénie Strong. London: William Heinemann; New York: Macmillan, 1900.

Wood, Susan. *Roman Portrait Sculpture 217–260 A.D.: The Transformation of an Artistic Tradition.* Columbia Studies in the Classical Tradition, no. 12. Leiden: E. J. Brill, 1986.

*Part Two*

# MYTHOLOGY

# ₁4₁

# Classical Mythology in Ancient and Later Literature

Hunger, Herbert. *Lexikon der griechischen und römischen Mythologie, mit Hinweisen auf das Fortwirken antiker Stoffe und Motive in der bildenden Kunst, Literatur und Musik des Abendlandes bis zur Gegenwart* (Lexicon of Greek and Roman Mythology with References to the Survival of Ancient Themes and Motifs in the Fine Arts, Literature, and Music of the West up to the Present). 8th ed. Vienna: Hollinek, 1988.

## ART FORM

In ancient literature, as in ancient art, mythology underwent a constant process of reshaping. Every literary recounting of an ancient myth is different in some respects from every other, and there are also general chronological changes in the way gods and heroes were viewed. One of the threads which can be followed, for example, is the changing conception of what constitutes heroic behavior. For the Greek and Trojan heroes of Homer's *Iliad*, the main goals were to achieve glory on the battlefield and honor for this achievement from their warrior peers. In Homer's *Odyssey*, Odysseus survives countless difficulties through his perseverance and resourcefulness. Heracles (Hercules), in Hesiod's *Theogony*, is an ethical hero who performs his exploits not for his own benefit, but to rid the world of destructive forces. In Pindar's odes for

71

victors at the Panhellenic games, the same hero is given a similar treatment; he eliminates enemies of man who are a threat to the established order.

The *Choephori* (the Libation-Bearers) and *Eumenides* (the Kindly Ones) from the *Oresteia*, by Aeschylus, present a new type of hero in the figure of Orestes. Caught between the command of Apollo to avenge his father Agamemnon's death at the hands of his mother Clytaemnestra and the wrath of the Furies that followed his murder of his mother, Orestes undergoes a trial for the matricide in Athens and is exonerated of guilt by Athena. Aeschylus' Orestes, then, is a figure who is more at the mercy of the gods than previous heroes; yet he attempts to make choices that are morally correct. In Euripides' *Electra* and *Orestes*, the son of Agamemnon is driven mad by the Furies and only Apollo is able to alleviate his difficulties. The Furies are absent in Sophocles' *Electra*, and Orestes is portrayed as following Apollo's instructions both in the murder of his mother and in the noble motivations of loyalty to his father and a desire to avenge his death.

Yet another heroic ideal is evident in Virgil's characterization of the Trojan Aeneas in the *Aeneid*. Aeneas' life is a story of subordination of his own personal wishes to his divinely sanctioned mission of establishing the Roman line in Lavinium. Thus he obeys the gods' command to abandon Queen Dido in Carthage in order that he may journey on to Italy. Finally, the urbane Ovid adds a comic dimension to his recountings of heroic legends. For example, in book 9 of the *Metamorphoses*, he describes Heracles' pose on the funeral pyre as bearing a resemblance to the reclining and festive posture of a banqueter (9.235-8). This is an entertaining note since overindulgence in food and drink was a trait frequently associated with the hero.

The foregoing brief survey demonstrates the quality and diversity of heroic characterization that ancient literature contains. There is no question that such recountings of ancient myths had an equal or greater influence on the post-ancient artistic tradition than surviving antiquities. It is essential, then, that the researcher seeking possible ancient sources for artistic renditions investigate the known literary variants in addition to the artistic prototypes. We know that some of these literary masterpieces were always available and others were inaccessible, but were rediscovered. Virgil's and Ovid's works fall into the former category. They were not lost during the Middle Ages and were first printed circa 1469 and 1471 A.D., with vernacular translations appearing in the late fifteenth and sixteenth centuries. Homer's *Iliad* and *Odyssey* belong to the second category, at least as far as Western Europe was concerned, being "virtually unknown" in the Medieval period (Bush, *Mythology and the Renaissance Tradition in English Poetry*—see Supplementary Sources below). However, Homer's epics were the first important Greek texts to be published in the Renaissance; they were published in the original in 1488, and in the following century in English, French, German, Italian, and Spanish translations. In the late fifteenth and sixteenth centuries, texts of the other Greek authors were printed, and in the sixteenth century translations of some of the plays of Euripides and Sophocles appeared.

By examining the different ancient literary variants of a myth and discovering which texts were available at a given place and time, the researcher can form well-grounded hypotheses regarding likely literary sources for specific artistic renditions. This type of investigation must not, however, omit a consideration of post-ancient literary renditions of the same theme. Such accounts often added to the previously established tradition new heroic aspects and new motifs which were borrowed by contemporary artists. In Medieval and Renaissance sources, for example, Heracles is transformed into a courtly, virtuous, and learned knight, aspects which are reflected in contemporary cycles of prints and paintings that feature Heraclean exploits. For suggestions on how to begin this type of research, see the Handbooks and Supplementary Sources below; also consult the Research Use portion of chapter 8, "Classical Mythology in Art after Antiquity."

# RESEARCH USE

For investigating the most persistent literary variants of ancient myths, as well as identifying the major scholarly discussions of these variants, an excellent starting point is the latest edition of Herbert Hunger's *Lexikon der griechischen und römischen Mythologie, mit Hinweisen auf das Fortwirken antiker Stoffe und Motive in der bildenden Kunst, Literatur und Musik des Abendlandes bis zur Gegenwart* (Lexicon of Greek and Roman Mythology with References to the Survival of Ancient Themes and Motifs in the Fine Arts, Literature and Music of the West up to the Present). The first part of an entry in Hunger's *Lexikon* summarizes the corpus of myths associated with a god or mortal in antiquity. Notes at the end of the entry cite specific passages from ancient literary works, as well as making reference to important alternate mythological traditions. The second part of the entry, also with notes, presents a survey of the interpretations of the character in ancient religious thought and in later commentaries and mentions significant ancient cults of divinities and heroes. In addition, ancient and later artistic, literary, and musical renditions of pertinent myths are listed, without bibliography. Finally, before the notes near the end of an entry is a list of major modern discussions of the mythological character; the primary emphasis of many of these references is a critical review of ancient literary sources.

Through consulting the literary sources which Hunger cites, and which his modern scholarly treatments discuss (see Complementary References below for these sources), the researcher can familiarize himself or herself with all known ancient variants of a particular myth. Furthermore, through the use of the Supplementary Sources (see below) that discuss the transmission of ancient texts after antiquity, the investigator can achieve some knowledge about the availability of texts that have been identified as possible sources of inspiration in postclassical times. Armed with these two types of information, the researcher can propose new relationships between ancient literature and the later literature and art that was inspired by it, or correct misinterpretations of artistic representations that have found their way into the art historical literature because they were founded on an incomplete knowledge of the literary tradition.

# ORGANIZATION

The main body of the text of Hunger's *Lexikon der griechischen und römischen Mythologie* consists of alphabetically arranged entries on divinities and mortals from classical mythology. The fullest entries are those that discuss major characters from Greek mythology. There are also long entries for important figures from Roman mythology, such as Aeneas and Romulus, and for the Oriental divinities, such as Isis and Serapis, who were worshipped by the Romans. Shorter entries and/or cross-references appear under the Roman names for characters who have Greek counterparts. Hunger states in the foreword to the first edition of the *Lexikon* that he does not aim for completeness in his selection of mythological characters, and that he has intentionally left out the more obscure personages.

The first part of the entry is the name of the divinity or mortal in bold-faced print. For Greek names, the correct ancient Greek form and accentuation of the name is given first. If there is an alternate Greek form for the name or an alternate accentuation that is in common modern usage, it is given next in parentheses. After the name of the mythological character there often appears basic information on his or her parentage, spouse, and position among the gods or mortals. An asterisk following the name of a parent or spouse indicates that there is an additional entry under this personage's name.

If information on the character is not contained in this entry but can be found under another entry, the title of the latter entry is cited next, preceded by "s." A typical cross-reference to another entry is: "**Skíron** s. Theseus" (Skíron see Theseus). Another form a cross-reference can take is: "**Megára** (Mégara), Gattin des Herakles," meaning "Megara (Megara), wife of Heracles." For information on Megara therefore, the researcher should consult the entry on Heracles.

In a standard entry, the name and basic information on the character are usually followed by three separate paragraphs of information, which are preceded by the letters *M, R,* and *N.* The paragraph marked "M" is a concise summary of the corpus of myths commonly associated with the character in important ancient literary sources. The ancient authors are named in notes at the end of the entry, with alternate literary traditions identified as well. In many cases, the text of paragraph "M" is followed by a brief genealogical chart in which women's names are written in italics. The paragraph marked "R" reviews the aspects of the character that are emphasized in ancient religious thought and elucidated in later commentaries, and it mentions significant ancient cults. Again, notes for this portion of the entry that refer to both ancient literature and modern commentary appear at the end of the entry. The third paragraph or paragraphs is introduced by "N," signifying the *Nachwirkung* or influence of the myths. This consists of lists, without bibliography, of works of art, literature, and music from antiquity to the twentieth century that illustrate events from the mythological career of the character. This portion of the entry is often broken down into several sections according to medium. The title of the work is given first, then the artist's or author's name, the date (if known), and finally, for works of art, the location.

The next-to-the-last portion of the entry, which appears immediately before the notes, is entitled "Literatur." Here, major modern discussions of the pertinent myths from journals, monographs, encyclopedias, and dissertations are cited. Most of these references discuss the myths in antiquity; special emphasis is given to their treatment in ancient literature.

As indicated above, the entries are not all of equal length. For example, many entries for Roman characters are abbreviated, particularly in the summary of myths (paragraph M), which is more fully presented in the entries for the corresponding Greek characters. Furthermore, if there is no material for any of the three categories—M, R, or N—or for "Literatur," Hunger simply omits this portion of the entry.

At the beginning of Hunger's *Lexikon* are forewords to the first and eighth editions, and at the end are lists of explanations of frequently used religious terms, general literature on Greek and Roman mythology and religious history, general and specific studies on the survival of classical mythology after antiquity, and bibliographic abbreviations. The studies of specific myths are arranged alphabetically by the mythological characters under consideration.

Accompanying the text are photographs of mythological representations, which are more numerous and cover a broader range of time and media in the later editions of Hunger's *Lexikon.*

## COMPLEMENTARY REFERENCES

For the researcher who wishes to consult fuller recountings of myths and more comprehensive lists of ancient literary sources than can be found in Hunger, Pierre Grimal's *Dictionary of Classical Mythology* is recommended. The myths are narrated in alphabetically arranged entries in Grimal, and the notes with the ancient sources are located in second entries at the back of the volume. The latter are immediately followed by a useful "Table of Sources" which names the ancient authors referred to in the notes and identifies published texts and, where possible, translations. In addition, Grimal's *Dictionary* includes photographs of antiquities with mythological content, genealogical charts, maps, and an index of ancient names. Mythological entries in Smith's three-volume *Dictionary of Greek and Roman Biography and Mythology* do not cite as many literary sources as Grimal, but after the description of a particular variant of a myth, specific authors and passages that follow the variant are often named. The same reference contains lengthy articles on the lives and works of ancient authors, as well as entries on artists and other figures from ancient history. These biographical articles cover personages who lived "to the extinction of the Western Empire in the year 476 of our era, and to the extinction of the Eastern Empire by the capture of Constantinople by the Turks in the year 1453."

No study of any ancient myth is complete until the researcher has consulted the two most important German encyclopedias of classical learning: Roscher's illustrated *Ausführliches Lexikon der griechischen und römischen Mythologie* (Detailed Lexicon of Greek and Roman Mythology); and *Paulys Realencyclopädie der classischen Altertumswissenschaft* (Pauly's Encyclopedia of Classical Knowledge). While not easy to use, both references contain a feature not present elsewhere: they provide complete discussions of the different literary variants of myths and make specific references to the authors and works where these variants are present. The researcher must remember not only to consult the main entries in both references, but also to look for supplements to the articles at the ends of the volumes. In addition, there are fifteen *Supplement* volumes for *Paulys Realencyclopädie*. Two guides, by Hans Gärtner and Albert Wünsch, and by John P. Murphy, provide quick access both to the articles in these *Supplement* volumes and to the supplementary materials at the ends of the original volumes in *Paulys Realencyclopädie*.

Another encyclopedic work is Daremberg and Saglio's illustrated *Dictionnaire des antiquités grecques et romaines d'après les textes et les monuments* (Dictionary of Greek and Roman Antiquities according to the Texts and the Monuments). Like the two German encyclopedias just discussed, this reference describes different variants of classical myths and identifies the literary sources for the variants in the notes. However,

Daremberg and Saglio's treatments of the mythological variants and literary sources are not as comprehensive as those in the German encyclopedias, and the only mythological characters for whom there are entries are the gods and heroes who were important in ancient cult, religious festivals, and art. The index volume for Daremberg and Saglio, entitled *Tables*, has a useful section on pages 8–10 ("5° Mythologie Grecque et Romaine"), in which all the articles that relate to a particular divinity or mortal are listed under the personage's name. For example, one of the items listed under Jupiter is Aetnaea, a festival celebrated at Etna in honor of Zeus Aitnaios. Daremberg and Saglio's *Dictionnaire* and the two German encyclopedias can also be used as sources for information on the roles of mythological characters in ancient cult and in ancient art, but the reader should remember that in these areas of research all three references are seriously outdated. (The latest volumes from the second series and the latest *Supplement* volumes for *Paulys Realencyclopädie* form an exception to this rule.)

Other encyclopedic treatments of mythology in classical literature are the two corpora by L. Preller: *Griechische Mythologie* (Greek Mythology), and *Römische Mythologie* (Roman Mythology). Preller's volumes describe literary variants of myths more fully than the three encyclopedias just discussed, and quotations from classical works are frequently provided in the notes at the bottoms of the pages. The only problem with using Preller's references lies in the absence of an index for volume 2 of *Griechische Mythologie*, the volume entitled *Die griechische Heldensage* (The Greek Heroic Legends). This difficulty is partially remedied by the detailed tables of contents which introduce the three parts of volume 2.

The researcher who wishes to discover whether a text of an ancient author in question or a translation was available to a postclassical artist or his patron can consult several valuable introductions to this type of investigation. The easiest of these references to use is *Harper's Dictionary of Classical Literature and Antiquities*, by Harry Thurston Peck. Among the alphabetically arranged entries in this reference are long articles on ancient authors, which survey the literary output of the authors and often include mentions of the most important manuscripts and the first printed editions of texts. Ancient literary works are also referred to in entries on particular mythological characters and events, such as the "Trojan War." In such entries additional discussion can sometimes be found of post-ancient literary treatments of the same themes. The same *Dictionary* contains entries on the great scholars of classical antiquity from the medieval period to the nineteenth century. The fullest accounts of the earliest printed editions of ancient texts that I have been able to locate appear at the ends of the author entries in Smith's *Dictionary of Greek and Roman Biography and Mythology*. Smith consistently cites the publication dates and places of publication of these early editions and often also provides the names of the publishers. *The Oxford Companion to Classical Literature*, by Paul Harvey, like the two dictionaries just described, surveys the literary output of ancient authors in articles bearing their names and often makes mention of important manuscripts and printed editions that were available after antiquity. Further articles can be found in the same volume under the titles of literary works. In both types of articles and in additional ones on mythological characters and events, frequent reference is made to literary works composed after antiquity which were influenced by ancient treatments of the same themes.

*Kleines Lexikon der griechischen und römischen Mythologie* (Small Lexicon of Greek and Roman Mythology), by Hannelore Gärtner, summarizes the most commonly used variants of classical myths as well as making mention of important postclassical renditions from literature, music, and art. Every major change in the literary tradition in the characterization of a mythological figure is emphasized, and many recent literary works from the twentieth century with mythological content are named. Thus Gärtner's useful handbook can be used to supplement the materials that are included in Hunger's *Lexikon*, particularly the lists of modern literary renditions.

*The MLA International Bibliography of Books and Articles on the Modern Languages and Literatures*, an annual bibliography on the literature of all periods and places except classical antiquity, published by the Modern Language Association of America, can be searched for material on mythological characters in postclassical literature. The paper copy of the *MLA International Bibliography* for each year consists of two volumes: the *Subject Index* and the *Classified Listings with Author Index*. The reader should consult the *Subject Index* under the name of the pertinent mythological character. Any books and articles will be described according to their contents in the *Subject Index*, and their numbers in the same year's *Classified Listings with Author Index* will be given. In order to find full bibliographic citations, the reader must then look up the number given for each book or article in the five-part *Classified Listings with Author Index;* periodical abbreviations are explained at the front of this index. The years 1981 and following of the *MLA International Bibliography* can also be searched for mythological character by consulting the compact disc published by the H. W. Wilson Company. Since this compact disc version of the *MLA International Bibliography* is published quarterly, it contains more recent citations than those in the latest volumes of the paper edition. In addition, the years 1963 and following for the same bibliography can be searched by computer through the Dialog database under the title *MLA Bibliography*. This database is updated ten times each year. *Bibliographie zur Symbolik, Ikonographie und Mythologie: Internationales Referateorgan* (Bibliography on Symbolism, Iconography and Mythology: International Review) is an annual review that covers books and journal articles on mythology in the literature of all periods. Most of the entries in this bibliography are summarized in abstracts in German, Italian, English, or

French. An index at the back of each volume provides access to the entries by the names of the mythological characters, and there is also a *Generalregister* (General Index) for the first ten volumes.

## Bibliographic Entries for Complementary References

*Bibliographie zur Symbolik, Ikonographie und Mythologie: Internationales Referateor-gan.* Baden-Baden: Librairie Heitz GMBH, 1968– . With *Generalregister zu Jahrgang 1/1968–10/1977.* Baden-Baden: Valentin Koerner, 1977.

Daremberg, Ch., and Edm. Saglio. *Dictionnaire des antiquités grecques et romaines d'après les textes et les monuments contenant l'explication des termes qui se rapportent aux moeurs, aux institutions, à la religion, aux arts, aux sciences, au costume, au mobilier, à la guerre, à la marine, aux métiers, aux monnaies, poids et mesures, etc., etc. et en général à la vie publique et privée des anciens.* 5 vols. Paris: Librairie Hachette, 1877–1919. *Tables.* Paris: Librairie Hachette, 1919. Reprint. Graz: Akademische Druck- u. Verlag Sanstalt, 1963–69.

Gärtner, Hannelore. *Kleines Lexikon der griechischen und römischen Mythologie.* Leipzig: Bibliographisches Institut, 1989.

Gärtner, Hans, and Albert Wünsch. *Paulys Realencyclopädie der classischen Alter-tumswissenschaft: Neue Bearbeitung. Register der Nachträge und Supplemente.* Munich: Alfred Druckenmüller, 1980.

Grimal, Pierre. *The Dictionary of Classical Mythology.* Translated by A. R. Maxwell-Hyslop. New York: Basil Blackwell, 1986.

Harvey, Paul. *The Oxford Companion to Classical Literature.* Oxford, New York: Oxford Univ. Press, 1984.

*MLA Bibliography.* Computer database, updated 10 times annually. New York: Modern Language Association of America, 1963– ; available through Dialog Information Services.

*MLA International Bibliography of Books and Articles on the Modern Languages and Literatures.* 1969– . New York: Modern Language Association of America, 1970. (Supersedes *MLA American Bibliography of Books and Articles on the Modern Languages and Literatures.* 1921– . Reprint from PMLA 37.1 ff.– . New York: Kraus Reprint Corp., 1964– .)

*MLA International Bibliography.* Compact disc, updated quarterly. Bronx, N.Y.: H. W. Wilson Co., 1981– .

Murphy, John P. *Index to the Supplements and Suppl. Volumes of Pauly-Wissowa's R. E.* 2d ed. Chicago: Ares, 1980.

Pauly, August Friedrich von, Georg Wissowa, and Wilhelm Kroll, eds. *Paulys Realencyclopädie der classischen Altertumswissenschaft: Neue Bearbeitung.* 24 vols. 2d ser. (R–Z), 19 vols. Stuttgart: J. B. Metzler, 1894–1972. *Supplement.* 15 vols. Stuttgart: J. B. Metzler, 1903–78.

Peck, Harry Thurston, ed. *Harper's Dictionary of Classical Literature and Antiquities.* 2d ed. New York, Cincinnati, Chicago: American Book, 1897. Reprint. New York: Hooper Square Pubs, 1962.

Preller, L. *Griechische Mythologie.* Vol. 1, *Theogonie und Götter.* Revised by Carl Robert. Vol. 2, *Die griechische Heldensage.* 4th ed. Rewritten by Carl Robert and revised in part by Otto Kern. Berlin: Weidmannsche Buchhandlung, 1894–1921. Reprint. Berlin: Weidmann, 1964–67.

———. *Römische Mythologie.* 3d ed. Revised by H. Jordan. Berlin: Weidmannsche Buchhandlung, 1881–83.

Roscher, W. H., ed. *Ausführliches Lexikon der griechischen und römischen Mythologie.* 6 vols. Leipzig and Berlin: B. G. Teubner, 1884–1937. Reprint. Hildesheim: Georg Olms, 1965.

Smith, William, ed. *A Dictionary of Greek and Roman Biography and Mythology.* 3 vols. London: J. Murray, 1902.

# HANDBOOKS

Three modern handbooks in English provide access to the most commonly transmitted versions of ancient myths. *Crowell's Handbook of Classical Mythology,* by Edward Tripp, has alphabetized entries for divinities and mortals from classical mythology in which the standard forms for myths are presented, along with references to important ancient literary sources. *A Handbook of Greek Mythology,* by H. J. Rose, presents the most widely accepted versions of myths in larger type in the text, and cites major ancient literary sources, compilations of further sources, and modern commentary in the notes. More obscure or late variants of myths are reported in smaller print in the text. *Mythology, Greek and Roman,* an illustrated handbook by Thomas H. Carpenter and Robert J. Gula, provides entertaining recountings of Greek and Roman myths pertaining to ancient gods, heroes, and monsters. Some commentary on variants in myths is also supplied, and at the back are notes (the "Index of Selected Sources") and an appendix (number IV) on ancient literary sources.

*Classical Mythology,* by Morford and Lenardon, has the aim of presenting the "dominant version" of each ancient myth. This goal is achieved through the extensive use of well-chosen excerpts in prose translations from Homer, Hesiod, the *Homeric Hymns,* Pindar, the Greek lyric poets, the Greek tragedians, and Virgil and Ovid; these excerpts are expertly linked by explanatory text and are presented in chapters dealing with the gods, the heroes, and Roman mythology. Numerous genealogical tables and maps accompany the text. The same reference has two chapters on the survival of mythology in literature, art, and music after antiquity; a valuable introduction summarizing modern explanations for classical mythology as well as the archaeological evidence for historic aspects of myths; and photographs of art works with mythological content from antiquity to this century.

The best ancient handbook of Greek mythology is *The Library,* an uncritical summary derived from classical literature that was composed in the first or second century A.D. The name of the author of this work is uncertain, but he is commonly called Apollodorus, after the author of an earlier work with the same title from the second century B.C. The Loeb Classical Library volumes of *The Library* present the Greek text, as edited by James George Frazer, and the same scholar's translations on facing pages; an excellent introduction to this text and mythology in general; and footnotes calling attention to "principal passages of other ancient writers where each particular story is told." Furthermore, the text is preceded by a concise summary of mythological contents and followed by a detailed index. Before the index is an interesting appendix of folktales from nonclassical sources that have motifs in common with classical myths.

The *Oxford Classical Dictionary,* edited by N. G. L. Hammond and H. H. Scullard, is the best source to consult for reliable biographical information on ancient authors, the works attributed to them, the dates of the works, and authoritative texts of and commentaries on the works. The second list of abbreviations at the front of the volume, entitled "Authors and Books," can be consulted for explanations of abbreviations that are commonly used for the names and works of ancient authors. *The Oxford Classical Dictionary* also has articles on the most important deities and mortals from Greek and Roman mythology. In these articles, historical aspects are emphasized, for example, evidence for cults and for any elements in the mythological traditions relating to heroes and heroines that seem to be derived from real ancient persons.

The *New Century Classical Handbook,* edited by Catherine B. Avery, has entries on ancient authors, works by the same authors, and characters from classical mythology. Avery states in her preface: "The aim of these articles is to present the material as it appeared to the ancients, rather than to apply modern interpretations." Particularly valuable are the detailed summaries of the plots of literary works with mythological content, which can be found under the titles of the works. Comments on the use of myths by the authors of the same literary works appear in the entries bearing the authors' names. For reasons unknown, Avery's recountings of myths connected with divinities and heroes do not refer to the pertinent entries for literary sources. Photos and drawings of antiquities that illustrate ancient myths accompany the entries in this reference.

The *Illustrated Dictionary of Greek and Roman Mythology,* by Michael Stapleton, is similar to *The New Century Classical Handbook* in its inclusion of entries on ancient literary works, classical authors, and mythological characters. Useful features in this handbook are the comments in entries on heroes regarding possible bases for their legends in the careers of real historical personages, and cross-references at the ends of entries to further entries on related mythological characters and pertinent literary works. Stapleton's *Dictionary* includes illustrations of myths, primarily from ancient art, and some examples from postclassical art up to the twentieth century.

For the researcher interested in the survival of mythology in the literature after antiquity, *Classical Mythology in Literature, Art, and Music,* by Philip Mayerson, traces the major variants of pagan myths in literature from antiquity to the twentieth century. Mayerson provides illustrations from the art of all periods and mentions important musical compositions, especially operas. He groups the myths chronologically, for example, chapter 7, "The Age of Heroes," deals with characters before the Trojan War, while chapter 8, "The Trojan War," discusses episodes leading up to and occurring during that conflict. An introductory chapter summarizes the content and mythological focus of major ancient literary sources. Mayerson also provides a helpful general bibliography at the end of the volume.

Usually following Ovid or Virgil (the ancient authors most commonly consulted by artists after antiquity), Thomas Bulfinch retells ancient myths and includes more modern recountings of myths by twenty-five English poets. At the back of *Bulfinch's Mythology* is a helpful "Dictionary and Index" containing concise summaries of the most significant episodes from the careers of mythological characters. Fifty plates of artistic representations of myths from antiquity to the nineteenth century accompany the 1970 edition of this reference, which is also provided with an appendix describing the finds at important archaeological sites. Charles Mills Gayley's *The Classic Myths in English Literature and in Art* recounts ancient myths and gives citations of major ancient literary sources; quotes English and American poetic renditions of the myths; and provides illustrations from art, with a preponderance of them ancient depictions. Additional examples besides the poems and art works included and illustrated in the text are cited in the commentary at the back of the volume. Indexes of mythological subjects and of authors and artists are also included, along with maps and genealogical tables.

John C. Traupman's bibliographic article, "Books for Teaching the Classics in English: 1990 Survey," includes lists of inexpensive and in-print handbooks of classical mythology (pp. 345–49) and of the classical tradition, including mythology, in literature after antiquity (pp. 337–38).

## Bibliographic Entries for Handbooks

Apollodorus. *The Library.* Edited with introduction, translation, and commentary by James George Frazer. 2 vols. The Loeb Classical Library. 1921. Reprint. Cambridge, Mass.: Harvard Univ. Press, 1976–79.

Avery, Catherine B., ed. *The New Century Classical Handbook.* New York: Appleton, 1962.

Bulfinch, Thomas. *Bulfinch's Mythology: The Age of Fable, The Age of Chivalry, Legends of Charlemagne.* New York: Crowell, 1970.

Carpenter, Thomas H., and Robert J. Gula. *Mythology, Greek and Roman.* New York and London: Longman, 1977.

Gayley, Charles Mills. *The Classic Myths in English Literature and in Art.* New ed. 1911. 29th printing. Waltham, Mass., and London: Blaisdell Publishing Co., 1968.

Hammond, N. G. L., and H. H. Scullard, eds. *The Oxford Classical Dictionary.* 2d ed. Oxford: Clarendon Press, 1970.

Mayerson, Philip. *Classical Mythology in Literature, Art, and Music.* Waltham, Mass., and Toronto: Xerox College Pub., 1971.

Morford, Mark P. O., and Robert J. Lenardon. *Classical Mythology.* 3d ed. White Plains, N.Y.: Longman, 1985.

Rose, H. J. *A Handbook of Greek Mythology.* 6th ed. New York: Dutton, 1959.

Stapleton, Michael. *The Illustrated Dictionary of Greek and Roman Mythology.* Introduction by Stewart Perowne. Library of the World's Myths and Legends. New York: Peter Bedrick Books, 1986.

Traupman, John C. "Books for Teaching the Classics in English: 1990 Survey." *Classical World* 83 (March–April 1990): 283–354.

Tripp, Edward. *Crowell's Handbook of Classical Mythology.* New York: Crowell, 1970.

## SUPPLEMENTARY SOURCES

One of the most rewarding ways to study myths in literature is to trace their chronological development in different ancient authors. In *The Creative Poet: Studies on the Treatment of Myths in Greek Poetry,* by Jennifer R. March, this approach is achieved for five myths—"Peleus and Achilles, Meleagros and the Kalydonian Boar, Deianeira and the death of Herakles, Klytaimestra and the *Oresteia* myth, and Oidipous." The study covers surviving Greek poems from the eighth to the fifth centuries B.C., as well as poems that are known only through fragments or titles. Attempts are made to reconstruct the latter through the examination of representations, particularly vase-paintings, that may have been inspired by these lost texts. March concludes "that poets made adaptations and innovations to a 'given' myth to a larger extent than has perhaps been generally realised, and that the literary form or the needs of the occasion for which a piece of poetry was produced often influenced to a high degree the poet's particular use of inherited mythological material." In *Roman Myth and Mythography,* by Bremmer and Horsfall, an attempt is made to distinguish two types of myths of the Romans: those which originated in Italy before "regular contact with Greek literature"; and those which fall into the category of "'secondary myth,' that are products of antiquarian industry, literary activity, a desire for impressive antecedents . . . ." A number of Roman myths are discussed from this perspective, the most important being the legends of Aeneas and Romulus. In establishing the antiquity or lack of it for particular stories, information from surviving literary texts is supplemented by archaeological evidence from pertinent sites and artistic representations.

*Greek Religion,* by Walter Burkert, discusses the relationship of Greek myths to Greek sacred rituals, "for which they frequently provide a reason, an aetiology . . ." The principal period covered by this study is from 800 to 300 B.C.; a chapter on Neolithic and Bronze-Age practices is also provided. Particularly valuable syntheses are found in the chapters entitled "The Gods" and "The Dead, Heroes, and Chthonic Gods"; here evidence from literature, archaeology, and art is used to explicate the cults and characters of important divinities and heroes. Other chapters examine parts of the Greek sanctuary and the rituals performed there, festivals, the general functions of cult, mystery cults, and religion according to the philosophers. While Burkert frequently refers to published representations of Greek myths throughout this volume, none is illustrated.

Since ancient literary works rather than ancient artistic prototypes often inspired post-ancient artists, the researcher needs to understand the evidence regarding the availability and reliability of ancient texts at any given time. *Scribes and Scholars: A Guide to the Transmission of Greek and Latin Literature,* by L. D. Reynolds and N. G. Wilson, begins its survey with the sixth century B.C., when texts seem to have first been written down, and continues to the improved scholarly methods used to establish the original versions of texts in the nineteenth and twentieth centuries. *History of Classical Scholarship from 1300 to 1850,* by Rudolf Pfeiffer, covers a more limited time-frame, places less emphasis on the corruption of texts, and devotes more attention to the publication through manuscript and printed copies of a wider range of works by particular authors. Both volumes have indexes at the backs which permit the researcher to look up specific authors, and notes to indicate further scholarship.

*The Classical Heritage and Its Beneficiaries,* by R. R. Bolgar, is a period-by-period account of what is known about "the classical education" from antiquity to the end of the Renaissance. A lengthy index at the back provides access to discussions of specific Greek and Latin authors, as well as to general topics such as "Greek language," "Greek studies," "Latin language," and "Latin studies." Particularly useful are the two appendixes that bring together information on manuscripts of Greek texts and published translations of Greek and Roman authors. Appendix 1 includes chronologically arranged lists of the manuscripts of Greek "Prose Writers" and "Poets" and the fifteenth-century Italian locations of the manuscripts. Appendix 2 lists translations of Greek and Roman authors in the English, French, German, Italian, and Spanish languages that were printed before 1600. John Edwin Sandys' *History of Classical Scholarship,* in three volumes, is older than the other works on the survival of classical literature just discussed, but in some respects it is the most complete. Beginning in antiquity and ending at 1900 A.D., this monumental study outlines the activities of major European and American scholars. Each volume has a detailed index containing extensive references to Sandys' textual mentions of ancient authors. The indexes of volumes 2 and 3 also provide numerous citations, with dates and often locations given, of printed editions of ancient works; the editions cited are not only those referred to in Sandys' text, but many additional ones. Several chronological charts are included in each volume, the most valuable being those in volume 2 of "Editiones Principes" (First Editions to appear in print) of Latin and Greek authors.

Works of literature which inspired great works of art were of course not all composed in antiquity. While the various references discussed in all portions of this entry facilitate the task of locating all ancient literary treatments of a particular myth, it is much more difficult to locate the often less famous later literary renditions of the same themes. The single volume that contains the most comprehensive listings of post-ancient literary sources is Hunger's *Lexikon der griechischen und römischen Mythologie* (above). The reader should consult the works that are listed under headings for the different genres of literature in section "N" of Hunger's entries. The last parts of the entries in *The Oxford Companion to Classical Literature* (described in Complementary References above) name additional works with mythological subject matter, particularly those from English literature.

The second edition of *Mythology and the Renaissance Tradition in English Poetry*, by Douglas Bush, investigates mythology in English literature. The author begins his discussion with "the uses of mythology in English non-dramatic poetry from the Middle Ages," and ends his examination in 1680. The main goal of this thoughtful study is "to show the persistence, for good and ill, of the medieval spirit." This spirit consists of a religious reverence for writings of the ancients and a belief that Christian truths were embedded in ancient texts. Bush traces the survival and then the dissolution of this attitude in the seventeenth century. At the back of this study is an appendix consisting of a chronologically arranged list of English mythological poems and English translations of Ovid up to 1680.

*Classical Myth and Legend in Renaissance Dictionaries: A Study of Renaissance Dictionaries in their Relation to the Classical Learning of Contemporary English Writers*, by Starnes and Talbert, investigates a type of reference that was frequently consulted by Renaissance writers and artists, but which is infrequently mentioned in modern scholarship on classical sources. Particularly valuable portions of this fascinating volume are the first two chapters, which provide general information on the dictionaries themselves. For typical dictionary entries, the reader should examine the chapters that compare mythological passages from literature with the dictionary entries which seem to have been their inspiration.

Further useful references are those which discuss a particular theme in literature through the ages. One of the best treatments of this kind is *The Herakles Theme*, by G. Karl Galinsky. In this scholarly work which can be used with profit to explain changes in the artistic tradition (such as the introduction of representations of Heracles learning the secrets of the universe from Atlas), Galinsky studies "the variety of his manifestations in literature and the many reasons—personal, historical, social and moral, and the reasons of genre—which conditioned an author's response to him." Illustrations of Heracles in Western art and a helpful bibliography accompany Galinsky's text. Another excellent survey of the characterization of a hero in Western literature—this time Odysseus/Ulysses—is *The Ulysses Theme*, by W. B. Stanford. This study demonstrates that unlike Heracles, who was generally favorably treated in the literature of all periods, wily Odysseus experienced long periods of disfavor, both in antiquity and in the medieval period. It was only in the fourteenth century, when Petrarch had the *Odyssey* translated into Latin, that some authors began to describe this hero in a more positive fashion. Five appendixes supplement the textual discussion and a sixth one lists representations from the ancient and later artistic tradition.

Finally, there are studies which present our knowledge of the survival of texts and translations of classical authors in manuscripts and printed editions. Excellent examples of such studies are *La survie d'Eschyle à la Renaissance: Éditions, traductions, commentaires et imitations* (The Survival of Aeschylus in the Renaissance: Editions, Translations, Commentaries and Imitations), by Monique Mund-Dopchie, and *The Early Printed Editions (1518-1664) of Aeschylus: A Chapter in the History of Classical Scholarship*, by J. A. Gruys. These monographs correct the previously held opinion that Aeschylus was totally unknown in the sixteenth century by demonstrating that during the sixteenth and seventeenth centuries there were twenty-one printed editions in Greek and in Latin translations of the playwright's tragedies. Furthermore, through comparisons of readings from different manuscripts and printed editions, Mund-Dopchie and Gruys establish the sources for specific printed editions. Gruys also provides extensive quotations from published explanations and contemporary correspondence that shed light on methods of scholarship.

*Bibliographic Entries for Supplementary Sources*

Bolgar, R. R. *The Classical Heritage and its Beneficiaries.* Cambridge: Cambridge Univ. Press, 1954.

Bremmer, J. N., and N. M. Horsfall. *Roman Myth and Mythography.* University of London. Institute of Classical Studies. Bulletin. Supplement 52. London: Institute of Classical Studies, 1987.

Burkert, Walter. *Greek Religion.* Translated by John Raffan. Cambridge, Mass.: Harvard Univ. Press, 1985.

Bush, Douglas. *Mythology and the Renaissance Tradition in English Poetry.* 2d ed. New York: Norton, 1963.

Galinsky, G. Karl. *The Herakles Theme: Adaptations of the Hero in Literature from Homer to the Twentieth Century.* Totowa, N. J.: Rowman & Littlefield, 1972.

Gruys, J. A. *The Early Printed Editions (1518–1664) of Aeschylus: A Chapter in the History of Classical Scholarship.* Bibliotheca Humanistica et Reformatorica 32. Nieuwkoop: B. de Graaf, 1981.

March, Jennifer R. *The Creative Poet: Studies on the Treatment of Myths in Greek Poetry.* University of London. Institute of Classical Studies. Bulletin. Supplement 49. London: Institute of Classical Studies, 1987.

Mund-Dopchie, Monique. *La survie d'Eschyle à la Renaissance: Éditions, traductions, commentaires et imitations.* Académie royale de Belgique. Ronds René Draguet. Classe des Lettres 1. Louvain: Peeters, 1984.

Pfeiffer, Rudolf. *History of Classical Scholarship from 1300 to 1850.* Oxford: Clarendon Press, 1976.

Reynolds, L. D., and N. G. Wilson. *Scribes and Scholars: A Guide to the Transmission of Greek and Latin Literature.* 2d ed. Oxford: Clarendon Press, 1974.

Sandys, John Edwin. *A History of Classical Scholarship.* Vol. 1, *From the Sixth Century B.C. to the End of the Middle Ages.* Vol. 2, *From the Revival of Learning to the End of the Eighteenth Century (in Italy, France, England, and the Netherlands).* Vol. 3, *The Eighteenth Century in Germany, and the Nineteenth Century in Europe and the United States of America.* Vol. 1, 3d ed., 1921; Vols. 2–3, 1908. Reprint. New York and London: Hafner Publishing, 1964–67.

Stanford, W. B. *The Ulysses Theme: A Study in the Adaptability of a Traditional Hero.* 2d ed. New York: Barnes & Noble, 1964.

Starnes, DeWitt T., and Ernest William Talbert. *Classical Myth and Legend in Renaissance Dictionaries: A Study of Renaissance Dictionaries in Their Relation to the Classical Learning of Contemporary English Writers.* Chapel Hill: Univ. of North Carolina Press, 1955.

## Additional Supplementary Sources

Norton, Dan S., and Peters Rushton. *Classical Myths in English Literature.* Introduction by Charles Grosvenor Osgood. New York: Rinehart, 1952.

Palmer, Henrietta Raymer. *List of English Editions and Translations of Greek and Latin Classics Printed before 1641.* Introduction by Victor Scholderer. London: Bibliographical Society, 1911.

Pfeiffer, Rudolf. *History of Classical Scholarship from the Beginnings to the End of the Hellenistic Age.* Oxford: Clarendon Press, 1968.

Pfister, Friedrich. *Greek Gods and Heroes.* Translated by Mervyn Savill. London: MacGibbon & Kee, 1961.

Sabin, Frances E. *Classical Myths That Live Today.* Edited by Ralph Van Deman Magoffin. New York: Silver, Burdett, 1927.

Tatlock, Jessie M. *Greek and Roman Mythology.* New York: Appleton, 1917.

Wilamowitz-Moellendorff, U. von. Hugh Lloyd-Jones, ed., introduction, notes. *History of Classical Scholarship.* Translated by Alan Harris. Baltimore: Johns Hopkins Univ. Press, 1982.

# ₁5₁

# Classical Mythology in Ancient Art

Lexicon Iconographicum Mythologiae Classicae (Iconographic Lexicon of Classical Mythology). Edited by John Boardman, Philippe Bruneau, Fulvio Canciani, Lilly Kahil, Nikolaos Kontoleon, Erika Simon, Nikolaos Yalouris, Hans Christoph Ackermann, Jean-Robert Gisler, et alii. v. 1– . Zurich and Munich: Artemis, 1981– .

## ART FORM

With the possible exception of several works from Mycenaean Greece of the Late Bronze Age, the first tentative representations of Greek myths appear in Greek Geometric art of the eighth century B.C. These depictions are difficult to interpret with any degree of certainty because standard arrangements for myths had not yet been established and the Geometric style permitted little figural detail. Many new myths were introduced in the stylistically awkward but animated Orientalizing depictions from the seventh century, and an elaborate mythological iconography was formulated. Hereafter, the iconography for any given myth did not remain static, but constantly underwent a process of reformulation. Archaic art of the sixth century B.C., when further myths were introduced, was the high point for Greek narrative art. Richly detailed and intensely vigorous depictions of myths that often contain central characters as well as numerous spectators were created at Greek city-states on the mainland and abroad. In the Classical period (480–330 B.C.), the number of figures in standard mythological scenes was often reduced in order to emphasize the key participants. These gods and heroes, garbed in flowing drapery or with their well-toned bodies displayed, assumed graceful and harmonious poses rather than the stiff stances of the preceding age. In short, Classical grandeur and naturalism supplanted Archaic liveliness and stylization. In the last great Greek age, the Hellenistic period (330–30 B.C.), Classical calm was replaced with the melodramatic Baroque and the sweet and sensual Rococo styles. The favorite subject of the former style was heroic conflicts, while the latter specialized in erotic and playful scenes from mythology and from daily life. These styles, with their virtuoso figural realism and emphases on heroic and languid postures, were the first in Greek art to make such a blatant appeal to the passions rather than to the intellect.

Etruscan art, which followed the same stylistic development as Greek art, featured both Greek and Etruscan myths. Etruscan representations of borrowed Greek myths did not exhibit a consistently Greek iconography, but often included unexpected details or personages. In some cases, these differences have been interpreted by modern scholars as misunderstandings of the stories depicted, while in other cases they seem to reflect an alternate Etruscan tradition. Purely Etruscan myths are incompletely understood because Etruscan literature has not survived. Like the Etruscans, the Romans used Greek myths in much of their art and modeled the cults of their Olympian gods after Greek counterparts. Often Greek myths were given new forms and new significance by the Romans, as in the case of the abbreviated labors of Heracles on Roman sarcophagi, which seem to have symbolized the trials of mortal existence. The Romans also created their own mythology of illustrious, god-sprung founding fathers of the Roman state, such as Aeneas and Romulus, who were claimed as forefathers by the emperors.

Greek, Etruscan, and Roman myths appeared on every ancient art form: vases, gems, coins and miniature reliefs on other types of objects, engraved metalware such as mirrors, statuettes, statues, sarcophagi, wall paintings, and architectural sculptures. Apparently this fondness for the myths of the gods and heroes arose from a combination of attitudes —reverence towards the power of the gods and the fortitude of the heroes; identification with the very human triumphs and failures of both; and fascination with the drama and complexity of the stories and with the beautiful or exotic forms and attributes of the characters.

## RESEARCH USE

Once its seven volumes and supplementary volume(s) are complete, the *Lexicon Iconographicum Mythologiae Classicae* (Iconographic Lexicon of

Classical Mythology) will be the most comprehensive illustrated encyclopedia of Greek, Etruscan, and Roman mythology. Adopting a fuller
format than Brommer's lists of representations (see the beginning of
chapter 6, "Greek Gods and Heroes in Ancient Art"), this reference
provides a brief description of each example from ancient art, extensive
bibliographic citations, and line drawings or photographs of a large
percentage of the examples. Literary recountings of the myths are also
reviewed, and commentary on the examples from art follows their
descriptions. In brief, this is a self-contained reference that provides
extensive information on the general iconographic development of
particular myths in ancient art and their relationship to the ancient
literary tradition. Its descriptions and illustrations are probably sufficient
to enable a researcher of a myth in medieval or later art to determine if
a postclassical representation has been influenced by or derived from a
surviving ancient prototype.

For those wishing to investigate particular ancient depictions of
myths, the *Lexicon* provides bibliographic citations to all major scholarship on each example. This is particularly valuable for examples with
unusual features and for those of uncertain interpretation. For representations that fall in the latter category, the numerous illustrations are
helpful: they encourage visual comparisons with depictions of certain
interpretation. Often there is more than one possible interpretation for
an example with a unique iconographic scheme. Once the *Lexicon* is
complete, it will be possible to compare such examples with illustrations
of all the different myths that are possible identifications. Without
consulting another reference, the researcher will thereby be able to form
a tentative hypothesis about the interpretation he or she finds most
convincing. This preliminary work can be followed up by further
consultation of the scholarship cited in the *Lexicon* under the several
myths. Finally, the *Lexicon* has another possible use. As new depictions
of myths are uncovered in future excavations and in unpublished
collections, their identifications can be confirmed through comparisons
with examples with similar arrangements in the *Lexicon*.

# ORGANIZATION

The *Lexicon Iconographicum Mythologiae Classicae* contains articles (i.e.,
rubrics) on characters from classical mythology in Greek, Etruscan, and
Roman art. The articles also devote some attention to Early Christian and
Islamic representations of the same mythological characters, and to the
Egyptian, Near Eastern, and barbarian figures whose representations were
influenced by the iconography or stylistic traits of classical counterparts.
While the coverage of narrative scenes is the primary emphasis of the

articles, "non-narrative images" are also presented. The complete *Lexicon* is intended to have seven volumes and one or more supplementary volumes. The scope of the *Lexicon* is outlined and an explanation for its use is provided in the introduction and in the "Notes for Readers" at the beginning of the first volume, and in the "Note for Readers" in volume two. The user of the *Lexicon* will find in it articles in German, English, French, and Italian, with no translations. The articles are arranged alphabetically according to the Greek names of the characters when these are known; the text and line drawings can be found in part 1 of each volume and the plates in part 2. The text of the longer articles is introduced by a table of contents. All articles begin with an outline of the lineage of the mythological personage and a survey of the significant episodes in his or her career. At this point and elsewhere in an article, cross-references to other articles in the *Lexicon* and to catalog entries in other articles are indicated by means of an arrow. The rest of the article is broken down into one or more sections, with each section devoted to a single myth or a group of related myths that are illustrated in ancient art.

Each of these sections is introduced by a summary of the literary sources relating to the pertinent myth(s). A bibliography of general discussions of the myth(s) in art and literature follows. Abbreviations that appear in the general bibliography are explained in the three lists of abbreviations at the front of all the volumes. These lists are labeled "A" (Abbreviations of Ancient Texts), "B" (Abbreviations of Reviews and Periodicals), and "C" (Other Abbreviations). Abbreviations in volume 1 are not repeated in later volumes, and so must be consulted by users of subsequent volumes. The next part of the article, located after the general bibliography, is the catalog of representations in ancient art. This is sometimes prefaced by an explanatory table. The researcher should remember that catalogs of representations are intended to be complete only for periods in which the number of examples is limited. Also, all the earliest examples are always included, and mention is made of "all iconographical types and their variations, as well as the range of objects on which they are represented." The catalog entries comprise several parts. The first is the catalog number, which may be followed by an asterisk to indicate that a photograph of the example is in the plate volume, or by a dot to indicate that there is a line drawing in the text volume. Next the object type is named, along with the artist, if known (note that vase-painters' names sometimes appear within the citations to the references by Beazley that are explained in chapter 10, "Athenian Vases"). The current location and inventory number of the object are then presented, along with the place of origin, which can appear before or after the current location. Bibliographic citations follow; note that some bibliographic abbreviations are the same as those used in the general bibliography at the beginning of the section (described above), while others are shortened forms for references whose complete citations can be found in the same general bibliography within the entry. The date of the object can be found after the bibliographic citations. A brief description of the mythological content, with inscriptions noted, is often the last part of each catalog entry. However, comments which summarize any controversy about the identification of individual characters or the entire mythological scene are sometimes provided after the description. The last part of each section dealing with a single myth or group of myths follows the catalog of examples and is the commentary on the examples. Here, general trends in the iconography of representations from different periods or media are summarized, and problematic examples are discussed in terms of the features they have in common with known standard arrangements.

While working on a particular myth, the researcher should not only consult the pertinent article, but also the addenda at the end of each text volume, which contain supplementary material for many of the articles. Additional helpful features are the "List of Illustrations in the Text," at the beginning of each text volume; and the "List of Plates" at the end of each volume of photographs. Authors of the articles in each volume are listed at the beginning of the volume. General abbreviations, in four languages, appear after abbreviations lists A, B, and C in volume 1. In the same position in volumes 3–5 are "Abbreviations of Museum Names."

## COMPLEMENTARY REFERENCES

The most frequently cited references in the catalog entries of the *Lexicon* are the same as those mentioned under the Complementary References for Brommer's *Vasenlisten* (Vase Lists) and *Denkmälerlisten* (Lists of Monuments) (see the beginning of chapter 6, "Greek Gods and Heroes in Ancient Art"). Brommer's references themselves, including the *Göttersagen in Vasenlisten* (Vase Lists of Myths of the Gods, see also chapter 6), should be regularly consulted for examples of the myths discussed in the *Lexicon*. This is necessary because citations to Brommer are not always provided in the *Lexicon*'s catalog entries. Since Brommer does not always identify examples in the same way as the multiple authors of the entries in the *Lexicon*, and since he is the only scholar who has mastered most of the vast material included in the *Lexicon*, his opinions should always be given very serious consideration.

## HANDBOOKS

For the researcher who is not proficient in all four languages used in the entries for the *Lexicon*, Pierre Grimal's *Dictionary of Classical Mythology* is recommended. This excellent handbook can be consulted for brief summaries in English of the corpora of myths associated with particular Greek and Roman characters. *The Dictionary of Classical Mythology* presents all important literary variants of each myth, and extensive citations of specific literary sources in the notes. In addition, this reference includes photographs of antiquities with mythological content, genealogical charts, maps, and an index of ancient names. *Hellenike Mythologiá* (Greek Mythology), written in modern Greek, is a five-volume recounting of variants of Greek myths in ancient literature, edited by I. Th. Kakrides. Volume 1 introduces Greek myths and the literary sources and includes a chapter on the interpretations of myths from antiquity to today; volume 2 concentrates on the myths of the gods; and volumes 3–5 examine heroic myths. The text in each volume is accompanied by many superb color photographs illustrating the myths under discussion from Greek vases, statues, architectural sculptures, reliefs, coins and seal stones, and from Roman wall paintings and mosaics. In *Greek Mythology,* John Pinsent points out the common elements that recur in different myths and attempts to explain them by their possible basis in real history or in psychological truth. This thought-provoking analysis is accompanied by numerous illustrations of the myths (some in color) from every medium of Greek art.

Another valuable though outdated handbook is Collignon's illustrated *Manual of Mythology in Relation to Greek Art.* Here the historical development of the standard artistic types for gods and some heroes is traced through discussions of statuary and other media such as painted vases and coins. Many of the art works referred to in the text are illustrated in drawings. Since the monuments depicting each god and hero are presented in separate chapters or units, Collignon's *Manual* can provide helpful introductions to the chronological development of characters whose myths are fully discussed in the *Lexicon. Greek Gods and Heroes,* which illustrates many myths appearing on antiquities from the Museum of Fine Arts in Boston, follows an arrangement similar to Collignon, with a separate discussion of each mythological character. While the text of this handbook was written for high-school students, the numerous photographs can be used to supplement Collignon's drawings, and there is a useful general introduction on the style and narrative content of the different phases of ancient art.

Additional handbooks are available which are general studies of classical myths in particular media and/or periods of art. For example, Jane Henle's *Greek Myths: A Vase Painter's Notebook* summarizes and illustrates the principal myths of the Greek gods and heroes found on Greek painted vases produced at Athens and elsewhere from the late eighth century to the fourth century B.C. Photographs of vases accompany the textual discussion, and an alphabetized "Index of Types" can also be found at the back. The latter consists of line drawings of vases illustrating all the myths discussed in the text. Extensive references to the scholarly literature on particular myths are supplied in the notes and bibliography. The earliest narrative representations in Greek art, dating from 725 to 600 B.C., are cataloged and discussed by Klaus Fittschen in the authoritative study, *Untersuchungen zum Beginn der Sagendarstellungen bei den Griechen* (Investigations on the Beginning of Representations of Legends by the Greeks). Fittschen's examples, from all regions of the Greek world, are thoroughly considered, and include reviews of previous scholarship and valuable suggestions with regard to possible or likely mythological identifications. At the back of Fittschen's illustrated volume is a chronological chart of the placement within each quarter-century of particular representations of the gods and heroes. Karl Schefold's *Myth and Legend in Early Greek Art* surveys narrative Greek art of all media, including architectural sculpture, from the broader period of the eighth century to 560 B.C., while *Götter- und Heldensagen der Griechen in der spätarchaischen Kunst* (Legends of the Gods and Heroes of the Greeks in Late Archaic Art), by the same author and Luca Giuliani, covers all media from the Greek Late Archaic period of 560 to 500 B.C. In these two studies, Schefold distinguishes five developmental phases of early Greek art which exhibit distinctive stylistic and narrative approaches. Many of the most important examples of early narrative art are described in Schefold's text and illustrated in the high-quality plates and drawings, and surviving or hypothesized literary sources for the artistic representations are suggested. Indexes at the back of each volume allow the researcher to follow the development of particular mythological characters. *Myth and Legend in Early Greek Art* is the easier of the two volumes to use because it exists in this English translation, but *Götter- und Heldensagen der Griechen in der spätarchaischen Kunst* is the only one which contains scholarly notes after the text. Two additional studies by Schefold and Jung—*Die Göttersage in der klassischen und hellenistischen Kunst* (The Legends of the Gods in Classical and Hellenistic Art) and *Die Urkönige, Perseus, Bellerophon, Herakles und Theseus in der klassischen und hellenistischen Kunst* (The Early Kings Perseus, Bellerophon, Heracles and Theseus in Classical and Hellenistic Art, discussed in chapter 6 under Handbooks)—are illustrated handbooks tracing the myths of Greek gods and the principal heroes in Classical and Hellenistic Greek art.

Ingrid Krauskopf's survey of Etruscan narrative art, *Der thebanische Sagenkreis und andere griechische Sagen in der etruskischen Kunst* (The Theban Cycle and Other Greek Legends in Etruscan Art), covers the same time frame as Schefold's four studies, that is, the sixth through the first century B.C. In her discussions of selected Etruscan depictions of Greek myths, Krauskopf identifies Greek literary sources as well as possible Greek and Etruscan artistic prototypes, and she emphasizes the original aspects of Etruscan iconography. The Romans also used Greek myths in various art forms, one of the most important of which was elaborate sarcophagus reliefs. A representative sample of Roman sarcophagi with Greek myths is described (with bibliographic citations) and lavishly illustrated by Hellmut Sichtermann and Guntram Koch in *Griechische Mythen auf römischen Sarkophagen* (Greek Myths on Roman Sarcophagi). In a thought-provoking introduction, the multiplicity of artistic sources for the sarcophagus reliefs is elucidated, and our problems in understanding the significance of Greek myths in Roman funerary contexts are outlined. Besides representing the myths of Greek gods and heroes, the Romans frequently illustrated the legends of their two most illustrious forefathers, Aeneas and Romulus. Roman depictions of all the legends associated with both of these early kings are brought together by Peter Aichholzer in *Darstellungen römischer Sagen* (Representations of Roman Legends). This illustrated survey contains discussions of sources for Roman representations in Roman literature and in Greek and Etruscan art, as well as a catalog of examples with bibliography; entries in the latter include the helpful feature of the history of pieces which have been known for centuries.

## Bibliographic Entries for Handbooks

Aichholzer, Peter. *Darstellungen römischer Sagen.* Dissertationen der Universität Wien 160. Vienna: VWGÖ, 1983.

Collignon, Maxime. *Manual of Mythology in Relation to Greek Art.* Translated and enlarged by Jane E. Harrison. 1899. Reprint. New Rochelle, N.Y.: Caratzas Brothers, 1982.

Fittschen, Klaus. *Untersuchungen zum Beginn der Sagendarstellungen bei den Griechen.* Berlin: Bruno Hessling, 1969.

*Greek Gods and Heroes.* 7th ed. Boston: Museum of Fine Arts, 1981.

Grimal, Pierre. *The Dictionary of Classical Mythology.* Translated by A. R. Maxwell-Hyslop. New York: Basil Blackwell, 1986.

Henle, Jane. *Greek Myths: A Vase Painter's Notebook.* Bloomington and London: Indiana Univ. Press, 1973.

Kakrides, I. Th., general ed. *Hellenike Mythologiá.* 5 vols. Athens: Ekdotike Athenon, 1986.

Krauskopf, Ingrid. *Der thebanische Sagenkreis und andere griechische Sagen in der etruskischen Kunst.* Mainz am Rhein: P. von Zabern, 1974.

Pinsent, John. *Greek Mythology.* Rev. ed. New York: Bedrick Books, 1983.

Schefold, Karl. *Myth and Legend in Early Greek Art.* Translated by Audrey Hicks. New York: Abrams, 1966.

————, and Luca Giuliani. *Götter- und Heldensagen der Griechen in der spätarchaischen Kunst.* Munich: Hirmer, 1978.

————, and Franz Jung. *Die Göttersage in der klassischen und hellenistischen Kunst.* Munich: Hirmer, 1981.

Schefold, Karl, and Franz Jung. *Die Urkönige, Perseus, Bellerophon, Herakles und Theseus in der klassischen und hellenistischen Kunst.* Munich: Hirmer, 1986.

Sichtermann, Hellmut, and Guntram Koch. *Griechische Mythen auf römischen Sarkophagen.* Bilderhefte des Deutschen Archäologischen Instituts Rom 5/6. Tübingen: E. Wasmuth, 1975.

## SUPPLEMENTARY SOURCES

As pointed out above, one of the most important and difficult questions that confront the modern researcher is the degree to which artistic representations are dependent in their arrangements and details on literary accounts of myths. Carl Robert's *Bild und Lied* (Picture and Poetry), written in straightforward German, is still a classic example of this type of scholarship. Robert presents myths from the standpoint of clarifying the forms that they assume in the art and poetry of the major periods, as well as suggesting the relationship that these artistic and poetic renditions have to each other. When consulting this study, however, the researcher should bear in mind that there has been considerable refinement in the dating of antiquities since the late nineteenth century. Therefore, Robert's dates for pieces should be checked against those in a more modern reference such as the *Lexicon*. Robert's discussions of specific myths can be located quickly through the use of the index at the back. Not all scenes from art depicting Greek gods and heroes represent myths which are explicated in ancient literature. Some show aspects of ritual instead. In addition, ritual motifs can appear in mythological scenes. For example, vases showing the grave mounds of heroes such as Patroclus or Agamemnon can bear the motif of a snake, an allusion to the cult belief that a dead hero dwelt in the tomb in the form of a snake. The researcher looking for an explanation of such ritual motifs in Greek art can consult Jane Harrison's *Prolegomena to the Study of Greek Religion,* which still presents the most complete although sometimes outdated coverage of this fascinating realm. Richly illustrated discussions of particular ritual aspects, such as "Snake, Erinys [Fury] as," can swiftly be found in this work through the use of the general index at the back. Besides literature, changing cult beliefs may have had an impact on changing mythological emphases in art. According to H. A. Shapiro, in *Art and Cult under the Tyrants in Athens,* the popularity of certain mythological scenes in sixth-century Athenian vase-painting suggests that the gods and heroes were similarly viewed in contemporary cult. For example, the frequency of depiction of the apotheosis of Heracles in Athenian vase-painting and architectural sculpture of 575–525 B.C. may reflect a cult situation in which the Athenians were the first to worship Heracles as a god. In the case of the goddess Athena, it is believed that an Early Archaic cult statue on the Athenian Acropolis was copied on Athenian vases and also influenced the pose of Athena in depictions on vases of the battle of gods and giants.

A familiarity with the known corpora of representations of commonly depicted myths, which can be acquired through the use of the *Lexicon* or Brommer's volumes (see chapter 6) and the references cited therein, has enabled researchers to propose tentative identifications for the mythological content of controversial works. It is especially important to attempt to decipher the mythological programs of public buildings, the type of monument which most clearly was intended to express community values. This process of deciphering becomes particularly complex in the case of architectural sculptures that are poorly and/or incompletely preserved, or that have been removed from the structures which they once decorated. When thematic identifications are proposed for such sculptures, they must always be appropriate for the function of the building and the propagandistic intent of the builders. Furthermore, the researcher must consider identifications involving thematic interrelationships between portions of the decoration from the same side of the building.

One way in which the mythological content of damaged monuments can be restored is through comparisons of ancient descriptions of these structures with the surviving remains. This methodology is followed by Jane E. Harrison in her old but still valuable study, *Mythology and Monuments of Ancient Athens*. Harrison introduces her discussions of monuments with their descriptions from Pausanias, the second-century A.D. author of the frequently consulted *Description of Greece*. She demonstrates, for example, that the battered fragments of sculptures from the pediments of the Classical Parthenon do not by themselves indicate the general themes of the original sculptural groups, which are only known through Pausanias's explanations. The Parthenon's other architectural sculptures, the exterior metopes and the interior frieze, are not mentioned in ancient literature, and are poorly preserved in some portions and have large gaps in others. Thus it is not surprising that modern scholars hold different opinions in regard to both sculptural sequences. For example, Frank Brommer, in *The Sculptures of the Parthenon*, is uncertain whether the west metopes show Greeks and Amazons or Greeks and Persians. His uncertainty arises from the inability to discern female breasts on the battered warriors in Oriental dress. On the other hand, John Boardman, in *The Parthenon and Its Sculptures*, believes that the opponents of the Greeks, some of whom are mounted, were Amazons. However, he suggests that reference was made to the Persian invasions through the Amazons' adoption of Persian dress.

The small temple or treasury from the Hera sanctuary at Foce del Sele near Paestum in South Italy, an earlier structure from the Early Archaic period, is even more difficult to interpret because, while most of its metopes are preserved, they were all dismantled from the building in antiquity. In *The Frieze from the Hera I Temple at Foce del Sele*, I have recently attempted a unified reconstruction based on the assumption that the reliefs were organized in mythological cycles. An earlier reconstruction of the metopes by P. Zancani Montuoro and U. Zanotti-Bianco, published in *Heraion alla Foce del Sele II* (The Hera Sanctuary at the Mouth of the Sele), is thematically disunified for all sides but the facade. For the earlier reconstruction, contemporary miniature art, which often combined apparently unrelated themes, was used as a basis for comparison, while the recent reconstruction was supported by other Early Archaic temples that seem to have exhibited coherent mythological programs.

In order to identify myths on ancient painted vases, which are our richest source for depictions with full casts of characters, the pieces have to be carefully scrutinized both for details of the figures themselves and for inscriptions identifying the figures. When the latter are lacking, as is often the case, other vases with inscriptions or more complete representations of the same myths need to be used to achieve correct interpretations. *Griechische Vasenmalerei: Auswahl hervorragender Vasenbilder* (Greek Vase-painting: Selection of Outstanding Vase-images), by Adolf Furtwängler and others, is an early model for this type of careful scholarship. This excellent corpus consists of textual discussions and large illustrations of high-quality painted vases from the major Greek workshops from the sixth through the fourth centuries B.C. Each vase included is fully described both in its decoration and technique. Where necessary or helpful, additional vases are referred to and illustrated, and ancient texts which provide clues to identification are also cited.

An interesting type of problem which one encounters in studying ancient vases is explaining changes in the thematic repertoire of a particular workshop. In *Les représentations dans la céramique attique du IV$^e$ siècle* (Representations on Attic Vases of the 4th Century), Henri Metzger attempts to explain the new thematic emphases on late Athenian painted vases of the fourth century. He demonstrates through representative examples that in this century many myths involving conflict were abandoned, and that erotic, marine, and banquet scenes predominated. By way of explanation, he tentatively suggests for such myths a funerary symbolism, according to which an actual person may have identified with the good or bad fortunes of mythological prototypes.

Etruscan representations of Greek myths, which are far from slavish copies of Greek examples, are often difficult to interpret. Hampe and Simon, in *Griechische Sagen in der frühen etruskischen Kunst* (Greek Legends in Early Etruscan Art), attempt to demonstrate that a number of early Etruscan black-figure vases and bronze reliefs depicting Greek myths exhibit original arrangements which show an intimate familiarity with both Greek literary and artistic prototypes. This view necessitates a revision in the earlier scholarship that suggested the Etruscans had an incomplete understanding of Greek myths, and used them for their decorative appeal, rather than for their narrative relevance. A more mass-produced medium in Etruscan art than painted vases was the sarcophagus-shaped cinerary urn. In *Studies Related to the Theban Cycle on Late Etruscan Urns,* Jocelyn Penny Small analyzes the corpus of Hellenistic examples that has previously been identified as representing Greek myths associated with Thebes. By separating the urns with similar arrangements into distinct types which are differentiated by "slight variations" such as "an alteration in the pose of one figure or the addition of a particular attribute," Small attempts to demonstrate that other stories outside the Theban cycle were often intended; in many cases the myths represented seem to be known or unknown Etrusco-Roman legends whose schemes were influenced by the iconography of Theban myths with similar story lines. Fifty-two myths on Hellenistic urns from Volterra, the most active Etruscan producer of these monuments, are examined by L. B. van der Meer in "Etruscan Urns from Volterra: Studies on Mythological Representations." Through a consideration of earlier representations of the same myths in other media that exhibit the same "basic schemes" as those on the urns, van der Meer demonstrates that models for the urns' schemes seem to have been transmitted "from south to north via central Italy." When discussing artistic centers that were major sources for models, he emends previous scholarship by excluding Pergamon, Rhodes, Attica, and Rome.

Another study by Jocelyn Penny Small, *Cacus and Marsyas in Etrusco-Roman Legend,* unravels the complex processes by which Cacus the Seer in Etruscan art was derived from Greek representations of the musical contest between Apollo and Marsyas. In Roman literature and art, both Cacus and Marsyas were transformed—Cacus to Virgil's concept of a fire-breathing son of Vulcan and thief of Heracles' cattle, and Marsyas to a respected augur who assumed the new artistic form of a standing figure with a wineskin, with arm raised to call attention to an omen in the sky. To arrive at her convincing conclusions, Small makes use of evidence from Greek, Etruscan, and Roman art, as well as ancient literary and historical sources that demonstrate the manipulation of myth by the Romans for political purposes.

Sperlonga in Central Italy, site of a summer dining hall in a grotto forming part of an Imperial villa, has produced one of our richest caches of Roman copies of lost Greek sculptural groups with mythological content. Discovered in 1957 broken into more than seven thousand marble pieces, these incomplete groups have posed problems for scholars attempting reconstructions. The two most complicated groups show Odysseus' blinding of the Cyclops Polyphemus and the encounter of Odysseus' ship with the monstrous Scylla. Belonging to one of these groups is a dramatic head of Odysseus in his traditional cone-shaped hat, the *pilos.* Giulio Iacopi, in *L'antro di Tiberio a Sperlonga* (The Cave of

Tiberius at Sperlonga), initially attributed the head to the Scylla group, but a Roman relief copy of the Polyphemus group led Gösta Säflund, in *The Polyphemus and Scylla Groups at Sperlonga*, to suggest the more convincing attribution of the head to that group. More copies, evidently of the Scylla group, supported Säflund's identification of a headless standing figure as the second Odysseus from the Scylla group. Many fragments from Sperlonga remain to be studied and pieced back together to form additional mythological groups.

## Bibliographic Entries for Supplementary Sources

Boardman, John. *The Parthenon and its Sculptures*. Austin: Univ. of Texas Press, 1985.

Brommer, Frank. *The Sculptures of the Parthenon: Metopes, Frieze, Pediments, Cult-Statue*. Translated by Mary Whittall. London: Thames & Hudson, 1979.

Furtwängler, Adolph, K. Reichhold, and Friedrich Hauser. *Griechische Vasenmalerei: Auswahl hervorragender Vasenbilder*. 3 vols. text and 3 vols. plates. 1904–32. Reprint. Rome: "L'Erma" di Bretschneider, 1967.

Hampe, Roland, and Erika Simon. *Griechische Sagen in der frühen etruskischen Kunst*. Mainz: P. von Zabern, 1964.

Harrison, Jane E. *Mythology and Monuments of Ancient Athens, Being a Translation of a Portion of the 'Attica' of Pausanias by Margaret de G. Verrall, with Introductory Essay and Archaeological Commentary*. London and New York: Macmillan, 1890.

———. *Prolegomena to the Study of Greek Religion*. 3d ed. 1922. Reprint. New York: Meridian, 1955.

Iacopi, Giulio. *L'antro di Tiberio a Sperlonga*. I Monumenti Romani 4. Rome: Istituto di Studi Romani, 1963.

Meer, Lammert Bouke van der. "Etruscan Urns from Volterra: Studies on Mythological Representations." *Bulletin Antieke Beschaving* 52–53 (1977–78): 57–98.

Metzger, Henri. *Les représentations dans la céramique attique du IV^e siècle*. Bibliothèque des Écoles françaises d'Athènes et de Rome 172. Paris: E. de Boccard, 1951.

Robert, Carl. *Bild und Lied: Archäologische Beiträge zur Geschichte der griechischen Heldensage*. Philologische Untersuchungen 5. Berlin: Weidmannsche Buchhandlung, 1881. Reprint. New York: Arno, 1975.

Säflund, Gösta. *The Polyphemus and Scylla Groups at Sperlonga*. Stockholm: Almquist & Wiksell, 1972.

Shapiro, H. A. *Art and Cult under the Tyrants in Athens*. Mainz am Rhein: P. von Zabern, 1989.

Small, Joselyn Penny. *Cacus and Marsyas in Etrusco-Roman Legend*. Princeton Monographs in Art and Archaeology, no. 44. Princeton: Princeton Univ. Press, 1982.

———. *Studies Related to the Theban Cycle on Late Etruscan Urns*. Archaeologica 20. Rome: Giorgio Bretschneider, 1981.

Van Keuren, Frances. *The Frieze from the Hera I Temple at Foce del Sele*. Archaeologica 82. Rome: Giorgio Bretschneider, 1989.

Zancani Montuoro, P., and U. Zanotti-Bianco, *Heraion alla Foce del Sele II: "Il Primo Thesauros."* Rome: La Libreria dello Stato, 1954.

## Additional Supplementary Sources

Andreae, Bernard, and Baldassare Conticello. "Skylla und Charybdis: Zur Skylla-Gruppe von Sperlonga." *Akademie der Wissenschaften und der Literatur. Abhandlungen der geistes- und sozialwissenschaftlichen Klasse* 14 (1987).

Holloway, R. Ross. "Early Greek Architectural Decoration as Functional Art." *American Journal of Archaeology* 92 (1988): 177–83.

———. "Le programme de la décoration sculpturale du temple 'C' de Sélinonte." *Revue des archéologues et historiens d'art de Louvain* 17 (1984): 7–15.

# ‹6›

# Greek Gods
# and Heroes
# in Ancient Art

Brommer, Frank. *Göttersagen in Vasenlisten* (Vase Lists of Myths of the Gods). Marburg: N.G. Elwert, 1980.

———. *Vasenlisten zur griechischen Heldensage* (Lists of Vases with Greek Heroic Legends). 3d ed. Marburg: N.G. Elwert, 1973.

Brommer, Frank, and Anneliese Peschlow-Bindokat. *Denkmälerlisten zur griechischen Heldensage* (Lists of Monuments with Greek Heroic Legends). Vol. 1, *Herakles*. Marburg: N.G. Elwert, 1971.

Brommer, Frank, Anneliese Peschlow-Bindokat, and Dagmar Kemp-Lindemann. *Denkmälerlisten zur griechischen Heldensage.* Vol. 2, *Theseus—Bellerophon—Achill*. Marburg: N.G. Elwert, 1974.

Brommer, Frank, and Dagmar Kemp-Lindemann. *Denkmälerlisten zur griechischen Heldensage.* Vol. 3, *Übrige Helden* (The Remaining Heroes). Marburg: N. G. Elwert, 1976. Vol. 4, *Register.* Marburg: N.G. Elwert, 1976.

Brommer, Frank. *Konkordanzlisten zu alter Vasenliteratur* (Lists of Concordances for Early Vase Literature). Marburg: N.G. Elwert, 1979.

## ART FORM

The stories of the Greek divinities and heroes were favorite themes for the best vase-painters and manufacturers of relief vases in the major centers of production in Greece, Asia Minor, South Italy, Etruria, and the

Roman world. Perhaps vases were a favorite medium for depicting these stories because their broad pictorial fields often encouraged the inclusion of not only the chief protagonists, but also their helpers and spectators in the composition. In addition, vases exhibited detailed renditions of specific facial expressions, lively gestures, active poses with straining muscles, fine articles of clothing, and weaponry and other attributes; all these details could be admired close at hand and contributed to the dramatic power of the mythological scenes.

Greek vases of the Archaic period (the period of the greatest production of mythological scenes on painted vases) depicted the gods, goddesses, and heroes as stiff but vigorous presences, each with his or her own distinctive dress and attributes; often there were large groups of helpers and spectators on each side of the central scene. By the Classical period, the richness of such superficial characterization had given way to more supple and dignified images. Compositions were now simpler and less cluttered, and did not include a superabundance of spectators.

The most common thematic motif featuring Greek gods is the pursuit of a mortal by an enamored divinity. Sometimes the god or goddess assumes an animal form in order to succeed in his or her amorous quest, as in the case of Zeus's metamorphosis as a gentle bull during his wooing of the Tyrian princess Europa. Other more serious myths are also depicted, such as the miraculous births of Athena and Dionysus from Zeus's head and thigh; the divine wrath of Apollo and Artemis, slayers of all the sons and daughters of Niobe; or the gods' confident superiority in the battle with the rebellious giants. Ancient vases illustrate the full spectrum of qualities that the Classical-period citizen assigned to his gods—their erotic passions, their divine anger and retribution, and their unconquerable strength as warriors.

Greek heroes were shown valiantly struggling with formidable human and monstrous foes. They were also depicted abducting women or sulking over their loss of the women, and they were shown sinking to the ground and breathing their last on the battlefield. For ancient peoples, the stories of Greek heroes seem to have exemplified human trials on a grand scale.

Besides being used to decorate ancient vases, the sagas of Greek gods and heroes were often among the themes chosen for the monumental wall paintings and architectural sculptures that decorated public buildings with sacred or secular functions. In addition, they were represented in ancient freestanding sculptures of monumental and miniature scale, in relief sculptures with non-architectural functions, in domestic wall paintings and mosaics, and on mirrors, gemstones, coins, and medallions. The compositions in these media varied from two-figure groups featuring the hero or god and an opponent or beloved to elaborate configurations comparable to the full casts of characters on vases.

# RESEARCH USE

Brommer's *Göttersagen in Vasenlisten* (Vase Lists of Myths of the Gods) consists of lists, without illustrations, of Greek, Etruscan, and Roman vases featuring myths in which the gods play leading roles; the same author's *Vasenlisten zur griechischen Heldensage* (Lists of Vases with Greek Heroic Legends) consists of unillustrated lists of vases with scenes of heroic exploits. Brommer's four-volume *Denkmälerlisten zur griechischen Heldensage* (Lists of Monuments with Greek Heroic Legends), is a compilation of Greek, Etruscan, and Roman representations of heroes from all media except vases. No comparable reference exists that brings together all representations of the gods on media other than vases. In the righthand column of the lists in these three references are citations of current publications containing illustrations of the examples that are cited. Thus, one possible research use for the volumes is as a source for publications of particular examples, which can easily be located within the lists through the use of the indexes of collections at the end of all three references (vol. 4 in the *Denkmälerlisten*).

By examining illustrations of the examples cited in Brommer's references, the researcher can also investigate various aspects of divine and heroic representations. For example, subtle changes in the role and appearance of a single god or hero can be studied through a chronological examination of one or more mythological incidents; the god's or hero's opponents can be scrutinized in the same developmental fashion to determine changes in their physical characteristics and behavior. Contemporary depictions of the same divinity or hero from different cities can also be compared to determine different regional concepts of the same mythological character. Furthermore, all the vases showing one god or hero can be contrasted with those showing another god or hero for evidence of the variety of ancient ideals for divine or heroic conduct. Another possible avenue of research would be to compare vases depicting gods from the *Göttersagen* with vases illustrating heroic exploits from the *Vasenlisten*. Such an investigation would provide the researcher with some insight into the fascinating issue of ancient man's differing views of the virtues of his gods and heroes.

Since the *Vasenlisten* are devoted exclusively to vases, and examples in the *Denkmälerlisten* are arranged by medium, the researcher interested in prototypes for heroic stories can systematically investigate the categories of likely and available sources for postclassical art, such as ancient vases, sarcophagi, gemstones, coins, or medallions. Comparisons can also be made of the standard iconographic types that are used for the same myth in different ancient media. Such a study permits the discernment of the possible influence of one ancient medium on another, or the determination of separate artistic traditions in different media.

Another possible route of investigation is the consideration of different heroic myths in one medium, for example, Etruscan mirrors. Common artistic conventions for the medium, such as standard heroic compositions, can thereby be discovered. Finally, the researcher wishing to track down all certain ancient representations of a single heroic myth from a specific period and/or region of ancient art, can collect examples from the appropriate volume of the *Denkmälerlisten* and from the *Vasenlisten*. A thorough examination of all pertinent examples of unquestioned mythological interpretation can help determine whether additional examples of uncertain mythological content can confidently be added to the corpus of representations of the same myth.

Brommer's *Konkordanzlisten zu alter Vasenliteratur* (Lists of Concordances for Early Vase Literature) can be used to identify ancient vases that are illustrated in the engraved plates of publications from the late eighteenth, nineteenth, and early twentieth centuries. Vases in these commonly cited publications are often difficult or impossible to identify, since details in the plates illustrating the vases are often erroneous and the textual descriptions of the vase shapes, places of manufacture, and dates are frequently incorrect. Furthermore, many of the vases contained in these publications are now in different locations, or are lost or destroyed.

## ORGANIZATION OF THE *VASENLISTEN*

Altogether an impressive eight thousand vases are cited in the third edition of Brommer's *Vasenlisten zur griechischen Heldensage*. The general thematic organization of the vase lists is outlined in the "Inhaltsverzeichnis" (Table of Contents) at the front of the volume. Within thematic groupings of related heroes, a separate section is devoted to each individual. Vases within each section are presented in lists devoted to separate myths, which are arranged alphabetically according to the names of specific opponents of the hero. A point of confusion for the researcher not familiar with the *Vasenlisten* is the unexplained Roman numerals that are used for the themes of vases with Heracles cycles (pp. 1–2). These numerals refer to the numbering system used for Heracles' labors in Brommer's *Denkmälerlisten* (vol. 1, p. 1).

At the beginning of many lists of vases in this work is a paragraph containing bibliographic citations of articles and monographs that feature general discussions of the myth. Any bibliographic abbreviations encountered here that are not included in the list of abbreviations at the beginning of the volume are standard ones used by the Deutsches Archäologisches Institut. They can be found in the abbreviations lists which appear every few years in the journal *Archäologischer Anzeiger* (see the volume for 1989, pp. 721–28). The vases in the lists are arranged in five different categories, "A" through "E" (explained in the "Sonstiges" section of the abbreviations). "A" signifies Attic (Athenian) black-figure; "B," Athenian red-figure; "C," Archaic painted vases manufactured outside of Athens; "D," post-Archaic painted vases produced outside of Athens; and "E," relief vases. Within every mythological list, each category of vases is numbered separately. Information on the vases is presented in three columns. In the first column, after the category letter and the number of the vase, its location and inventory number are given. In the center column is the abbreviation for the vase shape (see "Sonstiges," the second list of abbreviations). If a vase is a fragment or fragments, "fr" or "frr" will be added after the abbreviation for the vase shape. Another type of abbreviation, specifying the place or area of manufacture (again, see "Sonstiges"), often appears before the vase shape. The third column gives a bibliographic citation for each vase, including a citation to illustrations, if the vase has been published. The researcher looking up the vases in these publications should expect to regularly consult *Archäologischer Anzeiger* for bibliographic abbreviations that Brommer does not explain (see above).

There are no illustrations in the *Vasenlisten*, and there is no textual discussion except for some brief but useful generalizations in the "Vorwort" (Foreword) about the rarest and most popular exploits of Theseus and Heracles on vases.

The names of specific mythological protagonists and the page numbers where pertinent vase lists are located can quickly be found in the "Stichwörterverzeichnis" (Index) at the back. The *Vasenlisten* also has an appendix at the back in which the vases are listed alphabetically by location, with cross-references to the vase lists.

## ORGANIZATION OF THE *DENKMÄLERLISTEN*

Brommer's *Denkmäleristen zur griechischen Heldensage* is a four-volume reference consisting of lists of heroic representations from all media of Greek, Etruscan, and Roman art except vases. An interesting difference between this reference and Brommer's *Vasenlisten*, as Brommer notes in the "Vorwort" to volume 1, is the greater number of Roman examples in the *Denkmälerlisten*. The subtitles describe the specific contents of the four volumes of the *Denkmälerlisten*. The first one is devoted to Heracles, the most popular ancient hero. The legends of Theseus, Bellerophon, and Achilles comprise the second volume. The third, *Übrige Helden* (The Remaining Heroes), includes the myths of all the other heroes and heroines. The last volume consists of an index of the objects listed in the other three volumes, arranged by their current locations. (Objects with unknown locations are listed at the end of the index.)

Within volumes 1–3, the lists of representations of particular myths are broken down into media, which are identified by headings. Examples from each medium are numbered separately. The media are presented according to the following standard order: examples known only through ancient literary references; monumental freestanding sculptures; monumental reliefs, including architectural sculptures and Roman sarcophagi; wall paintings and mosaics; miniature bronze sculptures, reliefs, and mirrors; and other categories of miniature art, such as lamps, gems, and coins and medallions. In the Heracles volume, a separate heading can frequently be found between the literary references to lost monuments and the monumental sculptures. This heading consists of cross-references to representations from the mythological cycles that are listed at the beginning of the volume.

None of the three volumes of monument lists includes a thematic index at the back, although each has a table of contents at the front. The Heracles volume presents the myths in alphabetical order according to the names of the hero's opponents. The same holds true for Theseus and Bellerophon, while the illustrated episodes from Achilles's life are presented in the order in which they reputedly occurred. The heroes and heroines included in volume 3 are arranged alphabetically.

For all types of objects except coins, the *Denkmälerlisten* gives the location of the object in the left column. The object type, if incompletely identified by the heading for the medium, is specified in the central column, and bibliographic citations are found in the right column. Abbreviations not included in the lists at the beginning of volumes 1 and 3 can be found in the journal *Archäologischer Anzeiger*. Because of the multiplicity of examples of each type of coin, they are presented by mint location (left column), indication of date (center column), and bibliographic citations of published examples (right column).

# ORGANIZATION OF THE *GÖTTERSAGEN*

The vase lists in *Göttersagen in Vasenlisten* are arranged in alphabetical order according to the divinities' names. The entries in the lists have a format identical to that of the *Vasenlisten zur griechischen Heldensage* (see above). The abbreviations for vase shapes in the second column and the bibliographic abbreviations in the third column are also the same for both references. *Göttersagen in Vasenlisten* has two indexes at the back, one for mythological personages, and the other for figure types (e.g., "Jüngling" or Youth), fabulous creatures, and objects.

As Brommer explains in the "Vorwort" (Foreword), not all sagas of the gods are included in the *Göttersagen*. The stories omitted are the wedding of Peleus and Thetis, attended by all the gods except Eris; the return of Hephaestus to Mount Olympus to free his mother Hera from the throne with invisible bonds which he had sent to her; the birth of Athena in the company of the gods; and the battle of the gods and giants. In short, all the stories involving assemblies of gods are omitted.

## ORGANIZATION OF THE *KONKORDANZLISTEN*

The format of *Konkordanzlisten zu alter Vasenliteratur* is close to that used in Brommer's *Vasenlisten*. The left column includes both the plate number from the early publication of the vase and the vase's current location and inventory number. In the center is the vase shape, abbreviated as in the *Vasenlisten*. In the right column are bibliographic citations for vases which have been republished in the twentieth century. The abbreviations used here can be found in the *Vasenlisten* or in the journal, *Archäologischer Anzeiger* (1989, pp. 721–28). This reference by Brommer also contains a "Vorwort" (Foreword), with a list in alphabetical order of all the antiquarian publications included, and an explanation of the difficulty of compiling the *Konkordanzlisten*. The reference does not include any indexes.

## COMPLEMENTARY REFERENCES

When using Brommer's *Göttersagen* and *Vasenlisten*, the researcher unfamiliar with the standard shapes of Greek vases can consult the chart of shapes in Richter's *Handbook of Greek Art*. Fuller accounts of the vases and their functions can be found in Richter and Milne's *Shapes and Names of Athenian Vases*. In his bibliographic citations in the *Vasenlisten*, Brommer frequently refers to "ABV," "ARV²," and "Par." These are the abbreviations for Beazley's three studies (see the beginning of chapter 10) in which Attic vases are not organized according to their mythological content (as in Brommer), but are presented in lists of works attributed to particular vase-painters, groups of painters, and potters. Beazley gives bibliographic citations for all the published vases in his lists—information which Brommer does not repeat. Beazley's volumes also supplement the *Vasenlisten* by providing concise descriptions of all the figural scenes on the vases for which Brommer only indexes the heroic representations. Another publication to which Brommer constantly makes reference is the *Corpus Vasorum Antiquorum* (Corpus of Ancient Vases; "CV" in Brommer). This is an ongoing serial publication consisting of photographs and descriptions of ancient vases from collections in several nations (see chapter 10, under Complementary References).

    Several standard publications of narrative scenes in different media are frequently cited in abbreviated forms in volumes 1–3 of Brommer's

*Denkmälerlisten.* "Schefold, Wände" is the abbreviation for Schefold's *Die Wände Pompejis* (The Walls of Pompeii), an unillustrated catalog, with bibliographic citations, of all recorded figurative wall paintings from Pompeii (see chapter 17). Citations for Roman sarcophagi in *Denkmälerlisten* often take the form of "Robert II," or "Robert III,1," "III,2," or "III,3," which refer to volumes 2–3 of Robert's *Die antiken Sarkophag-Reliefs* (The Ancient Sarcophagus Reliefs). These are the volumes that describe and illustrate sarcophagi with scenes from the Trojan, Theban, and Argonaut cycles (vol. 2); and those with myths featuring additional gods and heroes, arranged alphabetically by the principal protagonist's name (vol. 3). Three different abbreviations are used for Brunn and Körte's *I rilievi delle urne etrusche* (The Reliefs of Etruscan Urns), a three-volume publication of Etruscan sarcophagus urns. They are: "Brunn," "Brunn-Körte," and "Rilievi." Miniature bronze narrative panels from the armbands of Greek shields dedicated at Olympia were published by Kunze in the volume entitled *Archaische Schildbänder* (Archaic Shield Bands), which is referred to by Brommer in the following ways: "Kunze, Ol. Forsch."; "Kunze"; and "OlForsch II." Additional material on shield bands can be found in the more recent publication by Peter Bol, *Argivische Schilde* (Argive Shields). Brommer's abbreviation "BMC" signifies *A Catalogue of Greek Coins in the British Museum*, by the Department of Coins and Medals at the British Museum and "BMC Gems" refers to Walters' *Catalogue of the Engraved Gems . . . in the British Museum*. Finally, in citations of ancient descriptions of lost monuments, "Paus." is the abbreviation for Pausanias' *Description of Greece* (composed in the second century A.D.), for which the translations and illustrated commentaries by Frazer and by Jones and Wycherley, are recommended. Also, Nik. D. Papachatze's edition, *Pausaniou Hellados periegesis* (Pausanias' Description of Greece; with a translation and commentary in modern Greek) contains many useful reconstructions of lost and damaged monuments, as well as bibliography at the ends of the volumes; and a new ancient Greek edition of Pausanias by Maria Helena Rocha-Pereira can be consulted regarding textual questions.

Summary articles on specific Greek gods and heroes in ancient art and literature can be found in four standard references: the illustrated *Enciclopedia dell'arte antica, classica e orientale* (Encyclopedia of Ancient Art: Classical and Oriental); Roscher's *Ausführliches Lexikon der griechischen und römischen Mythologie* (Detailed Lexicon of Greek and Roman Mythology), with line drawings; the authoritative *Pauly's Real-Encyclopädie der classischen Altertumswissenschaft* (Pauly's Encyclopedia of Classical Knowledge), without illustrations; and the *Lexicon Iconographicum Mythologiae Classicae* (Iconographic Lexicon of Classical Mythology; see the beginning of chapter 5, "Classical Mythology in Ancient Art"), which is the most comprehensive illustrated encyclopedia, but which is not yet complete. Recent monographs and periodical literature can be located by looking up the gods' and heroes' names in the "Index Nominum Antiquorum" (Index of Ancient Names) in the latest volumes of *L'Année philologique* (Philological Year). The researcher should be informed of the publications listing vases with myths that are not included in the *Göttersagen in Vasenlisten*. On page 320 of Brommer's *Vasenlisten zur griechischen Heldensage* is a list of vases showing the gods' arrival at the wedding of Peleus and Thetis. Representations of the same myth in other media are listed on page 365 of Brommer's *Denkmälerlisten zur griechischen Heldensage* (vol. 3). On pages 63–67 of Brommer's *Vasenlisten* are vases illustrating the battle of gods and giants that include Heracles; and on pages 52–54 of Brommer's *Denkmälerlisten* (vol. 1) are lists of depictions of gigantomachies with Heracles from other media. Examples of gigantomachies with Athena from all media are described in the article by Pierre Demargne, "Athena," from the *Lexicon Iconographicum Mythologiae Classicae* (vol. 2, 990–92, pls. 747–49 [see chapter 5]). Additional gigantomachies from all media can be found in Vian's *Répertoire des gigantomachies figurées dans l'art grec et romain* (Repertoire of Gigantomachies Represented in Greek and Roman Art). Depictions of the birth of Athena from Greek shield bands and vases and Etruscan mirrors are discussed in the article by Brommer, "Die Geburt der Athena" (The Birth of Athena), from the *Jahrbuch des Römisch-Germanischen Zentralmuseums Mainz;* and examples from every medium are discussed in "Athena," by Pierre Demargne, in the *Lexicon Iconographicum Mythologiae Classicae* (vol. 2, 986–90, pls. 742–47). Representations of Hephaestus in all media and myths (including the wedding of Peleus and Thetis, gigantomachies, the birth of Athena, and the god's return to Olympus) are discussed, listed, and illustrated in Brommer's *Hephaistos.*

   Finally, the researcher should be apprised of the fact that all the myths of the gods whose names fall at the beginning of the alphabet have received full discussion and illustration in the published volumes of the *Lexicon Iconographicum Mythologiae Classicae.* When all the volumes of the *Lexicon* have appeared, the media not covered in Brommer's *Göttersagen* will have been brought together in a single reference.

## Bibliographic Entries for Complementary References

*L'Année philologique: Bibliographie critique et analytique de l'antiquité gréco-latine.* Paris: Société d'édition "Les Belles Lettres," 1928– .

Bol, Peter. *Argivische Schilde.* Olympische Forschungen 17. Berlin and New York: de Gruyter, 1989.

British Musuem. Department of Coins and Medals. *A Catalogue of the Greek Coins in the British Museum.* 29 vols. London: The Trustees, 1873–1927.

Brommer, Frank. *Hephaistos. Der Schmiedegott in der antiken Kunst.* Mainz: P. von Zabern, 1978.

———. "Die Geburt der Athena." *Jahrbuch des Römisch-Germanischen Zentralmuseums Mainz* 8 (1961): 66–83.

Brunn, Heinrich von, and G. Körte. *I rilievi delle urne etrusche, pubblicati a nome dell' Instituto di Corrispondenza Archeologica.* 3 vols. Rome: Salviucci, 1870–1916.

*Enciclopedia dell'arte antica, classica e orientale.* Edited by Ranuccio Bianchi Bandinelli. 7 vols., *Supplemento,* and *Atlante dei complessi figurati.* Rome: Istituto della Enciclopedia Italiana, 1958–73.

Kunze, Emil. *Archaische Schildbänder. Ein Beitrag zur frühgriechischen Bildgeschichte und Sagenüberlieferung.* Olympische Forschungen 2. Berlin: Walter de Gruyter & Co., 1950.

Pauly, August Friedrich von, Georg Wissowa, and Wilhelm Kroll, eds. *Paulys Realencyclopädie der classischen Altertumswissenschaft: Neue Bearbeitung.* 24 vols. 2d ser. (R–Z), 19 vols. Stuttgart: J. B. Metzler, 1894–1972. *Supplement.* 15 vols. Stuttgart: J. B. Metzler, 1903–78.

*Pausaniae Graeciae descriptio.* Edited by Maria Helena Rocha-Pereira. Bibliotheca scriptorum Graecorum et Romanorum Teubneriana. Leipzig: Teubner, BSB, 1973–81.

Pausanias. *Description of Greece.* Translated by W. H. S. Jones, and commentary by R. E. Wycherley. Loeb Classical Library. 1918–35. Reprint. Cambridge, Mass.: Harvard Univ. Press, 1978–79.

*Pausanias's Description of Greece.* Translation and commentary by J. G. Frazer. 2d ed. 6 vols. London: Macmillan and Co., 1913. *Graecia Antiqua: Maps and Plans to Illustrate Pausanias's Description of Greece.* Compiled by James George Frazer, explanatory text by A. W. Van Buren. London: Macmillan and Co., 1930.

*Pausaniou Hellados periegesis: eisagoge . . . .* Translation and commentary by Nik. D. Papachatze. 5 vols. Athens: Ekdotike Athenon, 1974–81.

Richter, Gisela M. A. *A Handbook of Greek Art.* 9th ed. New York: Da Capo, 1987.

Richter, Gisela M. A., and Marjorie J. Milne. *The Metropolitan Museum of Art: Shapes and Names of Athenian Vases.* New York: Plantin Press, 1935.

Robert, Carl, ed. *Die antiken Sarkophag-Reliefs.* Vol. 2, *Mythologische Cyklen.* Berlin: G. Grote, 1890. Vol. 3.1–3, *Einzelmythen.* Berlin: G. Grote, 1897–1919.

Roscher, W. H., ed. *Ausführliches Lexikon der griechischen und römischen Mythologie.* 6 vols. Leipzig and Berlin: B. G. Teubner, 1884–1937. Reprint. Hildesheim: Georg Olms, 1965.

Schefold, Karl. *Die Wände Pompejis: Topographisches Verzeichnis der Bildmotive.* Berlin: Walter de Gruyter & Co., 1957.

Vian, Francis. *Répertoire des gigantomachies figurées dans l'art grec et romain.* Paris: Librairie C. Klincksieck, 1951.

Walters, H. B. *Catalogue of the Engraved Gems and Cameos Greek Etruscan and Roman in the British Museum.* London: The Trustees, 1926.

# HANDBOOKS

The most complete English recountings of divine and heroic legends can be found in Kerényi's two handbooks, *The Gods of the Greeks* and *The*

*Heroes of the Greeks.* Kerényi does not attempt to simplify the complex ancient literary tradition, but simply enumerates all the variants for each myth, citing the surviving literary sources for them in his notes. Interspersed throughout the text of both volumes are illustrations of Greek vases depicting some of the myths under discussion. The most complete summary in English of myths of the gods and heroes in Greek art is the recently published reference, *Art and Myth in Ancient Greece*, by Thomas H. Carpenter. This illustrated survey covers Greek art of all media from ca. 700 B.C. to 323 B.C. While the main purpose of this handbook is the tracing of myths in the art of different Greek cities, there is also some discussion of literary sources, particularly in the second chapter on method. At the back of Carpenter's book is a list of bibliographic abbreviations, a bibliography (arranged following the chapters of the text), and an annotated list of the illustrations.

The essential natures of the Greek gods in ancient literature, art, and cult are illuminated in Otto's *The Homeric Gods: The Spiritual Significance of Greek Religion.* Separate chapters clarify ancient man's concepts of the Olympians Athena, Apollo and Artemis, Aphrodite, and Hermes. Some illustrations from Greek vases accompany the text. In Hans Walter's *Griechische Götter* (Greek Gods), a chapter is devoted to each of the twelve Olympians. The gods' origins and major myths are described and illustrated with numerous examples from vase-painting and sculpture. These reproductions have a useful type of labeling in which the names of the mythological characters are placed immediately below their representations. Erika Simon's *Die Götter der Griechen* (The Gods of the Greeks) also contains a chapter on each Olympian. However, Simon emphasizes the history of worship of each divinity in citing and illustrating major temples, architectural sculptures, and cult statues. The roles of the Olympians in Greek cult, as indicated by literary and archaeological evidence, are described by Séchan and Lévêque in *Les grandes divinités de la Grèce* (The Great Divinities of Greece). Schefold and Jung's *Die Göttersage in der klassischen und hellenistischen Kunst* (Legends of the Gods in Classical and Hellenistic Art) organizes the discussion of Classical and Hellenistic representations of the gods in three chapters on their births, battles, and loves. Standard and important examples of each myth are described and illustrated, along with Roman copies of Greek prototypes. Unlike Walter's study, notes on the text and bibliographic citations for the illustrations are provided.

Vases and other media depicting heroic legends from the two principal producers of early Greek art, Corinth and Athens, are cataloged and described by Hans von Steuben in *Frühe Sagendarstellungen in Korinth und Athen* (Early Representations of Legends of Corinth and Athens). Von Steuben's catalog includes all the painted vases and other art forms illustrating important heroic episodes that were produced at

Corinth and Athens between 700 and 550 B.C. Most of the catalog entries are discussed in the text, and thirty-seven line drawings are provided. Representations of Heracles, Theseus, Perseus, and Bellerophon in all media of Classical and Hellenistic Greek art and in Roman copies of Greek art are described and illustrated in Schefold and Jung's *Die Urkönige* (The Early Kings). Another illustrated study by the same authors, *Die Sagen von den Argonauten, von Theben und Troia in der klassischen und hellenistischen Kunst* (The Legends of the Argonauts, of Thebes and Troy in Classical and Hellenistic Art), considers the depictions of additional heroes involved in group undertakings at Colchis (land of the Golden Fleece), Thebes, and Troy.

## Bibliographic Entries for Handbooks

Carpenter, Thomas H. *Art and Myth in Ancient Greece.* World of Art. New York: Thames & Hudson, 1990.

Kerényi, C. *The Gods of the Greeks.* Translated by Norman Cameron. London: Thames & Hudson, 1951.

———. *The Heroes of the Greeks.* Translated by H. J. Rose. London: Thames & Hudson, 1959.

Otto, Walter Friedrich. *The Homeric Gods: The Spiritual Significance of Greek Religion.* Translated by Moses Hadas. New York: Pantheon, 1954.

Schefold, Karl, and Franz Jung. *Die Göttersage in der klassischen und hellenistischen Kunst.* Munich: Hirmer, 1981.

———. *Die Sagen von den Argonauten, von Theben und Troia in der klassischen und hellenistischen Kunst.* Munich: Hirmer, 1989.

———. *Die Urkönige, Perseus, Bellerophon, Herakles und Theseus in der klassischen und hellenistischen Kunst.* Munich: Hirmer, 1986.

Séchan, Louis, and Pierre Lévêque. *Les grandes divinités de la Grèce.* Paris: E. de Boccard, 1966.

Simon, Erika. *Die Götter der Griechen.* 3d ed. Munich: Hirmer, 1985.

Steuben, Hans von. *Frühe Sagendarstellungen in Korinth und Athen.* Berlin: B. Hessling, 1968.

Walter, Hans. *Griechische Götter: Ihr Gestaltwandel aus den Bewußtseinsstufen des Menschen dargestellt an den Bildwerken.* Munich: R. Piper & Co., 1971.

# SUPPLEMENTARY SOURCES

Themes common to several of the gods, themes connected with single gods, and single myths have been investigated in the scholarly literature. Loeb's *Die Geburt der Götter in der griechischen Kunst der klassischen Zeit* (The Birth of the Gods in Greek Art of the Classical Period) discusses and provides lists of representations of births of the gods in Greek art. In this study, the birth of Athena (not included in Brommer's *Göttersagen in Vasenlisten*) is shown to be the only myth from this category to appear before 500 B.C.; the artistic development of the exotic births of other divinities and mortals during the Classical period is traced as well. The amorous pursuits of mortals by the gods in Attic vase-painting and sculpture from the fifth century B.C., the period of the greatest popularity of these myths, are examined in Kaempf-Dimitriadou's *Die Liebe der Götter in der attischen Kunst des 5. Jahrhunderts v. Chr.* (The Loves of the Gods in Attic Art of the 5th Century B.C.). The author takes special care to point out instances in vase designs where the monumentality of the figure types and compositions seems to be derived from lost wall paintings or sculptures. Schauenburg surveys the same theme as Kaempf-Dimitriadou, but in South Italian vase-painting, with lists of examples, in his article entitled "Göttergeliebte auf unteritalischen Vasen" (The Beloved of the Gods on South Italian Vases). In his text, Schauenburg makes it clear which myths are known for the first time on Greek vases from this region, and which ones are dependent on Attic prototypes. Assemblies of the gods from Attic art of the sixth and fifth centuries B.C. are reviewed in Knell's dissertation, *Die Darstellung der Götterversammlung in der attischen Kunst des VI. u. V. Jahrhunderts v. Chr.* (The Representation of Assemblies of Gods in Attic Art of the 6th and 5th Centuries B.C.). Particularly valuable and not collected elsewhere are the divine assemblies on Attic black-figure vases that do not refer to a particular myth. Beckel's *Götterbeistand in der Bildüberlieferung griechischen Heldensagen* (The Assistance of the Gods in the Pictorial Tradition of Greek Heroic Legends) investigates another interesting general facet of gods—their roles in Greek literature and in Archaic and Classical art as helpmates for Greek heroes.

In the realm of studies of particular gods, Cook's *Zeus: A Study in Ancient Religion* is of fundamental importance in its lengthy discussions of the different aspects of the cult of Zeus and related divinities. Whenever representations of an aspect of Zeus are known (such as Zeus wielding his thunderbolt), they are illustrated in line drawings or photographs. Gods other than the Olympians have also received scholarly attention. For example, the origin and development of the sun god in ancient art is the focus of Schauenburg's *Helios*. Cornelia Isler-Kerényi suggests ways to distinguish the identities of winged goddesses in early Greek art in her volume entitled *Nike: Der Typus der laufenden Flügelfrau in archaischen Zeit* (Nike: The Type of the Running Winged Female in the Archaic Period); and in *Personification of Abstract Concepts in Greek Art and Literature to the End of the Fifth Century B.C.*, Shapiro summarizes the evidence which provides solutions to some of the problems of identifying artistic representations of minor divinities with names that are also Greek nouns related in meaning to the goddesses' or gods' functions.

Eva Zahn's *Europa und der Stier* (Europa and the Bull), on the strange courting of Europa by Zeus in the form of a bull, exemplifies a study of a single myth with a divine protagonist. Besides discussing, listing, and illustrating uncontested representations of this myth, Zahn mentions examples that are forgeries or that seem to show Maenads rather than Europa on a bull.

Artistic traditions in representing gods and heroes did not develop independently of literary accounts. The exact nature of the dependence cannot often be determined, because frequently the literary sources are lost. In the case of Heracles, little correlation can be demonstrated between the early pictorial representations and literary accounts, since the first representations usually precede the surviving literary sources. Thus, in Brommer's *Heracles: The Twelve Labors of the Hero in Ancient Art and Literature*, specific sources cannot usually be suggested for the standard artistic arrangements of the canonic labors or for aberrations from them. With Homer's *Odyssey* extant, the situation is very different for depictions of Odysseus. In *Odysseus: Die Taten und Leiden des Helden in antiker Kunst und Literatur* (Odysseus: The Deeds and Sufferings of the Hero in Ancient Art and Literature), Brommer discusses Odysseus in ancient art from the standpoint of where the artistic tradition is consistent with Homer, and where it deviates. When the latter occurs, possible alternate sources, such as other literary accounts or artistic conventions that were not dependent on literature, are suggested. The influence of particular literary sources can vary from city to city, and from period to period. In *The Iliad in Early Greek Art*, Friis Johansen concludes that painted vases and miniature reliefs from the neighboring cities of Corinth and Argos demonstrate "a quite intimate knowledge of the great epic" a century before this familiarity is evident in the painted vases of Athens. Finally, changed interpretations of Odysseus's character mark every phase of Greek and Roman art and form the focus of Odette Touchefeu-Meynier's *Thèmes odysséens dans l'art antique* (Stories of Odysseus in Ancient Art).

## Bibliographic Entries for Supplementary Sources

Beckel, Guntram. *Götterbeistand in der Bildüberlieferung griechischer Heldensagen.* Waldsassen/Bayern: Stiftland, 1961.

Brommer, Frank. *Heracles: The Twelve Labors of the Hero in Ancient Art and Literature.* Translated and enlarged by Shirley J. Schwarz. New Rochelle, N.Y.: Aristide D. Caratzas, 1986.

———. *Odysseus: Die Taten und Leiden des Helden in antiker Kunst und Literatur.* Darmstadt: Wissenschaftliche Buchgesellschaft, 1983.

Cook, Arthur Bernard. *Zeus: A Study in Ancient Religion.* 3 vols. Cambridge: Univ. Press, 1914–40.

Friis Johansen, K. *The Iliad in Early Greek Art.* Copenhagen: Munksgaard, 1967.

Isler-Kerényi, Cornelia. *Nike: Der Typus der laufenden Flügelfrau in archaischer Zeit.* Zürich: Eugen Rentsch, 1969.

Kaempf-Dimitriadou, Sophia. *Die Liebe der Götter in der attischen Kunst des 5. Jahrhunderts v. Chr.* Antike Kunst. Beiheft 11. Bern: Francke, 1979.

Knell, Heinrich. *Die Darstellung der Götterversammlung in der attischen Kunst des VI. u. V. Jahrhunderts v. Chr.: Eine Untersuchung zur Entwicklungsgeschichte des "Daseinsbildes."* Diss., Albert-Ludwigs-Universität zu Freiburg im Breisgau, 1965.

Loeb, Ehud Herbert. *Die Geburt der Götter in der griechischen Kunst der klassischen Zeit.* Diss., Hebräische Universität Jerusalem. Jerusalem: Shikmona Publishing Co., 1979.

Schauenburg, Konrad. "Göttergeliebte auf unteritalischen Vasen." *Antike und Abendland* 10 (1961): 77–101.

———. *Helios: Archäologisch-mythologische Studien über den antiken Sonnengott.* Berlin: Gebr. Mann, 1955.

Shapiro, H. A. *Personification of Abstract Concepts in Greek Art and Literature to the End of the Fifth Century B.C.* Diss., Princeton Univ., 1977. Ann Arbor and London: University Microfilms International, 1980 (number 77–14,250).

Touchefeu-Meynier, Odette. *Thèmes odysséens dans l'art antique.* Paris: E. de Boccard, 1968.

Zahn, Eva. *Europa und der Stier.* Würzburg: Königshausen & Neumann, 1983.

## Additional Supplementary Sources

Beck, Irmgard. *Ares in Vasenmalerei, Relief, und Rundplastik.* Frankfurt/M. and New York: Peter Lang, 1984.

Bothmer, Dietrich von. *Amazons in Greek Art.* Oxford: Clarendon Press, 1957.

Brommer, Frank. *Der Gott Vulkan auf provinzialrömischen Reliefs.* Cologne and Vienna: Böhlau, 1973.

———. *Herakles, II: Die unkanonischen Taten des Helden.* Darmstadt: Wissenschaftliche Buchgesellschaft, 1984.

———. *Theseus: Die Taten des griechischen Helden in der antiken Kunst und Literatur.* Darmstadt: Wissenschaftliche Buchgesellschaft, 1982.

Carpenter, Thomas H. *Dionysian Imagery in Archaic Greek Art: Its Development in Black-Figure Vase Painting.* Oxford: Clarendon Press, 1986.

Coldstream, J.N. *Deities in Aegean Art before and after the Dark Age.* An Inaugural Lecture delivered in Bedford College on Wednesday 27th October 1976. London: Bedford College, 1977.

Hausmann, Ulrich. *Hellenistische Reliefbecher aus attischen und böotischen Werkstätten: Untersuchungen zur Zeitstellung und Bildüberlieferung.* Stuttgart: W. Kohlhammer, 1959.

Heimberg, Ursula. *Das Bild des Poseidon in griechischen Vasenmalerei.* Diss., Freiburg im Breisgau, 1968.

Hiller, Stefan. *Bellerophon: Ein griechischer Mythos in der römischen Kunst.* Munich: Wilhelm Fink, 1970.

Kemp-Lindemann, Dagmar. *Darstellungen des Achilleus in griechischer und römischer Kunst.* Bern: Herbert Lang: Frankfurt/M.: Peter Lang, 1975.

Long, Charlotte R. *The Twelve Gods of Greece and Rome.* Études préliminaires aux religions orientales dans l'Empire romain 107. Leiden: E. J. Brill, 1987.

Mariolea, Maria. *Die mythologischen Darstellungen auf lakonischen Vasen des sechsten Jahrhunderts v. Chr.: Bemerkungen zur Komposition, Ikonographie und Themenwahl lakonischer Vasenbilder.* Diss., Universität zu München, 1973.

Meyer, Hugo. *Medeia und die Peliaden.* Archaeologica 14. Rome: Giorgio Bretschneider, 1980.

Moret, Jean-Marc. *L'Ilioupersis dans la céramique italiote: Les mythes et leur expression figurée au IV^e siècle.* Bibliotheca Helvetica Romana 14. Rome: Institut Suisse de Rome, 1975.

Neils, Jenifer. *The Youthful Deeds of Theseus.* Archaeologica 76. Rome: Giorgio Bretschneider, 1987.

Raab, Irmgard. *Bei den Darstellungen des Parisurteils in der griechischen Kunst.* Frankfurt/M.: Peter Lang, 1972.

Rallo, Antonia. *Lasa: Iconografia e esegesi.* Studi e materiali di etruscologia e antichità italiche 12. Florence: Sansoni, 1974.

Schauenburg, Konrad. *Perseus in der Kunst des Altertums.* Bonn: Rudolf Habelt, 1960.

Voegtli, Hans. *Bilder der Heldenepen in der kaiserzeitlichen griechischen Münzprägung.* Aesch, Switzerland: The Author, 1977.

Vollkommer, Rainer. *Herakles in the Art of Classical Greece.* Oxford University Committee for Archaeology. Monograph no. 25. Oxford: Oxford Univ. Committee for Archaeology, 1988.

Ward, Anne G., W. R. Connor, Ruth B. Edwards, and Simon Tidworth. *The Quest for Theseus.* Preface by Reynold Alleyne Higgins. New York and London: Praeger, 1970.

Zanker, Paul. *Wandel des Hermesgestalt in der attischen Vasenmalerei.* Antiquitas 3.2. Bonn: R. Habelt, 1965.

Zindel, Christian. *Drei vorhomerische Sagenversionen in der griechischen Kunst.* Diss., Universität Basel. Basel: aku-Fotodruck, 1974.

# ι7ι

# Greek Drama
# in Ancient Art

Webster, Thomas Bertram Lonsdale. *Monuments Illustrating Tragedy and Satyr Play.* 2d ed. University of London. Institute of Classical Studies. Bulletin. Supplement 20. London: Institute of Classical Studies, 1967.
———. *Monuments Illustrating Old and Middle Comedy.* 3d ed. Revised and enlarged by John Richard Green. University of London. Institute of Classical Studies. Bulletin. Supplement 39. London: Institute of Classical Studies, 1978.
Green, John Richard. "Additions to Monuments Illustrating Old and Middle Comedy." *University of London. Institute of Classical Studies. Bulletin* 27 (1980): 123–31.
Webster, Thomas Bertram Lonsdale. *Monuments Illustrating New Comedy.* 2d ed. University of London. Institute of Classical Studies. Bulletin. Supplement 24. London: Institute of Classical Studies, 1969.

## ART FORM

One of the richest sources of Greek mythology is ancient drama. The stories of the heroes and gods unfold in Greek tragedies, satyr plays, comedies, and farces. Dramatic presentations always included new twists in previously recounted myths. Such unexpected elements must have intrigued ancient audiences, as well as lending moral fabric to the plays. The exotic masks, costumes, and stage sets must also have aided in conveying the story line and in capturing the viewers' interest.

Elements from dramatic performances were depicted in ancient art from the early fifth century B.C. to the fifth century A.D. Plays, characters from plays, Dionysus (god of the theater) and company with a mask, actors with masks, and masks alone were chosen as the subject for ancient vases, wall paintings, mosaics, reliefs, statuary, lamps, coins, jewelry, and vessels of glass and precious metals. In addition, masks of actors and members of the chorus were commonly reproduced in replicas of terra-cotta, metal, stone, and glass.

Scenes from fifth-century tragedies by Aeschylus, Sophocles, and Euripides appear on Greek vases from Athens and South Italy, and lost fourth-century tragedies by authors such as Astydamas and Chaeremon are illustrated occasionally on South Italian vases. These depictions differ from other representations of Greek myths in the presence of theater costumes, scenery, and (on some South Italian vases) the stage, or the *paidagogos*—the white-haired retainer who often functions as a witness. Aesthetically, these illustrations of tragedy lack the consistency of nondramatic representations of the same myths, since characters in nontheatrical dress are often mixed in with those in stage costumes. Nonetheless, the tragic scenes often have an unusual intensity of pose and gesture. Many vases also reproduce dramatic parodies of Greek myths from satyr plays, comedies, and farces. Unlike the unmasked characters on vases illustrating tragedies and satyr plays, the actors from comedies and farces are depicted in full costume, including the appropriate masks, and the stage is frequently shown. Scenes from satyr plays, comedies, and farces exhibit a lively, humorous verve that contrasts with the gravity of tragic representations.

# RESEARCH USE

The four references by Webster and Green that are cited at the beginning of this entry contain the most complete published catalogs of ancient reproductions of theatrical masks, actors, and scenes from drama. All four references can be used to investigate the general development of theatrical masks or costumes, or to study the masks or costumes of particular character types, regions, or periods. Representations from different periods of performances of the same plays can be compared to determine changes in the interpretation of the dramas. Furthermore, representations of dramatic presentations of myths can be compared with nondramatic ones (for these, use the references listed at the beginnings of chapters 5 and 6) to determine differences between art produced under the influence of the theater and art derived from other sources.

While a large number of illustrations of specific tragedies and satyr plays by Aeschylus, Sophocles, and Euripides can be identified, only a handful of illustrations of plays by other tragedians and by comedians has been discovered. Thus, Webster's *Monuments Illustrating Tragedy and Satyr Play*, with its appendix of specific scenes, is a far richer source for illustrations of performances of identified dramas than the other three compendia of elements from comedy. However, it should be noted that *Monuments Illustrating Old and Middle Comedy* lists figure types in the "Summary Index of Poses . . ."; and the "Supplementary List" from *Monuments Illustrating New Comedy* describes late Roman mosaics from Lesbian Mytilene that illustrate scenes from eleven of Menander's plays.

## ORGANIZATION

The main body of the text in Webster's three volumes and in Green's article consists of monument lists of ancient reproductions of masks, actors, and scenes from dramas. These lists are broken down into groups of examples that were produced in the same place and are the same type of object. Each group is identified by a distinct pair of letters constituting a prefix; each object has the appropriate prefix as well as a number indicating its position within the group. The first letter of the prefix stands for the place or region of manufacture and the second letter indicates the object type or material. The prefixes are explained at the beginning of the "Synopsis," which serves as the table of contents in Webster's references: the first letters of the prefixes can be found under "Local" for locality, and the second letters can be found under "Use or Material."

The standard entry format for objects listed in *Monuments Illustrating Tragedy and Satyr Play* and *Monuments Illustrating New Comedy* is the following. The basic factual information on each object is provided in five columns of information at the beginning of the entry. First the prefix is given, and then the number of the object. Numbers that appear in parentheses after the prefix and object number are those of Webster's unpublished inventory of objects located at the University of London Institute of Classical Studies. In the second column the object type is identified and the artist's name or the scale is sometimes given. The next column provides the current location, often with an inventory number. In the fourth column is the "find spot"; when this is unknown, the fourth column is blank. In the last column is the object's date; if the date is uncertain, the column is left blank and a tentative date is suggested at the end of the entry. Below the factual headings is a brief textual description of each object. It is followed by a section labeled "Ref.," with bibliography. Lists of bibliographic abbreviations can be found immediately before the "Catalogues" of these two volumes and at the end of the volume in *Monuments Illustrating Old and Middle Comedy*. For abbreviations not appearing in these lists, the researcher is advised to consult the *American Journal of Archaeology* (vol. 95 [1991], pp. 1–16). Miscellaneous comments can be found in the last optional portion of the entry entitled "Note." Often additional, more general comments introduce groups of objects.

The entries in Webster's *Monuments Illustrating Old and Middle Comedy* and Green's "Additions to Monuments Illustrating Old and Middle Comedy" contain the same information as those in Webster's other two references, but the categories of information are arranged differently. On the first line are the prefix and object number and the object type. On the second line are the current location with inventory number, the find spot (if known), and the scale (if known). The description of the object forms a separate paragraph, and bibliographic citations and notes appear at the end of the entry.

The researcher should be aware that at the back of Webster's *Monuments Illustrating Tragedy and Satyr Play* and in *Monuments Illustrating New Comedy* is a section entitled "Addenda and Corrigenda." This contains bibliographic additions to items in the main catalog and additional objects not listed in the catalog. In *Monuments Illustrating New Comedy*, insertion marks next to objects in the main catalog indicate that there are bibliographic additions, and insertion marks between entries inform the reader that he or she should consult the "Addenda and Corrigenda" for additional objects. *Monuments Illustrating New Comedy* also has a "Supplementary List" beyond the "Addenda and Corrigenda." Once again, insertion marks in the main catalog tell the reader to look for additional objects in this list.

Some objects are illustrated in plates at the back of Webster's volumes. In the catalog entries for *Monuments Illustrating Old and Middle Comedy* and in Green's "Additions . . . ," the plate number is cited for every illustrated object.

An invaluable part of Webster's volumes is the "Synopsis," or table of contents, which can be found after the introduction. It provides the dates for the groups of objects listed in each chapter, and identifies as well the place of manufacture and object type for each group, and the numbers of the specific objects. Researchers should be aware that objects from the same group, if they were produced during more than one timeframe, can be included in more than one chapter. Unfortunately, the synopsis does not summarize additional objects listed in the "Addenda and Corrigenda."

Besides the introduction in each of Webster's volumes, described under Research Use, the backs of the same references contain other useful features. Particularly valuable is the "Appendix: Illustrations of Particular Plays," in *Monuments Illustrating Tragedy and Satyr Play*. This not only repeats objects from the main catalog, regrouped under the titles of the plays, but it also includes additional representations that were probably inspired by the plays but do not include elements from performances.

All three of Webster's volumes include indexes of masks, provenances, and museums. Only the indexes in *Monuments Illustrating Tragedy and Satyr Play*, however, cite objects from the "Addenda and Corrigenda." All three references have a concordance in which correspondences between Webster's catalog numbers and other standard references are provided. The concordances should be consulted regularly since all the citations presented in them are not always repeated in the catalog entries.

## COMPLEMENTARY REFERENCES

The researcher must be forewarned that the appendix entitled "Illustrations of Particular Plays" in Webster's *Monuments Illustrating Tragedy and Satyr Play* is not complete. Many examples from Séchan's *Études sur la tragédie grecque* (Studies on Greek Tragedy; see also under Supplementary Sources) and from Brommer's *Satyrspiele: Bilder griechischer Vasen* (Satyr Plays: Pictures on Greek Vases) are not repeated by Webster. He concentrates rather on adding new bibliographic citations to the literature on previously known examples and on supplying new examples of dramatic representations. Thus anyone wishing to track down all known depictions of a particular tragedy or satyr play must collect examples from Séchan's or Brommer's book along with those in Webster's list. Depictions of the farce, a simple type of comedy consisting of parodies of heroic and divine sagas and scenes from daily life, are cataloged and illustrated by Trendall in *Phlyax Vases*. Trendall's reference should be used in conjunction with Webster's *Monuments Illustrating Old and Middle Comedy*, since the latter does not provide separate entries for many of these vases, but only cites them by the prefix "Ph" and Trendall's numbers.

For discussions of representations of Greek dramas and elements from Greek dramas that have been published after the major references under discussion, researchers are urged to consult the summary article by John Richard Green, "Theatre Production: 1971–1986." This article lists and describes scholarly literature of all types that deals with the theater in general, the origins of drama, Greek and Roman theater structures, staging, actors and performances, tragedies, satyr plays, and comedies.

*Bibliographic Entries for Complementary References*

Brommer, Frank. *Satyrspiele: Bilder griechischer Vasen*. 2d ed. Berlin: de Gruyter, 1959.

Green, John Richard. "Theatre Production: 1971–1986." *Lustrum: Internationale Forschungsberichte aus dem Bereich des klassischen Altertums* 31 (1989): 7–95.

Séchan, Louis. *Études sur la tragédie grecque dans ses rapports avec la céramique*. Paris: Champion, 1926. Reprint. Paris: Champion, 1967.

Trendall, Arthur Dale. *Phlyax Vases.* 2d ed. University of London. Institute of Classical Studies. Bulletin. Supplement 19. London: Institute of Classical Studies, 1967.

# HANDBOOKS

Trendall and Webster's *Illustrations of Greek Drama* is a companion volume for all the major references discussed above and for Trendall's *Phlyax Vases.* It does not attempt to provide comprehensive lists with brief descriptions and few illustrations, like the other references, but fully discusses and illustrates a more limited number of well-chosen examples. In addition, the beginning of Trendall and Webster's study includes a chapter entitled "Pre-dramatic Monuments," a category of representations not discussed elsewhere which depict the tragic and comic choral dances that preceded drama. The same chapter discusses several examples of choral dances honoring Dionysos, or *dithyrambs.* "Farce and Tragedy in South Italian Vase-painting," a forthcoming article by Trendall, summarizes Athenian vase-painting prototypes and South Italian vases illustrating scenes and myths from different types of Greek drama. This article, to appear in a festschrift in honor of R. M. Cook, emphasizes elements in the painted scenes such as masks, theatrical costumes, stages, and stage sets that are unquestionably copied from actual dramatic performances. In *The Dramatic Festivals of Athens*, Pickard-Cambridge concentrates on reconstructing the Athenian festivals whose high points were the dramatic competitions. This reference also includes chapters on costume, the actor, the chorus, the audience, and performers' guilds. Pickard-Cambridge constantly refers to and illustrates archaeological and artistic evidence. Surviving monuments are again cited and illustrated by Pickard-Cambridge in the related study *Dithyramb, Tragedy and Comedy.* This monograph summarizes evidence of all kinds that reveals the characteristics of dithyramb, early tragedy, and comedy.

## Bibliographic Entries for Handbooks

Pickard-Cambridge, Arthur Wallace. *Dithyramb, Tragedy and Comedy.* 2d ed. Revised by Thomas Bertram Lonsdale Webster. Oxford: Clarendon Press, 1962.

———. *The Dramatic Festivals of Athens.* 2d ed. Revised by John Gould and David Malcolm Lewis. Reissued with supplement and corrections. New York: Oxford Univ. Press, 1988.

Trendall, Arthur Dale. "Farce and Tragedy in South Italian Vase-painting." In *Looking at Greek Vases.* Ed. by N. Spivey and T. Rasmussen. New York: Cambridge Univ. Press, forthcoming 1991.

———, and Thomas Bertram Lonsdale Webster. *Illustrations of Greek Drama.* London: Phaidon; New York: Praeger, 1971.

## SUPPLEMENTARY SOURCES

Huddilston's outdated but still useful *Greek Tragedy in the Light of Vase Paintings* spells out the common and disparate aspects of extant texts and vases illustrating them. Séchan (see Complementary References above) focuses on the pertinent tragedy as the main inspiration, but also allows for possible influence from other dramas and from a separate artistic tradition. In *The Oresteia: Iconographic and Narrative Tradition*, Prag investigates all early representations of episodes from the Oresteia which do not show the influence of Aeschylus. In addition, he incorporates a few post-Aeschylean Attic red-figure vases into his discussion to demonstrate changes in the iconographic tradition, such as a new humanized form of the Furies which seems to reflect the impact of Aeschylean productions. In *Dramen des Aischylos auf westgriechischen Vasen* (Dramas of Aeschylus on Western Greek Vases), Kossatz-Deissmann adopts the similar point of view that sudden changes in the iconographic traditions of myths on Greek vases can reflect modifications of the myths by tragedians. Thus, in her catalog of South Italian vases showing the influence of Aeschylus's tragedies, she includes some vases without theater costumes which she believes, nonetheless, follow the Aeschylean versions of the myths. The *paidagogos*, the elderly witness figure on South Italian vases illustrating tragedies, is the focus of the final portion of Chamay and Cambitoglou's article in *Antike Kunst* (Ancient Art). Thirty-one examples of the figure type are listed, and conclusions are presented regarding his standard appearance and role. This stock figure type, who has no place in nondramatic representations, is extremely important because his presence signals that a scene from a tragedy is intended.

In a 1987 article, Oliver Taplin identifies an illustration of a specific scene from Aristophanes' *Thesmophoriazusae* in an Apulian bell crater of circa 370 B.C. Taplin suggests further that the vase reproduces a contemporary performance in Apulia of the late-fifth-century play. Previous scholarship assumed that only Attic tragedy, not Old Comedy, was revived in South Italy in the fourth century. Thus, if Taplin is correct, a number of the South Italian *phlyax* vases (believed to illustrate local farces or contemporary Middle Comedy) may have to be reinterpreted as representations of Attic Old Comedy. Taplin leads the way by singling out several *phlyax* vases that may fall in this new category. C. W. Dearden attempts to reconstruct the basic characteristics of *phlyax* comedies (i. e., farces) in Magna Graecia in a 1988 article. Using *phlyax* vases as evidence, Dearden concludes that South Italian farces were relatively sophisticated dramas performed on temporary stages, with plots that often parodied Greek tragedies.

Sutton's *The Greek Satyr Play* can be used to supplement Brommer's *Satyrspiele: Bilder griechischer Vasen* (see Complementary References). While Brommer's main purpose is to describe the artistic representations that seem to reflect the influence of lost satyr plays, Sutton's study reconstructs these plays from surviving fragments of text. Sutton also cautiously makes use of artistic representations of satyr plays as evidence for the productions of the plays.

Dithyrambs, as has already been mentioned under Handbooks, were another form of drama besides tragedies, comedies, and satyr plays. These choral dances honoring Dionysus had a mythological content which was narrated without actors; the dancers usually did not wear masks. In *Dithyrambos und Vasenmalerei in Athen* (Dithyramb and Vase-painting in Athens), Heide Froning attempts to provide correct interpretations for a number of Attic vases which she believes show the decoration of victory tripods won in dithyramb contests and the actual performances of dithyrambs.

In his recent article "Masks on Apulian Red-figured Vases," Trendall brings together all Tarentine vases that include theatrical masks. These masks usually belong to female or male characters from comedy, and they are most often shown along with Dionysus and his company of satyrs and maenads, or as a vase's sole decoration. Trendall's article adds a substantial number of new examples to the corpus of mask vases in his *Phlyax Vases* (see Complementary References above), and demonstrates that these vases were popular at Tarentum within the limited time frame of circa 370 to 350 B.C. In *Menandro e il teatro greco nelle terracotte liparesi* (Menander and the Greek Theater in the Terra-cottas of Lipari), Luigi Bernabò Brea catalogs the largest corpus of theatrical material from any site—one thousand terra-cotta masks and statuettes of actors from the island of Lipari (north of Sicily)—and illustrates many examples, some in color. These terra-cottas, the majority from tombs dating from circa 400 B.C. to Lipari's destruction in 252 B.C., represent characters from tragedies, satyr plays, and comedies. While most of them can only be vaguely identified by category of drama and character types, the third appendix in this work suggests specific identifications for some examples in characters from particular Attic and South Italian tragedies. The second appendix, by Madeleine Cavalier, presents the painted vases from the tombs of Lipari in a chronological sequence; a number of these illustrate Greek dramas.

Finally, rather than using art as his primary source in reconstructing the visual impact of Greek tragedy, Taplin (in *Greek Tragedy in Action*) points out how the speeches, dialogues, and choruses in the texts themselves accent and reiterate the physical activities of the actors and choral members. Several aspects, such as "actions and gestures," are investigated through discussions of textual references to them in nine surviving tragedies by Aeschylus, Sophocles, and Euripides. Taplin also briefly describes tragic costumes and masks, several of which he illustrates with photographs of Greek vases. Future research might be

possible in the area of comparisons between textual and artistic references to the same actions in specific tragic scenes.

## Bibliographic Entries for Supplementary Sources

Bernabò Brea, Luigi. *Menandro e il teatro greco nelle terracotte liparesi.* Appendix II
by Madaleine Cavalier. Genova: Sagep Editrice, 1981.

Chamay, Jacques, and Alexander Cambitoglou. "La folie d'Athamas par le
peintre de Darius" (The Madness of Athamas by the Darius Painter). *Antike
Kunst* 23 (1980): 35–43.

Dearden, C. W. "Phlyax Comedy in Magna Graecia—A Reassessment." In
*Studies in Honour of T. B. L. Webster.* Edited by J. H. Betts, J. T. Hooker, and
J. R. Green. Vol. 2, 33–41. Bristol: Bristol Classical Press, 1988.

Froning, Heide. *Dithyrambos und Vasenmalerei in Athen.* Beiträge zur Archäologie
2. Würzburg: Konrad Triltsch, 1971.

Huddilston, John Homer. *Greek Tragedy in the Light of Vase Paintings.* London and
New York: Macmillan, 1898.

Kossatz-Deissmann, Anneliese. *Dramen des Aischylos auf westgriechischen Vasen.*
Schriften zur antiken Mythologie 4. Mainz am Rhein: P. von Zabern, 1978.

Prag, A. J. N. W. *The Oresteia: Iconographic and Narrative Tradition.* Warminster,
Wiltshire: Arris & Phillips Ltd; Chicago: Bolchazy-Carducci Publications,
1985.

Sutton, Dana Ferrin. *The Greek Satyr Play.* Meisenheim am Glan: Anton Hain, 1980.

Taplin, Oliver. *Greek Tragedy in Action.* Berkeley and Los Angeles: Univ. of
California Press, 1979.

———. "Phallology, *Phlyakes,* Iconography and Aristophanes." *Proceedings of the
Cambridge Philological Society* 213 (1987): 93–104.

Trendall, Arthur Dale. "Masks on Apulian Red-figured Vases." In *Studies in
Honour of T. B. L. Webster.* Edited by J. H. Betts, J. T. Hooker, and J. R. Green.
Vol. 2, 137–54. Bristol: Bristol Classical Press, 1988.

## Additional Supplementary Sources

Bieber, Margarete. *Die Denkmäler zum Theaterwesen in Altertum.* Berlin and
Leipzig: Vereinigung wissenschaftlicher Verleger, 1920.

———. *The History of Greek and Roman Theater.* 2d ed. Princeton: Princeton Univ.
Press, 1961.

Blume, Horst-Dieter. *Einführung in das antike Theaterwesen.* Die Altertumswissenschaft. 2d ed. Darmstadt: Wissenschaftliche Buchgesellschaft, 1984.

Ghiron-Bistagne, Paulette. *Recherches sur les acteurs dans la Grèce antique.* Paris: Les
Belles Lettres, 1976.

Little, Alan MacNaughton Gordon. *Myth and Society in Attic Drama.* New York:
Columbia Univ. Press, 1942.

———. *Roman Perspective Painting and the Ancient Stage.* Wheaton, Md., 1971.

Simon, Erika. *The Ancient Theatre.* Translated by C. E. Vafopoulou-Richardson.
London and New York: Methuen, 1982.

Webster, Thomas Bertram Lonsdale. *The Greek Chorus.* London: Methuen, 1970.

———. *Greek Theater Production.* 2d ed. London: Methuen, 1970.

# ⟨8⟩

# Classical Mythology
# in Art
# after Antiquity

Pigler, A. *Barockthemen: Eine Auswahl von Verzeichnissen zur Ikonographie des 17. und 18. Jahrhunderts* (Baroque Themes: A Selection of Lists on the Iconography of the Seventeenth and Eighteenth Centuries). 2d ed. 3 vols. Budapest: Akadémiai Kiadó, 1974.

## ART FORM

It is significant that Christian themes in art, first introduced in the second century A.D., never supplanted pagan myths; instead, both thematic categories persisted in art after antiquity and up to our times. The reasons that classical myths never lost their appeal for artists and patrons may lie in their endless variety and their subtle moral content. These themes could be given widely divergent artistic interpretations without the doctrinal constraints that were imposed on Christian images.

Depictions of pagan myths in art after antiquity have sometimes followed traditional classical imagery, but more often they have exhibited new arrangements that have corresponded to new uses of the myths. In the Medieval period, manuscript illustrations with mythological themes were used to exemplify lessons of Christian morality. In some cases these illustrations seem to be copies of miniatures from Greco-Roman manuscripts, while in other instances new formulations with characters in contemporary dress are evident. The latter nonetheless betray some familiarity with the ancient stories as recounted in sources such as Ovid's popular *Metamorphoses*.

In the Renaissance and Baroque periods, the first serious study of antiquities was attempted, a phenomenon which prompted emulation of their beauty and harmonious proportions. In these periods, many myths were represented for which no prototypes from classical art were known. Thus new arrangements for myths in two- and three-dimensional works were invented which drew from ancient and later literary sources, but not from ancient art. For example, the myth of Heracles' choice between Virtue and Vice, first known in 1463, seems to have been inspired by a quotation from the philosopher Prodicus in Xenophon's *Memorabilia*. Renaissance and Baroque representations of other myths with an ancient iconographic tradition sometimes seem to reveal the influence of these artistic prototypes, and sometimes seem entirely independent of them. In the art of these periods myths were often used allegorically to express serious moral precepts, but many mythological works had the more frivolous function of evoking a carefree and erotic ancient paradise.

A more monumental and formal classicism is evident in the paintings and sculptures of Neoclassical artists such as David and Canova. Gone were the flourish and drama of Renaissance and Baroque works; in their place was a more restrained and severe treatment of classical themes acted out in archaeologically correct settings. This new style was judged to be consistent with classical ideals as exemplified by antiquities from the eighteenth-century excavations at Pompeii and other sites. Neoclassical works showing episodes from ancient mythology and history were always intended to instruct the viewer in virtuous conduct.

In the nineteenth century, Romantic artists such as Delacroix infused new life into classical myths by capturing intensely dynamic moments of conflict in innovative compositions. Contemporary opponents of Romanticism, such as Ingres, represented ancient myths in a calmer, more statuesque, but also more lifeless fashion. Classical myths persist in the art of this century, during which a remarkable variety of interpretations of ancient themes has been evident. The work of some twentieth-century artists such as Picasso preserves some aspects of the style or significance of ancient representations, while other artists such as Dali have given bold new shapes and symbolic functions to the Minotaur and other mythological characters.

## RESEARCH USE

The title of Pigler's reference, translated into English, is *Baroque Themes: A Selection of Lists on the Iconography of the Seventeenth and Eighteenth Centuries*. This three-volume reference encompasses lists of examples from painting and sculpture representing about one thousand themes from the Christian and pagan worlds. Volume 1 consists of annotated lists of examples with Christian themes, volume 2 lists pagan themes, and volume 3 contains plates of selected examples from the lists in the other two volumes. While the emphasis in the lists is on examples from the Baroque period, Pigler attempts to indicate the time frame up to the Baroque period when specific themes are attested. Thus he includes, where pertinent, selections of fifteenth- and sixteenth-century examples, and on occasion even earlier examples, particularly Roman wall paintings, sarcophagi, gems, and sculptural groups. In addition, in volume 2 Pigler names significant ancient literary sources that may have influenced Baroque artists' renditions of classical themes.

Volumes 2 and 3 of Pigler's reference can be used to identify the standard iconography or iconographies (if there are chronological or regional variants) for classical myths in the Renaissance and Baroque periods. Prints from these periods and additional paintings and sculptures from other periods can be located by using the pertinent references discussed in Complementary References below. Thus, for frequently represented myths, the researcher can compile a list including depictions from every period, and can investigate entire artistic traditions.

Since Renaissance and Baroque painters and sculptors were often influenced by ancient literary rather than artistic sources, the researcher also needs to examine classical texts recounting the myths that are known to have been available in these periods. Pigler's citations of textual sources provide the reader with starting points in this type of research. Further investigations can be carried out by consulting the references that are discussed in chapter 4, "Classical Mythology in Ancient and Later Literature." In addition, such research should be carried out on an artist-by-artist basis; that is, any modern literature which comments on an artist's or his patron's or adviser's familiarity with particular texts needs to be consulted, as does any information on the contents of available libraries and published editions. The most current modern literature on a specific artist can be speedily identified by a RILA (*Répertoire international de la littérature de l'art*) computer search (see Complementary References below).

## ORGANIZATION

Volume 1 of Pigler's reference is devoted to Christian themes, primarily those from the Old and New Testaments. Volume 2 deals exclusively with pagan themes. These are covered in chapters as follows: 1. Greek and Roman mythology; 2. Legends; 3. Greek and Roman history; 4. History after antiquity; 5. From poetry after antiquity; 6. Allegories; 7. Genre scenes; 8. Various. The categories within which some themes, particularly heroic ones, have been grouped are not always predictable. For example, all the Heracles myths can be found under "Greek and Roman mythology"; the episodes from Achilles's life are under "Legends"; and Romulus and Remus's suckling and quarrel are under "Greek and Roman history." Thus the researcher is cautioned to look up a character in the "Namen- und Sachregister" (Index of Names and Subjects) at the back of volume 2 before concluding that the myths of this personage are not included.

Each myth is introduced by a descriptive title in bold-faced type. For example, **Herkules auf dem Scheiterhaufen** is the heading for depictions of Heracles on the funeral pyre. Further description of the standard iconography for the myth often follows the title, along with the citation of ancient literary sources and modern scholarship. A list of representa- tions of the myth, primarily from painting and sculpture, follows the myth's introduction. The researcher looking for a specific example within such a list can make use of italicized headings in the margins for guidance. Headings such as *Ital.* for Italian indicate the break-down by country of depictions from the Baroque period (the 17th and 18th centuries). Within each country, works are arranged chronologically by the artists' birthdates. Sometimes all the Renaissance examples are presented in a single category labeled *15.–16. Jh.* (15th–16th Centuries) that precedes Baroque representations, and in other instances these examples are incorporated into the first parts of the country-by-country Baroque listings. Renaissance examples can also be listed under the heading *Frühere Beispiele* (Earlier Examples), a category which can also include Medieval images. When ancient examples are cited, they are labeled *Antike,* and appear first in the lists of representations. Sometimes examples from the nineteenth century are also included; these appear at the ends of the lists with the label *19. Jh.*

Entries in the lists provide the following information. The artist's name is given first. "Dess." appearing in the place of the artist's name signifies "Desselben" (The Same), and indicates that the same artist who executed the preceding work created this one as well. The artist's name is followed by the dates of his life, in parentheses. The medium of the work is mentioned next, often in an abbreviated form (see vol. 1, p. 13, for an explanation of these abbreviations). For example, "Gem." stands for "Gemälde" (Painting), and "Hz." is the abbreviation for "Hand- zeichnung" (Drawing). When a specific date for a work is provided, it follows the medium. The current location of the work is given next. If the work used to be in a particular location, but the current whereabouts are unknown, the location is preceded by "Ehe," for "Ehemals" (formerly), "Früher" (formerly), or "War" (was). "Verst." is the abbreviation for "Versteigert" (Sold at Auction), and "Erw." stands for "Erwähnt" (Mentioned). The latter appears in the place of a location in cases when the work has been mentioned in the art historical literature without a location given. The last part of the entry is citations for publications of the work, if it has been published. When "Abb." (for "Abbildung") precedes a bibliographic citation, it signals that the reference includes an illustration of the work. "Vgl." before a citation stands for "Vergleiche" (Compare). A few bibliographic abbreviations are explained by Pigler (vol. 1, p. 13). Most citations for books not included in the list of abbreviations are given in a full enough form, including date of publication, that they can easily be identified. Catalogs may pose the only difficulty. Formats such as "Kat. v. J. 1872" mean "Katalog vom Jahre 1872" (Catalog from the Year 1872). Journal titles, not explained in Pigler's abbreviations, are nonetheless often given an abbreviated form. For instance, "Burl. Magaz." denotes the *Burlington Magazine,* and "Gazette des B.-A." signifies *Gazette des Beaux-Arts.* Also, "Jb." in the titles of various German journals stands for Jahrbuch (Yearbook). With the help of a reference librarian, the researcher should be able to decipher all the journal titles.

Tables of contents listing all the myths included in volumes 1 and 2 can be found at the backs of the volumes. After the table of contents in volume 2 is the "Namen- und Sachregister" (Index of Names and Subjects). This index is arranged alphabetically and provides access to the lists of Christian and pagan themes in both volumes; references to volume 1 give only the page numbers of the lists, while citations for volume 2 with pagan themes have two parts—"II" signifying the volume number, followed by the page number(s) in Arabic numerals.

The plates in volume 3 are introduced by a list which is divided into two parts corresponding to volumes 1 and 2. Entries in this list give the plate number first, preceded by "Tafel" (Plate). The theme of the work is named next, and the page number in volume 1 or 2 where the list of examples can be found is provided in parentheses. In the right column is the page number of the plate. The artist's name can be found in the label under the actual plate; this can be matched with the citation for the same work in the corresponding list from volume 1 or 2. The plates from volume 3 are not cited in the lists in volumes 1 and 2.

Finally, for those readers who are proficient in German, the prefaces to the first and second editions of Pigler's reference, at the beginning of volume 1, are recommended. In them, Pigler stresses his concept of the work's main purpose—to eliminate inaccurate or insufficient identifications of the subject matter of Baroque art. Also, he explains his criteria for the selection of the themes and examples to be included in the reference.

## COMPLEMENTARY REFERENCES

The reference which is most frequently cited by Pigler is Thieme and Becker's *Allgemeines Lexikon der bildenden Künstler von der Antike bis zur*

*Gegenwart* (General Lexicon of Fine Artists from Antiquity to the Present). Pigler refers to this reference by the abbreviation "Th.-B." It is a multivolume international lexicon with entries on artists from antiquity to the present, which mentions many works but has no illustrations.

Someone interested in comparing classical representations with Renaissance and Baroque ones can supplement Pigler's ancient examples with examples from the *Lexicon Iconographicum Mythologiae Classicae* (Iconographic Lexicon of Classical Mythology, see chapter 5) or Brommer's references (see chapter 6).

The researcher who wishes to find additional examples of classical themes that are not included in Pigler may use a number of other references. For mythological representations in Italian art of all periods, the *Alinari Photo Archive* can be consulted. This microfiche edition reproduces about 120,000 photographs from the Alinari archives in Florence, along with the printed catalogs for the photographs. Many of these catalogs have subject indexes, which can be accessed through the table on pages 38–39 of the *Guide to the Microform Collection*. In addition, representations of classical heroes and heroines (but not gods and goddesses) can be located by consulting fiches 6–8 of the series 0–21 from the *Alinari Photo Archive*, which make up the "Index of Historical Persons in the Ancient World" (see the *Guide to the Microform Collection*, p. 43). Available at the Avery Library at Columbia University are these useful printed indexes of the Alinari photographs: *Repertorio di opere d'arte iconografica: La mitologia greco-romana, Catalogo delle fotografie edite da F.lli Alinari* (Iconographic Inventory of Works of Art: Greco-Roman Mythology, Catalog of the Photographs Printed by the Alinari Brothers); and *Mille Pitture di venti secoli* (A Thousand Paintings from Twenty Centuries).

*Attributs et symboles dans l'art profane 1450-1600: Dictionnaire d'un langage perdu* (Attributes and Symbols in Profane Art from 1450 to 1600: Dictionary of a Lost Language), by Guy de Tervarent, is an alphabetically arranged and illustrated dictionary of attributes of classical gods and heroes; symbols of all kinds including plants and animals; and gods and heroes who have symbolic values. All of these attributes and symbols are used in Renaissance art from 1450 to 1600. In the case of attributes, the first information that is provided is the identity or identities of the mythological character(s) to whom the attribute belongs. For symbols, the quality (or qualities) to which allusion is made through allegory is named. Both types of entries name sources in art and literature before the Renaissance (under "Source"), and selections of examples from all media of Renaissance art (under "Art"), with bibliography. At the beginning of the main volume of *Attributs et symboles* is a list of bibliographic abbreviations.

For prints from the sixteenth and seventeenth centuries, which Pigler cites only occasionally, the *Index Iconologicus* (Iconological Index) is the most complete corpus. This is a microfiche index consisting of reproductions, arranged alphabetically by theme, of the prints that are described in A. von Bartsch's multivolume compendium, *Le peintre graveur* (The Painter-Engraver). Many of the same prints are also published in larger, more legible reproductions in the *Illustrated Bartsch*. The researcher simply needs to match up the volume number from *Le peintre graveur* with the old volume number which is provided on the title pages of the *Illustrated Bartsch*. Besides reproducing prints dating from 1500 to 1700 A.D., the *Index Iconologicus* includes entries for prints from "as early as A.D. 1250 to as recently as 1940." For an explanation of the organization and all the symbols used in the *Index Iconologicus*, the researcher should devote careful study to *Index Iconologicus: A Guide to the Microform Edition*. In it, the most important symbols the researcher must understand are: > meaning consult another subject heading, which is identified by the placement of three dots under the main word signifying the heading; and an asterisk, which indicates that the other subject heading has an illustration. *Print Index: A Guide to Reproductions*, by Pamela Jeffcott Parry and Kathe Chipman, indexes illustrations of prints from the eighteenth century until circa 1975 which have been published in one hundred books and catalogs in English. For prints with mythological content, see "Mythological Themes" on pages 292–93.

Reproductions of two-dimensional works of all media (including tapestries) from 250 books and catalogs of collections are indexed by Yala M. Korwin in *Index to Two-dimensional Art Works*. The references indexed are all in English, were published between 1960 and 1977, and cover Western art from the Middle Ages to the twentieth century. Volume 2 of this index contains both subject entries, which are underlined, and title entries.

Mythological paintings from all periods, particularly the Renaissance and Baroque and the nineteenth and twentieth centuries, can be identified through the use of two indexes to reproductions in books and catalogs. One of these references, Havlice's *World Painting Index*, is a two-volume listing of the paintings reproduced in 1,167 books and catalogs. The first volume includes the bibliography of books and catalogs indexed as well as entries for paintings listed under artists' names. The second volume has an alphabetically arranged title index that can be consulted to locate paintings with particular themes. The *First Supplement 1973–1980* for the same reference also has a title index in volume 2. Isabel and Kate Monro's *Index to Reproductions of European Paintings: A Guide to Pictures in More than 300 Books* covers many earlier general studies and catalogs of collections in English, and includes a section on pages 443–47 called "Mythological Themes." Illustrations of American paintings from books and catalogs are indexed by the Monros in *Index to Reproductions of American Paintings: A Guide to Pictures Occurring in More than 800 Books* (see "Mythological Themes," pp. 452–53) and the *1st Supplement* to it (see

"Mythological Themes," p. 306); as well as in Smith and Moure's *Index to Reproductions of American Paintings, Appearing in More than 400 Books Mostly Published since 1960* (see "Illustrations from Literature: Mythological," pp. 711–12). The ongoing *Index to Reproductions in Art Periodicals (IRAP)* (see the "Myth" section in the subject index) is valuable for students of American art since it lists works illustrated in *Art in America*. *Contemporary Art and Artists: An Index to Reproductions*, by Pamela Jeffcott Parry, indexes "illustrations of works of art, dating from approximately 1940 to the present and covering all media except architecture." This reference indexes over sixty books and exhibition catalogs in English. For classical myths, see "Mythological Themes," (p. 318). Finally, 950 books and catalogs covering the sculpture of all periods, scales, and media are indexed by Jane Clapp in *Sculpture Index*, which integrates thematic headings into the alphabetical lists of sculptors and their works. When using all the indexes of reproductions mentioned in this paragraph, the researcher needs to first locate a work in the title or subject index where the artist's name will be given. Then the same work needs to be found in the list of works under the artist's name where the bibliographic citations are provided in abbreviated forms. (For explanations of these, consult the pertinent list of abbreviations.)

For further study of the examples which have been found in the indexes to reproductions and for additional examples, the researcher needs to consult all types of art historical publications. Six bibliographies which are published annually or more frequently provide access to this literature and can be searched both by a mythological subject and by an artist's name. *L'Année philologique* (Philological Year) is the annual annotated bibliography for journals, books, catalogs, and dissertations covering all aspects of antiquity, including ancient art. An "Index Nominum Antiquorum" (Index of Ancient Names) at the back of each volume includes names of mythological characters and ancient artists. *Bibliographie zur Symbolik, Ikonographie und Mythologie: Internationales Referateorgan* (Bibliography on Symbolism, Iconography and Mythology: International Review) is an annual review that covers books and journal articles on mythology in the art of all periods. Most of the entries in this bibliography are summarized in abstracts in German, Italian, English, or French. An index at the back of each volume provides access to the entries by the names of the mythological characters, and there is also a *Generalregister* (General Index) for the first ten volumes. *Art Index*, published quarterly, lists articles from about 125 journals covering all periods of art history. Since articles cited in *Art Index* have entries under subjects and artists, the printed volumes of this bibliography can be searched for literature in either category. *Art Index* can also be searched by computer on the Wilsonline online vendor service for the period from September 1984 onwards. The *Répertoire d'art et d'archéologie* (Repertoire

of Art and Archaeology), issued quarterly, lists and provides brief annotations for books, journal articles, proceedings, and catalogs. Currently
the publications included cover art from the Early Christian period to
1939. Each volume of four issues has an index of artists and of subjects.
In the latter, ancient mythological characters can be found under "Iconographie, Mythologie." *RILA: Répertoire international de la littérature de l'art*
(1975– ), appearing semiannually, has bibliographic annotations for all
types of art historical publications that discuss art from the fourth century A.D. to the present. It can be searched by mythological theme and
artist in the indexes for the printed volumes. In addition, under the title
*Art Literature International (RILA)* the same bibliography can be searched by
computer through the Dialog database. *ARTbibliographies Modern* (1969– )
is a semiannual annotated bibliography including books, articles, catalogs, and dissertations that discuss twentieth-century art. Mythological
subjects can be found under the heading "Mythology" within the
alphabetized entries, and all publications on artists are grouped under
headings with the artists' names. *ARTbibliographies Modern* can also be
searched by computer for the years 1974 and following through the
Dialog database. Authoritative monographs, catalogs, biographies, and
published dissertations on individual artists from all periods and places
are brought together in *Art Books: A Basic Bibliography of Monographs on
Artists*, by Wolfgang M. Freitag.

There are also important indexes to the holdings in three major art
libraries. *The Index to Art Periodicals* (compiled by the Ryerson Library at
the Art Institute of Chicago) begins its periodical indexing in 1907; since
the initiation of *Art Index* in 1930, *The Index to Art Periodicals* covers
museum bulletins and foreign periodicals not indexed there. Access to
the *Index's* periodical literature on the art of all periods is by subject and
artist. *The New York Public Library . . . Dictionary Catalog of the Art and
Architecture Division* indexes books, catalogs, and journal articles on the
art of all periods, with access by subject and by artist. The *Catalog* is
updated annually by the *Bibliographic Guide to Art and Architecture*. *The
Metropolitan Museum of Art, New York, Library Catalog* indexes books and
articles on the art of all periods by subject and artist. It indexes all of its
own periodical holdings from the nineteenth century and from the first
years of the twentieth century up to the initiation of the *Répertoire d'art et
d'archéologie* in 1910 and *Art Index* in 1930. Thereafter, it covers journals
not indexed in these two references and the publications of learned
societies. The *Library Catalog* has a series of supplements, the latest of
which was published in 1987.

Printed catalogs of the art collections in large museums, unless they
concentrate on works from a specific period or genre or those with a
limited thematic content, can only introduce the researcher to small
selections of the museums' vast holdings. However, with their huge

storage capacity and high resolution of visual images, videodiscs can present large numbers of art works that are unpublished or poorly known. Some videodiscs of this type have already been published and more will certainly appear in the future. For example, a videodisc entitled *The National Gallery of Art* contains color images, with captions, of 1,645 paintings, sculptures, drawings, and prints from this important museum in Washington, D.C. The accompanying computer program for an Apple Macintosh Plus or more advanced model, entitled *The National Gallery of Art LaserStack*, provides access to the 1,645 works by subject, style, medium, artist, nationality, period, and date. Three videodiscs entitled *The Louvre* contain thirty-five thousand color images of five thousand works of all media and from all periods that are located in the Louvre in Paris. At the time this entry was written, a computer access program for these videodiscs was not yet available.

## Bibliographic Entries for Complementary References

*Alinari Photo Archive from the Archivi Alinari, Florence.* Edited by L. D. Couprie. 7 vols. Microfiche. *Guide to the microform collection.* Leiden: IDC, 1988; distributed by Norman Ross Publishing Inc.

*L'Année philologique: Bibliographie critique et analytique de l'antiquité gréco-latine.* Paris: Société d'édition "Les Belles Lettres," 1928– .

*Art Index: A Cumulative Author and Subject Index to a Selected List of Fine Arts Periodicals and Museum Bulletins.* New York: H. W. Wilson, 1929/30– .

*Art Literature International (RILA).* Computer database, updated semiannually. Williamstown, Mass.: J. Paul Getty Trust, 1973– ; available through Dialog Information Services.

*ARTbibliographies Modern.* Santa Barbara, Calif.: ABC-Clio Press, 1973– . (Supersedes *LOMA. Literature on Modern Art: An Annual Bibliography.* 1969– . Boston: Worldwide Books, 1971– .)

Bartsch, Adam von. *Le peintre graveur.* 22 vols. Vienna: J. V. Degen, 1803–21.

———. *The Illustrated Bartsch. Le peintre graveur illustré.* General editor, Walter L. Strauss. Vol. 1– . New York: Abaris Books, 1978– .

*Bibliographic Guide to Art and Architecture.* Boston: G. K. Hall, 1975– .

*Bibliographie zur Symbolik, Ikonographie und Mythologie: Internationales Referateorgan.* Baden-Baden: Librairie Heitz GMBH, 1968– . With *Generalregister zu Jahrgang 1/1968–10/1977.* Baden-Baden: Valentin Koerner, 1977.

Clapp, Jane. *Sculpture Index.* 3 vols. Metuchen, N. J.: Scarecrow, 1970.

Freitag, Wolfgang M. *Art Books: A Basic Bibliography of Monographs on Artists.* New York and London: Garland Publishing, 1985.

Havlice, P. *World Painting Index.* 2 vols. Metuchen, N. J.: Scarecrow, 1977. *First Supplement 1973–1980.* 2 vols. Metuchen, N. J.: Scarecrow, 1982.

*Index Iconologicus.* Microfiche. *Index Iconologicus: A Guide to the Microform Edition.* Developed by Karla Langedijk. Sanford, N.C.: Microfilming Corp. of America, 1980.

*Index to Art Periodicals, Compiled in Ryerson Library, The Art Institute of Chicago.* 11 vols. Boston: G. K. Hall, 1962. *First Supplement.* Boston: G. K. Hall, 1975.

*Index to Reproductions in Art Periodicals (IRAP).* Seattle, Wash.: Data Arts, 1987– .

Korwin, Yala H. *Index to Two-dimensional Works.* 2 vols. Metuchen, N.J. and London: Scarecrow, 1981.

*The Louvre.* 3 videodiscs. Directed by André Hatala. Neuilly-sur Seine, France: ODA, 1989; distributed by the Voyager Company.

*The Metropolitan Museum of Art, New York, Library Catalog.* 23 vols. Boston: G. K. Hall, 1960. *Sales Catalogs.* 2 vols. Boston: G. K. Hall, 1960. *First Supplement* to *Eighth Supplement.* Boston: G. K. Hall, 1962–80. *First Supplement.* 2d ed. Boston: G. K. Hall, 1982. *Second Supplement.* 2d ed. 4 vols. Boston: G. K. Hall, 1985. *Third Supplement 1983–86.* 2d ed. 3 vols. Boston: G. K. Hall, 1987.

*Mille Pitture di venti secoli.* Florence: Fratelli Alinari S. A., Istituto di Edizioni Artistiche, 1949.

Monro, Isabel, and Kate M. Monro. *Index to Reproductions of American Paintings: A Guide to Pictures Occurring in More than 800 Books.* New York: H. W. Wilson, 1948. *1st Supplement.* New York: H. W. Wilson, 1964.

———. *Index to Reproductions of European Paintings: A Guide to Pictures in More than 300 Books.* New York: H. W. Wilson, 1956.

*The National Gallery of Art.* Videodisc no. VP1-NGA-84. Written, directed, and produced by Jerry Whiteley. New York: Videodisc Publishing, 1983; distributed by the Voyager Company.

*The National Gallery of Art LaserStack.* Computer program. Los Angeles: 1987; distributed by the Voyager Company.

*The New York Public Library . . . Dictionary Catalog of the Art and Architecture Division.* 30 vols. Boston: G. K. Hall, 1975. *Supplement 1974.* Boston: G. K. Hall, 1976.

Parry, Pamela Jeffcott. *Contemporary Art and Artists: An Index to Reproductions.* Westport, Conn., and London: Greenwood Press, 1978.

Parry, Pamela Jeffcott, and Kathe Chipman. *Print Index: A Guide to Reproductions.* Westport, Conn., and London: Greenwood Press, 1983.

*Répertoire d'art et d'archéologie.* Paris: Morance, 1910– .

*Repertorio di opere d'arte iconografica: La mitologia greco-romana, Catalogo delle fotografie edite da F.lli Alinari.* Florence: F.lli Alinari, 1936.

*RILA: Répertoire international de la littérature de l'art. International repertory of the literature of art.* Williamstown, Mass.: College Art Association of America, 1975– .

Smith, Lyn Wall, and Nancy D. W. Moure, *Index to Reproductions of American Paintings, Appearing in More than 400 Books Mostly Published since 1960.* Metuchen, N. J.: Scarecrow, 1977.

Tervarent, Guy de. *Attributs et symboles dans l'art profane 1450–1600: Dictionnaire d'un langage perdu.* Travaux d'humanisme et renaissance, no. 29. Geneva: Librairie E. Droz, 1958. *Supplément et index.* Travaux d'humanisme et renaissance, no. 29 bis. Geneva: Librairie E. Droz, 1964.

Thieme, Ulrich, and Felix Becker. *Allgemeines Lexikon der bildenden Künstler von der Antike bis zur Gegenwart.* 37 vols. Leipzig, East Germany: Seeman, 1907–50.

# HANDBOOKS

The basic story lines and the standard artistic arrangements and attributes of the characters in commonly represented Christian and pagan themes are summarized in Hall's useful handbook, *Dictionary of Subjects and Symbols in Art*. Frequent reference is made in Hall's entries to important passages from ancient and later literature. At the front of the volume is an annotated list of all of these sources and a general bibliography. *Myth and Religion in European Painting 1270–1700: The Stories as the Artists Knew Them*, by Satia and Robert Bernen, contains "quotations and summaries from the Bible and from ancient, medieval and Renaissance writers [that] tell the stories as the painters themselves might have known them . . . ." A list of authors cited appears at the back. Since a number of works by these writers, particularly mythological handbooks from the Renaissance, are not used by Hall, the reference by the Bernens provides useful supplementary material.

Distinctive motifs from myths as told by important Greek and Roman authors are indexed in *A Dictionary of Pictorial Subjects from Classical Literature: A Guide to Their Identification in Works of Art*, by Percy Preston. These motifs fall into the categories of "the objects, the creatures, the essential, distinguishing features of a figure, or a figure's various activities in a given scene." For example, under "Apple, *Golden*," one of the entries is:

> ERIS (Discord) tosses one among the divine guests at the wedding of Peleus and Thetis; being claimed by Hera, Athena, and Aphrodite, it and the three goddesses are taken by Hermes to Mt. Ida, where the shepherd Paris considers the bribes they offer him and awards the apple to Aphrodite (*Ep.* 3.2; *Fab.* 92).

The abbreviated citations to literary sources within parentheses are explained in the "List of Works Cited" at the beginning of the reference. Entries such as this one can be used as an aid in identifying artistic representations whose mythological content is uncertain. Drawings of mythological scenes from antiquities accompany the text of this reference.

*Classic Myths in Art*, by Julia deWolf Addison, forms an excellent introduction to myths that are frequently represented in art. Addison retells the myths in her text, often in the words of an important ancient author such as Euripides or Ovid, and she also discusses and illustrates outstanding artistic renditions from antiquity to the nineteenth century. *La mythologie dans l'art ancien et moderne* (Mythology in Ancient and Modern Art), by René Ménard, adopts a similar approach; ancient myths are recounted, with some citations of the classical literary sources, and line drawings show representations of the myths from ancient and later art. Special emphasis is given in the illustrations to French art; unillustrated works of art are also mentioned in the text.

*The Legends of Troy in Art and Literature*, by Margaret R. Scherer, encompasses a broader corpus of myths than its title implies, for its discussions begin with the wedding of the parents of Achilles—Peleus and Thetis—and include the major episodes before, during, and after Homer's *Iliad*, and episodes from the *Oresteia*, Homer's *Odyssey*, and Virgil's *Aeneid*. In all the chapters, including the Homeric and Virgilian ones, alternate accounts of the legends by authors from all periods are summarized, and there are numerous illustrations of art from antiquity to the twentieth century. The handbook also has these useful features at the back: notes to accompany the chapters, which include bibliography on art works illustrated and referred to in the text; mythological and general indexes; and two chronologically arranged appendixes which summarize pertinent literary and musical works and list additional examples from art, with bibliography.

In *Classical Myths in Sculpture*, Agard describes and illustrates stylistically representative sculptures with mythological content from every major period of art history from antiquity to the present. In his discussions of these examples, grouped in chapters according to their periods of production (such as chapter 5, "Baroque Sculpture"), Agard emphasizes the adherence or divergence of post-ancient works from the style or iconography of prototypes from different classical periods. He adopts the view that: "To the greatest sculptors . . . Greek and Roman mythological figures have been subjects for neither copy nor adaptation, but rather for study and inspiration" (p. 8). Bibliography and additional examples are supplied at the back of the volume, along with a "Glossary of Divinities and Heroes," arranged alphabetically.

Thirty-four paintings and sculptures with mythological personages from the National Gallery of Art in Washington, D. C., are illustrated and described by Sienkewicz in *Classical Gods and Heroes in the National Gallery of Art*. With the exception of several sculptures placed outside the galleries, most of these works, dating from the Renaissance to the twentieth century, are arranged both chronologically and by gallery number. Sienkewicz tells the story behind each work, often referring to ancient sources such as Ovid and Virgil, and explains the narrative details within the images. The handbook has a bibliography and an appendix of the main characters' Roman and Greek names and functions at the back.

A medium which is not normally discussed in handbooks of mythology in Western art is tapestries. (Scherer's *Legends of Troy in Art and Literature* is an exception.) Jack Franses illustrates a representative selection in *Tapestries and Their Mythology*. In this survey for the nonprofessional, the illustrations (some in color) accompany recountings of the major classical myths. A helpful index of thematic motifs ("Signs and Symbols") appears at the back of the volume and can be used to identify the myths in unstudied tapestries. Brief introductory chapters identify the major centers and some of the workshops that produced tapestries.

## Bibliographic Entries for Handbooks

Addison, Julia deWolf. *Classic Myths in Art.* Boston: L. C. Page & Co., 1904.

Agard, Walter Raymond. *Classical Myths in Sculpture.* Baltimore, Md.: Waverly Press, Inc., for the Univ. of Wisconsin Press, 1951.

Bernen, Satia and Robert. *Myth and Religion in European Painting 1270–1700: The Stories as the Artists Knew Them.* London: Constable, 1973.

Franses, Jack. *Tapestries and Their Mythology.* London: John Gifford, 1973.

Hall, James. *Dictionary of Subjects and Symbols in Art.* New York: Harper & Row, 1974.

Ménard, René. *Mythologie dans l'art ancien et moderne.* With an appendix on the origins of mythology by Eugène Véron. Paris: Ch. Delagrave, 1878.

Preston, Percy. *A Dictionary of Pictorial Subjects from Classical Literature: A Guide to Their Identification in Works of Art.* New York: Scribner, 1983.

Scherer, Margaret R. *The Legends of Troy in Art and Literature.* 2d ed. New York and London: Phaidon Press, for the Metropolitan Museum of Art, 1964.

Sienkewicz, Thomas J. *Classical Gods and Heroes in the National Gallery of Art.* Washington, D. C.: Univ. Press of America, Inc., 1983.

# SUPPLEMENTARY SOURCES

A number of studies of mythology in art focus on more limited spans of time than the handbooks described above. For example, *Greek Mythology in Byzantine Art*, by Kurt Weitzmann, investigates "the survival of representations of classical myths in Byzantine manuscripts and also ivories." These representations were created at the imperial workshops of Constantinople during the tenth and eleventh centuries. They preserve both the arrangements and style of presumed images from antiquity, which, it is suggested, were miniatures from illustrated manuscripts from the Roman Imperial period. Weitzmann considers representations of the same myths in Byzantine art of different media, and suggests that the lost manuscripts that apparently served as models were illustrated handbooks of mythological texts such as Apollodorus. The second printing of Weitzmann's illustrated study contains a preface which summarizes scholarly discoveries since the publication of the first printing about thirty years earlier. An old but exemplary article by Erwin Panofsky and Fritz Saxl, "Classical Mythology in Mediaeval Art," examines Medieval representations of constellations such as Hercules (between Corona Borealis and Lyra) and compares them with ancient and Renaissance depictions of the same figures. The interesting conclusion reached is that, unlike the court artists of Constantinople, Medieval artists in general tended to disconnect classical myths from their classical iconography, although they often made use of classical types for Christian figures. The successful reintegration of classical iconographic types with the correct mythological figures was an achievement of Renaissance artists.

The catalog for a 1987 exhibition at Brown University, *Survival of the Gods: Classical Mythology in Medieval Art*, attempts to explain the alteration of classical prototypes in the Medieval period from a functional standpoint. According to the introduction, "the survival of the gods in the Middle Ages cannot be explained as dim and disremembered recollections, but as conscious evocations which were perceived as suitable for specific medieval needs." For example, the "virtuous and imperial qualities" which Heracles assumes in Medieval art can be understood as a response to the desire on the part of many rulers to claim descent from the hero. *Survival of the Gods* presents Medieval mythological representations from several thematic categories: representations of gods and heroes; "Goddesses Transformed" into Christian figures such as the Virgin; secular uses of mythological representations in "Science, Medicine and Magic"; and the incorporation of ancient gems with mythological content in precious objects of Medieval date. Each work in the catalog is illustrated and described in detail, and its particular style and iconography are explained in the light of its function. Bibliographic citations accompany each catalog entry, and an excellent bibliography with several parts, including "General" and "Catalogues," appears at the volume's end.

*The Survival of the Pagan Gods: The Mythological Tradition and Its Place in Renaissance Humanism and Art*, by Jean Seznec, begins its consideration with antiquity and ends with the late sixteenth century. Rather than stressing the visual discontinuity of Medieval representations of myths, as do Panofsky and Saxl, Seznec emphasizes the ways in which classical gods and heroes are incorporated in and reflect changing concepts of "world history, natural science, and morals." He concludes that a fuller knowledge of ancient artistic prototypes prompted the reestablishment of ancient iconography, but that the unbroken conceptual heritage from antiquity onwards invested the classical figures with spiritual meanings which provided elements of continuity and ensured their preservation in art. Throughout his study, Seznec makes frequent reference to contemporary literature of the different genres that make use of mythology; these literary works are brought together in a bibliography of sources at the back of the volume, which is followed by a general bibliography. Illustrations from art appear throughout Seznec's text and support the author's conceptual history of mythology.

The illustrated exhibition catalog, *Gods and Heroes: Baroque Images of Antiquity*, by Eunice Williams brings together examples from seventeenth-century art of all media with mythological themes. In the introduction and catalog entries, Williams elucidates the more complete knowledge that seventeenth-century artists had of antiquity than their predecessors from the previous century, a situation which resulted in a consistently correct achievement of a classical style and iconography. She demonstrates the common usage of the myths of eminent heroes and gods as allegories for the achievements and ambitions of contemporary rulers such as Louis XIII and Louis XIV, and she also discusses the emergence of landscapes, often populated with ancient ruins, to create idyllic moods for both mythological and nonmythological scenes.

Representations of mythological character types from the art of particular periods and places can be interpreted as expressions of prevailing social attitudes. For example, in *Mythology and Misogyny: The Social Discourse of Nineteenth-Century British Classical-Subject Painting*, Joseph A. Kestner attempts to demonstrate that women in Victorian mythological paintings "were continually represented in one of two ways: either as irresponsible, outcast, prostituted, vicious, sensuous, demented, bestial, castrating, sinister, delusive, conniving, domineering, and fatal; or as submissive, passive, forlorn, abject, somnolent, dependent, unintelligent, enervated, helpless, nonsexual, ethereal, compliant, abandoned, and indecisive." Kestner frequently quotes interesting documentation from the papers and conversations of the artists themselves in support of his contention that they intended their female mythological characters to be understood by the viewer as either wicked or incompetent. However, many of the specific interpretations that are proposed for paintings seem forced into the mold of these two categories, and inadequate attention is given to the possible derivation of features such as small male genitalia from earlier artistic prototypes. Thus the researcher should not accept the conclusions in this study without checking them against earlier published discussions, and against the evidence contained in the paintings themselves and in the complete biographical materials on the artists' lives, attitudes, and sources. The real value of Kestner's book lies in the encyclopedic number of mythological representations that he refers to in his textual discussions, many of which are illustrated. Furthermore, a lengthy bibliography which brings together pertinent books, catalogs, journal literature, and unpublished papers can be found at the end.

Ovid, the single most influential ancient author with regard to both art and literature after antiquity, is the focus of a series of essays edited by Charles Martindale, *Ovid Renewed: Ovidian Influence on Literature and Art from the Middle Ages to the Twentieth Century*. While this fascinating volume is primarily devoted to tracing Ovid's multifaceted impact on English literature, the introduction by the editor contains some comments on artistic renditions of Ovidian themes, and Nigel Llewellyn's essay, "Illustrating Ovid," stresses the varying degrees of faithfulness to the text of illustrations from different periods, as well as the didactic or erotic purposes of these representations. The volume is accompanied by black-and-white plates and contains an appendix supplementing two articles by Niall Rudd that is a list of published representations of the theme, "Daedalus and Icarus in Art" (i.e., ancient through twentieth century).

## Bibliographic Entries for Supplementary Sources

Kestner, Joseph A. *Mythology and Misogyny: The Social Discourse of Nineteenth-Century British Classical-Subject Painting.* Madison: Univ. of Wisconsin Press, 1989.

Martindale, Charles, ed. *Ovid Renewed: Ovidian Influence on Literature and Art from the Middle Ages to the Twentieth Century.* Cambridge and New York: Cambridge Univ. Press, 1988.

Panofsky, Erwin, and Fritz Saxl. "Classical Mythology in Mediaeval Art." *Metropolitan Museum Studies* 4 (1933): 228–80.

Seznec, Jean. *The Survival of the Pagan Gods: The Mythological Tradition and Its Place in Renaissance Humanism and Art.* Translated by Barbara F. Sessions. Bollingen Series no. 38. New York: Pantheon, 1953.

*Survival of the Gods: Classical Mythology in Medieval Art.* Catalog of an exhibition in the Bell Gallery, Brown University, February–March, 1987. Providence, R. I.: Department of Art, Brown Univ., 1987.

Weitzmann, Kurt. *Greek Mythology in Byzantine Art.* Studies in Manuscript Illumination, no. 4. 1951. 2d printing, with addenda. Princeton: Princeton Univ. Press, 1984.

Williams, Eunice. *Gods and Heroes: Baroque Images of Antiquity.* Catalog of an exhibition at Wildenstein, New York, October 1968 to January 1969. New York and London: Garland Pub. Inc., 1968.

## Additional Supplementary Sources

Bosque, Andrée de. *Mythologie et Maniérisme: Italie, Bavière, Fontainebleau, Prague, Pays-Bas: Peinture et Dessins.* Paris: Albin Michel; Antwerp: Fonds Mercator, 1985.

Chadwick, Whitney. *Myth in Surrealist Paintings, 1929–1939.* Ann Arbor, Mich.: UMI Research Press, 1980.

Dacos, N. "Sopravvivenza dell'antico." In *Enciclopedia dell'arte antica, classica e orientale. Supplemento 1970,* 725–46. Rome: Istituto della Enciclopedia Italiana, 1973.

Gentili, Augusto. *Da Tiziano a Tiziano: Mito e allegoria nella cultura veneziana del Cinquecento.* Milan: Feltrinelli, 1980.

Jacobs, Michael. *Mythological Painting.* New York: Mayflower Books, 1979.

Prindle, Lester Marsh, ed. *Mythology in Prints: Illustrations to the Metamorphoses of Ovid, 1497–1824.* Burlington, Vt.: The editor, 1939.

Sox, David. *Unmasking the Forger: The Dossena Deception.* New York: Universe, 1988.

*Part Three*

# MEDIA STUDIES

# ˌ9ˌ

# Greek Sculpture

Richter, Gisela M. A. *The Sculpture and Sculptors of the Greeks.* 4th ed. New Haven: Yale Univ. Press, 1970.

## ART FORM

Our knowledge of Greek sculpture comes from two types of sources: Greek originals, most of whose sculptors' names are not known; and Roman copies and ancient literary accounts of lost masterpieces by the most famous Greek sculptors. The surviving unattributed originals are of a consistently high quality from the standpoints of both technique of execution and strength of design. However, it was the masterpieces by the most eminent sculptors, which we no longer have, that were most admired by the people of antiquity. One can only conclude that they must have been the very best Greek sculptures. This idea is reinforced by numerous references in surviving literature to important and influential innovations achieved by the master sculptors. In order to completely understand Greek sculpture, the researcher must study both original sculptures and copies of masterpieces. An appreciation of each type of sculpture is dependent on a knowledge of the other type. Greek original sculptures inform us of the technical and stylistic characteristics of each phase of development in Greek sculpture and give us some sense of the refinement that the best sculptures from each period must have exhibited. Roman copies and descriptions of lost originals allow us to reconstruct the complex compositions and costly materials of the masterpieces and to understand how they were revered by ancient viewers. Each masterpiece must also be restored in the mind's eye as being even more beautiful and majestic than the best originals from its period of production.

## RESEARCH USE

Richter's *Sculpture and Sculptors of the Greeks* is a comprehensive and reliable survey of Greek freestanding and architectural sculpture. Written in a remarkably lucid style, it facilitates initial research in two areas: the stylistic development of particular sculptural types and aspects of sculptures; and attempts at achieving reliable concepts of the original masterpieces by famous Greek sculptors. Part 1 of Richter's volume is organized for the first kind of research. It provides separate discussions that trace improvements in rendering various figure types and aspects of figures. Original Greek sculptures whose sculptors are not known are used as examples, along with attributed original masterpieces and ancient copies of masterpieces. In part 2, Richter gives separate consideration to each major Greek sculptor and surveys the evidence that survives in regard to their production. In a handful of cases, this evidence consists of actual originals. But all that is left most often are ancient copies and/or literary descriptions. The evidence Richter presents in part 2 can be used in several types of inquiries. The literary descriptions can be looked up and scrutinized in attempts at comprehending the theory behind ancient art (see Complementary References below). Copies of masterpieces by the same sculptor can be assigned a chronological order and an artist's development can thus be discerned. Further, the works of two or more sculptors can be compared to distinguish differences in their concepts of the ideal form of gods and humans.

## ORGANIZATION

Part 1 begins with chapters on the historical background and general characteristics of Greek sculpture. Next is a chapter on the development of the human figure from the Geometric through the Hellenistic periods. This is broken down into chronological considerations of the standing figure, the seated figure, the flying or running figure, and the crouching figure. The following chapter outlines the treatment of the head by first describing developments in the rendering of the features of the head, and then changes in the ability to express emotions through the head. The chapter on Greek dress characterizes the different treatments of drapery throughout the periods and explains how drapery can be used for the dating of sculptures. In the next chapter, Richter demonstrates that animals in Greek sculpture undergo the same type of development towards increased naturalism as human figures. The evolution of design principles in architectural reliefs and gravestones forms the subject matter for the chapter on composition. Technical aspects, such as the application of color to sculptures of stone, terra-cotta, and wood, are considered in the chapter on technique. The gradual mastery of perspective in relief sculpture is outlined in the chapter devoted to this medium. The last chapter in part 1 elucidates the differences in style and composition between original Greek sculptures and Roman copies and modern forgeries.

In part 2 of Richter's volume, there are chapters on Greek sculptors and groups of sculptors from the Archaic through the Hellenistic periods. The chapters on Classical and Hellenistic sculptors are divided into units of information on each sculptor or working group. Evidence for the sculptor's geographic origins and workshop connections and the dates for significant commissions is presented first. This consists of literary accounts of the sculptor's activities and corroborative evidence from surviving monuments (particularly inscribed bases). The works themselves are discussed next. General comments on characteristics found in all the sculptor's works are followed by discussions of particular works. All extant information on each work is elucidated, including: any surviving parts of the work; copies of the work reproduced full scale, as well as miniature reproductions in statuettes, reliefs, paintings, and coins; ancient descriptions of the appearance of the work and its aesthetic principles; literary evidence on the reasons for the commission of the work; and the history of the work after its completion, including any changes in its location and accounts of its final destruction.

Chapter 7 consists of a very useful chart of outstanding Greek sculptures arranged by their tentative dates. The sculptures are listed along with the external evidence for dating them. The fourth edition of Richter's book contains illustrations of 853 freestanding and architectural sculptures discussed in the text, in photographs at the back of the book. In addition, the text is accompanied by linear reconstructions of buildings showing the architectural sculptures in place. At the back of the book is a very thorough bibliography pertaining to Greek sculpture and sculptors. The index at the back of the book is arranged alphabetically; references are provided to textual discussions of the various sculptures and sculptors, cities and temples, heroes and gods, and terms. There is a second index to the illustrations; the works illustrated are listed by titles, subject matter, and building.

## COMPLEMENTARY REFERENCES

In her discussions of individual sculptors in part 2, Richter frequently cites but does not usually quote ancient texts. These texts can be found in three compilations: Stuart Jones's *Select Passages from Ancient Writers Illustrative of the History of Greek Sculpture;* Pollitt's *The Art of Greece 1400–31 B.C.: Sources and Documents;* and Overbeck's *Die antiken Schriftquellen zur Geschichte der bildenden Künste bei den Griechen.* In the compilation by Stuart Jones, the Greek and Latin texts are provided along with commentary and translations, while Pollitt supplies just translations and commentary. In most instances the same passages appear in both compilations, but each reference also includes texts which are not quoted in the other compilation. Overbeck's corpus consists of untranslated passages from Greek and Latin authors on Greek artists. Each passage quoted has a separate number. The numbers for all the passages which mention an artist can be found under the artist's name in the index at the back of the volume. Overbeck contains all the original texts on Greek sculpture which are translated by Pollitt (who cautions that in some cases he has used editions of texts later than Overbeck's) as well as many more texts that cannot be found in either Jones or Pollitt, including passages on Greek sculptors who lived during the Roman Empire.

Besides Richter's summaries of the work of major sculptors in *Sculpture and Sculptors,* articles on both major and less significant sculptors can be found in the illustrated *Enciclopedia dell'arte antica, classica e orientale* (Encyclopedia of Ancient Art: Classical and Oriental); Thieme and Becker's *Allgemeines Lexikon der bildenden Künstler von der Antike bis zur Gegenwart* (General Lexicon of Fine Artists from Antiquity to the Present); and *Paulys Realencyclopädie der classischen Altertumswissenschaft* (Pauly's Encyclopedia of Classical Knowledge). For all but the most recent major monographs and periodical literature on specific sculptors, see these articles and the bibliographies in Richter and in the Handbooks and Supplementary Sources described below. The most recent studies can be located by consulting the "Index Nominum Antiquorum" (Index of Ancient Names) in the latest volumes of the annual annotated bibliography called *L'Année philologique* (Philological Year).

Another way to locate recent literature on anonymous and attributed sculptures of large scale, both freestanding and architectural, is through consultation of a two-volume study entitled *Greek Sculpture: An Exploration,* by Andrew Stewart. In the bibliography at the end of volume 1 and in the notes which immediately precede the bibliography, Stewart emphasizes publications that have appeared after the latest edition of Richter's *Sculpture and Sculptors.* Stewart's eloquent text in volume 1 is divided into three sections: part 1, on the craft and role of the Greek sculptor; part 2, on the stylistic and iconographic development of Greek sculpture in the context of contemporary concerns and aspirations; and part 3, on the evidence for the lives and production of individual sculptors. The last part includes many translated passages from Greek and Latin sources and cross-references back to further discussion in part 2. In his textual discussion and notes, Stewart addresses controversial issues of importance by concisely elucidating the nature of the evidence and explaining what he feels are the most convincing conclusions. Three useful appendixes follow part 3 of volume 1: a chart, "Extant Greek Bronze Statues," arranged in order of discovery; a chart of original Greek sculptures—both freestanding and architectural—which can be attributed to specific sculptors whose names are known from ancient literary sources; and a chart of original sculptures whose dates have been determined "by inscriptions, literary texts, or precisely dated archaeological contexts." Volume 2 of Stewart's study contains detailed labels and plates of varying quality of reproduction; architectural reconstructions, with sculptures in place; and ground plans, with the positions and themes of architectural sculptures labeled.

## Bibliographic Entries for Complementary References

L'Année philologique: Bibliographie critique et analytique de l'antiquité gréco-latine. Paris: Société d'édition "Les Belles Lettres," 1928– .

Enciclopedia dell'arte antica, classica e orientale. Edited by Ranuccio Bianchi Bandinelli. 7 vols., Supplemento, and Atlante dei complessi figurati. Rome: Istituto della Enciclopedia Italiana, 1958–73.

Jones, H. Stuart. Select Passages from Ancient Writers Illustrative of the History of Greek Sculpture. Enlarged by Al. N. Oikonomides. Chicago: Argonaut Publishers, 1966.

Overbeck, Johannes Adolf. Die antiken Schriftquellen zur Geschichte der bildenden Künste bei den Griechen. Leipzig: Wilhelm Engelmann, 1868. Reprint. Hildesheim: Georg Olms Verlagsbuchhandlung, 1959.

Pauly, August Friedrich von, Georg Wissowa, and Wilhelm Kroll, eds. Paulys Realencyclopädie der classischen Altertumswissenschaft: Neue Bearbeitung. 24 vols. 2d ser. (R–Z), 19 vols. Stuttgart: J. B. Metzler, 1894–1972. Supplement. 15 vols. Stuttgart: J. B. Metzler, 1903–78.

Pollitt, J. J. The Art of Greece 1400–31 B.C.: Sources and Documents. Sources and Documents in the History of Art Series, edited by H. W. Janson. Englewood Cliffs, N.J.: Prentice-Hall, 1965.

Stewart, Andrew. Greek Sculpture: An Exploration. 2 vols. New Haven and London: Yale Univ. Press, 1990.

Thieme, Ulrich, and Felix Becker. Allgemeines Lexikon der bildenden Künstler von der Antike bis zur Gegenwart. 37 vols. Leipzig: Seeman, 1907–50.

## HANDBOOKS

Besides Richter's scholarly volume, there are several excellent general surveys of Greek sculpture. For example, the richly illustrated German text by Fuchs, *Die Skulptur der Griechen* (The Sculpture of the Greeks), follows the format of part 1 in Richter by outlining the stylistic evolution of figure types and compositions for both freestanding and architectural sculptures. However, instead of presenting all known works by each sculptor as a unit (as Richter does in part 2), Fuchs incorporates his discussions of copies of lost masterpieces into his considerations of figure types. The same author, with Joseph Floren, presents Greek sculpture from the Geometric through the Archaic periods in the first volume of *Die griechische Plastik* (Greek Sculpture), entitled *Die geometrische und archaische Plastik* (Geometric and Archaic Sculpture). Here, examples from the same period and same sculptural school are discussed as units—a type of organization which allows the researcher to form clear concepts of the characteristics of particular regional schools. Extensive bibliographic citations at the beginning of the volume and the chapters, and in the footnotes, make this an invaluable reference tool. Indexes for artists and the museum locations of works discussed provide access to the text.

A full consideration of the stylistic development of all periods of Greek sculpture can be found in the four-volume reference by Ludger Alscher, *Griechische Plastik* (Greek Sculpture). This scholarly study provides numerous photographs—both general views and details—of the sculptures discussed. A fine selection of beautifully illustrated and thoroughly described Greek sculptures can be found in *Greek Sculpture*, by Reinhard Lullies. Nearly all the freestanding and architectural sculptures included in this survey are Greek originals.

Boardman's *Greek Sculpture: The Archaic Period* is the most straightforward and fully illustrated survey of the many original early Greek sculptures. A second handbook by the same author, *Greek Sculpture: The Classical Period: A Handbook*, deals with fifth-century Classical sculpture. The majority of surviving works pertaining to this period are original architectural sculptures and Roman copies of masterpieces. In *Anticlassicism in Greek Sculpture of the Fourth Century B.C.*, Blanche Brown outlines stylistic changes in surviving monuments from the late fifth and fourth centuries (the Late Classical period). *The Sculpture of the Hellenistic Age*, by Margarete Bieber, surveys the variety of sculptural styles attested by original sculptures and copies from the succeeding Hellenistic period (ca. 330–30 B.C.). Monuments of the same type, period, and place or region of manufacture are presented as units.

## Bibliographic Entries for Handbooks

Alscher, Ludger. *Griechische Plastik*. Vol. 1, *Monumentale Plastik und ihre Vorstufen in der griechischer Frühzeit*. 1954. Vol. 2, pt. 1, *Archaik und die Wandlung zur Klassik*. 1961. Vol. 3, *Nachklassik und Vorhellenismus*. 1956. Vol. 4, *Hellenismus*. 1957. Berlin: Deutscher Verlag der Wissenschaften.

Bieber, Margarete. *The Sculpture of the Hellenistic Age.* Rev. ed. New York: Columbia Univ. Press, 1961.

Boardman, John. *Greek Sculpture: The Archaic Period.* New York and Toronto: Oxford Univ. Press, 1978.

———. *Greek Sculpture: The Classical Period: A Handbook.* New York: Thames & Hudson, 1985.

Brown, Blanche R. *Anticlassicism in Greek Sculpture of the Fourth Century B.C.* New York: New York Univ. Press, for the Archaeological Institute of America and the College Art Association of America, 1973.

Fuchs, Werner. *Die Skulptur der Griechen.* 3d ed. Munich: Hirmer Verlag, 1983.

Fuchs, Werner, and Josef Floren. *Die griechische Plastik.* Vol. 1, *Die geometrische und archaische Plastik.* Handbuch der Archäologie. Munich: C. H. Beck, 1987.

Lullies, Reinhard, and Max Hirmer, photographer. *Greek Sculpture.* 2d ed. Translated by Michael Bullock. New York: Abrams, 1960.

## SUPPLEMENTARY SOURCES

Various characteristics of Greek sculptures have been studied in order that their chronology and places of manufacture may be correctly ascertained. Particularly important aspects that have received attention are advances in production techniques, the increase in accuracy of anatomical representation, and methods of depicting the human form that are unique to specific media. In *Greek Sculpture: A Critical Review,* Carpenter attempts to reconstruct the basic technical processes utilized by Greek sculptors. He relates changes in these processes to apparent changes in the sculptors' desire and ability to convincingly reproduce the appearance of living beings. Adam's *The Technique of Greek Sculpture in the Archaic and Classical Periods* is a good companion volume for Carpenter's study, since it summarizes our knowledge of the use of sculptors' tools.

For the complex problem of interpreting the various types of Roman copies, the recent study by Ridgway, *Roman Copies of Greek Sculpture: The Problem of the Originals,* is recommended. In addition to Roman copies, our knowledge of the commissions of ancient sculptors is enhanced by a considerable number of signed statue bases. Usually belonging to lost statues, these bases are described and illustrated by Marcadé, in *Recueil des signatures de sculpteurs grecs* (Collection of Signatures of Greek Sculptors).

Additional studies discuss technical, functional, and stylistic aspects of Greek sculptures of the same material. The best general survey of Greek bronzes of all types, including hollow-cast figures and solid-cast statuettes, is Rolley's *Greek Bronzes.* In this study, casting techniques, the functions of bronze statuary and utilitarian objects, regional schools of production, and statuette types are reviewed. Excellent photographs in black-and-white and color accompany the text. Greek terra-cotta statuettes and small reliefs are presented in chronological groups that are broken down into regional schools in the comprehensive monograph by Higgins, *Greek Terracottas.*

Further scholarly treatments define sculptural types through the presentation of large corpora of examples. For instance, the most complete studies of the Archaic *kouroi* and *korai* are the lavishly illustrated volumes by Richter, *Kouroi: Archaic Greek Youths* and *Korai: Archaic Greek Maidens.* In both studies, approximately two hundred examples are arranged in six chronologically consecutive groups which Richter established through a careful discrimination of the stages in the Archaic sculptor's mastery of human anatomy and drapery. Portraits of Greeks who lived from the eighth through the first centuries B.C. and during Roman times are brought together by Richter in her three-volume corpus, *The Portraits of the Greeks.* Nearly all the original Greek portraits and Roman copies of them are described and illustrated in the more than two thousand fine photographs. In 1972, Richter published a *Supplement* containing additions and corrections to her original volumes, and Smith recently finished an abridged and updated edition which Richter herself was unable to complete.

A combination of research approaches is utilized by Ridgway in *The Archaic Style in Greek Sculpture.* The major monument types are presented, with examples from each geographic region given separate consideration. This study contains many new suggestions on problematic aspects of Archaic sculpture and on controversial pieces. The same author considers Early Classical sculpture in *The Severe Style in Greek Sculpture.* Through separate discussions of Greek originals and Roman copies, Ridgway attempts to achieve a secure definition of the style. A similar separation of originals from Roman copies is used by Ridgway in *Fifth Century Styles in Greek Sculpture.* Here the phase of Classical commonly called High Classical (ca. 450–400 B.C.) is discussed. The incomplete evidence in terms of surviving monuments and the apparent blurring of previously distinct regional sculptural schools during the Early Hellenistic period are reviewed by Ridgway in *Hellenistic Sculpture I: The Styles of ca. 331–200 B.C.* These factors cause the author to confess an inability to "reach a unifying vision of sculptural trends with the third century." She admits that she has to "acknowledge the coexistence of many [styles], occasionally even in the same monument" (p. xxiii). In *Greek Sculpture of the Archaic Period: The Island Workshops,* Pedley assigns Archaic island statues to three regional schools at Naxos, Paros, and Samos. The basis for this arrangement lies in the establishment of a nucleus of pieces securely attributed to each island because of their provenances and inscriptions. Stylistically similar sculptures were then assigned to the same groupings. Like Ridgway and Pedley, Holloway attempts to define regional sculptural styles in *Influences and Styles in the*

Late Archaic and Early Classical Greek Sculpture of Sicily and Magna Graecia. Holloway discerns in South Italy a "coroplastic" style whose conventions arose from terra-cotta sculpture, and he distinguishes three styles in Sicily.

## Bibliographic Entries for Supplementary Sources

Adam, Sheila. *The Technique of Greek Sculpture in the Archaic and Classical Periods.* London: Thames & Hudson, for the British School of Archaeology at Athens, 1966.

Carpenter, Rhys. *Greek Sculpture: A Critical Review.* Chicago: Univ. of Chicago Press, 1960. 2nd impression. Chicago and London: Univ. of Chicago Press, 1971.

Higgins, Reynold Alleyne. *Greek Terracottas.* London: Methuen, 1967.

Holloway, R. Ross. *Influences and Styles in the Late Archaic and Early Classical Greek Sculpture of Sicily and Magna Graecia.* Louvain: Institut Supérieur d'Archéologie et d'Histoire de l'Art, 1975.

Marcadé, J. *Recueil des signatures de sculpteurs grecs.* 2 vols. Athens: École Française d'Athènes, 1953–57.

Pedley, John Griffiths. *Greek Sculpture of the Archaic Period: The Island Workshops.* Mainz: P. von Zabern, 1976.

Richter, Gisela M. A. *Korai: Archaic Greek Maidens: A Study of the Development of the Kore Type in Greek Sculpture.* London and New York: Phaidon Press, 1968. Reprint. New York: Hacker Art Books, Inc., 1988.

———. *Kouroi: Archaic Greek Youths: A Study of the Development of the Kouros Type in Greek Sculpture.* 3d ed. London and New York: Phaidon Press, 1970.

———. *The Portraits of the Greeks.* 3 vols. London: Phaidon Press, 1965. Supplement London: Phaidon Press, 1972. Abridged and rev. ed. by R. R. R. Smith. Ithaca, N.Y.: Cornell Univ. Press, 1984.

Ridgway, Brunhilde Sismondo. *The Archaic Style in Greek Sculpture.* Princeton: Princeton Univ. Press, 1977.

———. *Fifth Century Styles in Greek Sculpture.* Princeton: Princeton Univ. Press, 1981.

———. *Hellenistic Sculpture I: The Styles of ca. 331–200 B.C.* Madison: Univ. of Wisconsin Press, 1990.

———. *Roman Copies of Greek Sculpture: The Problem of the Originals.* Ann Arbor: Univ. of Michigan Press, 1984.

———. *The Severe Style in Greek Sculpture.* Princeton: Princeton Univ. Press, 1970.

Rolley, Claude. *Greek Bronzes.* Translated by Roger Howell. Foreword by John Boardman. London: Sotheby's Pubns./Chesterman Pubns., 1986.

## Additional Supplementary Sources

Fittschen, Klaus, ed. *Griechische Porträts.* Darmstadt: Wissenschaftliche Buchgesellschaft, 1988.

Houser, Caroline. *Greek Monumental Bronze Sculpture of the Fifth and Fourth Centuries B.C.* With a new bibliography. Outstanding Dissertations in the Fine Arts. New York and London: Garland Publishing, 1987.

Houser, Caroline, and David Finn, photographer. *Greek Monumental Bronze Sculpture.* New York and Paris: Vendome Press, 1983.

Jenkins, R. J. H. *Dedalica: A Study of Dorian Plastic Art in the Seventh Century B.C.* Cambridge: University Press, 1936.

Kaulen , Georg. *Daidalika: Werkstätten griechischer Kleinplastik des 7. Jahrhunderts v. Chr.* Munich: Wasmuth, 1967.

Mattusch, Carol C. *Greek Bronze Statuary from the Beginnings through the Fifth Century B.C.* Ithaca and London: Cornell Univ. Press, 1988.

Schneider, Lambert A. *Asymmetrie griechischer Köpfe vom 5. Jh. bis zum Hellenismus.* Wiesbaden: Franz Steiner Verlag GmbH, 1973.

Schweitzer, Bernhard. *Greek Geometric Art.* Translated by Peter and Cornelia Usborne. London: Phaidon Press, 1971.

Vermeule, Cornelius C. *Greek Sculpture and Roman Taste: The Purpose and Setting of Graeco-Roman Art in Italy and the Greek Imperial East.* Jerome Lectures, Twelfth Series. Ann Arbor: Univ. of Michigan Press, 1977.

# ₁10₁

# Athenian Vases

Beazley, J. D. *Attic Black-figure Vase-painters*. Oxford: Clarendon Press, 1956.
———. *Attic Red-figure Vase-painters*. 2d ed. 3 vols. Oxford: Clarendon Press, 1963.
———. *Paralipomena: Additions to Attic Black-figure Vase-painters and to Attic Red-figure Vase-painters (second edition)*. Oxford: Clarendon Press, 1971.
Carpenter, Thomas H., et al. *Beazley Addenda: Additional References to ABV, ARV² and Paralipomena*. 2d ed. Oxford: Oxford Univ. Press, 1989.

## ART FORM

The vases of ancient Athens are referred to as Attic or Athenian. Exhibiting a remarkable clarity and forcefulness in their shapes and designs, painted Athenian vases have long been recognized as the finest pottery from the Greek and Etruscan world. By circa 630 B.C., Athenian vases of the black-figure technique were being produced. This technique, involving the painting of the figures in black glaze, with incised (i.e., engraved) details, persisted at Athens until circa 450 B.C. About twenty thousand of these valued products have been unearthed in ancient tombs and sanctuaries throughout the Mediterranean world. The vases adhere to a limited number of well-proportioned shapes and are decorated with elegant figured scenes and neatly executed bands of ornament. The names of about a dozen Athenian painters and sixty potters are known through their signatures on black-figure vases. Additional unsigned vases have been attributed to the known painters on the basis of stylistic similarities in the painted motifs, and similarities in shape have permitted attributions of unsigned vases to the known potters. Over three hundred anonymous black-figure painters and potters have also been identified through their own distinctive products and have been assigned modern names. Furthermore, vases painted in similar styles by groups of painters evidently within the same workshops have been distinguished.

On Attic red-figure vases, the figural decorations were left the natural color of Athenian clay. The contours and inner details of the figures were drawn in and the background was painted in black glaze. Figures executed in this more naturalistic technique display greater vitality and grace than the silhouetted figures on black-figure vases. Attic red-figure vases were manufactured in Athens during the late Archaic and Classical periods, from circa 530 to 320 B.C. The Attic red-figure workshops were even more active than the black-figure ones, as is demonstrated by the fact that the hands of over five hundred red-figure painters have been distinguished. About fifty actual names of painters and potters working in this technique are known.

Between circa 510 and 400 B.C., another vase-painting technique called white-ground was current in Athens. This method involved the coating of the entire background of the vase with a white slip on which the figures were sensitively painted in outline, with inner details added. The *lekythos*, an oil flask for daily and funerary use, was frequently decorated with eloquent scenes in this technique.

The subjects of Attic vases are Greek myths, illustrations of dramas, scenes from daily life, and occasionally, events from recent history. The arrangements used to depict myths and everyday scenes are more standardized in black- than in red-figure. Also, most of the Attic illustrations of drama are restricted to fifth-century red-figure vases. This same century is also noted for its red-figure vases with complicated, tiered compositions that seem to have been influenced by lost wall paintings. The vast majority of Attic vases, however, exhibit simpler designs which are perfectly suited for the limited repertoire of controlled vessel shapes.

## RESEARCH USE

The four references named above are the most comprehensive compilations of attributed Attic black- and red-figure vases. They consist of attribution lists, without illustrations but with brief descriptions of thematic content and bibliographic citations, of the majority of the black- and red-figure and white-ground vases known to the great mastermind of attributions, J. D. Beazley. These vases are located in museums and collections all over the world. By using Beazley's lists as a means of access to the vases and reviewing all the published work of a single painter or potter, the researcher can become familiar with products spanning the artist's entire career. Different stylistic phases of the artist's work can be distinguished and an attempt can be made to reconstruct the original order of production of these phases. The researcher can also examine vases by a single painter that exhibit the same theme. Such an investigation will indicate any development in the painter's narrative technique. In addition, comparative stylistic or thematic studies of the work of two or more artists can be made to determine their interdepen- dence or independence.

# ORGANIZATION OF *ATTIC BLACK-FIGURE VASE- PAINTERS* AND *ATTIC RED-FIGURE VASE-PAINTERS*

A single list in Beazley's *Attic Black-figure Vase-painters* or in his *Attic Red-figure Vase-painters* is composed of all the products by a single painter, a group of painters, or a potter (whose works are referred to as being from the same class). *Attic Red-figure Vase-painters* includes the products of both red-figure and white-ground painters. In both works, lists of vases related to each other in style of painting and/or shape are presented in the same chapter. The chapters in *Attic Black-figure Vase-painters* are arranged in two chronological sequences: part 1 is devoted to artists who specialized in large vases, and part 2 to artists who worked with small vases. *Attic Red-figure Vase-painters* has ninety chapters which are grouped together to form twenty books, each containing vases from the same period by painters specializing in the same or related shapes.

At the beginning of each list of vases in both works, Beazley provides a brief bibliography of what he considers "the more comprehensive or more pointed accounts of the Painter" (*Attic Black-figure Vase-painters*, p. x); occasionally Beazley also includes a paragraph of discussion about an important point or issue concerning the work of the painter. All the vases attributed to a single painter or group are numbered consecutively from one (1) to the last vase in the list. The "Instructions for Use" section, which immediately follows the preface in both publications, should be consulted for help in understanding and interpreting the information contained in the individual vase entries. In each entry the information is given in the following order: the city name (Beazley uses only the city name to indicate the main museum collection in that city); the museum inventory or collection number; an indication if the vase is only a fragment; the provenance, if known; the publication or publications in which illustrations can be found; and a concise description of the subject matter depicted.

Since the *Attic Red-figure Vase-painters* published in 1963 is a second edition, Beazley provides the entry number the vase had in the first edition in parentheses immediately after the current entry number for the vase. Occasionally the number in parentheses is preceded by an "a" or an "ℓ" to indicate a change in attribution. The "a" stands for "adjunct," and means that in the first edition this vase was considered to be "in the manner of" or "near" a painter or group, but it is attributed to the painter or group in the second edition. The "ℓ" stands for "list," and means the opposite of "a"; in the first edition the vase was attributed to a painter or group, but in the second edition it is placed in an adjunct relationship to the painter or group. The descriptions of the subjects depicted on the vases are usually briefer in *Attic Red-figure Vase-painters* than in *Attic Black-figure Vase-painters*. Beazley states that if a museum number is available to aid in the identification of the vase, then the subject description refers only to the main figure(s) and not to the other figures that might be present. But if "a vase or a fragment has no museum number, or if it is in less permanent possession—in the market, or in private hands—, it may be described in detail to assist identification" (*Attic Red-figure Vase-painters*, p. xlvi). Artists' signatures and *kalos*- and *kale*-names are always reproduced. (These are names of contemporary persons that are accompanied by the Greek adjective meaning "good" or "beautiful.") If the vase was attributed to the vase-painter by scholars before Beazley, the name of the first scholar to propose the attribution is in brackets. At the end of the entry the word "restored" can often be found. By this Beazley means that "the ancient portions [of the vase] have been repainted or retouched in places, or modern pieces added, or both. It is a warning" (*Attic Black-figure Vase-painters*, p. ix). In *Attic Red-figure Vase-painters*, Beazley also uses the phrase "now cleaned" if "the restorations have been removed, either since the publications were made, or since I described the vase as 'restored'." He also cautions that "a 'restored' vase may naturally have been cleaned since I saw it; and a vase, clean when I saw it, may have been tampered with since" (p. xliv).

Two addenda immediately follow the text in *Attic Black-figure Vase-painters*, and three addenda appear at the back of volume 2 in *Attic Red-figure Vase-painters*. These should be consulted regularly since they include a variety of additional information on vases described in the text, such as inventory numbers that were omitted in the original entries, additional publications that illustrate the vases, new information Beazley received about the condition of the vases or the subjects depicted, and corrections regarding the attributions of the vases. The addenda also include completely new entries. Each addenda entry begins with the page numbers of the text to which the entry applies, in bold-faced type. If an addenda entry gives additional information or corrects the original entry in the text, the researcher must locate the initial entry in the text by matching the vase's list number or its city and the inventory number that are given in the addenda entry with the same information in the appropriate entry in the text. New entries are treated as insertions. Beazley indicates where in the list he wishes to insert the new vase by providing the number of the vase in the text which precedes the insertion. The number is followed by "bis" if this is the first vase to be inserted. For second insertions, "ter" is used, and "quater" is used for third insertions. For any subsequent insertions, superscript numerals are used.

Five indexes follow the addenda; they are located at the back of *Attic Black-figure Vase-painters*, and in volume 3 of *Attic Red-figure Vase-painters*. The indexes cover the following subjects: index 1, proveniences (or provenances); index 2, mythological subjects; index 3, collections (public or private); index 4, publications; and index 5, painters, potters, groups, and classes. In all of the indexes, the numbers refer to pages in the text. The corresponding entry in the text can be found by matching the information in the index entry with the pertinent information in the entry or entries on the cited page in the text. For index 1, match the find spots; for index 2, the subject matter; for index 3, the city names (and the museum if it is not the main one in the city) and the inventory numbers (if they are known); and for index 4, match the bibliographic citations. The reader should be cautioned that index 3 only includes vases listed in the text; it does not necessarily reflect each museum's or collection's complete holdings of Attic black-figure pottery. Index 3 consists of two sections: the main section, which covers vases whose current location in a specific collection is known, and a much smaller section, "vases of which the whereabouts is unknown." The latter section is divided into two categories: vases "formerly in private or public collections" (vases whose owner was not recorded are listed as a separate subdivision at the end of this category), and "vases now or at one time in the market." Index 4 consists of a list of major publications of Attic black-figure vases, arranged by plate number, with cross-references to the Beazley entries. The types of publications indexed include monographs, scholarly journals, and catalogs of both public and private collections. This index is particularly useful for nineteenth-century publications, which often describe black-figure vases so inaccurately that the vases cannot be traced in later literature.

There are three other very useful tools in Beazley's volumes. The "Principal Shapes" section, which follows the "Instructions for Use" at the beginning of the volumes, lists the vase shapes commonly decorated by Attic vase-painters working in the pertinent techniques. Illustrations of the shapes are cited. Lists of abbreviations for the publications cited in the vase lists can be found after "Principal Shapes." The third tool is an appendix which lists instances where the name of a contemporary person (male or female) is inscribed, joined with the Greek adjective *kalos* or *kale*. It is located immediately before the addenda in both *Attic Black-figure Vase-painters* and *Attic Red-figure Vase-painters*. The latter reference contains three additional addenda on the head vase (a vase in the form of a human head); signatures of potters; and fragmentary signatures of potters, of potters or painters, or of painters.

## ORGANIZATION OF THE *PARALIPOMENA*: *ADDITIONS TO ATTIC BLACK-FIGURE VASE-PAINTERS AND TO ATTIC RED-FIGURE VASE-PAINTERS*

Beazley's *Paralipomena* updates the information on vases previously listed in *Attic Black-figure Vase-painters* and *Attic Red-figure Vase-painters* and includes new entries. The text of *Paralipomena* is divided into two books: book 1 includes all the additions to *Attic Black-figure Vase-painters* (*ABV*), and book 2 does the same for *Attic Red-figure Vase-painters* (*ARV²*). As in *ABV* and *ARV²*, there is a separate list of vases for each painter, group of painters, or potter (i.e., class). Underneath the painter, group, or class name, given in boldfaced type, the appropriate pages for the entire oeuvre in *ABV* or *ARV²* are cited. All page numbers refer to either *ABV* or *ARV²*, unless they are accompanied by "above" or "below," which indicates a page reference in *Paralipomena*. The lists of vases contain two types of entries. For entries that give updated information, one must locate the initial entry in *ABV* or *ARV²* by matching the number of the vase within the original vase list or its city name and inventory number. New entries are treated as insertions. Beazley indicates where in the *ABV* or *ARV²* lists he wishes to insert a new vase by providing the number of the vase which precedes the insertion. The number is followed by "bis" if this is the first vase to be inserted. For second insertions, "ter" is used, and "quater" is used for third insertions. For any subsequent insertions, superscript numerals are used.

## ORGANIZATION OF *BEAZLEY ADDENDA*: *ADDITIONAL REFERENCES TO ABV, ARV², AND PARALIPOMENA*

*Beazley Addenda*, now available in a second edition, updates the bibliographic citations for the vases in Beazley's *Attic Black-figure Vase-painters*,

*Attic Red-figure Vase-painters,* and *Paralipomena,* and provides corrections for the factual contents of Beazley's entries. The corrections indicate when the location of a vase or its inventory number has changed and when the subject has been misidentified. This reference does not include citations of additional illustrations for Haspels' *Attic Black-Figured Lekythoi* (see Complementary References below); another publication serving this purpose is in preparation. *Beazley Addenda* generally does not include any citations for illustrations of vases that Beazley did not see or attribute. However, some additional vases are listed along with bibliographic citations in the two appendixes, "Additional Vases with *Kalos* Names" and "Additional Vases with Potter or Painter Signatures." Information about attributed and unattributed vases can also be obtained from the Beazley Archive database project at the Ashmolean Museum, Oxford (see the two prefaces). For the organization of *Beazley Addenda,* which is similar to that of the *Paralipomena,* see the "Instructions for Use."

# COMPLEMENTARY REFERENCES

In his bibliographic citations of individual vases, Beazley frequently refers to illustrations in the *CV.,* or *Corpus Vasorum Antiquorum* (Corpus of Ancient Vases). This is an ongoing publication of fascicles, arranged by country and museum collection, that consist of photographic plates of the vases and catalog entries. It is important to note that in his citations to the plates from the *Corpus Vasorum Antiquorum* that appear in *Attic Black-figure Vase-painters,* Beazley leaves out the name of the collection and the rubric "III H e" (signifying the category of Attic black-figure vases; see page ix of the "Instructions for Use"). In his citations to the same work in *Attic Red-figure Vase-painters,* Beazley leaves out the name of the collection and the rubric "III I c" (signifying Attic red-figure vases). He also omits the number of the fascicle where the vase is published. Researchers can quickly find fascicle numbers by using the chapter "II Index of Fascicles by City" of Carpenter's *Summary Guide to Corpus Vasorum Antiquorum.* He or she should take care, however, when using Carpenter's aid, to look up the plate number under the correct city and the correct rubric for the vase category.

Not all attributed Attic vases are included in the four references described at the beginning of this chapter. In *Attic Black-figure Vase-painters,* Beazley only cited *lekythoi* which were included in E. Haspels' *Attic Black-figured Lekythoi* if he had new information on them; he also provided new entries for *lekythoi* which were additions to Haspels' lists. The lists of attributed *lekythoi* in Haspels' study are accompanied by a textual discussion of selected examples. Her detailed descriptions of the vase-painters' styles and characteristic *lekythos* shapes and the numerous black-and-white photographs illuminate her method of attribution.

### Bibliographic Entries for Complementary References

Carpenter, Thomas H. *Summary Guide to the Corpus Vasorum Antiquorum*. New York: Oxford Univ. Press, 1984.

*Corpus Vasorum Antiquorum*. Paris et al.: 1923– .

Haspels, C. H. Emilie. *Attic Black-figured Lekythoi*. 2 vols. Paris: E. de Boccard, 1936.

# HANDBOOKS

Beazley's four references do not include any textual discussion of individual vases or illustrations. The revised edition of Beazley's *Development of Attic Black-figure* (with footnotes containing updated bibliographic citations) partially fills the gap by providing a well-illustrated general discussion of the black-figure technique, in which its development is traced through important vases by major black-figure vase-painters. Additional examples of work by the same vase-painters can be found in Beazley's lists in *Attic Black-figure Vase-painters*, and can be looked up in other references. John Boardman's illustrated volume, *Athenian Black Figure Vases: A Handbook*, can be consulted for summaries of the major vase-painters' entire oeuvres. Gisela Richter's *Attic Red-Figured Vases* surveys the surviving vases and the painting styles of major red-figure vase-painters. In *Athenian Red Figure Vases: The Archaic Period* and in *Athenian Red Figure Vases: The Classical Period*, John Boardman discusses the stylistic development of the red-figure technique from its introduction in the Late Archaic period down to its abandonment in the late fourth century. The products of vase-painters working in this technique, as well as the frequency with which the various genre and mythological scenes occur, are reviewed. Robert Folsom's *Attic Black-Figured Pottery* and *Attic Red-Figured Pottery* survey stylistic developments in the treatment of the human figure in black- and red-figure and white-ground vase paintings, and trace the evolution and decline of particular vase shapes in the same three techniques. Finally, much of Arias' *History of One Thousand Years of Greek Vase Painting* is devoted to Attic vases of the black- and red-figure and the white-ground techniques. This beautiful book has over two hundred full-page, black-and-white and color photographs of Attic vases by the renowned photographer Max Hirmer. The vases illustrated are by the best Attic vase-painters; accompanying the plates are extensive descriptions of every vase, with bibliographic citations and introductions to the general stylistic traits and thematic preferences of each vase-painter. The bibliographies of these handbooks and Beazley's references, as well as the "Index Nominum Antiquorum" (Index of Ancient Names) from the latest volumes of *L'Année philologique* (Philological Year), should be consulted for the monographs and periodical literature available on individual vase-painters and potters.

### Bibliographic Entries for Handbooks

*L'Année philologique: Bibliographie critique et analytique de l'antiquité gréco-latine.* Paris: Société d'édition "Les Belles Lettres," 1928– .

Arias, Paolo Enrico. *A History of One Thousand Years of Greek Vase Painting.* Translated and revised by B. B. Shefton. New York: Abrams, 1962.

Beazley, J. D. *The Development of Attic Black-figure.* Rev. ed. Sather Classical Lectures, no. 24. Berkeley: Univ. of California Press, 1986.

Boardman, John. *Athenian Black Figure Vases: A Handbook.* World of Art. New York: Thames & Hudson, 1985.

———. *Athenian Red Figure Vases: The Archaic Period: A Handbook.* World of Art. New York: Thames & Hudson, 1985.

———. *Athenian Red Figure Vases: The Classical Period: A Handbook.* World of Art. New York: Thames & Hudson, 1989.

Folsom, Robert S. *Attic Black-Figured Pottery.* Park Ridge, N.J.: Noyes Press, 1975.

———. *Attic Red-Figured Pottery.* Park Ridge, N.J.: Noyes Press, 1976.

Richter, Gisela M. A. *Metropolitan Museum of Art: Attic Red-Figured Vases: A Survey.* Rev. ed. New Haven: Yale Univ. Press, 1958.

## SUPPLEMENTARY SOURCES

Von Bothmer's exhibition catalog, *The Amasis Painter and His World: Vase-painting in Sixth-Century B.C. Athens,* is an example of a study of the products of a single Attic black-figure vase-painter. The catalog gives detailed descriptions of half the painter's surviving vases, along with extensive bibliography and photographs, some in color, of both sides of every vase. When problems arise in interpreting figural scenes, the answers are searched for in similar scenes from other vases by the Amasis Painter. Another recent study, *The Phiale Painter,* by John H. Oakley, examines the style, thematic content, and vase shapes and their ornaments of a major Attic red-figure and white-ground vase-painter who worked during the third quarter of the fifth century. Oakley concludes that the Phiale Painter had an unusually "lively style of drawing" and a rich repertoire of subject matter drawn from a variety of sources. *The Meidias Painter,* by Lucilla Burn, investigates the subject matter of this important Attic red-figure vase-painter from the late fifth century. By cataloging, illustrating, and discussing vases by the Meidias Painter and his associates that fall into specific thematic categories, Burn determines two main emphases that are new to Attic vase-painting—the elimination of violence in myths where it was previously required, and the use of a lush garden as a setting for these newly tranquil idylls. Both tendencies are interpreted as "evocations of a far-off time when life was simpler and more stable."

Thomas Bertram Lonsdale Webster's *Potter and Patron in Classical Athens* investigates the relationship between painters and potters both within the individual workshops and among the different workshops, and the relationship between the patrons and the scenes depicted on the vases. *A City of Images: Iconography and Society in Ancient Greece* is a collection of essays by Claude Bérard and other authors in which nonmythological images from various thematic categories that appear on Athenian vases are investigated as a source of evidence for "the social construction of reality in classical Athens."

In *Shapes and Names of Athenian Vases,* Richter and Milne describe the standard vase shapes and the evidence for their ancient names from the sixth through the fourth centuries, that is, the period of Attic black- and red-figure. A more recent discussion of the standard shapes of Attic vases can be found in *Containers of Classical Greece: A Handbook of Shapes,* by Maxwell George Kanowski. Illustrated with many line drawings and featuring a general bibliography as well as references on each shape, Kanowski's handbook supplements and updates but does not replace Richter and Milne's standard study. Besides covering Attic vase shapes within the same time frame encompassed by Richter and Milne, Kanowski devotes some attention to Attic shapes from 1100 to 600 B.C., and supplies some information on shapes popular in Corinth and South Italy. A number of studies are also devoted to the evolution of particular shapes and their decorations; a good example is *The Attic Pyxis,* by Sally Rutherfurd Roberts. The methods of the potting, painting, and firing of Attic black- and red-figure pottery are reconstructed by Noble in *The Techniques of Painted Attic Pottery.*

For the researcher wishing to survey the periods of Attic vase-painting before the introduction of the black-figure technique circa 630 B.C., these studies are recommended: Desborough's *Protogeometric Pottery;* Coldstream's *Greek Geometric Pottery;* Davison's *Attic Geometric Workshops;* and Kübler's *Altattische Malerei* (Early Attic Painting [on Proto-Attic vases from the seventh century]). After the abandonment of the Attic red-figure technique circa 320 B.C., the fine ware of the Hellenistic period consisted primarily of black moldmade bowls with relief decorations, which usually functioned as wine cups. Susan Rotroff's *Hellenistic Pottery: Athenian and Imported Moldmade Bowls* is devoted to bowls of this type that were found in the Athenian agora.

## Bibliographic Entries for Supplementary Sources

Bérard, Claude, et al. *A City of Images: Iconography and Society in Ancient Greece.* Translated by Deborah Lyons. Princeton: Princeton Univ. Press, 1989.

Bothmer, Dietrich von. *The Amasis Painter and His World: Vase-painting in Sixth-Century B.C. Athens.* Introduction by Alan L. Boegehold. Catalog of an exhibition in the Metropolitan Museum of Art, New York, September–October, 1985. Malibu, Calif., and New York/London: J. Paul Getty Museum and Thames & Hudson, 1985.

Burn, Lucilla. *The Meidias Painter.* Oxford Monographs on Classical Archaeology. Oxford: Clarendon Press, 1987.

Coldstream, J. N. *Greek Geometric Pottery: A Survey of Ten Local Styles and their Chronology.* London: Methuen, 1968.

Davison, Jean M. *Attic Geometric Workshops.* Yale Classical Studies, no. 16. New Haven: Yale Univ. Press, 1961.

Desborough, V. R. d'A. *Protogeometric Pottery.* Oxford: Clarendon Press, 1952.

Kanowski, Maxwell George. *Containers of Classical Greece: A Handbook of Shapes.* St Lucia and London: Univ. of Queensland Press, 1984.

Kübler, Karl. *Altattische Malerei.* Tübingen: E. Wasmuth, 1950.

Noble, Joseph Veach. *The Techniques of Painted Attic Pottery.* Rev. ed. New York: Thames & Hudson, 1988.

Oakley, John H. *The Phiale Painter.* Kerameus 8. Mainz/Rhein: P. von Zabern, 1990.

Richter, Gisela M. A., and Marjorie J. Milne. *The Metropolitan Museum of Art: Shapes and Names of Athenian Vases.* New York: Plantin Press, 1935.

Roberts, Sally Rutherfurd. *The Attic Pyxis.* Chicago: Ares Pubs., 1978.

Rotroff, Susan I. *Hellenistic Pottery: Athenian and Imported Moldmade Bowls.* The Athenian Agora, no. 22. Princeton, N.J.: American School of Classical Studies at Athens, 1982.

Webster, Thomas Bertram Lonsdale. *Potter and Patron in Classical Athens.* London: Methuen, 1972.

## Additional Supplementary Sources

Brann, Eva T. H. *Late Geometric and Protoattic Pottery, Mid 8th to Late 7th Century B.C.* The Athenian Agora, no. 8. Princeton, N.J.: American School of Classical Studies at Athens, 1962.

Hambidge, Jay. *Dynamic Symmetry: The Greek Vase.* New Haven: Yale Univ. Press, 1920.

Kurtz, Donna Carol. *Athenian White Lekythoi: Patterns and Painters.* Oxford: Clarendon Press, 1975.

Mertens, Joan R. *Attic White Ground: Its Development on Shapes Other Than Lekythoi.* Outstanding Dissertations in the Fine Arts. New York: Garland Publishing, 1977.

Moore, Mary B., Mary Zelia Pease Philippides, and in collaboration with Dietrich Von Bothmer. *Attic Black-Figured Pottery.* The Athenian Agora, no. 23. Princeton, N.J.: American School of Classical Studies, 1986.

Richter, Gisela M. A. *Red-figured Athenian Vases in the Metropolitan Museum of Art.* Drawings by Lindsley F. Hall. 2 vol. New Haven: Yale Univ. Press; London: Humphrey Milford; Oxford: Oxford Univ. Press, 1936.

Scheibler, Ingeborg. *Griechische Töpferkunst: Herstellung, Handel und Gebrauch der antiken Tongefäße.* Beck's Archäologische Bibliothek. Munich: C. H. Beck, 1983.

Sparkes, Brian A., and Lucy Talcott. *Black and Plain Pottery of the 6th, 5th and 4th Centuries B.C.* The Athenian Agora, no. 12. Princeton, N.J.: American School of Classical Studies at Athens, 1970.

Wehgartner, Irma. *Attisch weissgrundige Keramik: Maltechniken, Werkstätten, Formen, Verwendung.* Mainz am Rhein: P. von Zabern, 1983.

# ᐟ11ᐟ

# South Italian and
# Sicilian Vases

Trendall, Arthur Dale. *The Red-figured Vases of Lucania, Campania and Sicily.* Vol. 1, *Text.* Vol. 2, *Indexes and Plates.* Oxford: Clarendon Press, 1967. *First Supplement.* University of London. Institute of Classical Studies. Bulletin. Supplement 26. London: Institute of Classical Studies, 1970. *Second Supplement.* University of London. Institute of Classical Studies. Bulletin. Supplement 31. London: Institute of Classical Studies, 1973. *Third Supplement (Consolidated).* University of London. Institute of Classical Studies. Bulletin. Supplement 41. London: Institute of Classical Studies, 1983.

Trendall, Arthur Dale, and Alexander Cambitoglou. *The Red-figured Vases of Apulia.* Vol. 1, *Early and Middle Apulian.* Oxford: Clarendon Press, 1978. Vol. 2, *Late Apulian.* Oxford: Clarendon Press, 1982. *Indexes.* Oxford: Clarendon Press, 1982. *First Supplement to the Red-figured Vases of Apulia.* University of London. Institute of Classical Studies. Bulletin. Supplement 42. London: Institute of Classical Studies, 1983. *Second Supplement to the Red-figured Vases of Apulia.* University of London. Institute of Classical Studies. Bulletin. Supplement 60, Parts 1–2. London: Institute of Classical Studies, forthcoming.

Trendall, Arthur Dale. *The Red-figured Vases of Paestum.* Rome: British School at Rome, 1987.

# ART FORM

After Athens, the Greek workshops which produced the most painted vases were those located in South Italy and Sicily. Over 20,000 red-figure vases from the workshops of these Greek colonies in Magna Graecia have survived, of which about 18,500 have been attributed to specific vase-painters or groups. The attributed vases, belonging to the period between circa 440 and 300 B.C., can be separated into five regional styles: Lucanian (1,500 vases), produced in the area forming the toe of South Italy, with workshops first in Metaponto and perhaps Heraclea, and then in the barbarian interior; Apulian (10,000 vases), made in South Italy's heel, with Tarentum the main center and other workshops at inland towns such as Canosa; Campanian (4,000 vases), produced in the region adjacent to the Bay of Naples, with workshops at coastal Cumae and probably at inland Capua; Paestan (2,000 vases), made only at its name city of Paestum; and Sicilian (1,000 vases), manufactured first at Syracuse and Himera, and later at other sites in Sicily and on the island of Lipari to the north.

During the late eighteenth and the nineteenth centuries, South Italian red-figure vases were found in great numbers in ancient chamber-tombs in the region. Until they were distinguished from Attic products in the late nineteenth century, they were greatly admired; they subsequently fell into disfavor because they were judged to be aesthetically inferior to Attic vases. Since 1950, however, excavations have uncovered many new examples, which, along with the tireless research efforts in the area of artistic attributions, by Arthur Dale Trendall and other scholars, have stimulated renewed interest in the colonial products.

South Italian red-figure has many characteristics that distinguish it from Attic red-figure. South Italian clays, less rich in iron than Attic clay, fire a paler red color, and the black glaze background of South Italian vases is less lustrous, often taking on a greenish tinge. An interesting difference is that while the real names of dozens of Attic vase-painters are known, only two South Italian vase-painters, both from Paestum, signed their vases. Perhaps the most significant distinct traits of South Italian red-figure are the greater exuberance of its floral and figural decoration and the popularity of large vases, which were not produced at Athens after circa 370 B.C. The subject matter of the complex figural scenes found on the large vases is also far richer than in contemporary Attic ware in several ways. First, illustrations of drama, nonexistent on Attic vases after the early fourth century B.C., are abundant on South Italian vases from the same century. These examples outnumber the earlier fifth-century Attic vases belonging to the same genre, and they are also more valuable because costumes, scenery, and the stage are more frequently shown. Second, in contrast to the simpler contemporary

Attic representations, South Italian depictions of Greek myths are often spread out on two or three levels, with the Olympian gods occupying the uppermost sphere; some of these elaborate compositions seem to have been influenced by lost literary sources or wall paintings. The third important thematic category of decoration for large South Italian vases is scenes of offering at the tomb, which are indicated by a handsome columned shrine (not found on Attic vases), a grave stele, a single column, or a mound of earth.

While some may conclude that the combination of elaborate floral motifs and the often complex figural compositions of South Italian vases creates the impression of overworking, everyone must admit that individual figures are often skillfully drawn. Perhaps most significantly, South Italian vases comprise a fascinating branch of inquiry and yield extensive information about the many-faceted culture of the wealthy Greek colonists of Magna Graecia.

# RESEARCH USE

The three references and five supplements listed above bring together all the larger South Italian red-figure vases that have been attributed to specific vase-painters or groups of vase-painters from the same workshops. (Comprehensive coverage is not attempted for smaller vases.) Lists of attributed vases which identify figural decorations and cite publications of the vases form the main body of the text of these volumes; also, numerous illustrations and introductory discussions of stylistic and thematic traits of artists and groups accompany the lists.

One way in which the references and supplements can be used is as a source for information on specific vases, which can be located in the volumes' indexes to collections. (The researcher should be cautioned to use the correct volume for the regional style in looking up a vase.) Since the supplements contain citations to new publications of vases previously listed, as well as to newly attributed vases, the supplements should also be consulted regularly. A further use for the references and supplements is to examine the artistic development of a single painter or workshop. This type of investigation is facilitated by the introductory discussions and plates, and also by the frequent presentation of vases attributed to a single artist or group in two or more developmental phases. As unattributed vases by the same artists or groups are unearthed in excavations or discovered in museums or private collections, Trendall's volumes and the references cited therein should provide sufficient evidence to permit correct attributions.

Further possible uses of Trendall's references are comparisons of the products from contemporary or noncontemporary workshops from the same city, from different cities within the same regional style, or from different regional styles. Questions of possible interaction between workshops or of the influence of workshops on each other can thereby be investigated. Such investigations cannot, of course, be accomplished through stylistic considerations alone. They must be accompanied by an examination of the associations of vases from different workshops in the same archaeological contexts.

Finally, indexes to mythological content help the researcher trace a particular theme through vases produced at all the South Italian centers. Representations of myths from drama are included in these indexes.

## ORGANIZATION OF *THE RED-FIGURED VASES OF LUCANIA, CAMPANIA AND SICILY, THE RED-FIGURED VASES OF APULIA,* AND *THE RED-FIGURED VASES OF PAESTUM*

These three references present attributed South Italian vases in chapters, each of them devoted to a single vase-painter, a workshop with several vase-painters, or a group of stylistically related vases. The first reference includes the vases from all the chapters on the Lucanian style in a single numerical sequence; the same is done for the vases from all the chapters on the Sicilian style, thereby creating a second long list of vases. The chapters on Campanian vases are grouped in four larger parts corresponding to four workshops, with a separate numerical sequence established for each workshop. In contrast, *The Red-figured Vases of Apulia* has a separate list of vases for each chapter. *The Red-figured Vases of Paestum* presents its vases in three sequences corresponding to the volume's three parts: part 1 lists the Sicilian precedents for Paestan red-figured ware; part 2, the vases from the workshops of Asteas and Python; and part 3, the vases from two late Paestan workshops. (For further explanation of the numbering of the vases, see the paragraph below on the "Index to Collections.")

The text of all three references begins with helpful general bibliographies and general introductions. Each regional style or subdivision within a regional style is also prefaced by an introduction; the same holds true for each chapter. In the introductions to the chapters, traits common to all the painters considered in the chapter are outlined, and often an indication of the general chronology is given. The entries for vases attributed to a specific painter or group of painters are also introduced by prose descriptions of the painter's or group's unique traits of style and thematic repertoire.

The vases in each list of attributions to the same painter or group of painters are arranged so that all examples with the same shape can be found under a single italicized heading naming the shape (for standard South Italian shapes, see *The Art of South Italy: Vases from Magna Graecia,* pp. 310–11, figs. 1–42, pp. 308–10; see Handbooks below). On the first line of each separate entry is the number of the vase in the list; this is preceded by an asterisk (*) when the vase is illustrated. Next is the current location of the vase and its inventory number; for major museums, only the city name is given (except that "B.M." denotes the British Museum in London). The provenance of a vase, when known, is supplied after the location. The heights of many vases, in centimeters, are provided in *The Red-figured Vases of Lucania, Campania and Sicily,* and in *The Red-figured Vases of Paestum.* The first line of each entry concludes with the plate number for vases that are illustrated. When only the back of the vase is shown, the plate number is preceded by (b); otherwise, the front or both sides are shown.

If a vase has been published elsewhere, bibliographic citations are provided next. Most bibliographic abbreviations are explained in lists of abbreviations at the beginnings of the references. The reader should be aware that in *The Red-figured Vases of Lucania, Campania and Sicily* and in *The Red-figured Vases of Apulia* additional abbreviations can be found in the bibliographies of the introductions to the regional styles and their subdivisions, and in the introductions to the chapters. Volume 2 of *The Red-figured Vases of Apulia* does not repeat the general abbreviations from volume 1, but adds some additional ones. The abbreviation "R.I.," which frequently appears, means "Rome Institute," and refers to the Photo-Archive of the German Archaeological Institute in Rome.

A brief description of the vase's figural decoration is usually the last part of the vase entry. Here, the scenes or figures on both sides of the vase are identified, and for cups, also the designs on circular interiors. Mythological scenes are usually more summarily described than non-mythological ones; full discussions of the former can be found in the cited literature. Sometimes a comment comparing the vase with similar examples appears beneath the vase's thematic identification. In *The Red-figured Vases of Paestum,* some entries end with a list of other vases from the same tomb.

Besides the vase entries in the main chapters, entries for additional vases and additional information on and bibliography for previously listed vases can be found at the back of the text volume of *The Red-figured Vases of Lucania, Campania and Sicily,* and at the backs of both volumes of *The Red-figured Vases of Apulia;* entries for additional vases appear at the back of *The Red-figured Vases of Paestum.* The text volume of *The Red-figured Vases of Lucania, Campania and Sicily* includes these additional parts: appendix 1, a list of vases from the Owl-Pillar Group, which consists of poor Campanian imitations of Attic vases from 475–425 B.C. (not included in the Index to Collections from volume 2); appendix 2, a list of late Campanian vases from the *Kemai* Group, that is, small vases whose most complex decorations are female heads (not indexed); and appendix 3, a list of Sicilian vases with vegetable motifs painted in added colors (not indexed). Other additional parts include: addenda 1, comprising "I. Additions to the Vase-lists" (indexed in the Index to Collections in volume 2) and "II. Additional References" (not indexed); addenda 2, with new vases (included in the Index to Collections for the first and third supplements) and additional bibliography for vases from the main text (not indexed); "Supplement to Book I—Lucanian," with additional vases (indexed in the first and third supplements); and "Supplement to Book II—Campanian," with additional vases (described more fully and indexed in the first supplement, and indexed in the third supplement).

Volume 1 of *The Red-figured Vases of Apulia* has addenda with additional vases (included in the Index to Collections in the *Indexes* volume) and additional bibliography (not indexed). Volume 2 of the same reference has an appendix containing "1. New Vases" (indexed); "2. Vases with New Inventory Numbers" (indexed); and "3. Additional Bibliographical References" (some indexed). *The Red-figured Vases of Paestum* has the following three appendixes and two addenda containing additional vases: "Appendix I. Paestan Vases decorated in applied red" (i. e., vases decorated with red color applied over black glaze; indexed in section 2 of the Index of Collections); "Appendix II. Paestan black-figure from the Pagenstecher Class" (not indexed); "Appendix III. Campanian Vases from the Laghetto-Caivano Workshop found at Paestum" (some made of Paestan clay; not indexed); addenda with additional red-figure vases by the painters from the volume's main chapters (not indexed); and addenda with additional vases decorated with applied red (not indexed). The foregoing summary should leave no doubt in the reader's mind regarding the necessity of regular consultations of the appendixes and addenda.

The Index to Collections is the third index in volume 2 of *The Red-figured Vases of Lucania, Campania and Sicily,* the first index in the *Indexes* volume of *The Red-figured Vases of Apulia,* and the first index in *The Red-figured Vases of Paestum.* In all three cases, the Index to Collections has three parts: vases in museums and private collections; vases on the market and/or formerly in private collections; and published vases whose current location is unknown. The Index of Collections in *The Red-figured Vases of Paestum* is also divided into two sections: "I. Red-figured Vases" (for vases from the volume's main chapters), and "II. Vases decorated in applied red (Appendix I)." The researcher should note that the Index to Collections in all three references does not cite the page number where a vase entry is located. Instead, it cites a vase's serial number and, where necessary, its part number within Campanian or Paestan, or its chapter number within Apulian. Thus a Campanian vase, labeled *"Campanian,"* has a number such as *"4/419,"* which means vase 419 in part 4 of

Campanian. A Lucanian or Sicilian vase is labeled *"Lucanian"* or *"Sicilian,"* and is given a single number. A Paestan vase also has a two-part number such as *"3/366,"* which signifies vase 366 in part 3. An Apulian vase is given a number such as *"21/93,"* meaning vase 93 from chapter 21. To find a vase, the researcher must be certain to look for its number in the vase list for the appropriate region; in addition, a Campanian or Paestan vase number must be located in the list corresponding to the appropriate part of Campanian or Paestan, and an Apulian vase number needs to be searched for in the appropriate chapter.

All three references also include subject indexes (with an emphasis on mythology and drama); general indexes (combined with the subject index in *The Red-figured Vases of Lucania, Campania and Sicily*); indexes to painters and groups (under *"Vase-painters"* in the general index for *The Red-figured Vases of Paestum*); indexes to sites (under *"Proveniences"* in the general indexes for *The Red-figured Vases of Apulia* and *The Red-figured Vases of Paestum*); and a *"Concordance with CVA and other Publications."* Vases included in the concordances for all three references and the thematic indexes in *The Red-figured Vases of Apulia* and *The Red-figured Vases of Paestum* are cited with the same numeration system as in the Index to Collections, while the other indexes cite page numbers. Volume 2 of *The Red-figured Vases of Lucania, Campania and Sicily* also has an "Index of Greek Inscriptions," in alphabetical order. Maps can be found on pages 6, 191, and 578 of *The Red-figured Vases of Lucania, Campania and Sicily*, and on page 445 of volume 1 of *The Red-figured Vases of Apulia*. Chronological charts that group the major Apulian artists by workshops are located on page 447 of volume 1 and pages 1302–3 of the *Indexes* volume for the latter reference. The "List of Plates" and the plates appear in volume 2 of *The Red-figured Vases of Lucania, Campania and Sicily*, in both volumes of *The Red-figured Vases of Apulia*, and in the single volume of *The Red-figured Vases of Paestum*. Although the photographs are often rather small, they "give a representative selection of the more interesting or most typical vases by each of the principal painters."

## ORGANIZATION OF THE FIRST, SECOND AND THIRD SUPPLEMENTS TO *THE RED-FIGURED VASES OF LUCANIA, CAMPANIA AND SICILY*, THE FIRST SUPPLEMENT TO *THE RED-FIGURED VASES OF APULIA*, AND THE *SECOND SUPPLEMENT TO THE RED-FIGURED VASES OF APULIA*

The same kind of information that is in the addenda for the two references discussed above is contained in the supplements, that is, additional bibliography and new information on previously listed vases and entries for new vases. The additional references are not indexed at the backs of the volumes, but the new vases are. Besides the information on specific vases, the supplements include additions to the general bibliographies (some references are given abbreviated forms that are used in the vase entries) and, where necessary, prose summaries of new conclusions regarding workshops and painters, and of the evidence, often from new excavations, that has led to the conclusions. Each supplement also has a substantial number of photographs of vases from museums, private collections, and auction houses. These plates are at the backs of the supplements, while the "List of Plates" follows the preface of each volume. Before the plates in each supplement are an "Index to Collections" and a concordance, whose vases are referred to with the same numeration system as that in the same indexes in the two major references discussed above. The second and third supplements for *The Red-figured Vases of Lucania, Campania and Sicily* and the *First Supplement to the Red-figured Vases of Apulia* list vases which have been assigned new or different inventory numbers. In addition, the third supplement for *The Red-figured Vases of Lucania, Campania and Sicily* and the *First Supplement to the Red-figured Vases of Apulia* include thematic indexes which refer to the vases, by page number and serial number.

The third supplement for *The Red-figured Vases of Lucania, Campania and Sicily* repeats new vases from the previous two supplements in an abbreviated fashion, as well as adding more new ones. Thus the indexes for the third supplement include new vases from all three supplements. Also, all previously listed vases whose new locations are indicated in the first, second or third supplement are indexed by their new locations in the third supplement. Furthermore, all previously listed Lucanian, Campanian, and Sicilian vases which have been reattributed are listed in the third supplement, with both the new and the old attribution numbers given.

All three supplements for *The Red-figured Vases of Lucania, Campania and Sicily* include three appendixes which correspond in content to the three appendixes in the original publication (see above), and which add new information and examples. Vases from these appendixes are not indexed. Also not indexed are a few new vases in the addenda of pages 390–92 of the third supplement.

In a letter of March 14, 1991, Arthur Dale Trendall describes the appearance dates and contents of the forthcoming *Second Supplement to the Red-figured Vases of Apulia:* "Part 1 is already in process of being printed and should be ready by the middle of the year (it includes chapters 1–20 + bibliography); Part 2 has been typeset except for some of the indexes; it should be ready for printing in May and should appear at the end of the year. It includes chapters 21–30 + indexes, concordances and a few late 'addenda.' "

# COMPLEMENTARY REFERENCES

The reference most frequently cited in Trendall and Cambitoglou's *Red-figured Vases of Apulia* is *CVA*, the *Corpus Vasorum Antiquorum* (Corpus of Ancient Vases). This is an ongoing publication of fascicles containing photographs and catalog entries for vases in museums around the world. Trendall and Cambitoglou's citations are easy to locate, since the abbreviation *CVA* is followed by the number of the fascicle for the museum, the number for the vase category, and the plate number; for example, "Bologna PU 497. *CVA* 3, IV Gr, pl. 1, 11–12" means Bologna, Museo Civico number PU 497, third fascicle for this museum, plate 1 figures 11–12 from vase category IV Gr. The catalog entries for the vases in the *CVA* often include bibliographic citations which are not repeated by Trendall and Cambitoglou.

The researcher also should have on hand three references containing lists, plates, and discussions of attributed Apulian and Lucanian vases. The first two references, which are corpora of Apulian vases of the "Plain" or simple style, are Cambitoglou and Trendall's *Apulian Red-figured Vase-painters of the Plain Style*, and their "Addenda to *Apulian Red-figure Vase-painters of the Plain Style*." Vases from both references are also listed in their later publication of all styles of Apulian, *The Red-figured Vases of Apulia*. However, these later entries for "Plain"-style vases have an abbreviated form; what is not repeated are the citations of publications of the vases. The third reference, Trendall's *Early South Italian Vase-painting*, should be available to the researcher because its bibliographic citations for early Apulian vases also are not repeated in *The Red-figured Vases of Apulia*. *Early South Italian Vase-painting* also lists and discusses hundreds of early Lucanian vases, whose entries in *The Red-figured Vases of Lucania, Campania and Sicily* and its first and second supplements are cited. A further use for all three references is as sources for illustrations of vases not reproduced in *The Red-figured Vases of Apulia* and *The Red-figured Vases of Lucania, Campania and Sicily*.

Four additional illustrated references by Trendall which list and discuss attributed Paestan red-figure vases are necessary for research, since many of their bibliographic citations for vases are not repeated in his latest, most comprehensive corpus, *The Red-figured Vases of Paestum*. Trendall's *Paestan Pottery* (1936; abbreviated *PP*), with 404 vases, was the earliest corpus. "Paestan Pottery: A Revision and Supplement" (1952; abbreviated *PPSupp*) added over a hundred new vases. Close to a hundred more vases, over fifty of them from an excavation near the Temple of Hera II at Paestum, are included in "Paestan Post-script" (1953; abbreviated *PP-s*). Further excavations at different sites at Paestum yielded an additional three hundred vases, listed in "Paestan Addenda" (1959; abbreviated *PAdd*). The latest Trendall corpus, *The Red-figured Vases of Paestum* (1987), repeats vase entries (often without bibliographic citations) from the earlier publications and provides cross-references to these publications as well as adding one thousand new vases, to bring the number of attributed Paestan vases to nearly two thousand. Concordances for *Paestan Pottery,* "Paestan Pottery: A Revision and Supplement," and "Paestan Addenda" appear before the subject indexes in *The Red-figured Vases of Paestum;* these enable the researcher to quickly locate vases from the earlier publications in *The Red-figured Vases of Paestum.*

### Bibliographic Entries for Complementary References

Cambitoglou, Alexander, and Arthur Dale Trendall. *Apulian Red-figure Vase-painters of the Plain Style.* Monographs on Archaeology and Fine Arts. New York: Archaeological Institute of America, 1961.

———. "Addenda to *Apulian Red-figure Vase-painters of the Plain Style.*" *American Journal of Archaeology* 73 (1969): 423–33.

*Corpus Vasorum Antiquorum.* Paris et al.: 1923– .

Trendall, Arthur Dale. *Early South Italian Vase-painting.* Mainz: P. von Zabern, 1974. Rev. ed. of *Frühitaliotische Vasen.* Bilder Griechischer Vasen 12. Leipzig: Heinrich Keller, 1938.

———. "Paestan Addenda." *Papers of the British School at Rome* 27 (1959): 1–37.

———. "Paestan Post-script." *Papers of the British School at Rome* 21 (1953): 160–67.

———. "Paestan Pottery: A Revision and Supplement." *Papers of the British School at Rome* 20 (1952): 1–53.

———. *Paestan Pottery: A Study of the Red-figured Vases of Paestum.* Rome: British School at Rome, 1936.

## HANDBOOKS

The most authoritative and recent handbook is Trendall's *Red Figure Vases of South Italy and Sicily.* Six chapters of text, along with hundreds of photographs, provide a thorough introduction to the five South Italian and Sicilian styles and to the major painters and workshops. In addition, the first chapter explains the circumstances that fostered the growth of vase-painting in South Italy and discusses general aspects, such as vase shapes (see figs. 2–3), technique, and chronology. The final chapter summarizes the thematic content of the figured scenes, which are derived from mythology, drama, everyday life, and the cult of the dead. Following this chapter are a chronological chart of major painters from all the regional styles and an up-to-date bibliography. A shorter handbook by the same author, *South Italian Vase Painting,* features the excellent collection in the British Museum, and provides concise summaries of the subject matter of the different South Italian fabrics. Unlike Trendall's longer handbook, *Red Figure Vases of South Italy and Sicily,* this attractive study presents four color photographs and a more complete chart of common vase shapes (see fig. 2).

Although originally intended as an exhibition catalog, *The Art of South Italy: Vases from Magna Graecia*, edited by Margaret Ellen Mayo, can also be used as a source for general information and for some color photographs. Particularly valuable are the introductions to the five red-figure vase-painting styles by Trendall, who also wrote the catalog's general essay; the introduction to vases from different regions that were painted in the Gnathia technique (colors painted over black glaze), by J. R. Green; and the brief introduction to the catalog's two funerary vases in the fugitive polychrome technique of Centuripe, in eastern Sicily, by J. R. Green. Also important are an essay on the thematic content of South Italian vases by the leading expert, Margot Schmidt; a detailed explanation of the method of producing South Italian red-figure vases by Joseph Veach Noble; and a chart of vase shapes which illustrates several shapes not included in Trendall's charts (see above) and which has accompanying textual descriptions of the shapes and their functions by Margaret Ellen Mayo. At the back of the catalog is a useful bibliography, with references broken down by their regional and archaeological focus, and by their emphasis regarding thematic content.

## Bibliographic Entries for Handbooks

Mayo, Margaret Ellen, ed. *The Art of South Italy: Vases from Magna Graecia.* Catalog of an exhibition in the Virginia Museum of Fine Arts, Richmond, May–August, 1982. Richmond: Virginia Museum of Fine Arts, 1982.

Trendall, Arthur Dale. *Red Figure Vases of South Italy and Sicily: A Handbook.* World of Art. New York: Thames & Hudson, 1989.

———. *South Italian Vase Painting.* 2d ed. London: British Museum Publications Ltd., 1976.

# SUPPLEMENTARY SOURCES

The study of large collections of South Italian vases permits the researcher to observe the stylistic development in products manufactured in a single workshop, and to note interrelationships between workshops and between imported and local products. The Vatican in Rome owns one of the most representative collections of South Italian vases, with vases of all scales and degrees of simplicity and ornateness included. In *Vasi antichi dipinti del Vaticano* (Ancient Painted Vases of the Vatican), Trendall provides detailed descriptions, with bibliography, of many of these vases; all of those he discusses are illustrated, usually with both front and back shown. Ruvo di Puglia (ancient Rubi), a wealthy South Italian city located northwest of Tarentum, had an extensive ancient necropolis from whose tombs a large collection of vases was assembled by the Jatta family and housed in the Jatta Museum. In *Griechische Vasen in Unteritalien aus der Sammlung Jatta in Ruvo* (Greek Vases in South Italy from the Jatta Collection in Ruvo), by Hellmut Sichtermann, a representative selection of vases from this collection is illustrated and described in brief catalog entries which emphasize thematic content as well as relationships between imported vases and the vases—particularly Apulian ones—that were manufactured in the region. Also, where applicable, sources for vase-paintings in Greek drama are noted. Bibliographic citations for all the published vases are provided.

   *Le peintre de Darius et son milieu: Vases grecs d'Italie méridionale* (The Darius Painter and His Circle: Greek Vases of South Italy) is a catalog by Christian Aellen and others for some of the South Italian vases that were included in a 1986 exhibition at the Musée d'art et d'histoire at Geneva. In this scholarly work, illustrated by black-and-white and color photographs, particularly detailed descriptions are presented of Apulian vases, especially those by the eminent draftsman and narrator, the Darius Painter, and by his predecessors and followers. Bibliography is provided for the published vases in the exhibition, and for additional vases, art works in other media, and literary works that are mentioned for comparative purposes in the catalog entries.

   One of the most difficult problems the scholar encounters is unraveling the lost meaning of scenes on South Italian vases which clearly have a ritual intent, or contain ritual objects. Schmidt, Trendall, and Cambitoglou combined their efforts in an interesting publication that addresses this problem, *Eine Gruppe apulischer Grabvasen in Basel* (A Group of Apulian Funerary Vases in Basel). In this study, an attempt is made to arrive at correct interpretations of the decorations of thirteen Apulian funerary vases in Basel (seven by the same painter and from the same tomb). The vases fall into the thematic categories of offerings at the tomb of the deceased and Greek myths. Both types of scenes are interpreted as ones in which a hope is expressed that after death there will be new life for the deceased. This conclusion arises out of the liveliness of the figures identified as the deceased, who are shown in the center of offering scenes; the mingling of mortals with immortals in mythological abductions and images of the blessed afterlife; and the emphasis in other mythological scenes on the rescue of mortals from suffering or death. Hans Lohmann discusses, catalogs, and illustrates South Italian vases depicting funerary monuments in *Grabmäler auf unteritalischen Vasen* (Funerary Monuments on South Italian Vases). Most of the grave monuments he considers fall into the categories of statues, shrines with one or more figures inside (intended to be statues?), and shrines with plants or vases inside. In *Grabmäler auf unteritalischen Vasen*, Lohmann adopts a viewpoint parallel to that of the authors of *Eine*

*Gruppe apulischer Grabvasen in Basel* in suggesting that different types of funerary monuments, such as plants in shrines, symbolize hopes for immortality. In *Funerary Symbolism in Apulian Vase-painting*, Henry Roy William Smith goes farther than the two German monographs just described in his attempt to demonstrate that all Apulian red-figure vases were funerary in function. To support this thought-provoking hypothesis, he suggests that many attributes of mythological and nonmythological figures, such as mirrors, were references to blissful marriages which were to take place in the afterlife.

The *nestoris*, a strange jar shape with upswung handles that are usually embellished with disks, is the focus of *Red-figured Lucanian and Apulian Nestorides and Their Ancestors*, by G. Schneider-Hermann. In this illustrated monograph, Schneider-Hermann convincingly demonstrates that the *nestoris*, produced only by Greek workshops in Lucania and Apulia, was derived from a related shape called the *trozzella* that was a characteristic product of local non-Greek workshops. This non-Greek derivation, the appearance on some *nestorides* of figures in native (i. e., non-Greek) costumes, and a total absence of provenances from Tarentum lead Schneider-Hermann to the hypothesis that this aesthetically inharmonious shape was manufactured for the native Oscans and Samnites of the hinterland.

Current research, particularly finds from South Italian tombs, is demonstrating that beginning in the fourth century B.C., monochrome relief vases were manufactured in several South Italian regions. *Les gutti et les askoi à reliefs étrusques et apuliens: Essai de classification et de typologie* (Etruscan and Apulian Relief Gutti and Askoi: Attempt at Classification and Typology), by Marie-Odile Jentel, examines two shapes (*gutti* and *askoi*) of small perfume vases that were made by Greeks in Apulia and by Etruscans in Etruria. She organizes her examples in groups of *gutti* and *askoi* whose relief medallions have the same thematic content and arrangement; to examples of these two shapes she adds additional relief vases of other shapes that have medallions with the same theme and arrangement, as well as red-figure vases with similar relief medallions on the handles. Significantly, in some instances vases of different shapes exhibit medallions that were fashioned from the same mould. The ultimate sources for at least some of these moulds were metal reliefs and coins. Jentel's tables of examples make use of abbreviations that are explained in the bibliography at the front of volume 1.

## Bibliographic Entries for Supplementary Sources

Aellen, Christian, Alexander Cambitoglou, and Jacques Chamay. *Le peintre de Darius et son milieu: Vases grecs d'Italie méridionale.* Catalog of an exhibition at the Musée d'art et d'histoire, Geneva, April–August, 1986. Hellas et Roma 4. Geneva: Hellas et Roma, 1986.

Jentel, Marie-Odile. *Les gutti et les askoi à reliefs étrusques et apuliens: Essai de classification et de typologie.* 2 vols. Céramiques hellénistiques à reliefs 1. Québec: Les Presses de l'Université de Laval; Leiden: E. J. Brill; Toronto: Samuel Stevens Hakkert & Co., 1976.

Lohmann, Hans. *Grabmäler auf unteritalischen Vasen.* Deutsches Archäologisches Institut: Archäologische Forschungen 7. Berlin: Gebr. Mann, 1979.

Schmidt, Margot, Arthur Dale Trendall, and Alexander Cambitoglou. *Eine Gruppe apulischer Grabvasen in Basel: Studien zu Gehalt und Form der unteritalischen Sepulkralkunst.* Veröffentlichungen des Antiken-Museums Basel 3. Basel: Archäologischer Verlag, 1976.

Schneider-Hermann, G. *Red-figured Lucanian and Apulian Nestorides and Their Ancestors.* Allard Pierson Series, no. 1. Amsterdam: Allard Pierson Museum, 1980.

Sichtermann, Hellmut. *Griechische Vasen in Unteritalien aus der Sammlung Jatta in Ruvo.* Bilderhefte des Deutschen Archäologischen Instituts Rom 3/4. Tübingen: Wasmuth, 1966.

Smith, Henry Roy William. *Funerary Symbolism in Apulian Vase-painting.* Edited by J. K. Anderson. University of California Publications: Classical Studies, no. 12. Berkeley: Univ. of California Press, 1976.

Trendall, Arthur Dale. *Vasi antichi del Vaticano: Vasi italioti ed etruschi a figure rosse.* Rome: Città del Vaticano, 1953–55.

# ＼12＼

# Etruscan Mirrors

De Grummond, Nancy Thomson, ed. *A Guide to Etruscan Mirrors.*
Tallahassee, Fla.: Archaeological News, 1982.

## ART FORM

We have a better knowledge of Etruscan hand-mirrors than of any other
type of Etruscan antiquity. Altogether, about three thousand Etruscan
mirrors are known, scattered in collections all over the world. They are
believed to have originally been the prized possessions of Etruscan
women and to have been buried with them at their deaths. Etruscan
mirrors were produced from the tenth century to circa 100 B.C. Made of
bronze, they consist of a round flat plate which has a highly polished,
reflective surface on the slightly convex front side. By circa 530–520 B.C.,
the back was usually decorated with an engraving of a mythological or
genre scene, or sometimes consisted of a low relief, evidently a more
expensive form of ornament. The engravings, admired and imitated for
their delicacy of line and imaginative compositions within the circular
format, are a valuable source of information about Etruscan mythology,
religion, and daily life.

# RESEARCH USE

*A Guide to Etruscan Mirrors,* by Nancy de Grummond and others, is the most general survey of this subject. The researcher can use it as an introduction to Etruscan and other ancient mirror types, the methods of producing Etruscan mirrors, the range of subjects and styles in their engraved scenes, and evidence on their original uses. In addition, the dictionaries of personages from Greek and Etruscan mythology who appear on Etruscan mirrors form a valuable starting point for research in iconography, since most of the mirrors cited as examples have the personages' names inscribed. As the dictionaries point out, Etruscan mirrors with scenes from mythology fall into four classes: those whose characters and myths are derived from Greek art; those whose characters are Greek but whose myths are not; those whose myths are Greek but whose characters are both Greek and Etruscan; and those whose characters are all Etruscan. It may prove valuable to make comparisons between these classes of mirrors, since such research may lead to a better understanding of the relationship of Etruscan to Greek art.

# ORGANIZATION

The book begins by describing the basic types of Etruscan mirrors, differentiating between those cast in one piece and those with the handles cast separately. The designs and uses of mirrors of the Egyptians, Greeks, and Romans are then reviewed in order to bring out any common features of Etruscan and non-Etruscan examples. Theories on the casting and cold-working techniques of Etruscan mirrors are presented together with detailed quantitative analyses of the metallic composition of the bronze. The book outlines the problems of conservation and restoration, as well as the types and detection of forgeries. Next, the inscriptions on the mirrors in the form of captions, funerary dedications, owners' names, and artists' signatures are described, and their value in the study of the Etruscan language is considered.

Knowledge of Etruscan daily life as depicted in the engravings is discussed, and the thematic content of mirrors with mythological scenes is then summarized by means of dictionaries of Greek and Etruscan mythological figures. The dictionary entries outline the mythological roles and attributes exhibited by each figure on the mirrors where his or her name is inscribed. The patterns of flora and fauna, which usually form a decorative border around the figured scenes, are then discussed with regard to our knowledge about their periods of use, cities of manufacture, and compositional relationship with the scenes. A review of changes in the engraving styles of Etruscan mirrors in the Archaic,

Classical, and Hellenistic periods follows. The most significant conclusions of the book are presented in chapter 9, "The Usage of Etruscan Mirrors." It seems that in general, Etruscan mirrors were used by women during their lifetimes and then placed in their tombs. The Etruscans evidently believed that an Etruscan woman needed a mirror after death to ensure that she was properly adorned for the afterlife.

A Guide to Etruscan Mirrors includes 115 illustrations. Many of them represent pieces in the exhibition, "Reflections on Etruscan Mirrors," which was held at the Museum of Florida History in Tallahassee from October 1 to November 30, 1981. A handlist for the exhibition is included, along with an extensive bibliography on mirrors.

# COMPLEMENTARY REFERENCES

In the footnotes of A Guide to Etruscan Mirrors, constant reference is made to Etruskische Spiegel (Etruscan Mirrors), which is cited by the abbreviation ES. This work is the classic five-volume study by Eduard Gerhard and others that contains plates with line drawings of about nine hundred mirrors which are all described in detail in the accompanying text. In addition, the engraved containers for mirrors and cosmetics, called cistae, are discussed and illustrated in nineteen plates in volume 1.

In the short article, "Corpus Speculorum Etruscorum," Nancy de Grummond summarizes the contributions that have been made to the study of Etruscan mirrors by the publication of 121 mirrors in the first four fascicles of the ongoing international series. Corpus Speculorum Etruscorum (Corpus of Etruscan Mirrors). When complete, this work will publish line drawings and photographs of "an estimated 2,500–3,000 mirrors," along with descriptions of their decoration, including narrative scenes, chemical analyses of some examples, and bibliography for previously published examples. In her article, De Grummond adds conclusions contained in other studies published after A Guide to Etruscan Mirrors. These are particularly interesting as far as identifying the workshops that produced Etruscan mirrors and the most popular themes used for their decoration.

*Bibliographic Entries for Complementary References*

Corpus Speculorum Etruscorum. 1981– .
De Grummond, Nancy Thomson. "Corpus Speculorum Etruscorum." Archaeological News 13, no. 3/4 (Fall/Winter 1984): 85–87.
Gerhard, Eduard, A. Klügmann, and G. Körte. Etruskische Spiegel. Vol. 1, Allgemeines und Götterbilder, text to pl. 1–30 and pl. 1–120. Vol. 2, Heroische Mythologie, pl. 121–240. Vol. 3, pl. 241–80 and text to pl. 31–280. Vol. 4, pl.

281–430 and text to pl. 281–430. Vol. 5, new series of pl. 1–160 and text to these plates. Berlin: Georg Reimer, 1843–97.

# HANDBOOKS

*Etruscan Art*, by Otto J. Brendel (see chapter 2, "Etruscan Art and Architecture"), has useful summaries of the compositions, stylistic traits, and thematic content of Etruscan mirrors from the Archaic through the Hellenistic periods. These summaries can be found on pages 201–2, 284–87, 359–70, and 414–17.

In *The Etruscan Language: An Introduction*, by Giuliano and Larissa Bonfante, ten Etruscan mirrors with inscriptions are illustrated and the inscriptions are explained. Two dictionaries in the same reference—the "Glossary" and "Mythological Figures"—aid the reader who wishes to decipher unpublished inscriptions on Etruscan mirrors.

## Bibliographic Entries for Handbooks

Bonfante, Giuliano, and Larissa Bonfante. *The Etruscan Language: An Introduction*. New York and London: New York Univ. Press, 1983.
Brendel, Otto J. *Etruscan Art*. Prepared for press by Emeline Richardson. The Pelican History of Art. New York: Penguin, 1978.

# SUPPLEMENTARY REFERENCES

Two period studies of Etruscan mirrors are available. For the themes and border designs of mirrors from the Archaic period the researcher should consult the scholarly volume by Ilse Mayer-Prokop, *Die gravierten etruskischen Griffspiegel archaischen Stils* (The Engraved Etruscan Mirrors with Handles in the Archaic Style). Mirrors from the early and high classical phases (480–400 B.C.) are presented in typological/stylistic groups by Gabriele Pfister-Roesgen in *Die etruskischen Spiegel des 5. Jhs. v. Chr.* (The Etruscan Mirrors of the 5th Century B.C.). In *Spiegelwerkstätten in Vulci* (The Mirror Workshops in Vulci), Ulrike Fischer-Graf attributes 110 mirrors from the fifth through the early third century to the workshops at the important Etruscan city of Vulci. Finally, all aspects of the seventy mirrors in the Bibliothèque Nationale, Paris, are described by Denise Rebuffat-Emmanuel in *Le miroir étrusque d'après la collection du Cabinet des Médailles* (The Etruscan Mirror as Represented in the Collection of the Cabinet des Médailles). Volume 2 of the publication includes not only the standard photographs and drawings of the engraved mirror backs, but also views of the mirrors' polished fronts and sides.

## Bibliographic Entries for Supplementary Sources

Fischer-Graf, Ulrike. *Spiegelwerkstätten in Vulci.* Deutsches Archäologisches Institut. Archäologische Forschungen, vol. 8. Berlin: Gebr. Mann, 1980.

Mayer-Prokop, Ilse. *Die gravierten etruskischen Griffspiegel archaischen Stils.* Mitteilungen des Deutschen Archäologischen Instituts. Römische Abteilung, vol. 13. Heidelberg: F. H. Kerle, 1967.

Pfister-Roesgen, Gabriele. *Die etruskischen Spiegel des 5. Jhs. v. Chr.* Archäologische Studien, no. 2. Bern: Herbert Lang; Frankfurt/M.: Peter Lang, 1975.

Rebuffat-Emmanuel, Denise. *Le miroir étrusque d'après la collection du Cabinet des Médailles.* 2 vols. Collection de l'Ecole Française de Rome, no. 20. Rome: Palais Farnèse, 1973.

## Additional Supplementary Sources

Moscati, Paola. *Ricerche matematico-statistiche sugli specchi etruschi.* Contributi del Centro Linceo Interdisciplinare di Scienze Matematiche e loro Applicazioni, no. 66. Rome: Accademia Nazionale dei Lincei, 1984.

# , 13 ,

# Ancient Engraved Gems

Richter, Gisela M. A. *The Engraved Gems of the Greeks, Etruscans, and Romans.* Pt. 1, *Engraved Gems of the Greeks and the Etruscans: A History of Greek Art in Miniature.* London: Phaidon Press, 1968. Pt. 2, *Engraved Gems of the Romans: Supplement to the History of Roman Art.* London: Phaidon Press, 1971.

## ART FORM

Ancient coins and engraved gems have several common features. Both media survive in vast numbers, which allows for fairly complete reconstructions of their stylistic and thematic developments. Furthermore, artisans of surpassing skill were obviously employed to work in both media, for there are many exquisite miniature masterpieces in both. On the other hand, unlike coins, the designs of ancient gems were usually worked in intaglio, and a greater variety of materials—various colored stones and glass as well as metals—were used in their manufacture. In addition, while coins were minted by government authorities for public circulation, gems were usually made for private individuals for use as personal seals. Thus each gem was unique, and had a special significance for the person for whom it was created. Gems were often perforated to

188

serve as bezels in swivel rings or as pendants; unperforated examples were set into finger rings.

The designs on engraved gems exhibit a great variety, as would be expected for this personalized art form. Common themes on the gems are gods and goddesses, heroes, monsters, religious and secular scenes from daily life, animals, and various objects and symbols with magical powers. Portraits frequently appear on Hellenistic and Roman gems, and they are often less damaged and more delicately worked than portraits on coins. Three types of inscriptions are present amid these pictorial motifs: labels for the figures represented, the names of the gem owners, and artists' signatures. The first two types are usually in larger letters and in more conspicuous positions than the occasional artists' signatures.

The stylistic progression towards greater naturalism that can be observed in Greek sculpture is paralleled in engraved gems. In Greek gems, therefore, Geometric, Orientalizing, Archaic, Classical, and Hellenistic phases can be discerned. Stylistic changes in Greek gems were imitated in Etruscan products, as were Greek myths. Roman Republican gems were influenced by both contemporary Hellenistic and Etruscan gems. Many Roman Imperial gems recall Greek prototypes from various periods with mythological themes, while others show detailed scenes of contemporary life. The latter category of genre themes on Roman gems does not appear in the more formal repertoire of ancient coin types.

# RESEARCH USE

Richter's two-volume study provides a comprehensive introduction to the engraved gems of the Greeks, Etruscans, and Romans. Her stated goal in part 1, on Greek and Etruscan gems, is "to trace the evolution of styles and subjects within the framework of our present knowledge of Greek and Etruscan art" (p. xi). Part 2, devoted to Roman gems, presents the gems "in two broad categories of Republican and Imperial," within which the examples are arranged by thematic content (p. vii). While not attempting to include all known ancient gems, Richter describes and illustrates a large representative selection from major museums in Europe and the United States: 870 gems are cataloged in part 1, and 800 in part 2. Bibliographic citations are provided for all the gems that have been published previously, and both volumes also include general bibliographies. Thus Richter's volumes are invaluable for the researcher beginning work on a particular period of ancient gems; the stylistic progression in the treatment of standard figure types; the materials used for gems; engravers; classes of themes and specific themes; and the ancient literary sources and modern bibliography on gems.

# ORGANIZATION

Each of the two volumes in *The Engraved Gems* opens with a preface in which Richter outlines the scope of the contents. It is important to note that part 1 describes intaglio engravings on gemstones and on rings made entirely of metal. Both volumes include examples of molded glass gems with intaglio designs. Part 1 also presents a number of cameos from the Hellenistic period, and part 2 describes many Roman cameos. Unlike the designs of other classes of gemstones, the designs of cameos were worked in relief. All the gems discussed are illustrated with black-and-white photographs. The impression of each gem is always shown in a photo enlarged to triple the diameter of the actual gem. Wherever possible, a photograph of the gem which reproduces its actual scale is placed next to the enlargement of the gem's impression. Pages 10–11 of part 1 display color photos of a representative sample of the types of stones and other materials that were commonly decorated with engraved designs in antiquity.

The "Directions for the Use of the Book" immediately follows the preface in parts 1 and 2. Here Richter specifies the standard information supplied for each gem: the material, dimensions, provenance (when known), present location with inventory number, description of the engraved design and the transcription and translation of any inscriptions, and bibliographic citations. In part 1, a brief description of a gem's shape is often provided. Any evidence in the form of artistic parallels from additional gems, coins, or other media that is helpful in dating the gem or identifying the engraved motifs is also discussed.

General information relevant to all periods discussed in each volume is contained in a chapter entitled "General Introduction." Here, aspects such as the main uses of the gems, popular engraved devices, techniques of execution, materials, and engravers' signatures are reviewed.

The Greek and Etruscan gems in *The Engraved Gems*, part 1, are presented in twelve chapters of text which follow the "General Introduction." Each chapter is devoted to a particular period of gem production and, where it is discernible, a regional style. The periods covered are Geometric through Hellenistic. The Roman gems from *The Engraved Gems*, part 2, are discussed in four chapters covering broader time-frames. Republican gems are arranged stylistically into chapters on Etruscanizing and Hellenizing examples. All unsigned Imperial gems can be found in a single long chapter. A shorter chapter begins with a summary of our scanty knowledge—derived from ancient literary sources and signatures on gems—regarding the careers of Roman gem engravers whose names are known; the Imperial gems bearing the engravers' signatures are then described. A final chapter outlines ways in which ancient gems can be distinguished from modern forgeries. This chapter includes descriptions and illustrations of forgeries that were signed by eighteenth- and early-nineteenth-century engravers, with signatures consisting of Greek transliterations of their actual names.

The chapters in both volumes always open with a valuable prose introduction outlining common features of style, format, thematic content, and usage. Briefer comments often precede the groups of gems within the chapters. Groups of gems are composed of gems with different themes but with the same figure type (such as "Nude male figures showing the development in the rendering of the structure of the human body") and gems exhibiting the same thematic content. The most important categories of themes considered are deities, monsters, heroes, scenes from daily life, animals, and portraits of revered men of the past and contemporary figures.

In both volumes, the plates immediately follow the text. After the plates are the general bibliographies, "Sources of Photographs," "List of Inscribed Gems" (only in part 1), indexes of collections whose gems are described, and the indexes of the gems' themes and of people and places mentioned in the text (the latter index includes gem engravers whose names are known).

## COMPLEMENTARY REFERENCES

Richter does not include engraved gems from the Bronze Age in her two-volume study. One reference by Paul Yule, *Early Cretan Seals: A Study of Chronology*, presents a comprehensive classification of all Minoan seals from the Early and Middle Bronze Ages (the latter includes the First Palace-Building phase on Crete). Different chapters of this reference review "the stratigraphic basis for dating, the typology of shape/material combinations, decorative elements (i.e., thematic content), syntax, materials and carving techniques." A final chapter describes the style groups, which are based on the evidence outlined in previous chapters. All known examples from each group are listed, and bibliographic citations are provided for them in the form of the abbreviations explained at the front of the reference. Drawings and photographs of seal shapes and motifs accompany the textual discussion. An encyclopedic corpus of motifs on Late Bronze Age gems and signet rings—*The Iconography of Late Minoan and Mycenaean Sealstones and Finger Rings*—has been compiled by J. G. Younger. This reference presents more than 2,600 Late-Bronze-Age motifs that comprise both major thematic components and subsidiary components on sealstones and rings. Motifs consist of animals, human figures in various activities including religious ones, and plants. For the arrangement of motifs, the researcher should consult the table of contents; the introduction and abbreviations explain the complicated format of the entries for motifs. The lengthy catalog of motifs is accompanied by line drawings of selected examples. At the back of the reference is a general bibliography and a bibliography of readings on specific motifs (the "Iconographic Bibliography").

Another useful source of bibliography beyond what is listed in Richter's work is the second edition of *Greek and Roman Jewellery*, by Reynold Alleyne Higgins. The abbreviations at the front of this volume refer to a number of general references and archaeological reports of excavated caches of ancient jewelry and gems, and the bibliography at the back lists more general studies, catalogs of collections, works on different jewelry-making techniques, and reports on important finds of jewelry (the last are arranged in accordance with their introduction in the text). Finger rings, which often incorporated engraved seals or sealstones, are among the categories of jewelry that are discussed in the chronologically arranged and illustrated chapters. This reference summarizes our knowledge of jewelry from the Greek Bronze and Iron Ages, and from the different phases of Etruscan and Roman production.

Three surveys of the literature on ancient gems can be consulted as supplements to both the bibliography and the methodology in Richter's reference. Two of them are by Marianne Maaskant-Kleibrink: "A Survey of Glyptic Research in Publication During 1960–1968"; and "A Critical Survey of Studies on Glyptic Art Published Between ca. 1970–1980." In both review articles, the author attempts to "bring out which problems have been solved and which ones remain to be discussed." The third survey, a book catalog by Derek J. Content, is entitled *Glyptic Arts— Ancient Jewelry: An Annotated Bibliography.* Like the two review articles by Maaskant-Kleibrink, this catalog covers the literature on Greek Bronze-Age gems as well as later Greek, Etruscan, and Roman gems. It also includes literature on Near Eastern and postclassical gems.

On page 145 of "A Critical Survey," Maaskant-Kleibrink claims that in part 2 of Richter's *Engraved Gems* (the part devoted to Roman gems), "the dating . . . is no longer 'up to date.' " Researchers who wish to examine what Maaskant-Kleibrink considers to be current dating techniques may use as an examplar the same author's dissertation, *Classification of Ancient Engraved Gems: A Study Based on the Collection in the Royal Coin Cabinet, The Hague, with a History of That Collection.* Here the determining criteria for dating were: "the material and the shape of the stone since it may be supposed that these features were most dependent on changes in 'fashion' . . . style and engraving techniques . . . (and) the motif the gem bore." The selected catalog entries in this dissertation include detailed descriptions of all these aspects for each gem, along with citations of additional gems with the same engraved motifs.

*Die antiken Gemmen* (Ancient Gems), by Peter Zazoff, supplements both the bibliography and the scope of material in Richter's two volumes. Besides the general references in the "Abkürzungsverzeichnis" (List of Abbreviations), each chapter has a bibliography at the beginning; further literature is cited in the footnotes, and the first part of the text in many chapters summarizes past and current research. This exhaustive handbook thoroughly investigates Iron-Age Greek, Etruscan, and Roman gems, and also introduces periods of gem production not discussed by Richter—the Bronze Age, Christian, Medieval, and Renaissance to contemporary times. All types of gems are discussed except cameos and metal rings. The style, thematic content, materials, and provenances are elucidated in the chapters on gems from the different ancient periods. Information on engravers is presented when evidence is available. This reference is illustrated with line drawings and black-and-white photos.

### Bibliographic Entries for Complementary References

Content, Derek J. *Glyptic Arts—Ancient Jewelry: An Annotated Bibliography.* Contributions by Bernadette H. Willette. Houlton, Maine: Derek J. Content Rare Books, 1985.

Higgins, Reynold Alleyne. *Greek and Roman Jewellery.* 2d ed. Berkeley and Los Angeles: Univ. of California Press, 1980.

Maaskant-Kleibrink, Marianne. *Classification of Ancient Engraved Gems: A Study Based on the Collection in the Royal Coin Cabinet, The Hague, with a History of That Collection.* Diss., Rijksuniversiteit at Leiden, 1975. Leiden: Boerhaavezalen, 1975.

———. "A Critical Survey of Studies on Glyptic Art Published Between ca. 1970-1980." *Bulletin Antieke Beschaving* 58 (1983): 132-77.

———. "A Survey of Glyptic Research in Publication During 1960-1968." *Bulletin Antieke Beschaving* 44 (1969): 166-80.

Younger, J. G. *The Iconography of Late Minoan and Mycenaean Sealstones and Finger Rings.* Bristol: Bristol Classical Press, 1988.

Yule, Paul. *Early Cretan Seals: A Study of Chronology.* Marburger Studien zur Vor- und Frühgeschichte, no. 4. Mainz am Rhein: P. von Zabern, 1980.

Zazoff, Peter. *Die antiken Gemmen.* Handbuch der Archäologie. Munich: C. H. Beck, 1983.

# HANDBOOKS

In *Engraved Gems: The Ionides Collection,* John Boardman reviews the principal shapes, materials, themes, and styles of Greek gems from the sixth century B.C. onwards, and of Etruscan and Roman gems. Additional chapters outline the differences between ancient and postclassical gems and give the history of the Ionides Collection in London, whose gems are presented throughout the volume as examples of different periods. The influence of Greek gems on Etruscan and Roman products is emphasized throughout, and any common features of style and thematic content that relate gems to other ancient art forms are pointed out. Color and black-and-white enlargements and actual-size photographs of gems from the Ionides Collection accompany the textual discussion. Annotated catalog entries and a brief bibliography and list of abbreviations appear at the back.

*The Engraved Gems of Classical Times with a Catalogue of the Gems in the Fitzwilliam Museum,* a handbook and catalog by J. Henry Middleton which was first published in 1891, contains much useful information, although it is clearly outdated in some regards. (For example, the conclusion, stated on page 17, that the gold signet rings from the tombs at Mycenae were "Oriental imports" has now been supplanted by the belief that the rings were made by Cretan artists.) Particularly valuable portions of the text are the chapters on Roman gems, cameos, and inscriptions of owners' and artists' names on gems. These chapters summarize information on gem use, themes, and engravers that has been derived from extant ancient gems and from surviving comments from ancient literary sources. Chapters 8 ("The Characteristics of Ancient Gems") and 10 ("Gems in Mediaeval Times") familiarize the reader with the distinguishing features of postclassical gems from two classes: gems that were intended to be considered contemporary creations, and gems that were passed off as ancient works. The illustrated catalog of the gems in the Fitzwilliam Museum, which includes Iron-Age Greek and Roman pieces and postclassical creations and forgeries, can be found at the back of the volume. At the front is a bibliography of eighteenth- and nineteenth-century references on gems.

While some phases of development have been broken down further, by later researchers, Adolf Furtwängler's classification of ancient gems in *Die antiken Gemmen: Geschichte der Steinschneidekunst im klassischen Altertum* (Ancient Gems: History of Engraved Stones in Classical Antiquity) is still the standard framework for gem attribution and chronology. The first volume of Furtwängler's reference consists of actual-size photoengravings of impressions from Near Eastern, Greek, Etruscan, Roman, and postclassical engraved gems. The second volume contains detailed descriptions of the gems illustrated in volume 1, with bibliography; for any given description, the reader also needs to consult the additions and corrections at the back of volume 2. In the third volume, Furtwängler explains the basis for his broad chronological groupings and describes the gems in each group. This volume also includes a brief chapter on postclassical gems and forgeries, a chapter on different types of ancient gemstones and the techniques of working them, and an overview of the literature, beginning in the sixteenth century. Indexes can be found at the backs of volumes 2 and 3.

*Greek Gems and Finger Rings: Early Bronze Age to Late Classical*, a second study by John Boardman, provides a more comprehensive coverage than in *Engraved Gems: The Ionides Collection* of the Greek material while adopting a similar emphasis on gem shapes, materials, themes, and styles, and on the relationship between gems and other media such as vase-painting. As the title indicates, this large study begins with gems from the Bronze Age and ends its detailed treatment with the Late Classical period. Boardman states on page 9 that the gems from the eighth through the sixth centuries B.C. are treated from an historical standpoint. He advises the reader to consult his additional studies, *Island Gems* and *Archaic Greek Gems* (see Supplementary Sources below), for a full explanation of his stylistic groupings of the gems from these centuries. A brief chapter in *Greek Gems and Finger Rings* introduces Greek Hellenistic and Roman Republican and Early Imperial gems, and the final chapter reviews the different materials and techniques of gem production. More than one thousand Greek gems from different periods are discussed in the text, cataloged, and illustrated with black-and-white and color enlargements, making Boardman's selection of Greek specimens more extensive than Richter's. Notes for the text, a list of abbreviations, and a "Summary Gazetteer of Collections" appear at the back of the volume.

*Ashmolean Museum, Oxford. Catalogue of the Engraved Gems and Finger Rings: I. Greek and Etruscan*, by John Boardman and Marie-Louise Vollenweider, complements the material in *Greek Gems and Finger Rings*, *Island Gems*, and *Archaic Greek Gems*. Extensive introductory information and detailed catalog entries, both by Marie-Louise Vollenweider, are provided on gems and rings from the Hellenistic period, an era not covered in Boardman's three references. Vollenweider's introduction includes a valuable chart of the stones that were commonly used for Hellenistic gems. Briefer introductions and catalog entries are provided by Boardman for Greek Geometric through Classical, Greco-Persian, and Etruscan gems and rings in the Ashmolean Museum. Besides the black-and-white enlargements of the gems and their impressions, this catalog includes drawings of many of the gems' shapes. Abbreviations for publications referred to in the notes and the catalog entries can be found at the front of the volume.

Two comprehensive references attempt to reconstruct the sequence of production of Etruscan gems. The corpus by Peter Zazoff, entitled *Etruskische Skarabäen* (Etruscan Scarabs), presents a series of chronological groups and a complete catalog of Etruscan scarabs, that is, gems shaped like beetles. The catalog is arranged according to the thematic content of the engraved bases of the beetle-shaped gems. In the second reference, *Die etruskische Ringsteinglyptik* (Etruscan Engraved Ring

Stones), Wolfram Martini proposes a series of chronological groups for the second category of Etruscan engraved gems, the ring stones; significantly, Martini demonstrates that the earliest ring-stone engravings are stylistically and iconographically related to the designs on contemporary scarab bases. Martini's catalog of examples, including many but not all known ring stones, is organized chronologically. Thematic access to this catalog is provided by the index entitled "Themenkatalog" (Thematic Catalog).

"Gemme romane di età imperiale: produzione, commerci, committenze" (Roman Imperial Gems: Production, Markets, Commissions), by Gemma Sena Chiesa and Giuliana M. Facchini, is an up-to-date review of major studies pertaining to Roman gems; archaeologically recorded finds of gems; ancient Roman centers of production that are attested by caches of discards and unfinished pieces; and all the stylistic phases of Late Republican and Imperial gems. This model of careful scholarship is accompanied by color and black-and-white plates, a list of bibliographic abbreviations, and copious footnotes.

In her book entitled *Die Steinschneidekunst und ihre Künstler in spätrepublikanischer und augusteischer Zeit* (Engraved Gems and Their Artists in Late Republican and Augustan Times), Marie-Louise Vollenweider uses the style and thematic content of Roman gems from the Late Republican period and the age of Augustus as her evidence for a reconstruction of the cultural climate and political ideals of Roman leaders during this important century in Rome's history. In this study, Vollenweider summarizes our knowledge of the careers of specific Roman gem engravers, and draws conclusions regarding the significance of the engraved motifs and the use of the gems by Roman leaders and members of their families. This reference has black-and-white photos of gems and their impressions and of stylistically related coins; these are accompanied by a descriptive catalog ("Verzeichnis der Tafeln"), which refers the reader to textual discussions. Following the catalog is a list of bibliographic abbreviations and a table of Greek inscriptions that appear on the gems.

*Die Porträtgemmen der römischen Republik* (The Portrait Gems of the Roman Republic), also by Vollenweider, is a compilation of all known Roman portraits on gems from the Republican era. These portraits must be studied separately from coin portraits because their style is often very different. In terms of significance, they seem to embody various ethical ideals, and they also fill in gaps in historical evidence; falling into the latter category are the gems from Augustus's early supremacy in which the revered leader was shown as Neptune and as other gods. The first volume of this reference consists of the illustrated catalog, which is divided into Italic portraits in a local style, and later portraits of Roman leaders, which took on new, more individualized forms as a result of influence from Greek Hellenistic portraiture. The second volume explains the author's chronologically arranged stylistic groups, along with her hypotheses on the significance of the gem portraits. Immediately following the text in volume 2 is a list of bibliographic abbreviations.

*Musée d'art et d'histoire de Genève: Catalogue raisonné des sceaux cylindres et intailles* (Museum of Art and History at Geneva: Catalogue Raisonné of the Cylinder Seals and Intaglios), a lengthy catalog by Vollenweider of a major gem collection in Geneva, supplements the same author's other major studies with the inclusion in volume 2 of a series of gem portraits of Roman emperors. The catalog entries for these portraits include lengthy descriptions and justifications for dating. Stylistically similar portraits from coins often provide the basis for dating. Volume 2 of this catalog also includes Hellenistic and Roman Republican portraits, Roman gems bearing motifs from the theater, and Greek and Roman gems displaying symbols of different types. Volume 1 of the catalog has entries for Near Eastern, Greek, and Etruscan gems. In addition to its detailed catalog entry, each gem is always illustrated with an enlargement taken from an impression of the gem or the gem itself.

Cameos from the first and second centuries of the Roman Imperial period form the focus of the study by Wolf-Rüdiger Megow entitled *Kameen von Augustus bis Alexander Severus* (Cameos from Augustus to Alexander Severus). In the introduction, the author argues that our surviving Imperial cameos once belonged to Imperial collections which were dispersed through Europe from Constantinople by events such as the plundering that took place at the time of the fourth Crusade in 1204. The text of this reference consists of explanations of the different stylistic phases of cameo production. These chapters are followed by an exhaustive illustrated catalog of examples, arranged chronologically.

## Bibliographic Entries for Handbooks

Boardman, John. *Engraved Gems: The Ionides Collection.* Evanston, Ill.: Northwestern Univ. Press, 1968.

——. *Greek Gems and Finger Rings: Early Bronze Age to Late Classical.* New York: Abrams, 1970.

Boardman, John, and Marie-Louise Vollenweider. *Ashmolean Museum, Oxford. Catalogue of the Engraved Gems and Finger Rings: I. Greek and Etruscan.* Oxford: Clarendon Press, 1978.

Furtwängler, Adolf. *Die antiken Gemmen: Geschichte der Steinschneidekunst im klassischen Altertum.* Vol. 1, *Tafel.* Vol. 2, *Erklärung der Tafeln.* Vol. 3, *Geschichte der Steinschneidekunst im klassischen Altertum.* Leipzig and Berlin: Giesecke & Devrient, 1900. Reprint. Amsterdam: A. M. Hakkert, 1963.

Martini, Wolfram. *Die etruskische Ringsteinglyptik.* Mitteilungen des Deutschen Archäologischen Instituts. Römische Abteilung. Ergänzungsheft 18. Heidelberg: F. H. Kerle, 1971.

Megow, Wolf-Rüdiger. *Kameen von Augustus bis Alexander Severus.* Antike Münzen und geschnittene Steine 11. Berlin: Walter de Gruyter, 1987.

Middleton, J. Henry. *The Engraved Gems of Classical Times with a Catalogue of the Gems in the Fitzwilliam Museum.* Cambridge: Univ. Press, 1891. Reprint. *Ancient Gems: The Engraved Gems of Classical Times.* Chicago: Argonaut, 1969.

Sena Chiesa, Gemma, and Giuliana M. Facchini. "Gemme romane di età imperiale: produzione, commerci, committenze." In *Aufstieg und Niedergang der römischen Welt: Geschichte und Kultur Roms im Spiegel der neureren Forschung 2, Principat* 12.3, 3–31. Berlin and New York: Walter de Gruyter, 1985.

Vollenweider, Marie-Louise. *Musée d'art et d'histoire de Genève: Catalogue raisonné des sceaux cylindres et intailles.* Vol. 1. Geneva: Musée d'art et d'histoire, 1967. Vol. 2, *Les portraits, les masques de théatre, les symboles politiques: Une contribution à l'histoire des civilisations hellénistique et romaine.* Mainz am Rhein: P. von Zabern, 1976–79.

——. *Die Porträtgemmen der römischen Republik.* Vol. 1, *Katalog und Tafeln.* Vol. 2, *Text.* Mainz am Rhein: P. von Zabern, 1972–74.

——. *Die Steinschneidekunst und ihre Künstler in spätrepublikanischer und augusteischer Zeit.* Baden-Baden: Bruno Grimm, 1966.

Zazoff, Peter. *Etruskische Skarabäen.* Mainz am Rhein: P. von Zabern, 1968.

# SUPPLEMENTARY SOURCES

The first step in the study of seals from any given period is their classification, or organization into a series of sequential groupings. Such a classification is attempted by John Boardman for the Early Iron-Age seals of stone and ivory from the eighth, seventh, and sixth centuries B.C. Boardman's study, entitled *Island Gems: A Study of Greek Seals in the Geometric and Early Archaic Periods*, summarizes our knowledge of the Greek gems from these centuries that were manufactured in the Cycladic Islands and on the Greek mainland. Emphasis is given to seals from recorded excavations; these are used as foundations for both the chronology and the attribution of classes of seals, which are separately described and accompanied by comprehensive lists of examples. The author claims to have included "all published examples as well as the unpublished stones in the major collections." An article by the same author, "Island Gems Aftermath," records "additions and corrections to *Island Gems*" and discusses "a class of engraved stones which was not properly distinguished in that book." This class of gems is attributed by Boardman to workshops in the Cycladic Islands and is dated to "the middle and second half of the sixth century."

Another reference by John Boardman, *Archaic Greek Gems: Schools and Artists in the Sixth and Early Fifth Centuries B.C.*, classifies Greek gems with a different appearance and of different material, which were produced during the Archaic period. Unlike the simpler shapes of the gems discussed in *Island Gems*, these gems were cut in the scarab shape. Furthermore, instead of being made of steatite or ivory, these gems were manufactured out of harder stones from the chalcedony family, which required the use of the drill and cutting wheel. According to the author, *Archaic Greek Gems* is a "first attempt to sort out the material and present it in a manageable form." The "material" consists of Greek and Etruscan Archaic gemstones called scarabs which were cut in an articulated shape resembling the beetle that bears this name; and gemstones called scaraboids which are roughly blocked out but unarticulated beetle shapes. Both scarabs and scaraboids bear engraved designs on their flat, oval bases. In this reference, Boardman presents groups of Archaic scarabs and scaraboids from major collections in Europe and the United States, and from publications. He lists all known examples from each group, explains the common features of their engraved bases, and when it is possible, suggests a region or place of manufacture. The latter were determined on the basis of provenances, scarab shapes, and features of style that were shared with other art forms which have established places of manufacture.

Aquileia, a Roman city on the Adriatic, is unique among Roman settlements in being the known provenance for over 1,500 Roman gems, now in the city's Museo Nazionale. Of additional interest is evidence, in the form of unworked blocks of semiprecious stones and unfinished gems, which points to the conclusion that most of the gems found at Aquileia were also manufactured there in local workshops. In the publication *Gemme del Museo Nazionale di Aquileia* (Gems from the Museo Nazionale of Aquileia), Gemma Sena Chiesa suggests attributions of some of the gems from the lengthy catalog to specific workshops. She also proposes, on the basis of the gems from Aquileia, a refined chronology for Roman gem production which breaks down Furtwängler's periods into more subtle developments. Unfortunately, as Maaskant-Kleibrink has already observed (see "A Survey of Glyptic Research," pp. 173–74, from Complementary References above), the quality and size of Sena Chiesa's photographs of gem impressions are too fuzzy and small to allow the reader to independently evaluate the validity of the workshop attributions, or to easily observe the stylistic differences in Sena Chiesa's developmental phases.

The issue of whether certain themes on gems were popular with certain classes of society is a fascinating one. In the article "The Veneration of Heroes in the Roman Army: The Evidence of Engraved Gemstones," Martin Henig proposes that gems with heroic themes were frequently the property of officers in the Roman army because these men saw themselves as "inheritors of a glorious tradition established by heroes who had overcome all difficulties" (p. 249). He concludes further that "heroic gems were worn as a spur to action: the deeds of Hercules, Achilles, Odysseus, Theseus and Romulus were patterns for the soldier to follow" (p. 263). Besides presenting these conclusions, Henig's article reviews the evidence of gems with heroic themes and their archaeological contexts, which are often identified as the forts Roman soldiers lived in. Also surveyed are heroic scenes in other artistic media, which often appear to come from Roman military contexts.

One of the most difficult problems that confronts the archaeologist is determining the accuracy of miniature copies of lost statues. In *Statuen auf Gemmen* (Statues on Gems), Gertrud Horster investigates the conventions evident in copies of Greek statues on Roman gems. By comparing gem copies with coin copies of the same statues, the author concludes that engravers of both media generally did not work directly from the statues themselves. Instead they used as the basis for their designs drawings of the statues, which were altered when new aesthetic preferences required changes such as different viewing angles. This interesting study is illustrated by reproductions of gem and coin copies of the same statues.

Gems and a knowledge of them have been preserved through the ages by independent collectors. One of the most superb early cabinets of ancient gems was formed by the renowned Flemish painter, Peter Paul Rubens. His collecting activities, with special emphasis on his gem collection, form the focus of the study by Marjon van der Meulen entitled *Petrus Paulus Rubens Antiquarius: Collector and Copyist of Antique Gems.* Using the evidence of previously unpublished inventories of some of the gems in Rubens's collection, as well as descriptions from correspondence, and drawings and engravings of the gems by Rubens and others, van der Meulen has been able to reconstruct a large part of the collection and actually locate some of the gems and impressions made from them in the Bibliothèque Nationale in Paris. Studies such as this one, with an emphasis on discovering specific information about collections, can be used as foundations for suggestions regarding the copying of particular antiquities.

*Bibliographic Entries for Supplementary Sources*

Boardman, John. *Archaic Greek Gems: Schools and Artists in the Sixth and Early Fifth Centuries B.C.* Evanston, Ill.: Northwestern Univ Press, 1968.

———. *Island Gems: A Study of Greek Seals in the Geometric and Early Archaic Periods.* Supplementary Paper no. 10. London: Society for the Promotion of Hellenic Studies, 1963.

———. "Island Gems Aftermath." *Journal of Hellenic Studies* 88 (1968): 1–12.

Henig, Martin. "The Veneration of Heroes in the Roman Army: The Evidence of Engraved Gemstones." *Britannia: A Journal of Romano-British and Kindred Studies* 1 (1970): 249–65.

Horster, Gertrud. *Statuen auf Gemmen.* Habelts Dissertationsdrücke: Reihe klassische Archäologie 3. Bonn: Rudolf Habelt, 1970.

Meulen, Marjon van der. *Petrus Paulus Rubens Antiquarius: Collector and Copyist of Antique Gems.* Alphen aan den Rijn: Canaletto, 1975.

Sena Chiesa, Gemma. *Gemme del Museo Nazionale di Aquileia.* 2 vols. Aquileia: Associazione nazionale per Aquileia, 1966.

## Additional Supplementary Sources

Boardman, John. "Greek Gem Engravers, Their Subjects and Style." In *Ancient Art in Seals,* edited by Edith Porada, 101–19. Princeton: Princeton Univ. Press, 1980.

Femmel, Gerhard, and Gerald Heres. *Die Gemmen aus Goethes Sammlung.* Goethes Sammlungen zur Kunst, Literatur und Naturwissenschaft. Leipzig: E. A. Seemann, 1977.

Richter, Gisela M. A. "Inscriptions on Engraved Gems of the Roman Period and Some Modern or Problematical Representations." *Archeologia Classica* 25–26 (1973–74): 631–38.

Weingarten, Judith. *The Zakro Master and His Place in Prehistory.* Göteborg: Paul Astrom, 1983.

Zazoff, Peter and Hilde. *Gemmensammler und Gemmenforscher: Von einer noblen Passion zur Wissenschaft.* Munich: C. H. Beck, 1983.

# ⟨14⟩

# Greek Coins

Head, Barclay Vincent. *Historia Numorum: A Manual of Greek Numismatics.* 2d ed. Oxford: Clarendon Press, 1911. Reprint. London: Spink & Son, 1977.

Head, Barclay Vincent, and John N. Svoronos. *The Illustrations of Historia Numorum: An Atlas of Greek Numismatics.* 2d ed. Chicago: Ares, 1976.

## ART FORM

Our knowledge of ancient coins is far more complete than the fragmentary record of larger types of artifacts. Not only are single coins discovered in excavations, but also groups of coins from ancient hoards (small or large caches of coins buried in ancient times) are constantly being unearthed both on excavation sites and in modern construction projects. Coins were first minted in Asia Minor in the seventh century B.C. The earliest Greek coins were irregularly shaped metallic nuggets, usually of electrum, that were stamped with a recognizable design. The principal design represented is called the "type." From the sixth century onwards, relief designs were stamped on both the obverse (front) and reverse (back) of coins. From the early fifth century until the late fourth century B.C., the obverse design often consisted of the head of a god or hero. On the reverse was a symbol associated with the god appearing on the obverse (such as Apollo's lyre), a sacred animal, a local product, or a representation of a local myth or monument. After the death of Alexander the Great, portraits of rulers as well as heads of divinities frequently appeared on the obverses of Hellenistic coins. The obverses of Greek coins minted under Roman rule often bore the head of the current Roman Emperor as a compliment to his authority, while the reverses advertised a local feature.

Numismatics, the study of coins, is important not only because coins are official state documents, affording evidence on political, historical, and economic questions, but also because they can be miniature masterpieces of harmonious design and idealized form. The heads on the obverses of Greek coins are rendered in high relief and exhibit a stylistic development which parallels contemporary large-scale sculptures. The reverses of Greek coins are carefully designed for the coins' circular shape and often achieve graceful naturalism in the treatment of individual figures.

## RESEARCH USE

*Historia Numorum* (History of Coins) is the most comprehensive handbook of Greek coins. Not only does it supply surveys of the entire coin production of cities, kings, and dynasts from all the Greek periods (700–27 B.C.), but it also outlines the numismatic history of all cities except Rome during the Roman Imperial age (27 B.C.–268 A.D.). Therefore, this reference can be used by researchers wishing to review the entire minting activity of a single ancient city or ruler, or to compare the coin outputs of more than one city from the same region or under the same or a similar government. In his accounts of the coinages of particular cities, Head stresses the relationship between specific historical events and coins issued in response to these events. Thus his reference is especially valuable for the initial investigation of a limited series of issues (outputs of coinage by the same minting authority), since it permits them to be perceived in their proper historical context. The broad scope of Head's reference and the general index (no. 7) also enable researchers to discover what mints throughout the ancient world used the same coin types and weight standards.

## ORGANIZATION

The introductory chapter of *Historia Numorum* contains information on the metrical standards of the various regions, and essays on coin types, symbols, major stylistic divisions, and inscriptions. It also lists the titles of office and the honorary titles of the issuing authority found on coins, public games and sacred festivals celebrated by coin issues, and titles and epithets of cities. The rest of the manual is composed of three main chapters on the continents of Europe, Asia, and Africa, respectively. These chapters are arranged by countries or districts that are often further broken down into regions, following a clockwise sequence of areas around the Mediterranean. The consideration of each region begins with a bibliography; individual mints are then listed alphabetically.

Each mint is introduced with basic information about its location, historical significance, and the date of the earliest coinage. The specific issues of each mint are divided where possible into dated historical phases, which often include introductory paragraphs about the relationship between contemporary events and coin output, as well as descriptions of the coins themselves. Not all known coins from every chronological subdivision are mentioned. Instead, as Head states on page xix, his aim was to "draw attention to the leading and most characteristic coin types. . . ." The coins from the separate phases are usually described in two columns, with the obverse on the left and the reverse on the right. The following information is provided: identification of the coin types; inscriptions; the material of the coin ("AV" signifies gold, "AR" silver, "AE" bronze, and "EL" electrum); the denomination (explained on page xliv in the introduction) or the diameter, given in tenths of inches (a measurement conversion table appears on page xxxii); and the weight, given in grains. A table of weights to translate grains (abbreviated "grs.") into grams (which is the standard unit of weight for numismatists today) appears at the end of the volume.

On page xxi can be found a general bibliography of the monographs, as well as the periodicals and sales catalogs frequently consulted by the author. Six indexes at the back of the volume provide access to information from the following categories: regions and cities where coins were minted; kings and dynasts whose names appear on coins; remarkable coin inscriptions in Greek, Latin, Phoenician, Aramaic, Punic, and Hebrew (particularly references to divinities, heroes, and government bodies); Greek and Latin inscriptions from coins, giving titles and epithets of cities and mentions of sites; Greek and Latin inscriptions with "magisterial titles, offices, etc. and honorary distinctions"; and the names of Greek coin engravers. The seventh index is a general index of things, mythological personages, geographical locations exclusive of the regions and cities in index 1, and historical people other than the kings and dynasts in index 2. Along with the indexes at the end of the book are tables of all the alphabets which appear on coins.

In addition to studying the occasional illustration found in the text, the researcher can make use of the supplementary volume, *Illustrations of Historia Numorum*. Here the plates are arranged in the same order as Head's original text. After the description of each coin is a citation to the page number in *Historia Numorum* (abbreviated HN) where the coin was first presented.

## COMPLEMENTARY REFERENCES

For a more complete selection of coin types and illustrations than can be found in *Historia Numorum*, see the twenty-nine volume *Catalogue of Greek Coins in the British Museum*. This publication of one of the world's largest collections of Greek coins gives the catalog numbers, weights, metals, and sizes, with a brief description of the obverse and reverse of each coin. Plates illustrating selected coins are located at the back of many of the volumes. The catalog is not complete because the collection has been substantially augmented during this century.

Two illustrated references by David R. Sear, *Greek Coins and Their Values*, and *Greek Imperial Coins and Their Values: The Local Coinages of the Roman Empire*, can be used to update the conclusions, particularly those relating to chronology, that are presented by Head. Sear states in the preface to the first work that he has "tried to incorporate most of the current views on chronology, attribution, and interpretation of types which are the result of the immense amount of research undertaken over the past few decades by scholars in Europe and America." He also explains that he has included "representative examples of each period of issue for every mint." In the preface to *Greek Imperial Coins and Their Values*, Sear states his more limited aim of including "representative examples from the majority of mints active under each reign" of the Roman emperors. Besides covering the Archaic, Classical, and Hellenistic coins produced by mints in the different Greek regions, *Greek Coins and Their Values* discusses "Celtic issues of western Europe (including Britain) and the Danubian area" and the issues of "the Persian Empire, the Hellenistic Kingdoms and subsequent autonomous issues, North Africa and Carthage." *Greek Imperial Coins and Their Values* presents the coins minted by Greek cities during the period of Roman rule and "the coinages of independent kingdoms and client states whose issues were contemporary with Roman Imperial times." Both references present bibliographies at the fronts of the volumes, and maps showing the locations of mints at the backs.

*Archaic and Classical Greek Coins*, by Colin Kraay, provides an excellent modern overview of Greek coins from the period 600 to 280 B.C. Since Kraay provides fuller accounts than Head of the historical circumstances behind the minting activities of Greek cities and often proposes revisions in Head's chronology, this reference should always be consulted along with *Historia Numorum*. It has the added benefit of reproducing in its plates more than twice the number of coins in Head's *Illustrations of Historia Numorum*. A forthcoming publication, which will appear about June 1991, is Otto Mørkholm's *Early Hellenistic Coinage from the Accession of Alexander to the Peace of Apamea (336–188 BC)*. The press release for this book states: "This is the first full study of early Hellenistic coinage to be published. It provides a general history of the coinage of Alexander the Great and his successors, and of the cities of Greece and Asia Minor, over the century and a half 336–188 BC. Dr. Mørkholm's detailed descriptions of the coins and the 40 pages of plates illustrating over 600 items, will provide a standard work of reference for ancient historians, numismatists and collectors."

Another reference, *Die griechische Münze* (Greek Coins), by Peter Robert Franke, discusses Greek coins from the introduction of coinage to the end of the Hellenistic world, and thus can be used to supplement Head's treatments of periods not covered by Kraay. Some valuable aspects of this reference are the excellent enlarged photographs by Max Hirmer of select coins from each mint considered, which are accompanied by catalog descriptions with introductory comments on each mint; and the bibliography ("Schrifttum") at the end of the volume, which is arranged by regions and mints. *Greek Coins*, by Colin M. Kraay, has the same beautiful plates as *Die griechische Münze*, but the English text is different. Besides being in English, Kraay's study has several other features which facilitate its use. One is the subheadings, such as "The Types of Greek Coins," which break up the text in the first chapter. Furthermore, unlike Franke's book, where all the bibliography is at the end, Kraay handily follows his introductions to different regions and mints with bibliography. Only general references appear in the "Select Bibliography" at the end of the volume.

Most general handbooks on Greek coinage do not consider coins with Greek inscriptions that were mostly bronzes minted in the eastern Mediterranean under Roman rule (but see Sear's *Greek Imperial Coins and Their Values* discussed above). An exception to this rule is *A Guide to the Principal Coins of the Greeks from circ. 700 B.C. to A.D. 270 Based on the Work of Barclay V. Head*, by G. F. Hill. Here, four plates and the accompanying descriptions are devoted to these interesting coins which often reproduce local monuments. Unfortunately, emperors' names, but not their dates, are provided. A selection of these same late Greek bronze coins is discussed, cataloged (with dates given) and illustrated in the recent study by Cornelius C. Vermeule, *Divinities and Mythological Scenes in Greek Imperial Art*. The notes which precede Vermeule's illustrations provide bibliography on each coin. A fuller presentation of the late Greek coins from Asia Minor (Western Turkey) appears in *Sylloge Nummorum Graecorum Deutschland: Sammlung v. Aulock* (Corpus of Greek Coins, Germany: The von Aulock Collection), the eighteen-volume publication of coins from the large von Aulock collection, which forms part of the ongoing worldwide series of numismatic catalogs, *Sylloge Nummorum Graecorum* (Corpus of Greek Coins). *Roman Provincial Coins: An Introduction to 'Greek Imperials,'* by Kevin Butcher, presents a representative sample of coins produced during the Roman Empire in the Roman provinces. This concise reference forms an introduction not only to Greek "imperials" (Greek coins minted during the period of the Roman Empire) but also to provincial coins minted in other areas such as Spain, Gaul, and North Africa. Butcher includes all locally minted issues of limited circulation in his definition of provincial coinage.

In the fascicles of the *Sylloge Nummorum Graecorum* (mentioned in the previous paragraph), the obverse and reverse of every coin from a particular mint are reproduced at actual size. The denominations and types of all the coins are identified in the descriptions. In addition, die axes, coin weights, and inscriptions are recorded. This ongoing series often suggests dates for the coins and it provides bibliographic citations for previously published coins, and often for similar coins or coins struck from the same dies. The complete publication of all Greek coins in major collections, as in the *Sylloge*, is extremely important, for the numismatist thereby has available the resources to reconstruct the sequence of issues of a city through a mint study. A mint study involves the identification, through careful visual comparison of examples, of all the obverse and reverse dies that were used to strike the surviving coins. By noting die links, small or large groups of coins that were minted sequentially can be established. Examples that turn up in the future with the same pairs of dies as previously cataloged coins, even if the dies are imperfectly preserved, can then be identified as coins struck at the same mint and at the same time as the previously known examples.

Coins are usually found by chance in hoards. The ancient caches of coins yield extensive information that numismatists use to date coins as well as to determine their circulation, and they provide examples, besides those in already published collections, that can be included in mint studies. *An Inventory of Greek Coin Hoards*, edited by Margaret Thompson, Otto Mørkholm, and Colin Kraay, lists the major Greek coin hoards from the sixth century B.C. to 30 B.C. that have been found in the areas of Greek influence around the Mediterranean and in Asia. The entries are listed geographically and contain the following information for each hoard: the place where it was found (find spot), date of discovery, burial date, general contents of the hoard (i.e., the total number of coins and their metallic abbreviation), the context in which the hoard was found (when known), the specific contents of the hoard (i.e., the mints and the number of coins and denominations from each mint), the disposition (current location), and references (where the hoard was published). For hoards discovered or known after the publication of *An Inventory of Greek Coin Hoards,* all volumes of an ongoing series entitled *Coin Hoards* should be consulted. The index at the back of each volume lists hoards by the mints, the places of discovery (in bold type), and the current locations (in italics).

Two alphabetically arranged dictionaries can be consulted for quick identifications of unpublished Greek coins with legible Greek inscriptions. Both dictionaries contain inscriptions from Greek coins of all periods, including the Roman Empire. *Dictionary of Greek Coin Inscriptions,* by Severin Icard, lists words from inscriptions of all types, such as parts of titles, and also lists fragments of inscribed words—a valuable feature since often the first letters in words are missing on coins. For brief inscriptions of one or several letters that refer to the minting city, *Geographic Lexicon of Greek Coin Inscriptions,* by A. Florance, is the easiest reference to consult. Both references provide identifications of the minting city, as well as the region where the city is located. Once a tentative reading of an inscription is made and it has been matched with a reading given by Icard or Florance, the researcher must be certain that the coin's pictorial types appear under the city's coinage as described by Head or another authority.

Richard Plant's *Greek Coin Types and Their Identification* provides another rapid method of identifying Greek coins—by the types that are shown on their reverses. The author's types are derived from Greek coins from the periods of Greek independence and Roman Imperial rule, and they include gods, heroes, monsters, animals, plants, inanimate objects, and geometric shapes. Nearly three thousand examples of these reverse coin types are illustrated with line drawings. They are accompanied by catalog entries that identify the region where the coin was minted, the mint itself, and the coin's date; describe the reverse and obverse coin types; and identify the metal, give the coin's scale, and provide weights when the coin is silver or gold. A glossary at the back, "Some Gods, Goddesses and Heroes," provides descriptions of standard numismatic types. An older typological index, but one which has photographs rather than drawings of coins and provides bibliographic citations for further publications (a feature that is absent in Plant's book), is L. Anson's six-volume *Numismata Graeca: Greek Coin Types Classified for Immediate Identification.* As Anson explains in the introduction to the first volume, his corpus is devoted to "all coin-types representing inanimate objects, plants, etc., which occur either alone or as symbols in conjunction with figures, animals, etc." As in the case of Plant's reference, Anson's corpus includes Greek coins from all periods including the Roman Imperial era. At the back of each volume is an alphabetically arranged index to the volume's contents, and there is also a general index to all six volumes.

*Numismatic Bibliography,* by E. E. Clain-Stefanelli, introduces the researcher to different categories of literature on Greek numismatics— bibliographies, general references, important collections, the coins of the different regions settled by the Greeks, and special topics that include "Coin Types and Iconography" and "Portraits." Indexes at the back provide access to literature on mythological and historical personages found on coins; mints; and coin types (for the last, see "Index of Numismatic Terms").

For the most recent books and articles on Greek numismatics in general, as well as on specific mints, the researcher is advised to consult the latest numbers of *Numismatic Literature,* published semiannually by the American Numismatic Society. The alphabetical subject index at the back of each number lists pertinent publications under each mint. Another excellent source of numismatic literature is the ongoing publication *A Survey of Numismatic Research.* Published in preparation for the meetings of the Congrès International de Numismatique (International Numismatic Congress), which are held every six years at a different location, the *Survey* includes prose summaries of research in Greek numismatics from all periods. Besides identifying trends in scholarly literature, the *Survey* suggests areas in which research is needed. Publications on particular mints can be located by consulting the summaries of the pertinent geographic regions. For additional sources of bibliography, a useful survey of the history of numismatic research, and a description of resources in major numismatic libraries and their published catalogs, the researcher should consult Francis D. Campbell's article, "Numismatic Bibliography and Libraries."

### Bibliographic Entries for Complementary References

Anson, L. *Numismata Graeca: Greek Coin Types Classified for Immediate Identification.* Part 1, *Industry: Vases, Recipients, Tripods, etc.* Part 2, *War: Arms, Weapons, Armours, Standards, etc.* London: L. Anson, 1911. Part 3, *Agriculture: Plants and Trees, Fruits, Flowers, etc.* 1912. Part 4, *Religion: Altars, Attributes of Deities, Sacrifice, etc.* 1913. Part 5, *Architecture: Buildings, Edifices, Monuments, Temples, etc. Naval and Marine: Galley and parts of, Shells, Trident, etc.* 1914. Part 6, *Science and the Arts. Various.* 1916. London: Kegan Paul, Trench, Trübner. *General Guide-Index.* London: L. Anson, 1910.

British Museum. Department of Coins and Medals. *A Catalogue of the Greek Coins in the British Museum.* 29 vols. London: The Trustees, 1873–1927.

Butcher, Kevin. *Roman Provincial Coins: An Introduction to "Greek Imperials."* London: Seaby, 1988.

Campbell, Francis D. "Numismatic Bibliography and Libraries." In *Encyclopedia of Library and Information Science.* Vol. 37, Supplement 2, 272–310. Edited by Allen Kent. New York and Basel: Marcel Dekker, 1984. Reprint. Dallas: Numismatics International, 1986.

Clain-Stefanelli, E. E. *Numismatic Bibliography.* Munich: Battenburg, 1985.
*Coin Hoards.* Vol. 1– . London: Royal Numismatic Society, 1975– .
Florance, A. *Geographic Lexicon of Greek Coin Inscriptions.* Argonaut Library of Antiquities. Chicago: Argonaut Publishers, 1966.
Franke, Peter Robert. *Die griechische Münze.* 2d ed. Munich: Hirmer, 1972.
Hill, G. F. *British Museum, Department of Coins and Medals: A Guide to the Principal Coins of the Greeks from circ. 700 B.C. to A.D. 270 Based on the Work of Barclay V. Head.* Revised by John Walker. 2d ed. London: British Museum, 1959.
Icard, Severin. *Dictionary of Greek Coin Inscriptions: Identification of Coins By the Key-Letter and Fragmented Letter Method Applied to Greek and Gallic Coins.* Translated by Elizabeth Swain. Reprint, with introduction translated. New York: Sanford J. Durst Numismatic Publications, 1979.
Kraay, Colin M. *Archaic and Classical Greek Coins.* Berkeley: Univ. of California Press, 1976.
———. *Greek Coins.* New York: Abrams, 1966.
Mørkholm, Otto. *Early Hellenistic Coinage from the Accession of Alexander to the Peace of Apamea (336–188 B.C.).* Ed. Philip Grierson and Ulla Westermark. Cambridge: Cambridge Univ. Press, forthcoming.
*Numismatic Literature.* No. 1– . New York: American Numismatic Society, 1947– .
Plant, Richard. *Greek Coin Types and Their Identification.* London: Seaby, 1979.
Sear, David R. *Greek Coins and Their Values.* Vol. 1, *Europe.* Vol. 2, *Asia and North Africa.* London: Seaby, 1978–79.
———. *Greek Imperial Coins and Their Values: The Local Coinages of the Roman Empire.* London: Seaby, 1982.
*A Survey of Numismatic Research 1960–1965; 1966–1971; 1972–1977; 1978–1984.* International Numismatic Commission, 1967– . Preceded by *Congrès Internationale de Numismatique Paris 6–11 juillet 1953.* Vol. 1, *Rapports;* and *Congresso Internazionale di Numismatica Roma 11–16 settembre 1961.* Vol. 1, *Relazioni.*
*Sylloge Nummorum Graecorum.* Ongoing international series with fascicles for Austria, Denmark, France, Germany, Great Britain, Greece, Italy, Sweden, Switzerland, and U.S.A. 1931– .
*Sylloge Nummorum Graecorum Deutschland: Sammlung v. Aulock.* Edited by Gerhard Kleiner. 18 vols. Berlin: Mann, 1957–68.
Thompson, Margaret, Otto Mørkholm, and Colin M. Kraay, eds. *An Inventory of Greek Coin Hoards.* New York: American Numismatic Society, 1973.
Vermeule, Cornelius C. *Divinities and Mythological Scenes in Greek Imperial Art.* Art of Antiquity 5.1: Numismatic Studies. Cambridge and Everett, Mass.: CopyQuik Corp., 1983.

# HANDBOOKS

*A Dictionary of Ancient Greek Coins,* by John Melville Jones, is an illustrated and alphabetically arranged handbook which provides brief "articles on specific names and technical terms," including coin types. Bibliography is not provided for the articles. *Wörterbuch der Münzkunde*

(Dictionary of Numismatics), edited by Friedrich von Schrötter, contains explanations of the denominations of Greek coins, with further bibliography cited. An excellent modern handbook that surveys Greek coin types, denominations, and minting techniques is *Ancient Greek Coins* by G. K. Jenkins. The author outlines general trends in coin types and styles from the introduction of coinage through the end of the Hellenistic period. Black-and-white and color enlargements permit a study of the coins' subtlety of execution. *Coin Types: Their Origin and Development*, by George McDonald, describes the introduction and persistence of classes of obverse and reverse coin types (e.g., heads of divinities and heroes). For the researcher wanting a brief introduction to numismatics, *Greek Coinage*, by N. K. Rutter, is recommended. Rather than attempting to survey the minting activities of all Greek cities, Rutter limits his discussion to South Italy and Sicily, Classical Athens, and the Hellenistic kingdoms. Numerous illustrations, most of them from the Hunter Coin Cabinet at the University of Glasgow, accompany Rutter's lucid text. *Coinage in the Greek World*, by Ian Carradice and Martin Price, is a sophisticated and current explanation of the minting activities of Greek city-states as responses to changing political and economic circumstances. Extensive use is made by the authors of evidence from Greek coin hoards, which often include denominations of varying values from several Greek city-states and therefore demonstrate important patterns of circulation and commercial ascendancy. Ian Carradice has also written a brief but excellent summary of a single aspect of Greek numismatics in his pamphlet, *Ancient Greek Portrait Coins*. Using coins from the British Museum as illustrations, Carradice traces coin portraits of living rulers from their introduction in fifth-century Asia Minor to the end of the Hellenistic period.

## Bibliographic Entries for Handbooks

Carradice, Ian. *Ancient Greek Portrait Coins*. London: British Museum Publications, 1978.

Carradice, Ian, and Martin Price. *Coinage in the Greek World*. London: Seaby, 1988.

Jenkins, G. K. *Ancient Greek Coins*. 2d rev. ed. Coins in History. London: Seaby, 1990.

McDonald, George. *Coin Types: Their Origin and Development*. Glasgow: J. Maclehose & Sons, 1905.

Melville Jones, John. *A Dictionary of Ancient Greek Coins*. London: Seaby, 1986.

Rutter, N. K. *Greek Coinage*. Shire Archaeology. Aylesbury, Bucks: Shire Publications Ltd., 1983.

Schrötter, Friedrich von, ed. *Wörterbuch der Münzkunde*. 1930. Reprint. Berlin: W. de Gruyter & Co., 1970.

## SUPPLEMENTARY SOURCES

Coins are extremely useful documents for reconstructing history; they can confirm accounts by ancient historians, negate them, or offer entirely new information. *The Hellenistic Kingdoms: Portrait Coins and History,* by Norman Davis and Colin M. Kraay, demonstrates the usefulness of coins as a source of evidence in "successive accounts of the kings and queens of that age, illustrated by their portrait coins." Here the lengthy captions to the coin photos, which are often enlargements, point out references on the coins to events described in the text. In *Greek Coins and History: Some Current Problems,* Colin M. Kraay utilizes evidence from hoards with Greek coins to rule out some incorrect associations of coin issues with known historical figures and events. These associations had resulted in some improbable reconstructions of the minting activities of major and less important Greek city-states. Very little is known about local politics of the Greeks living in the eastern Mediterranean during the late second and most of the third century of the late Roman Empire. Kenneth W. Harl's study, *Civic Coins and Civic Politics in the Roman East A.D. 180-275,* demonstrates how information gleaned from local bronze coins sheds some light on this dark period of history. For example, an increased emphasis on Roman coin types, such as the goddess Roma, the infants Romulus and Remus suckled by the she-wolf, and the Roman Senate personified, seems to indicate political ties of local nobility with institutions like the Senate in Rome.

One of the greatest difficulties which confronts the numismatist is the attribution of coin dies to particular artists. Since most dies are unsigned or bear abbreviated names which may not belong to artists, attributions are often made on the basis of style alone. In *Masterpieces of Greek Coinage,* Charles Seltman attempts to reconstruct the artistic careers of some eminent Greek die-engravers. Using signed dies and stylistically similar unsigned dies as evidence, Seltman suggests that the most skilled die-engravers often worked at more than one city. All coins discussed are reproduced in enlargements and in actual size, and Seltman's comments on each accent their aesthetic excellence. A more recent discussion of the problems of attributing Greek coins to specific engravers can be found in *Art and Coinage in Magna Graecia,* by R. Ross Holloway. Here the author adopts a more cautious approach than Seltman and limits most of his attributions to coins signed "in minuscule letters inconspicuously placed on the die" (p. 67). Holloway also suggests some sources in non-numismatic art forms for the designs of South Italian coins.

Coin reverses showing lost ancient monuments have been studied for the information that they yield. *Ancient Coins Illustrating Lost Masterpieces of Greek Art,* by F. W. Imhoof-Blumer and Percy Gardner, compares the written evidence from Pausanias' *Description of Greece* (see chapter 6 under Complementary References) with the pictorial evidence on coins. In *Coins and their Cities*, Martin J. Price and Bluma L. Trell discuss problems in interpreting a selection of coins which illustrate lost or incompletely preserved buildings from everywhere in the Roman Empire except Rome. *Archaeology and the Types of Greek Coins*, by Percy Gardner, surveys the artistic development and aesthetic qualities of coin types with mythological content. Types from the Archaic through the Hellenistic periods are summarized, with special attention given to coins that copy statues. Lacroix's *Les reproductions de statues sur les monnaies grecques: Le statuaire archaïque et classique* (Reproductions of Statues on Greek Coins: Archaic and Classical Statuary) reviews coin reproductions of Archaic and Classical statues from mainland Greece and Asia Minor. Greek coins reproducing statues that were minted in these regions before the fourth century B.C. seem to be free adaptations of the statues' compositions. Thus most of the coin reproductions which Lacroix discusses fall between the fourth century and the Roman Imperial age. *Statues on Coins of Southern Italy and Sicily in the Classical Period*, by Phyllis Williams Lehmann, presents the evidence of ten coin types from Magna Graecia and Sicily that were minted between 480 and 323 B.C. and which Lehmann proposes are faithful reproductions of contemporary statues. Each of the ten coin types is also known in Greek or Roman statuette or statuary copies. A list of additional coin types which appear to reproduce statues but for which no statuary copies survive is appended at the end of the volume.

## Bibliographic Entries for Supplementary Sources

Davis, Norman, and Colin M. Kraay. *The Hellenistic Kingdoms: Portrait Coins and History.* London: Thames & Hudson, 1973.

Gardner, Percy. *Archaeology and the Types of Greek Coins.* Introduction by Margaret Thompson. Chicago: Argonaut Publishers, 1965.

Harl, Kenneth W. *Civic Coins and Civic Politics in the Roman East A.D. 180–275.* The Transformation of the Classical Heritage no. 12. Berkeley, Los Angeles, and London: Univ. of California Press, 1987.

Holloway, R. Ross. *Art and Coinage in Magna Graecia.* Bellinzona: Edizioni Arte e Moneta, [1978].

Imhoof-Blumer, F. W., and Percy Gardner. *Ancient Coins Illustrating Lost Masterpieces of Greek Art: A Numismatic Commentary on Pausanias.* Enlarged ed. with introduction, commentary and notes by Al. N. Oikonomides. Chicago: Argonaut Publishers, 1964.

Kraay, Colin M. *Greek Coins and History: Some Current Problems.* London: Methuen, 1969.

Lacroix, Léon. *Les reproductions de statues sur les monnaies grecques: La statuaire archaïque et classique.* Liège: Faculté de Philosophie et Lettres, 1949.

Lehmann, Phyllis Williams. *Statues on Coins of Southern Italy and Sicily in the Classical Period.* New York: H. Bittner, 1946.

Price, Martin Jessop, and Bluma L. Trell. *Coins and their Cities: Architecture and the Ancient Coins of Greece, Rome, and Palestine.* London: Vecchi; Detroit: Wayne State Univ., 1977.

Seltman, Charles. *Masterpieces of Greek Coinage.* Oxford: Bruno Cassirer, 1949.

## Additional Supplementary Sources

Alföldi, Maria R.-. *Antike Numismatik.* Vol. 1, *Theorie und Praxis.* Kulturgeschichte der antiken Welt 2. Vol. 2, *Bibliographie.* Kulturgeschichte der antiken Welt 3. Mainz am Rhein: P. von Zabern, 1978.

Boehringer, Christof. *Zur Chronologie mittelhellenistischer Münzserien 220–160 v. Chr.* Antike Münzen und geschnittene Steine. Berlin: Walter de Gruyter & Co., 1972.

Martin, Thomas R. *Sovereignty and Coinage in Classical Greece.* Princeton: Princeton Univ. Press, 1985.

Vacano, Otfried von. *Typenkatalog der antiken Münzen Kleinasiens.* Edited by Dietmar Kienast. Berlin: Dietrich Reimar, 1986.

Weidauer, Liselotte. *Probleme der frühen Elektronprägung.* Typos: Monographien zur antiken Numismatik 1. Fribourg: Office du livre, 1975.

# ι15ι

# Roman Republican Coins

Crawford, Michael H. *Roman Republican Coinage.* 2 vols. London: Cambridge Univ. Press, 1976.

## ART FORM

Roman Republican coins are a valuable source of evidence for Rome's early economic and political history as well as for her artistic development. The first Roman Republican coinage consisted of unmarked and marked bronze bars. Large bronze coins of a circular shape were also cast. The first struck coins were silver didrachms with the Roman ethnic (the inscription signifying "of the Romans"), which may have been introduced circa 280 B.C. Bronze double-litrae were possibly struck shortly thereafter, circa 275 B.C. These denominations imitating contemporary Greek didrachms and litrae were first struck at Greek mints in South Italy, and then at Rome. In 214 B.C., the first silver denarii and the first gold coins were struck at Rome. Throughout the second century B.C., Rome was the principal minting center, but there were additional mints in other Italian cities. In the first century B.C., Rome continued to be the main mint in Italy; however, many military issues were minted outside of Italy.

Since they were minted by Greek artisans or under their influence, Republican didrachms exhibit a Greek style, with a powerful idealized head of a god or hero on the obverse and a well-planned motif on the reverse. Many denarii in a more Roman style fail to show the same degree of refinement. The reverse types (principal designs) often seem overly crowded, with a summary treatment of individual figures. However, they are interesting from a thematic standpoint, since in them actual historical events such as military scenes or triumphal processions appear for the first time on ancient coins. In the last twenty years of Republican coinage, strong, unflattering portraits of living leaders were introduced, and they became an important facet of the subsequent coinage of the Roman Empire. If Crawford is correct in his conclusions, Republican die engravers did not derive either the style or the compositions of their coins from other media. Instead, they seem to have maintained an independent artistic tradition that is much better attested by surviving examples than other Republican art forms, and that apparently moved more single-mindedly away from Greek prototypes to a more purely Roman mode of expression.

## RESEARCH USE

Although not easy to use, Michael Crawford's *Roman Republican Coinage* provides the most reliable and complete survey of "mainstream" issues from the Republic, that is, the coins that were the accepted medium of exchange throughout Roman territory. The introductory chapters familiarize the reader with the proposed chronology of Republican coins, relying heavily on evidence from coin hoards. The illustrated catalog of issues (outputs of coinage by the same minting authority), which describes the obverse and reverse types, symbols and inscriptions, and supplies references to previous scholarship, is invaluable for the researcher. It provides the data for thorough investigations of aspects of Republican coinage, such as changes in the style of the obverse heads of divinities or leaders, or the introduction and persistence of particular themes or symbols on the reverses.

## ORGANIZATION

The first volume of *Roman Republican Coinage* reconstructs the history of the denarius and provides a brief discussion of the didrachm, which the denarius superseded. It considers what numismatic components made up the earliest denarius coinage (i.e., the silver denarius with its related smaller denominations in silver [fractions] and gold pieces, the bronze with its related bronze fractions, and the silver victoriatus), identifies what coins were products of the mints of Rome and the mints outside Rome, and discusses how accurately and on what grounds they can be dated. The coins of the second century B.C. are divided into periods on the basis of the hoards in which the issues of each period first appeared, and on dated historical events (such as the probable foundation of Narbo in 118 B.C.). The first-century B.C. framework is provided by prolific hoard evidence and by numerous issues for which dates can be independently determined.

The first volume also contains the catalog, which is introduced by notes on its use and abbreviations for publications and collections (p. 123). The catalog presents Republican coins in groupings of issues. Each of the 550 entries for issues contains the following information: the issuing authority, the mint, the approximate date of the issue, bibliographic references to previous scholarship, type descriptions, and commentary. The types within each issue are separately numbered and a specific example of each type is cited. In addition, if a type is illustrated in the plates at the back of volume 2, the appropriate plate number is provided. The appendix to the first volume lists coins which have at one time or another been wrongly thought to be official issues of the Republic. These include modern forgeries, misread coins, plated coins, and unofficial issues of bronze coins.

The second volume of *Roman Republican Coinage* contains surveys of technical, administrative, and artistic aspects of Republican coins. In chapter 1, our current knowledge about the metallic content of silver, gold, and bronze coins is summarized, and analytical tables of sixty-two silver and forty-seven bronze coins are presented. Chapter 2 explains the units of weight used for coins of different metals and surveys changes in the weight standards. The duties of "moneyers" and other monetary magistrates are described in the next chapter. Chapter 4 lists the moneyers who placed inscriptions referring to the public treasury or Senatorial decrees on their coins, and seeks to find historical reasons for the presence of these inscriptions. In chapter 5, changes in the laws regulating the various denominations of Republican coinage are reviewed, and the roles of the Senate and the moneyers in managing the minting of coins are reconstructed. The next chapter outlines the major denominations and their fractions, and explains the conversion equivalencies of coins of different metals. In chapter 7, Crawford masterfully reconstructs sources of income and expenditures of the public treasury, using literary evidence and surviving coins—the latter being presented in tables. Chapter 8 presents in the form of a chronological table the careers of the moneyers who can be identified from the abbreviations of their names on coins. In the next chapter, Crawford provides guidelines for distinguishing public coin types, which refer to the Roman state, from private types, which advertise the status and accomplishments of the families of the monetary magistrates. Finally, in the last chapter, "Art and Coinage," Crawford expresses his conclusion that Republican die engravers did not reproduce sculptures or paintings, but worked in an independent tradition, only imitating other coins. He includes a table of portrait types on Republican coins, with all examples of each type being assigned to the same hand or workshop.

Volume 2 of *Roman Republican Coinage* contains the plates (in chronological order, although divided between the large cast bronze coins [A–I], and the smaller struck coins [I–LXV]) and the key to the plates (which gives the location of the struck coins). All the struck coins are illustrated at actual size. The bibliography (using abbreviations from *L'Année philologique* [see chapter 1, under Complementary References] and M. H. Crawford's *Roman Republican Coin Hoards*, pp. 148–55 [see Complementary References below]) does not repeat works cited in the abbreviations in volume 1. Five indexes located at the end of the volume provide access to information in the following categories: types, legends, ancient sources referring to coins (papyri, inscriptions, and Greek and Latin authors), personal names on coins (the "RE" number is from the *Paulys Realencyclopädie der classischen Altertumswissenschaft* entry for persons' names [see Bibliographic Entries for Complementary References below]), and general. The concordances at the end of volume 2 are discussed below under Complementary References.

## COMPLEMENTARY REFERENCES

The reader should note that in volume 1 of Crawford's *Roman Republican Coinage*, frequent reference is made to *Coin Hoards*, an unexplained abbreviation for Crawford's *Roman Republican Coin Hoards*. Coin hoards (caches of coins buried in ancient times) are so frequently cited because they provide the most reliable evidence for the correct sequence of Republican issues. In *Roman Republican Coin Hoards*, the contents of hoards from 300 to 2 B.C. are presented in chronological groups with the following information given for each one: the place of discovery, the date of discovery (when known), the present-day country in which the place of discovery is situated, the type of receptacle containing the hoard (when known), the contents of the hoard (listed by denomination, with the number of coins for each), any publication of the hoard, and the current location of the hoard (when known). The hoard study also contains eighteen chronological tables in which the coins from each group are broken down into subgroups, with approximate dating provided. For hoards discovered or known after the publication of *Roman Republican Coin Hoards*, all volumes of an ongoing series entitled *Coin Hoards* should be consulted. The index at the back of each volume lists hoards containing Republican coins minted by Roman authorities under Rome; entries for these hoards identify Republican coins by citing the appropriate catalog numbers from volume 1 of Crawford's *Roman Republican Coinage*.

The concordances at the back of volume 2 of *Roman Republican Coinage* provide correspondences between Crawford's coin numbers and those in E. A. Sydenham's *The Coinage of the Roman Republic* and Ernest Babelon's *Description historique et chronologique des monnaies de la république romaine* (Historical and Chronological Description of the Coins of the Roman Republic). The former is a reference first published in 1952. Although Sydenham's chronology has been superseded by Crawford's, his introduction provides valuable background information not presented by Crawford, such as the locations and organizations of Republican mints. This reference also contains a catalog of issues, a feature duplicated by Crawford. The article "Sydenham in Retrospect . . .," by Charles A. Hersh, provides additions and corrections to Sydenham's study. Babelon's work is a two-volume catalog published in 1885–86 of a large collection of Republican coins located at the Bibliothèque Nationale in Paris. All the coins in the catalog are fully described and many are illustrated by line drawings. Volume 1 of Babelon's study describes in chronological order the Republican coins for which the moneyer is unknown. Babelon's volume 2 presents coins by known moneyers in alphabetical order according to the moneyers' family names. When more than one member of the same family had the office of a moneyer, names of individual family members are arranged chronologically within the larger grouping of the family. Thus this volume is valuable for the researcher wishing to look for possible common elements in the coin types of moneyers from the same family.

*Moneta: Recherches sur l'organisation et l'art des émissions monétaires de la République romaine (289–31 av. J.-C.)* (Coinage: Investigations on the Organization and the Art of the Monetary Emissions of the Roman Republic, 289–31 B.C.), by Hubert Zehnacker, can be used to supplement the evidence presented by Crawford on aspects of coinage such as mint marks that indicate systems of controlling Republican coin emissions. Zehnacker also provides lengthy discussions of the progression of types on Republican coins and their stylistic evolution. Particularly valuable are his chapters on coin types that represent historical events, and on the development of realistic portraiture on coins.

Andrew Burnett's brief but up-to-date survey, *Coinage in the Roman World*, presents a current view of the problem of dating Rome's earliest coins; this can be found in the chapter, "The Beginning of Coinage in the Third Century B.C." Burnett also reviews the history of the Roman denarius, in use from the late third century B.C. until the middle of the third century A.D. A useful appendix at the back of the book correlates events from Republican history with innovations in Rome's early coinage.

*Roman Historical Coins*, by Clive Foss, is a useful corpus of Roman coin types which refer to contemporary events and policies. This corpus begins its consideration with the second century B.C. and is thus a source of information on historical coins from the last two centuries of the

Republic. Descriptions of Republican coin types in Foss' illustrated reference are arranged in three parts: "the first of them, 'The Republic', covers the years 121–54 BC, the second the supremacy of Caesar, and the third the Civil Wars from 44–31 BC" (p. xi). The complex format of the coin descriptions and the abbreviations utilized are explained in the introduction. Coin entries include the identification and date of the event or policy referred to, the coin inscription, and a description of the coin's visual image or type. Citations of ancient historical texts are not provided, but references are given to standard numismatic publications, particularly to Crawford's *Roman Republican Coinage*, abbreviated "*Cr.*" At the back of the reference is an index of coin types.

In *Numismatic Bibliography*, E. E. Clain-Stefanelli lists different categories of literature on Roman Republican coinage—bibliographies, general references, sale catalogs, studies of coinage down to the time of Julius Caesar and from the period of Caesar, and special topics, including iconography. Indexes at the back provide access to literature on mythological and historical personages found on coins; mints; and coin types (for the last, see "Index of Numismatic Terms").

For the most recent books and articles on Roman Republican coinage, the researcher should consult the latest numbers of *Numismatic Literature*; material on this coinage can be located under "Roman, Roman Republic" in the subject index at the back of each number. Further literature on Republican coins can be found in the ongoing publication, *A Survey of Numsimatic Research*. Each issue includes a summary of current research on coinage from this controversial period. For additional sources of bibliography, a useful survey of the history of numismatic research, and a description of resources in major numismatic libraries and their published catalogs, the researcher should consult Francis D. Campbell's "Numismatic Bibliography and Libraries."

*Bibliographic Entries for Complementary References*

Babelon, Ernest. *Description historique et chronologique des monnaies de la république romaine vulgairement appelées monnaies consulaires.* 2 vols. Paris: Rollin et Feuardent, 1885–86.
Burnett, Andrew. *Coinage in the Roman World.* London: Seaby, 1987.
Campbell, Francis D. "Numismatic Bibliography and Libraries." In *Encyclopedia of Library and Information Science.* Vol. 37, Supplement 2, 272–310. Edited by Allen Kent. New York and Basel: Marcel Dekker, 1984. Reprint. Dallas: Numismatics International, 1986.
Clain-Stefanelli, E. E. *Numismatic Bibliography.* Munich: Battenburg, 1985.
*Coin Hoards.* Vol. 1– . London: Royal Numismatic Society, 1975– .
Crawford, Michael H. *Roman Republican Coin Hoards.* Special Publication no. 4. London: Royal Numismatic Society, 1969.
Foss, Clive. *Roman Historical Coins.* London: Seaby, 1990.

Hersh, Charles A. "Sydenham in Retrospect: Revisions, Corrections, and Some Rare and Unpublished Additions to That Author's 'The Coinage of the Roman Republic.'" In *Mints, Dies and Currency: Essays dedicated to the Memory of Albert Baldwin.* Edited by R. A. G. Carson, 9–32. London: Methuen, 1971.

*Numismatic Literature.* No. 1– . New York: American Numismatic Society, 1947– .

Pauly, August Friedrich von, Georg Wissowa, and Wilhelm Kroll, eds. *Paulys Realencyclopädie der classischen Altertumswissenschaft: Neue Bearbeitung.* 24 vols. 2d ser. (R–Z), 19 vols. Stuttgart: J. B. Metzler, 1894–1972. *Supplement.* 15 vols. Stuttgart: J. B. Metzler, 1903–78.

*A Survey of Numismatic Research 1960–1965; 1966–1971; 1972–1977; 1978–1984.* International Numismatic Commission, 1967– . Preceded by *Congrès Internationale de Numismatique Paris 6–11 juillet 1953.* Vol. 1, *Rapports;* and *Congresso Internazionale di Numismatica Roma 11–16 settembre 1961.* Vol. 1, *Relazioni.*

Sydenham, Edward A. *The Coinage of the Roman Republic.* Revised by G. C. Haines and edited by L. Forrer and C. A. Hersh. London: Spink & Son, 1952. Rev. ed. with indexes by G. C. Haines. New York: Arno, 1975. Reprint. New York: Sanford J. Durst, 1976.

Zehnacker, Hubert. *Moneta: Recherches sur l'organisation et l'art des émissions monétaires de la République romaine (289–31 av. J.-C.).* 2 vols. Bibliothèque des Écoles Françaises d'Athènes et de Rome 222. Rome: École Française de Rome, 1973.

# HANDBOOKS

There are many unresolved questions about Republican coins, such as the date of the minting of the first silver didrachms. Pliny the Elder and Livy state respectively that the Romans first minted silver coins in 269 or 268 B.C. Yet the contents of hoards seem to place this event earlier, perhaps circa 280 B.C. or earlier still. Because scholarly conclusions on matters such as this are currently undergoing revision, only relatively recent handbooks are reliable. The two best ones on the Republican period, which also offer excellent surveys of Imperial coinage, are *Roman Coins,* by C. H. V. Sutherland, and a second book with the same title, by J. P. C. Kent. Sutherland's reference has a remarkably readable but still scholarly text (accompanied by footnotes) that masterfully distinguishes between known facts and unresolved problems. At the back of the volume, immediately before the index, is a helpful glossary which explains the complex interrelationships of different Roman coin denominations as well as some of the components of coin types. J. P. C. Kent's handbook has briefer general discussions without footnotes, but his arguments are convincing and based on solid criteria such as the relationship of the lowering of weight standards to economically demanding conflicts. Numerous sharp enlargements illustrating nearly eight hundred coins (by Max and Albert Hirmer) and full catalog descriptions, with bibliography, provide a thorough introduction to Republican and Imperial Roman coins.

An even briefer but still reliable survey of Republican coinage is volume 1 of *Principal Coins of the Romans*, by R. A. G. Carson. Here, carefully selected coins of the Republic from the British Museum are presented in chronological groups, with introductory explanations. Each coin is illustrated at actual size and described. The concordance at the back refers the reader to the previous publication of most of the coins in the larger catalog for the same collection, *Coins of the Roman Republic in the British Museum*, by H. A. Grueber. This catalog of the largest collection of Republican coins in the world arranges the coins by mints (i.e., the mint of Rome, the mints of Italy outside Rome, and the mints of the provinces), and the coins within each mint are presented chronologically. Grueber's indexes and plates are located in volume 3. Many of Grueber's dates are no longer accepted and should be revised through consultation of the dates given in the introductions and catalog entries of Carson's *Principal Coins*.

*A Dictionary of Ancient Roman Coins*, by John Melville Jones, can be used to help identify unpublished Republican coins; this can be achieved by looking up the types on the coins. The researcher should be aware, however, that the *Dictionary* is not encyclopedic, nor does it provide further bibliography in its alphabetically arranged entries.

### Bibliographic Entries for Handbooks

Carson, R. A. G. *Principal Coins of the Romans*. Vol. 1, *The Republic c. 290–31 B.C.* London: British Museum Pubns., 1978.

Grueber, H. A. *Coins of the Roman Republic in the British Museum*. 3 vols. London: The Trustees, 1910. Reprint. London: British Museum, 1970.

Kent, J. P. C. *Roman Coins*. New York: Abrams, 1978.

Melville Jones, John. *A Dictionary of Ancient Roman Coins*. London: Seaby, 1990.

Sutherland, C. H. V. *Roman Coins*. New York: Putnam, 1974.

## SUPPLEMENTARY SOURCES

Coins, along with ancient historical accounts, document Rome's political and economic expansion in the Republican period. A valuable new book that adopts this type of approach is another study by Crawford, *Coinage and Money under the Roman Republic*. This work traces the introduction of Roman coinage and its spread throughout Italy and the Mediterranean. Frequent reference is made to the catalog entries in Crawford's *Roman Republican Coinage*, and coins of other ancient peoples that influenced Republican issues are discussed and illustrated. Arguments on the patterns of coin circulation are based on the contents of hoards.

While *Roman Republican Coinage* describes all Republican coins from the third century through the end of the Republic, Rudi Thomsen's *Early Roman Coinage* limits its consideration to the problematic coins of the third century. Volume 1 presents a comprehensive survey of numismatic evidence and scholarly literature: the ancient written sources in Greek and Latin concerning early coinage; the coins themselves; coin hoards, overstrikes, and type and weight standard parallels in contemporary Greek coins; and a summary of previous scholarship. Volumes 2 and 3 present a new chronology based on a synthesis of this evidence. This chronology is followed by Crawford except in minor details.

A general discussion of the artistic development of Republican coins (in which other art forms are more closely related to the development of coinage than Crawford hypothesizes) can be found in Strong's *Roman Art*. Finally, in *Architekturdarstellungen auf römischen Münzen der Republik und der frühen Kaiserzeit* (Architectural Representations on Roman Coins of the Republic and the Early Empire), Günter Fuchs traces representations of buildings on Roman coins from their introduction circa 130 B.C. to the early Empire. He attempts to define the spatial conventions which were used by the coin engravers, thereby allowing the modern viewer to reconstruct the flattened coin images in three dimensions.

## Bibliographic Entries for Supplementary Sources

Crawford, Michael H. *Coinage and Money under the Roman Republic: Italy and the Mediterranean Economy*. Berkeley: Univ. of California Press, 1985.

Fuchs, Günter. *Architekturdarstellungen auf römischen Münzen der Republik und der frühen Kaiserzeit*. Edited by Jochen Bleichen and Manfred Fuhrmann. Antike Münzen und geschnittene Steine 1. Berlin: W. de Gruyter, 1969.

Strong, Donald. *Roman Art*. 2d ed. Preface by and prepared for press by Jocelyn M. C. Toynbee; revised by Roger Ling. Harmondsworth, Middlesex, and New York: Penguin, 1988.

Thomsen, Rudi. *Early Roman Coinage: A Study of the Chronology*. 3 vols. Copenhagen: Nationalmuseet, 1957–61.

## Additional Supplementary Sources

Alföldi, Maria R.-. *Antike Numismatik*. Vol. 1, *Theorie und Praxis*. Kulturgeschichte der antiken Welt 2. Vol. 2, *Bibliographie*. Kulturgeschichte der antiken Welt 3. Mainz am Rhein: P. von Zabern, 1978.

Berger, Frank. *Die Münzen der Römischen Republik im Kestner-Museum Hannover*. Hannover: Kestner-Museum, 1989.

# ᛁ16ᛁ

# Roman Imperial Coins

Mattingly, Harold, Edward A. Sydenham, C. H. Sutherland, and R. A. G. Carson, eds. *Roman Imperial Coinage*. Vols. 1–9. London: Spink & Son, 1923–1981.
Sutherland, C. H. V., and R. A. G. Carson, eds. *Roman Imperial Coinage*. Vol. 1, rev. ed. London: Spink & Son, 1984.

## ART FORM

During the period of the Civil Wars (49–31 B.C.) at the end of the Republic and during the reign of the first Roman Emperor Augustus, Roman coinage took on new characteristics that persisted throughout the Roman Empire. Julius Caesar was the first emperor to regularly issue gold coins; their weight was later standardized by Augustus. The latter also supplanted bronze coins with coins in brass and pure copper. Further reforms of Augustus were the removal from the Senate of the authority to mint gold and silver, and the issuing himself of coins in these metals in the provinces. The Augustan Senate was allowed to continue to strike coins in Rome in the base metals of brass and copper. Caligula transferred the Imperial mint of gold and silver back to Rome (ca. 38 A.D.), but later (beginning 193 A.D.) a gradual shift back to the provinces can be traced.

Much information can be derived from Imperial coin types. The practice of placing realistic portrait heads of living persons (i.e., the emperor and his family) on coin obverses, introduced by Caesar in 44 B.C., was standard during the Empire. These inscribed and often closely dated coin portraits show a wide variety of personalities and hairstyles, rendered with a remarkably consistent fineness of execution. Not only are these coin portraits valuable for their own artistic merit, but also they are the basis for identifying uninscribed portraits of the emperors and their families in other media such as statuary. Furthermore, portraits of unidentified private individuals, which copy the hairstyles of contemporary emperors and empresses, can be assigned approximate dates by matching their hairstyles with those of Imperial family members on coin portraits.

Coin reverses were used as a propaganda tool, the types, or principal designs, reflecting the messages for which the rulers wished the widest possible circulation. The reverses of coins present a great variety of images, with as many as one hundred different types produced in a single year. The majority of these types are sacred subjects, including images of gods, demigods, heroes, and allegorical personifications. About one-third of the reverse types are devoted to the emperor, his family, and the Empire. These include images of the emperor in peacetime activities, such as distributing gifts, or in military roles, such as arriving from or departing for war; happy events in the emperor's family, such as births and betrothals; personifications of the Senate and the people; personifications of the provinces in the form of women accompanied by emblems; public events (e.g., the regulation of provisions for the Roman people symbolized by a corn-measure filled with ears of corn); and prayers for the emperor, with the legend within a laurel wreath. Public monuments such as altars, triumphal arches, temples, forums, columns, aqueducts, circuses, and baths are also depicted on coins. The presence of these specific types, along with the mention of very specific titles and offices of the emperors, helps numismatists assign Imperial coins a more exact chronological framework than is possible for the coins of the Republic.

# RESEARCH USE

*Roman Imperial Coinage* is the most comprehensive compilation of coin issues from the Roman Empire. As volumes were published, from 1923 onwards, they became progressively more complete, so that volumes 8–9 and the revised edition of volume 1 are authoritative corpora. Sutherland states in the latter (p. x): "The currently conceived purpose of the series is to inform both numismatists and historians of as much of the structure and detail of Roman imperial coinage as it is possible to do with adequate justifying argument . . . ." This purpose is achieved by the description in each volume of the coin issues from a chronological segment of the Roman Empire. Groups of related issues are presented as units, with introductory comments and then catalog entries; there are illustrations of some coins in the plates at the back.

Because it is the most comprehensive treatment of a vast body of material, *Roman Imperial Coinage* can be used to initially define the evidence for several types of research. For example, it could provide an indication of the geographic and chronological range of coins that demonstrate stylistic or iconographic differences in the rendition of the head or full figure of a single emperor, or of a series of rulers. It could also provide material for historians who wish to supplement information about emperors in literary sources with numismatic evidence. Policies and accomplishments of emperors which are not mentioned in literature but which are illustrated on coin reverses could thereby be incorporated into modern accounts of their rules. Furthermore, *Roman Imperial Coinage* could be used by architectural historians who wish to investigate coin representations of lost or damaged monuments from a single city or from a class of structures. A detailed depiction on a coin permits reconstruction of a totally lost monument or of lost parts of a monument. Sometimes the appearance of whole quarters of cities, such as harbors and their surrounding architecture, is reproduced on Roman coins.

# ORGANIZATION

Each of the nine volumes of *Roman Imperial Coinage* deals with coins from a particular time frame. These are presented either in a strict chronological arrangement or according to mints. The time-frame for each volume is as follows: volume 1 (rev. ed. 1984)—Augustus to Vitellius (31 B.C. to 69 A.D.); volume 2 (1926)—Vespasian to Hadrian (69–138 A.D.); volume 3 (1930)—Antoninus Pius to Commodus (138–192); volume 4, part 1 (1936)—Pertinax to Geta (193–217), part 2 (1938)—Macrinus to Pupienus (217–238), and part 3 (1949)—Gordian II to Uranius Antoninus (238–253); volume 5, part 1 (1927)—Valerian to the interregnum (253–275), and part 2 (1933)—Probus to the reform of Diocletian (276–293); volume 6 (1967)—the reform of Diocletian to the death of Maximinus (294–313); volume 7 (1966)—Constantine and Licinius (313–337); volume 8 (1981)—the family of Constantine (337–364); volume 9 (1983)—Valentinian to Theodosius (364–392). The coinage of each emperor's reign or mint is introduced by an historical survey in which coin issues from various classes are outlined (e. g., Imperial and Senatorial issues, the mint of Rome and provincial mints, dated and undated coins, etc.). Following this survey are tables with catalog entries for the same classes of coins as those covered in the introduction. In the first column of each table are the coin numbers for that table only and not for the plates. The second and third columns are headed by the symbols for gold (AV) and silver (AR), or brass (Or./Orich., meaning orichalcum) and copper (AE). Under these headings are the abbreviations for the coin denominations, which are explained on page 40 of volume 1. The next two columns briefly describe the obverse and reverse types and record any coin inscriptions in bold-faced type. The degrees of rarity are indicated beginning with volume 2, and mint marks are given beginning with volume 5. The last column provides plate numbers and bibliographic references. All the volumes contain a "Select Bibliography" of works pertinent to the volume. Volumes 1, 4 (part 3), 5 (part 1), and 6–9 include general introductions summarizing the characteristics of all the coins in the volume.

The second edition of volume 1 (1984) is an expanded and rewritten account of the first century of Imperial coinage. It contains nine hundred new coin entries along with updated information on mint attribution, chronological sequence, mint organization, and die-analysis.

## COMPLEMENTARY REFERENCES

The reference most frequently cited in volumes 1–9 of the original edition of *Roman Imperial Coinage* is the large corpus by Henry Cohen, entitled *Description historique des monnaies frappées sous l'Empire romain communément appelées médailles impériales* (Historical Description of the Coins Struck during the Roman Empire commonly called Imperial Medals). Referred to simply as "C." in *Roman Imperial Coinage*, this outdated eight-volume reference catalogs more than thirty thousand Roman Imperial coins, many of which are illustrated with drawings. On page xxvii of volume 1, Cohen explains his abbreviations; for example, "G. B." stands for "Grand bronze" (large bronze). *Monete imperiali romane* (Roman Imperial Coins), a catalog of the now dispersed collection which previously belonged to the author G. Mazzini, can be used along with Cohen's reference, for it follows Cohen's order of coins and provides photographs of many of the coin types for which Cohen has only drawings or no illustrations at all. The revised edition of volume 1 of *Roman Imperial Coinage* frequently cites *Coins of the Roman Empire in the British Museum*, edited by Mattingly and others, which it abbreviates "BMC." Like *Roman Imperial Coinage*, the British Museum catalog has been published over a long period of time, so that its more recent volumes are more reliable than the earlier ones. Another reference which is commonly cited in the revised edition of volume 1 is *Roman Imperial Coins in the Hunter Coin Cabinet, University of Glasgow*, by Anne S. Robertson. Referred to as "Hunter," this catalog is particularly valuable because it revises the chronology and mint attribution of outdated volumes of *Roman Imperial Coinage* and *Coins of the Roman Empire in the British Museum*, and it extends its coverage farther than either of the other references: up to 491 A.D. Robertson introduces each volume with a helpful bibliography which is broken down into general and more chronologically limited sections, and a "List of Abbreviations." Where necessary, she includes textual explanations of her new reconstructions of numismatic history.

A recently published corpus of all the Julio-Claudian coins in Milan's Civiche Raccolte Numismatiche is the three-volume catalog, *Sylloge Nummorum Romanorum, Italia: Milano, Civiche Raccolte Numismatiche* (Corpus of Roman Coins, Italy: Milan, Municipal Numismatic Collections). The preface to the first volume of the catalog expresses the hope that Milan's *Sylloge Nummorum Romanorum*, with the same format as the *Sylloge Nummorum Graecorum* (see chapter 14, "Greek Coins," under Complementary References), will be the first in an ongoing international series of catalogs of collections of Roman Imperial coins.

Unpublished Imperial coins can be tentatively identified by using the old but still useful *Dictionary of Roman Coins, Republican and Imperial*, by Stevenson and others. Identification can be achieved by looking up a coin's legend in this alphabetically arranged reference, or its type (listed under its Latin name). *A Dictionary of Ancient Roman Coins*, by John Melville Jones, contains more up-to-date but less complete explanations of Roman coin types. Once the researcher has the information supplied by one or both of these dictionaries, he or she can look up the coin in the appropriate volume(s) of *Roman Imperial Coinage*.

*Roman Historical Coins*, by Clive Foss, is a useful corpus of Roman coin types which refer to contemporary events and policies. This corpus covers the entire period of the pagan Roman Empire and also considers the fourth and fifth centuries A.D. Descriptions of Imperial coin types in Foss' illustrated reference are arranged chronologically, according to the dates of the emperors' reigns. The complex format of the coin descriptions and the abbreviations utilized are explained in the introduction. Coin entries include the identification and date of the event or policy referred to, the coin inscription, and a description of the coin's visual image or type. Citations of ancient historical texts are not provided, but references are given to standard numismatic publications, particularly to *Roman Imperial Coinage* (whose numbers are always given at the end of the entry). The coin types of each emperor's reign are prefaced by an historical introduction. At the back of the reference is an index of coin types.

*Numismatic Bibliography*, by E. E. Clain-Stefanelli, introduces the researcher to different categories of literature on Roman Imperial coins— bibliographies, general references, sale catalogs, studies of coins of the emperors and the Roman provinces, and special topics including "Coin Types and Iconography" and "Portraits and Art in Coinage." Indexes at the back provide access to literature on mythological and historical personages found on coins; mints; and coin types (for the last, see "Index of Numismatic Terms").

For the most recent articles and books on Roman Imperial coins, the researcher should consult the latest numbers of *Numismatic Literature,* a semiannual bibliographical publication of the American Numismatic Society. The subject index at the back of each number provides access to literature through the names of emperors and the cities where Imperial mints were located. Further literature on Imperial coins can be found in the ongoing publication *A Survey of Numismatic Research,* each issue of which contains a critical summary of pertinent research from the past six years. For additional sources of bibliography, a useful survey of the history of numismatic research, and a description of resources in major numismatic libraries and their published catalogs, the researcher should consult Francis D. Campbell's article, "Numismatic Bibliography and Libraries."

## Bibliographic Entries for Complementary References

Campbell, Francis D. "Numismatic Bibliography and Libraries." In *Encyclopedia of Library and Information Science.* Vol. 37, Supplement 2, 272–310. Edited by Allen Kent. New York and Basel: Marcel Dekker, 1984. Reprint. Dallas: Numismatics International, 1986.

Clain-Stefanelli, E. E. *Numismatic Bibliography.* Munich: Battenburg, 1985.

Cohen, Henry. *Description historique des monnaies frappées sous l'Empire romain communément appelées médailles impériales.* 2d ed. 8 vols. Paris: Rollin & Feuardent, 1880–92. Reprint, with special dictionary. Graz: Akademische Druck u. Verlagsanstalt, 1955.

Foss, Clive. *Roman Historical Coins.* London: Seaby, 1990.

Mattingly, Harold, R. A. G. Carson, P. V. Hill and P. Brunn, eds. *Coins of the Roman Empire in the British Museum.* 8 vols. London: The Trustees, 1923–80. Vols. 1–6 reprinted with revisions: London: British Museum Publications, 1966–76.

Mazzini, G. *Monete imperiali romane.* Vol. 1, *Da Pompeo Magno a Domizia.* Vol. 2, *Da Nerva a Crispina.* Vol. 3, *Da Pertinace a Filippo Figlio.* Vol. 4, *Da Pacaziano a Valeria.* Vol. 5, *Da Severo II a Romolo Augustolo, Tessere, Contorniati.* Milan: Mario Ratto, 1957–58.

Melville Jones, John. *A Dictionary of Ancient Roman Coins.* London: Seaby, 1990.

*Numismatic Literature.* No. 1– . New York: American Numismatic Society, 1947– .

Robertson, Anne S. *Roman Imperial Coins in the Hunter Coin Cabinet, University of Glasgow.* 5 vols. New York: Oxford Univ. Press, for the Univ. of Glasgow, 1962–82.

Stevenson, Seth William, C. Roach Smith, and Frederic W. Madden. *A Dictionary of Roman Coins, Republican and Imperial.* 1889. Reprint. Hildesheim: Georg Olms, 1969.

*A Survey of Numismatic Research 1960–1965; 1966–1971; 1972–1977; 1978–1984.*
International Numismatic Commission, 1967– . Preceded by *Congrès Internationale de Numismatique Paris 6–11 juillet 1953.* Vol. 1, *Rapports;* and *Congresso Internazionale di Numismatica Roma 11–16 settembre 1961.* Vol. 1, *Relazioni.*
*Sylloge Nummorum Romanorum, Italia: Milano, Civiche Raccolte Numismatiche I. Giulio-Claudii.* Vol. 1, *Augustus-Tiberius.* Vol. 2, *Caius-Claudius.* Vol. 3, *Nero.*
Edited by Rodolfo Martini. Milano: Comune di Milano, Civiche Raccolte Numismatiche, 1990.

# HANDBOOKS

*Coinage of the Roman World,* by Andrew Burnett, contains an up-to-date survey of Roman Imperial coinage. Burnett adopts the sensible approach of "giving some historical explanation of them (the coins)" and of treating "coins as economic objects, . . . explaining both how and why they circulated, and how they can illuminate economic history." Besides discussing the coinage of the pagan Roman Empire in these ways, Burnett reviews the new system of coinage in the fifth century A.D. The chapter of Burnett's handbook that probably holds the most interest for the art historian, entitled "Designs and propaganda," surveys the principal types of Roman coins, including those of the provinces, and their apparent significance. Unfortunately, apart from the explanation of sources for passages from ancient literature found before the first chapter, Burnett provides no bibliography for his otherwise scholarly survey.

The two separate handbooks by J. P. C. Kent and C. H. V. Sutherland—both entitled *Roman Coins,* which are discussed in chapter 15, "Roman Republican Coins," under Handbooks, are recommended for their reliable text and enlarged photographs. Harold Mattingly's handbook, also entitled *Roman Coins,* is a somewhat older but still valuable survey of historical, economic, and iconographic aspects of Republican and Imperial Roman coinage. Especially useful for the art historian are Mattingly's detailed descriptions of classes of coin types. For example, under the coin types of the early Empire, type "a" is "Types of the Emperor and His Family," "e" is "Religious types," and "h" is "Buildings." Volumes 2 and 3 of *Principal Coins of the Romans,* by R. A. G. Carson, catalog and illustrate a selection of Imperial coins in the British Museum. Unlike the larger catalog, *Coins of the Roman Empire in the British Museum,* this survey includes coins up to the end of the fifth century. Since Carson's two volumes have the advantage of recent scholarship not available at the time of publication of *Coins of the Roman Empire in the British Museum,* his chronology, rather than that of the older catalog, should be followed. A concordance at the back of volume 2 of

*Principal Coins of the Romans* facilitates comparisons of dating and mint attribution of specific coins.

*Roman Imperial Money,* by Michael Grant, introduces the reader to some of the "historically noteworthy features" of Roman Imperial coins. For example, Grant traces the effective use in Augustan coinage of types that call attention to the preservation of Republican traditions in the new Empire. *Roman Imperial Coins: Their Art and Technique,* by Laura Breglia, describes and illustrates ninety-nine Roman Imperial coins and medallions from the Museo Nazionale in Naples. These descriptions, and the two introductions by Breglia and Bianchi Bandinelli, emphasize the stylistic evolution of Roman coinage, which is easy to follow visually in the full-page enlargements that accompany the actual-size photos of each coin.

Two handbooks written for Roman coin collectors are also valuable for the scholar, since they present useful compilations of evidence. *Roman Coins,* by Richard Reece, is a chronologically arranged survey that describes basic characteristics of commonly available coins, such as their types and inscriptions, and relates them to known historical events. Unifying traits in specific emperors' coinages are emphasized, as are any changes in their portraits during their reigns. *Roman Coins and Their Values,* by David R. Sear, has many useful features, perhaps the most valuable being the "Tables of Titles and Powers" which are provided for the surveys of the more important Roman emperors. These tables specify the years when particular titles and offices were conferred on emperors. Since these titles and offices are often named on the coins, they can be used to establish dates within reigns for many coins. Another helpful feature in Sear's surveys of the important emperors' coinages is his mention of all the mints known to have been in operation. The introductory portions of Sear's volume include a concise chronological survey of coin denominations and alphabetically arranged and illustrated dictionaries of deities and personifications who commonly appear on Roman coins. In each case, standard attributes are mentioned, and in the case of the deities, commonly used titles are listed.

All building types of ancient Rome that are represented on coins are considered by Philip V. Hill in *The Monuments of Ancient Rome as Coin Types.* Hill explains the organization of his book thus: "Each chapter deals with one particular type of building or monument, arranged geographically within the chapter, according to the administrative regions of the city. . ." (p. 7). The locations of these buildings depicted on coins, when they are known, are shown on two topographical maps of all of Rome and of the center of the city, found in appendix 1 at the back of the volume. In the text, a brief history of each building—illustrated by one or more coins—is provided, along with an explanation of the features visible on the coin(s). For preserved buildings, a photograph of the building as well as the coin(s) is provided. Numismatic conventions that cause deviations from the actual appearance of the buildings are rarely commented on. Appendix 2 lists the coins illustrated, as well as others, with references given to "BMC" and "RIC" (see the "Bibliography and Abbreviations"). After appendix 2 is a glossary explaining coin denominations, terms pertaining to buildings and statues, and titles used on coins.

### Bibliographic Entries for Handbooks

Breglia, Laura. *Roman Imperial Coins: Their Art and Technique.* Introduced by Ranuccio Bianchi Bandinelli; translated by Peter Green. New York: Praeger, 1968.

Burnett, Andrew. *Coinage of the Roman World.* London: Seaby, 1987.

Carson, R. A. G. *Principal Coins of the Romans.* Vol. 2, *The Principate 31 BC–AD 296.* Vol. 3, *The Dominate AD 294–498.* London: British Museum Publications, 1980–81.

Grant, Michael. *Roman Imperial Money.* London, New York: Nelson, 1954. Reprint. Amsterdam, Hakkert, 1972.

Hill, Philip V. *The Monuments of Ancient Rome as Coin Types.* London: Seaby, 1989.

Kent, J. P. C. *Roman Coins.* New York: Abrams, 1978.

Mattingly, Harold. *Roman Coins from the Earliest Times to the Fall of the Western Empire.* 2d ed. London: Methuen, 1960. Reprint. London: Spink, 1977.

Reece, Richard. *Roman Coins.* Practical Handbooks for Collectors. London: Ernest Benn, 1970.

Sear, David R. *Roman Coins and Their Values.* 4th ed. London: Seaby, 1988.

Sutherland, C. H. V. *Roman Coins.* New York: Putnam, 1974.

## SUPPLEMENTARY SOURCES

More than any other ancient people, the Romans attempted to achieve accurate characterization in their portraits. Yet the form that this characterization assumed varied from complete truthfulness, with every facial blemish reproduced, to an idealized treatment in which a recognizable facial structure was retained, but non-ideal details were eliminated. As stated under Art Form above, coins provide the most complete and certain record of changes in stylistic conventions in Roman portraits. Two volumes—*Römische Kaiserporträts im Münzbild* (Portraits of Roman Caesars on Coins), by Peter Robert Franke, and *Women of the Caesars: Their Lives and Portraits on Coins*, by Giorgio Giacosa—describe and illustrate (with enlarged photos) a sufficient number of coin portraits of male and female members of the Imperial families that the researcher can quickly grasp the main lines of stylistic development in Roman portraiture. Franke places emphasis in his descriptions of the emperors' portraits on the propagandistic concept of leadership projected by each head, while Giacosa concentrates on the actual characters of the Imperial women as they are known from historical accounts, and demonstrates how these traits are conveyed on the coins.

The obverses of Roman Imperial coins, with their fine portrait heads, are generally better designed and executed than the crowded reverses. A consistent quality of design, however, is maintained for both the obverses and reverses of Roman medallions. This numismatic genre, like coins, was struck from bronze, silver, and gold. Unlike coins, however, medallions seem to have been commemorative pieces that were given to specially chosen military and civilian officials. In a general study, entitled *Roman Medallions*, Jocelyn M. C. Toynbee attempts to arrive at an accurate definition of the characteristics that distinguish medallions from coins. She surveys the contents of the types on medallions, as well as the provenances of medallions to determine the sorts of occasions which were commonly commemorated by them and the people who were recipients of them. Toynbee also presents a long discussion of the general development of medallions, and their value as sources of evidence on Roman politics and religion and as reflections of art in other media. In the reprint edition of *Roman Medallions*, Toynbee's bibliography (at the back) is supplemented by a bibliography by William E. Metcalf (at the front). In the introduction, Metcalf also adds to Toynbee's discussion of the provenances of medallions an additional "List of Finds," and updates some of the arguments with more recent literature.

As indicated above, Roman coins are an excellent source of information for the historian. Yet the scholar making use of them must always bear in mind that they were issued by Roman rulers as propaganda tools. Thus they tended to present a ruler's policies and actions in the best possible light. On the other hand, an ancient historian could describe the same emperor's reign in an opposite fashion, with a completely negative bias. In *Roman History from Coins*, Michael Grant demonstrates how each contrasting version of the rule of a controversial emperor, such as Nero, can be seen to contain some truth, and a comparison of two versions quickly highlights the bias in each. Grant also elucidates the ways in which coins provide information not reported elsewhere. For example, a number of the third-century Soldier-Emperors are only known from coins, and many of the emperors' activities, such as the restoration of particular public buildings, are also only known from coins.

Representations on coins of buildings in Rome, while accurate in many respects, make use of certain conventions which must be understood for the correct interpretation of these miniature illustrations. In *Temples of Rome as Coin Types*, Donald Frederic Brown lucidly explains the types of features that are abbreviated or enlarged in illustrations of Roman temples on coins. For example, the numbers of columns in temples are often reduced so that the depiction will fit into the limited space of a coin or medallion. On the other hand, cult statues are often enlarged, and the central columns of the temple facade are spread apart to permit full visibility of the statues. Appendix A at the end of this study is a chronologically arranged list of temples illustrated on late Republican and Roman Imperial coins, with plate numbers cited. A fuller discussion of the same material can be found in Brown's dissertation, *Architectura Numismatica, Part One: The Temples of Rome* (Numismatic Architecture . . . ).

Another type of monument which was frequently represented on coins is the Roman triumphal arch. Often a single arch in Rome was reproduced on coins that were struck from several dies at mints in Rome and elsewhere. When these multiple coin illustrations disagree with one another in important architectural details, and when the arch itself does not survive to resolve such disagreements, the modern scholar must be equipped to judge the relative degrees of accuracy of the coins. *The Arch of Nero in Rome,* by Fred S. Kleiner, proposes a methodology for this type of dilemma. According to Kleiner, the coin dies which were cut in Rome are likely to be more accurate than those designed elsewhere, since Roman artisans would have had a first-hand familiarity with the monuments. Furthermore, the dies which can be demonstrated to have been executed earliest have a greater likelihood of being based on the actual monuments, while later dies seem to copy other coins rather than the monuments themselves. Kleiner's numerous photographs of the different coin copies of Nero's Capitoline arch and of earlier triumphal arches from the Republican and Julio-Claudian periods make it easy to follow the technical aspects of his argument.

## Bibliographic Entries for Supplementary Sources

Brown, Donald Frederic. *Architectura Numismatica, Part One: The Temples of Rome.* Ph.D. diss., New York University, 1941.

———. *Temples of Rome as Coin Types.* Numismatic Notes and Monographs no. 90. New York: American Numismatic Society, 1940.

Franke, Peter Robert. *Römische Kaiserporträts im Münzbild.* Munich: Hirmer, 1968.

Giacosa, Giorgio. *Women of the Caesars: Their Lives and Portraits on Coins.* Translated by R. Ross Holloway. Milan: Arte e moneta, [1977].

Grant, Michael. *Roman History from Coins: Some Uses of the Imperial Coinage to the Historian.* Cambridge: Cambridge Univ. Press, 1958. Paperback ed. Cambridge: Cambridge Univ. Press, 1968.

Kleiner, Fred S. *The Arch of Nero in Rome: A Study of the Roman Honorary Arch before and under Nero.* Archaeologica 52. Rome: Giorgio Bretschneider, 1985.

Toynbee, Jocelyn M. C. *Roman Medallions.* 1944. Reprint with introduction by William E. Metcalf. New York: American Numismatic Society, 1986.

## Additional Supplementary Sources

Alföldi, Maria R.-. *Antike Numismatik*. Vol. 1, *Theorie und Praxis*. Kulturgeschichte der antiken Welt 2. Vol. 2, *Bibliographie*. Kulturgeschichte der antiken Welt 3. Mainz am Rhein: P. von Zabern, 1978.

Alram, Michael. *Die Münzprägung des Kaisers Maximinus I. Thrax (235/238)*. Vol. 27, *MIR—Moneta Imperii Romani*. Vienna: Verlag der Österreichischen Akademie der Wissenschaften, 1989.

Donaldson, T. L. *Architecttura Numismatica or Architectural Medals of Classic Antiquity*. 1859. Reprint. *Ancient Architecture on Greek and Roman Coins and Medals*. With new preface and bibliography by John Emerson McCarthy. Argonaut Library of Antiquities. Chicago: Argonaut Publishers, 1966.

Hill, Philip V., J. P. C. Kent, and R. A. G. Carson. *Late Roman Bronze Coinage A.D. 324–498. Part I, The Bronze Coinage of the House of Constantine A.D. 324–346. Part II, Bronze Roman Imperial Coinage of the Later Empire A.D. 346–498*. Reprint with addenda. 1956–59. Reprint with addenda, indexes and plates. London: Spink & Son, 1978.

*Kritische Neuaufnahme der Fundmünzen der römischen Zeit in Deutschland (FMRD), Cohen-RIC-Konkordanz. Pt. 1, Von Augustus bis zur Follis-Reform Diocletians (Cohen² Bd. 1–6 und RIC Bd. I–V/1–2)*. Edited by Maria R.-Alföldi. Antiquitas, Series 1, Abhandlungen zur alten Geschichte 30. Bonn: Habelt, 1978.

Küthmann, Harald, et al. *Bauten Roms auf Münzen und Medaillen*. Catalog of an exhibition at Staatliche Münzsammlung, Munich, October–December, 1973. Munich: E. Bechenbauer, 1973.

Seaby, H. A. *Roman Silver Coins*. Vol. 1, *The Republic to Augustus*. 3d ed. Revised by David R. Sear and Robert Loosley. London: Seaby, 1978. Vol. 2, *Tiberius to Commodus, Arranged according to Cohen*. 3d ed. Revised by Robert Loosley. London: Seaby, 1979. Vol. 3, *Pertinax to Balbinus and Pupienus, Arranged according to Cohen*. 2d ed. Revised by David R. Sear. London: Seaby, 1982. Vol. 4, *Gordian III to Postumus, Arranged according to Cohen*. 2d ed. Revised by David R. Sear. London: Seaby, 1982. Vol. 5, *Carausius to Romulus Augustus, Arranged according to Cohen*. By C. E. King, with valuations by David R. Sear. London: Seaby, 1987.

Sutherland, C. H. V. *Roman History and Coinage 44 BC–AD 69: Fifty Points of Relation from Julius Caesar to Vespasian*. Oxford: Clarendon Press, 1987.

Szaivert, Wolfgang. *De Münzprägung der Kaiser Marcus Aurelius, Lucius Verus und Commodus (161–192)*. Vol. 18, *MIR—Moneta Imperii Romani*. Vienna: Verlag der Österreichischen Akademie der Wissenscharften, 1986.

———. *Die Münzprägung der Kaiser Tiberius und Caius (Caligula) 14/41*. Vols. 2–3, *MIR—Moneta Imperii Romani*. Vienna: Verlag der Österreichischen Akademie der Wissenschaften, 1984.

# ₁17₎

# Greek and Roman Interior Decoration

Schefold, Karl. *Die Wände Pompejis. Topographisches Verzeichnis der Bildmotive* (The Walls of Pompeii: A Topographical Catalog of the Pictorial Motifs). Berlin: Walter de Gruyter & Co., 1957.

## ART FORM

The Greeks who built Bronze-Age palaces initiated the ancient practice of decorating walls, floors, and ceilings of architectural interiors with figurative and abstract motifs. After an apparent break of several hundred years during the Dark Ages, interior decoration seems to have been resumed by the Greeks of the seventh century B.C. Thereafter, the tradition was unbroken, and was continued after the collapse of the Greek Hellenistic kingdoms by the Romans of the late Republican and Imperial eras.

One great period of Greek painting was the Classical development, when large wooden screen paintings that often celebrated the exploits of local heroes were set up in Greek public buildings. These lost monumental compositions are known in part through literary descriptions and through what appear to be copies of figure groups on vases and other media. By the early Hellenistic period, another more permanent technique of painting on plastered wall surfaces was frequently being utilized by the Greeks. Small panel pictures also seem to have been produced by Greek artists from the Classical period onward. Preserved examples demonstrate that floor mosaics with figural scenes were being executed by Greek craftsmen as early as the late fifth century B.C., and the first stucco reliefs from walls and vaulted ceilings were produced by Roman artisans of the first century B.C.

The Romans were great appreciators of Greek painting, and they often included copies of Greek panel paintings among the wall decorations of their homes and temples. But when more than one Roman copy after the same Greek original survives, there are often many differences in execution and composition; this phenomenon requires the researcher to exercise caution in assuming too close a correlation between a lost original and a surviving copy. Extensive evidence permits us to conclude that the Romans included copies of Greek originals and works that seem to be their own creations in ensembles of interrelated themes. These coherent programs of decoration for single rooms had the purpose of advertising the erudition or religious attitudes of the Romans who commissioned the works. Our less complete evidence concerning the thematic content of interior decorations in Greek public buildings—most of it from ancient literary descriptions—suggests that Classical and Hellenistic cycles existed, and that they glorified Classical city-states and Hellenistic rulers.

The eruption of Mount Vesuvius in 79 A.D. buried and preserved for posterity several sites containing our most extensive collection of surviving ancient interiors, that is, the Roman city of Pompeii and some neighboring settlements of a smaller scale, such as Herculaneum and Stabiae. The excavations at Pompeii, which began in the mid-eighteenth century, have uncovered many richly decorated houses, temples, and other public buildings. These structures, particularly the houses, belonged to all Roman social classes. Their interior decorations can therefore be used as indicators of the tastes, levels of culture, and religious beliefs of Roman society in general. In addition, the wall, ceiling, and floor decorations from Pompeii are a rich source of Roman copies based on lost Greek masterpieces.

# RESEARCH USE

The main reference for this topic is *Die Wände Pompejis: Topographisches Verzeichnis der Bildmotive* (The Walls of Pompeii: A Topographical Catalog of the Pictorial Motifs), by Karl Schefold. This is the most comprehensive survey, with bibliography, of the thematic content of the paintings, mosaics, and stucco reliefs from Pompeii. The main text in *Die Wände Pompejis* consists of nine chapters on the buildings from the nine regions inside the city walls. Each building from each region is fully described, with a separate paragraph devoted to the surviving or known decorations from each room. None of the decorations that are described is illustrated.

This reference can be used as a source of evidence for several different types of study. One type of investigation would focus on the decorations from rooms within the same structure that are known to have had different functions. Such a study would reveal the impact of the function of a room on the thematic contents of its decoration. Another type of investigation would compare the decorations from contemporary or noncontemporary buildings which were used for the same purpose. An investigation of the decorations of houses of different sizes and degrees of luxuriousness would be particularly valuable, since it would reveal the range of thematic emphases and tastes in domestic interior decoration. A third type of research would concentrate on all the examples from Pompeii with the same theme. Such a study would demonstrate the various contexts in which the same theme was used, and it would help us to understand the different possible significances this theme held for the Romans. This type of research might also turn up groups of two or more copies that are based on the same Greek originals.

## ORGANIZATION

As the title of Schefold's book indicates, the main body of the text consists of the *Topographisches Verzeichnis* (the Topographical Catalog), in which the themes of Pompeii's paintings, stucco reliefs, and mosaics are presented in an arrangement that corresponds to their original location in the city. All the decorations from one building are presented as a unit. All the buildings from a city block, or *insula*, form a larger group of material. All the *insulae* from one city region comprise the largest organizational element, a chapter. Since Pompeii—inside the city walls—has been divided by archaeologists into nine regions, most of the catalog is taken up with nine chapters for these regions. Each of these nine chapters catalogs all the preserved and known wall, floor, and ceiling decorations from every type of building, including houses as well as public buildings. Additional chapters are devoted to the Villa Imperiale (also referred to as the Villa Suburbana di Porta Marina) in southwest Pompeii under the Temple of Venus Pompeiana, and to the Villa of Mysteries, located outside the city walls to the northwest. For the page numbers of these chapters, see the "Inhalt" (Table of Contents), which can be found immediately after the "Vorwort" (Foreword).

The location of each building included in the nine chapters on the city regions is indicated in the page margin by three numbers which provide all the necessary topographical information. The Roman numeral gives the number of the region, the first Arabic number indicates the *insula*, and the second Arabic number identifies the building within the *insula*. All the buildings in each regional chapter are arranged consecutively according to their *insula* and building numbers.

Opposite the three numbers that identify a building's location is the name of the building. Three terms are used interchangeably in the book to signify "house"—the Latin "Domus," the Italian "Casa" and the German "Haus." When it is known, the name of the owner of the house is given; or if a house is commonly referred to by a descriptive name, this appellation is used. (For example, "Casa del Fauno," Italian for "the House of the Faun," is the name given to the large house in which a bronze figure of a faun was discovered in the pool in the atrium.) A Latin dictionary can be consulted for an explanation of most of the other types of structures in Pompeii; for example, "Taberna mit Thermopolium" is a shop dispensing hot drinks. Another type of name for a structure combines Latin and German words; for example, "Larenheiligtum" means a shrine of the Lares, deities who protected the Romans and brought them prosperity. Bibliographic references to major scholarly discussions follow the name of each building. Bibliographic abbreviations that appear here are explained in the "Verzeichnis der Abkürzungen" (List of Abbreviations) at the end of the volume.

Following the general information on a building is a series of paragraphs, each of which is devoted to the description of the decoration of one room. Rooms are usually labeled by lowercase letters in parentheses, but other labeling systems that correspond to plans which are mentioned in the bibliographic citations following a building's name may also be used. Next to these labels are the names of the identifiable room types. The latter are usually in Latin, and again a Latin dictionary can be consulted. A glossary explaining the standard room types in Roman houses and villas, and good labeled plans showing the locations of these room types can be found in A. G. McKay's *Houses, Villas and Palaces in the Roman World* (Ithaca, N.Y.: Cornell Univ. Press, 1975). After the name of the room type in the Schefold work is a directional indicator of the location of the decoration within the room. For example, "S-Wand" means the work to be described is on the south wall. When a painting is being described, the next information given is its thematic identification. When a mosaic or stucco relief is under discussion, both the medium and the theme are named. Unless indicated otherwise, a mosaic ("Mosaik" in German) is located on the floor. A stucco relief can either be on a wall surface, as when the term "Stuckwand" (stucco wall) is used, or it can be on the ceiling, as in cases when the term "Stuckdecke" (stucco ceiling) is used.

The thematic descriptions of the figurative elements in paintings, mosaics, and stucco reliefs consist of brief identifications of mythological and genre scenes, mythological figures outside of a mythological context, plants, animals, and objects. The reader should be cautioned that both Latin and Greek names for the same mythological characters are used in thematic descriptions, while only the Greek names are listed in the "Index der Bildmotive" (The Index of Pictorial Motifs) at the back of the volume (see below). When a representation that is described no longer survives, it is marked with a cross inside parentheses (+); and when it is partially destroyed, there is an "x" inside parentheses (x). For works that survive but are currently in Naples' Museo Archeologico Nazionale, the German rendering of Naples (Neapel) is given, along with the inventory number.

The paragraphs that describe the decorations of particular rooms often provide additional bibliography. Some indication of the chronology of the decorations from a specific room is also often given. For example, the last information on a room might simply be "Vespasianisch" (Vespasianic, i.e., 69–79 A.D.), or a more detailed explanation of the proposed chronology might be presented.

Even for the researcher who knows German, the descriptions of interior decorations in this reference can be difficult to understand because of their abbreviated format. For example, directional indicators may cause confusion, especially since they occur in both uppercase and lowercase letters. "N" and "n." both mean north; "S" and "s." are south; "O" and "o." are east; and "W" and "w." are west. A similar system is used for two indicators. For example, "SO" and "so." are southeast. The reader should note that the abbreviations for southeast are very close to "So," which Schefold commonly uses as the bibliographic abbreviation for Sogliano's 1879 catalog of paintings (see the "Verzeichnis der Abkürzungen"). Another frequently encountered abbreviation is "Z.", which stands for "Zimmer," or room. "L." and "l." stand for left, and "R." and "r." indicate right. In addition, the abbreviation "v." stands for "von," or of. When dates are given, "v. Chr." means "vor Christi," or B.C., and "n. Chr." means "nach Christo," or A.D. In bibliographic citations, "S." stands for "Seite," or page, and "Taf." stands for "Tafel," or plate. Finally, Helbig's frequently cited catalog of 1868 (see below for title) is referred to simply as "H."

Schefold provides valuable background information on the history of Pompeian scholarship in the "Vorwort" (Foreword) to his catalog. He explains that only two catalogs of a similar nature have previously been attempted—those by Helbig and Sogliano, mentioned in the previous paragraph. Since these early catalogs were published in 1868 and 1879, respectively, they are seriously outdated. Furthermore, they are less complete than Schefold's catalog, making reference only to the principal motifs from pictorial ensembles. In the "Vorwort," Schefold states his more ambitious goals of listing all figurative motifs, dating every room, and citing the most important published illustrations and scholarly discussions for every work. He justifies this full accounting of motifs by pointing out that according to current opinion, all the representative motifs in Roman interiors were intended to work together to create a spiritual whole, often of religious significance (see Complementary References below).

Schefold's "Vorwort" also outlines the chronological divisions and subdivisions of the four styles of Pompeian wall paintings: the First Style (often called Incrustation), before 80 B.C.; the Second Style (often called Architectural), from circa 80 to 15 B.C.; the Third Style (often called Ornate), from circa 15 B.C. to circa 60 A.D.; the Fourth Style (often called Intricate), under Nero, beginning after Pompeii's disastrous earthquake of 62 A.D., and continuing up to the emperor's death in 68 A.D.; the Fourth Style as a continuation of the Neronian Style under Vespasian; and the Pure Vespasianic Fourth Style (characterized by Schefold as classicizing), lasting up to the eruption of Vesuvius in 79 A.D.

Besides the "Vorwort," text, and "Verzeichnis der Abkürzungen" (List of Abbreviations), Schefold's reference has some other valuable features. Immediately after the "Inhalt" (Table of Contents) is a chronological table, "Vermutliche Daten wichtiger in Pompeji oder Neapel erhaltener Dekorationen" (Probable Dates of Important Surviving Decorations in Pompeii or Naples).

At the back of the volume before the "List of Abbreviations" is the useful "Index der Bildmotive deren Standort in Pompeji bekannt ist" (Index of Pictorial Motifs Whose Provenance in Pompeii Is Known). References in this index are made to page numbers in the text. On page 299 of the "Vorbemerkung zu den Registern" (Preliminary Observations on the Indexes), Schefold points out that he does not include the Lares, Penates, and still lifes in this index, since these themes are indexed in two other references which he names. As explained above, the "Index der Bildmotive" cites the names of mythological characters in their Greek forms, while the text uses both Latin and Greek forms. Anyone having difficulties in discovering the Latin equivalents for Greek names should consult H. J. Rose's *Handbook of Greek Mythology* (6th ed., New York: Dutton, 1959). The entries in Rose's first index, "Mythological Names, Greek and Latin, Including Fabulous Places," cite Greek names first, and then their Latin equivalents.

Another index can be found immediately before Schefold's "Index der Bildmotive." This is the "Gebäudeverzeichnis von Pompeji" (Index of Buildings in Pompeii). Here the commonly used names of buildings are arranged in alphabetical order and the topographical coordinates for each building are provided (for an explanation of these, see above). Thus, the reader who wants to become acquainted with the pictorial motifs in a particular building whose name he or she knows, can look up the name of the building in this index. Once the building's three topographical coordinates are known, it can be located easily in the appropriate regional chapter of the text. Buildings not described in the text, that is, buildings inside the walls of Pompeii which do not have preserved interior decorations, and those outside the walls, are marked with an asterisk. Buildings in the latter category are so indicated by the Latin "Extra moenia," meaning "Outside the Walls," and their locations are described. The reader should note that house names are alphabetized by the proper noun identifying them; for example, the "Casa delle Colombe" can be found under "Colombe." Also, when the letter "s." precedes the topographical numbers for a building, it stands for "siehe," or see, and alerts you to the fact that Schefold uses a different name for the same building in his textual description.

Two concordances precede the two indexes. The more useful of the two is the "Konkordanz zu den Inventarnummern des Museo Nazionale, Neapel" (Concordance to the Inventory Numbers of the Museo Nazionale, Naples). The purpose of this concordance is to enable the visiter to Naples' Museo Archeologico Nazionale to imagine the decorations housed there in their original settings. The majority of the works in this concordance are from Pompeii, but decorations from Herculaneum and Stabiae are also included. In the first of six columns in the concordance are the Naples museum inventory numbers, arranged sequentially. Schefold has put quotation marks around the numbers which he has discovered were incorrectly restored on the frames of the paintings after the original numbers had faded. In the second column is usually the number of the public exhibition hall in the museum where the work is currently displayed. If a picture is in the Gabinetto Segreto (the Private Cabinet) of the museum, this fact is indicated by the letters "G.S." Works which Schefold thinks might be in the museum's storerooms are marked "Mag.?" (for *Magazin* or *magazzino,* German and Italian for storeroom). The third and fourth columns in the same index provide bibliographic references to the published catalogs of the museum. The fifth column lists citations to Helbig's 1868 catalog, *Die Wandgemälde der vom Vesuv verschütteten Städte Campaniens* (The Wall Paintings from the Campanian Cities Buried by Vesuvius). The last column—the widest—provides a brief thematic identification of each work. In addition, when a work has a known provenance within Pompeii, the topographical coordinates of the building from which the work was removed are cited here. These coordinates enable the reader to look up the building in the appropriate regional chapter of Schefold's text. The letters "VdC." in the last column stand for the Villa of Cicero at Pompeii, a structure that is not described in Schefold's text. The letter "P." appears when a work is from Pompeii, but its exact point of origin within the city is unknown, and the letters "H." or "St." indicate that a work is from Herculaneum or Stabiae. When no provenance is given in the last column, the researcher should conclude that this information is not known. In cases of this type, Schefold enlarges the thematic identification to include a date and supplementary citations to the scholarly literature, if the work has been published.

The last page of the museum concordance consists of a single-page list, "Bilder ohne Inventarnummern" (Pictures without Inventory Numbers). The left column of this list gives the number of the museum room where a work is located. The right column identifies the theme of a work and, where possible, provides its date, provenance within Pompeii, and bibliographic citations. The reader should note that here "H" does not mean Herculaneum, but is the abbreviation for Helbig's 1868 catalog.

The second concordance is to the Helbig catalog. The reader fortunate enough to have access to this rare book can find an explanation of the arrangement of the second concordance on page 298 of Schefold's "Vorbemerkung zu den Registern" (Preliminary Observations on the Indexes).

## COMPLEMENTARY REFERENCES

As explained above, *Die Wände Pompeijis* has no illustrations. *Vergessenes Pompeji: Unveröffentlichte Bilder römischer Wanddekorationen in geschichtlicher Folge herausgegeben* (Forgotten Pompeii: Unpublished Illustrations of Roman Wall Decorations Arranged in Historical Sequence), by the same author, helps to fill this gap with nearly two hundred plates that are mostly black-and-white and color photographs. In order to discover whether a room from a house that is described in *Die Wände Pompejis* is illustrated and/or discussed in *Vergessenes Pompeji*, the reader should first turn to the "Topographischer Index" (The Topographical Index), found immediately after the black-and-white plates in *Vergessenes Pompeji*. He or she should search here for the three topographical indicators of the house's location and the label, in parentheses, of the specific room. If this room is discussed in *Vergessenes Pompeji*, page numbers for the discussion are given; if it is illustrated, the plate number is given, preceded by "Taf." (for "Tafel," or plate). Any room whose decorations are illustrated in the plates is also fully described in the text, as in Schefold's *La peinture pompéienne* (see below). The second appendix ("Anhang II") of *Vergessenes Pompeji* lists examples of different types of unified painted programs of the Second, Third, and Fourth Styles, for rooms from Pompeii and elsewhere.

Another excellent source of black-and-white and color photos and drawings of the interior decorations of Pompeii is *La peinture murale romaine: Les styles décoratifs pompéiens* (Roman Wall Painting: The Pompeian Styles of Decoration), by Alix Barbet. In this reference, the entire decorations of rooms with different functions from the four styles of Pompeian paintings are discussed and illustrated; mosaic pavements and ceiling designs in painting and stucco relief are considered along with wall paintings. To learn whether a particular house is described by Barbet, the reader should look up the house under the name it is commonly known by in the index (for example, the House of the Faun can be found under "maison du Faune"); after this name, the citation of the three topographical indicators of the house's location (the same indicators used in *Die Wände Pompejis*), placed inside parentheses, assures that an exact match between Schefold's and Barbet's descriptions has been made. Barbet's handbook includes a number of useful chronological tables, such as the one on page 182 that summarizes the divergent datings that leading scholars have proposed for the four Pompeian styles.

Volume 1 of *Le Collezioni del Museo Nazionale di Napoli: I Mosaici, le Pitture, gli Oggetti di uso quotidiano, gli Argenti, le Terracotte invetriate, i Vetri, i Cristalli, gli Avori* (The Collections of the Museo Nazionale at Naples: The Mosaics, the Paintings, the Objects of Daily Use, the Works in Silver, the Glazed Terra-cottas, the Glassware, the Ivories), edited by Borriello and others, can be consulted as a source of black-and-white and color photos of mosaics and paintings from Pompeii that are now housed in the Naples Museum. To determine whether a work is included in this catalog, the researcher needs to look up the Naples inventory number, which is provided by Schefold in *Die Wände Pompejis* in the concordance for volume 1 of *Le Collezioni del Museo Nazionale di Napoli*. The concordance then provides the catalog number used in this catalog, as well as the explanatory symbols "m" for mosaics and "p" for paintings. Preceding the entries in the catalog, which are illustrated by small black-and-white photos, are general introductory chapters on the museum's mosaics and paintings; in these chapters there are a number of excellent color photos. The catalog entries give the scale for each work, the find spot (including the names of buildings and the topographical coordinates for works from Pompeii), the painting style, bibliographical citations (for an explanation of abbreviations, see the back of the volume), and brief descriptions of works.

A good source for drawings of paintings and mosaics that are described by Schefold in *Die Wände Pompejis* is Salomon Reinach's *Répertoire de Peintures Grecques et Romaines (RPGR.), avec 2720 gravures* (Corpus of Greek and Roman Paintings [RPGR.], with 2720 Engravings). Schefold refers to Reinach's corpus with the abbreviation "RP," and cites the page and illustration number for each example from Reinach that he includes. At the bottom of each page of drawings in Reinach's reference are captions for the drawings. The provenance of each drawing is given first—"Pomp." stands for Pompeii; this information is preceded by "Mos." if an example is a mosaic. The theme of each example is then identified, and bibliography is provided (see the back for an explanation of bibliographic abbreviations). Reinach's drawings are of paintings and mosaics found all over the Roman Empire. Furthermore, since it groups examples of the same theme together, this reference is a useful starting point for research on variations in Roman copies after the same Greek originals. *Pitture murali e mosaici nel Museo Nazionale di Napoli* (Wall Paintings and Mosaics in the Museo Nazionale at Naples), by Olga Elia, can be consulted for detailed descriptions, dimensions, and some black-and-white photos of wall and floor decorations from Pompeii that are located in two galleries in the Naples Museum. In *Die Wände Pompejis*, Schefold makes references to this guidebook by citing "Elia," and then the author's catalog number.

For scholars who wish to order photographs of the interior decorations from a particular Pompeian house, or who wish to update the bibliography on a house with more current literature than is cited in Schefold's *Die Wände Pompejis*, the following reference, edited by Irene Bragantini and others, is recommended: *Pitture e pavimenti di Pompei: Repertorio delle fotografie del Gabinetto Fotografico Nazionale* (Paintings and Pavings from Pompeii: Corpus of the Photographs from the Gabinetto Fotografico Nazionale). This three-volume reference has entries for all the structures in Pompeii's nine regions (except region 4) whose interior decorations were photographed *in situ* in recent campaigns by the Istituto Centrale per il Catalogo e la Documentazione, formerly called the Gabinetto Fotografico Nazionale. Entries for the houses and other structures are arranged according to their three topographical coordinates. Within an entry for a particular house, decorations are grouped by rooms, which are referred to by the same numbering system as Schefold's in *Die Wände Pompejis*. The specific positions of works within rooms are often given; "N," "E," "S," and "O" stand respectively for north, east, south and west. The thematic content of each decoration— whether it be a painting (referred to by the abbreviation A), mosaic (P), or stucco relief (S)—is always described. The dating of a work is often given simply by a citation of the appropriate Roman numeral for its Pompeian style. Bibliographic citations use the abbreviations that are explained in the "Elenco delle abbreviazioni" (List of Abbreviations) at the front of each volume. The number of the photograph in the Istituto Centrale per il Catalogo e la Documentazione in Rome forms the last part of the entry (for an explanation of the abbreviations for other photographic archives whose photos are cited, see "Altre abbreviazioni" [Other Abbreviations] at the front of each volume). At the back of each volume are plans of the buildings included, with the rooms labeled as in the textual entries. In addition, there is an "Indice alfabetico degli edifici" (Alphabetical Index of Buildings) at the end of volume 3, in which the researcher can look up a building by its commonly used name;

here cross-references are given to the building's topographical coordinates and to its entry in *Pitture e pavimenti*.

In the article entitled "The Monumental and Literary Evidence for Programmatic Painting in Antiquity," Mary Lee Thompson discusses the types of mythological cycles that can be found in rooms from the houses at Pompeii and the prototypes for such cycles in Greek painting—prototypes known, for the most part, only through literary descriptions. According to Thompson, the programs of paintings at Pompeii show an "emphasis on Dionysus and Aphrodite, the contrasts . . . between the realms of Aphrodite and Artemis, and the use of biographical cycles of heroes" (p. 77). Thompson states on page 66 that the conclusions presented in her article were based on the analysis, contained in her dissertation ("Programmatic Painting in Pompeii: The Meaningful Combination of Mythological Pictures in Room Decoration," Ph.D. diss., Institute of Fine Arts, 1960), of the paintings from 277 rooms at Pompeii. Schefold's *Die Wände Pompejis* describes the thematic content of over a thousand additional rooms; a portion of these could form the focus of future research.

While scholars now generally accept Thompson's conclusions regarding the programmatic nature of Roman wall painting (but see Ling's *Roman Painting* under Handbooks below), they disagree on the significance of these cycles. Thompson (see pp. 40–41 of the article discussed in the previous paragraph) concludes, I believe correctly, that "the idea behind a combination of paintings is frequently on a superficial level, using a play on mythological and compositional motives just as a writer might delight in a witty play on words. The programs usually do not represent any profound religious or intellectual idea." In *La peinture pompéienne: Essai sur l'évolution de sa signification* (Pompeian Painting: Essay on the Evolution of Its Significance), Karl Schefold adopts a completely different point of view and insists that most cycles had the very serious religious purpose of being an "exaltation de l'existence terrestre" (an exaltation of terrestrial existence). Regardless of whether the reader accepts Schefold's main hypothesis regarding the apotheosis symbolism of Roman cycles, his examination of specific programs from the four different phases of Pompeian wall painting brings together and illustrates a useful corpus of examples. Furthermore, the commentary for his illustrations updates the bibliography on the same examples that appears in *Die Wände Pompejis*. Preceding the illustrations, *La peinture pompéienne* has two chronological tables outlining the dates Schefold accepts for Roman houses with painting cycles, and the dates for the Greek originals whose copies are included in these cycles.

The interior decoration of Roman buildings constructed after the destruction of Pompeii in 79 A.D. is surveyed by Hetty Joyce in *The Decoration of Walls, Ceilings, and Floors in Italy in the Second and Third*

*Centuries A.D.* According to Joyce, these stylistically debased but imaginatively designed interiors from the second and third centuries A.D. fall into three broad systems of decoration: "the modular, the architectural, and the figural" (p. 21). Only the figural compositions, consisting primarily of garden and aquatic scenes (some of the latter are mythological), exhibit thematic unity, while the isolated figures or panels that appear in rooms with modular or architectural schemes are often thematically unrelated. Significantly, Joyce arrives at two conclusions regarding second- and third-century interiors: "1) walls and ceilings are thought of as a decorative ensemble; 2) the floor is considered separately and treated as a neutral zone" (p. 99). As in the case of the earlier Pompeian interiors considered by Thompson and Schefold, future researchers might test and possibly refine Joyce's conclusions through the analysis of additional late Roman interiors.

For the researcher who wishes to compare surviving Roman interiors with texts describing famed Greek and Roman interiors, two source books with English translations of Greek and Latins texts by J. J. Pollitt are recommended: *The Art of Greece 1400–31 B.C.*, and *The Art of Rome c. 753 B.C.–337 A.D.* Pollitt's Greek sourcebook contains a separate collection of literary passages on painting in each of the chapters on a period of Greek art, and in the last chapter on art theory. *The Art of Rome* also treats painting separately in the chronologically arranged selections of passages. Artist, geographical, and general indexes at the back of each reference allow the reader to look up a passage on a work according to its artist, location, or subject matter. Literary passages on Roman mosaics, not always included in the selections of passages on painting, can be located by looking up "mosaic" in the general index of *The Art of Rome*. *Recueil Milliet: Textes grecs et latins relatifs à l'histoire de la peinture ancienne* (The Milliet Anthology: Greek and Latin Texts Relating to the History of Ancient Painting), by Adolphe Reinach, is a collection of texts in Greek and Latin alongside translations of the texts in French. The texts deal with Greek painting and are arranged chronologically. Quick access to texts on a particular painter is possible through the use of the "Index alphabétique des noms de peintres mentionnés dans ce volume" (Alphabetical Index of the Names of Painters Mentioned in This Volume), on pages 456–58. This anthology also includes footnotes that indicate when works named in texts are known through copies. The 1985 reprint has a new introduction by Agnès Rouveret on the significance of the original 1921 edition. The following new features, by the same author, are found at the back: an alphabetically arranged index of ancient authors that names the latest authoritative editions of their works and indicates corrections and additions to specific literary passages, referred to by number, in bold-faced type; and a bibliography with a particularly useful section on recent archaeological discoveries (pp. 450–55).

*Histoire et imaginaire de la peinture ancienne (V$^e$ siècle av. J.-C.–I$^{er}$ siècle ap. J.-C.)* [Imaginary History of Ancient Painting (Fifth Century B.C.– First Century A.D.)], by Agnès Rouveret, can be used along with Pollitt's and Reinach's Greek sourcebooks because it attempts to discover correspondences between the ancient history and theory of Greek Classical and Hellenistic painting and the surviving paintings themselves. Among the monuments discussed is the dynamic fourth-century painting from a tomb at Vergina in Macedonia, discovered in 1977, which is evidently an early copy of Nikomachos' *Rape of Persephone* (for the text referring to this work, see Pollitt, *The Art of Greece*, p. 172). A lengthy and current bibliography on the literary texts relating to ancient painting, and on surviving paintings and mosaics, appears at the back of this reference. Before Rouveret's bibliography is a table, arranged alphabetically by location, of famous lost paintings whose ancient locations are known from literary sources. This table names the subjects of the paintings and provides specific citations of literary passages. It also provides cross-references for paintings that were moved from their original locations to Rome.

*Antike Gemäldekopien* (Ancient Copies of Paintings), by Georg Lippold, investigates the complex problems that surround the identification of copies on ancient vases, reliefs, and wall paintings and mosaics from sites such as Pompeii and Herculaneum, with specific Greek paintings known through literary descriptions. In textual discussion and footnotes, Lippold reviews previous scholarship on controversial questions relating to the possible authorship of Greek originals. Black-and-white plates at the back often reproduce more than one copy of the same Greek original.

The researcher desiring to keep current on the literature on ancient mosaics should consult the irregular publication, *Bulletin de l'Association Internationale pour l'Étude de la Mosaïque Antique: Bibliographie* (Bulletin of the International Association for the Study of Ancient Mosaics: Bibliography). This bibliography lists articles and books on ancient mosaics along with abstracts of their contents (in French). Furthermore, reviews of books listed in previous volumes can be found in subsequent volumes. Entries are arranged by general works, and by works on the thematic content of mosaics, on technique, and on mosaics from different regions and cities within the regions. Each volume has a list of abbreviations of journals and other frequently cited publications at the front.

Two papers from a 1983 colloquium, published in the volume *L'Iconographie minoenne* (Minoan Iconography), suggest that frescoes from Minoan cult rooms had carefully conceived religious programs. In "Pictorial Programmes in Minoan Palaces and Villas?" Robin Hägg concludes that "the walls of Minoan cult rooms and connected areas were decorated mostly 1) with perpetuated cult scenes . . . , sometimes 2) with pictures that were guiding and directing the humans who took part in the ritual, sometimes 3) with divine images, which invited divine presence at the festival" (p. 214). The second article, "The Function and Interpretation of the Theran Frescoes," by Nanno Marinatos, concludes that the frescoes from the well-preserved cult rooms on the Cycladic island of Thera had ritual functions consistent with the religious activities that took place in the chambers. These authors' conclusions are significant because they support the hypothesis that coherent programming in interior decorations began with the first Greek wall paintings of the Bronze Age.

## Bibliographic Entries for Complementary References

Barbet, Alix. *La peinture murale romaine: Les styles décoratifs pompéiens*. Introduction by Filippo Coarelli. Paris: Picard, 1985.

Borriello, Maria Rosaria, et al. *Le Collezioni del Museo Nazionale di Napoli: I Mosaici, le Pitture, gli Oggetti di uso quotidiano, gli Argenti, le Terracotte invetriate, i Vetri, i Cristalli, gli Avori*. Introduction by Enrica Pozzi. 2 vols. Rome: De Luca Edizioni d'Arte; Milan: Leonardo, 1989.

Bragantini, Irene, ed., et al. *Pitture e pavimenti di Pompei: Repertorio delle fotografie del Gabinetto Fotografico Nazionale*. Vol. 1, *Regioni I, II, III*. Vol. 2, *Regioni V, VI*. Vol. 3, *Regioni VII, VIII, IX, Indici delle Regioni I-IX*. Rome: Istituto Centrale per il Catalogo e la Documentazione, 1981–86.

*Bulletin de l'Association Internationale pour l'Étude de la Mosaïque Antique: Bibliographie*. 1978– . Paris: Association Internationale pour l'Étude de la Mosaïque Antique. 1978– . (Supersedes *Bulletin d'information de l'Association Internationale pour l'Étude de la Mosaïque Antique*. 1968– . Paris: Association Internationale pour l'Etude de la Mosaïque Antique, 1968– .)

Elia, Olga. *Pitture murali e mosaici nel Museo Nazionale di Napoli*. Ministero della Educazione Nazionale, Direzione Generale delle Belle Arti: Le guide dei musei italiani. Rome: La Libreria dello Stato, 1932.

Hägg, Robin. "Pictorial Programmes in Minoan Palaces and Villas?" In *L'Iconographie minoenne: Actes de la Table Ronde d'Athènes (21–22 avril 1983)*, edited by Pascal Darcque and Jean-Claude Poursat, 209–17. Bulletin de correspondance hellénique, Supplément 11. Paris: École Française d'Athènes, 1985.

Joyce, Hetty. *The Decoration of Walls, Ceilings, and Floors in Italy in the Second and Third Centuries A.D.* Archaeologica 17. Rome: Giorgio Bretschneider, 1981.

Lippold, Georg. *Antike Gemäldekopien*. Abhandlungen der Bayerischen Akademie der Wissenschaften, Philosophisch-historische Klasse, N.F. 33. Munich: C. H. Beck, 1951.

Marinatos, Nanno. "The Function and Interpretation of the Theran Frescoes." In *L'Iconographie minoenne: Actes de la Table Ronde d'Athènes (21–22 avril 1983)*, edited by Pascal Darcque and Jean-Claude Poursat, 219–30. Bulletin de correspondance hellénique, Supplément 11. Paris: École Française d'Athènes, 1985.

Pollitt, J. J. *The Art of Greece 1400–31 B.C.: Sources and Documents*. Sources and Documents in the History of Art Series, edited by H. W. Janson. Englewood Cliffs, N.J.: Prentice-Hall, 1965.

Pollitt, J. J. *The Art of Rome c. 753 B.C.–337 A.D.: Sources and Documents.* Sources and Documents in the History of Art Series, edited by H. W. Janson. Englewood Cliffs, N.J.: Prentice-Hall, 1966. Reprint. New York: Cambridge Univ. Press, 1983.

Reinach, Adolphe. *Recueil Milliet: Textes grecs et latins relatifs à l'histoire de la peinture ancienne.* Introduction by S. Reinach. Paris: Klincksieck, 1921. Reprint, with new introduction and notes by Agnès Rouveret. Collection Deucalion. Paris: Macula, 1985.

Reinach, Salomon. *Répertoire de Peintures Grecques et Romaines (RPGR.), avec 2720 gravures.* Paris: E. Leroux, 1922. Reprint. Rome: "L'Erma" di Bretschneider, 1970.

Rouveret, Agnès. *Histoire et imaginaire de la peinture ancienne (V^e siècle av. J.-C.–I^er siècle ap. J.-C.).* Bibliothèque des Écoles Françaises d'Athènes et de Rome 274. Rome: École Française de Rome, Palais Farnèse, 1989.

Schefold, Karl. *La peinture pompéienne: Essai sur l'évolution de sa signification.* Translated by J.-M. Croisille. Collection Latomus 108. Brussels: Latomus, Revue d'études latines, 1972.

———. *Vergessenes Pompeji: Unveröffentlichte Bilder römischer Wanddekorationen in geschichtlicher Folge herausgegeben.* Bern and Munich: Francke, 1962.

Thompson, Mary Lee. "The Monumental and Literary Evidence for Programmatic Painting in Antiquity." *Marsyas* 9 (1961): 36–77.

# HANDBOOKS

There are a number of useful general handbooks on ancient painting, mosaics, and stucco reliefs. The most comprehensive and up-to-date handbook in English on Roman wall painting, mosaics, and stucco reliefs is Roger Ling's *Roman Painting*. This reference provides in-depth considerations of the four Pompeian styles in Italy and the provinces and of Roman painting and other interior decorations from the middle and late Empire; it also includes an introductory survey of Greek and Etruscan antecedents. In the chapter on mythological and historical paintings, Ling presents a view contrary to that of Thompson, who finds different types of thematic links between paintings within the same rooms (see Complementary References above). Ling concludes that "the chief factor which seems to have dictated the choice of pictures in a given room was the possibility of achieving a formal (i.e. a compositional and coloristic) balance" (p. 138). Additional chapters in Ling's handbook are "Other Paintings," "Technique," and "Painters and Patrons." A brief final chapter reports on the influence of Roman wall paintings on artists and interior decorators of the fifteenth century and later. *Roman Painting* has black-and-white and color photos and line drawings. The labels for illustrations of decorations from Pompeii give the three topographical coordinates of the buildings where the decorations were found; museum inventory numbers are also provided for Pompeian decorations that have been moved to Naples. At the back of the volume are a list of abbreviations and an extensive bibliography; the latter is divided into general references and those pertaining to the contents of the different chapters. Another comprehensive reference is *Malerei und Zeichnung der klassischen Antike* (Painting and Drawing of Classical Antiquity), by Andreas Rumpf. This is a stylistic history, written in straightforward German, of each period of ancient painting. The consideration begins with the Greek Geometric phase and ends with the late Roman era of the fifth century A.D. Evidence of all kinds—vases, original paintings and copies, mosaics, and literary sources—is discussed as manifestation of the variations in the style of each period. Photographs and drawings accompany the text. There are authoritative footnotes, and at the front is a list of abbreviations. *La pittura antica* (Ancient Painting) is a collection of essays and book reviews by the leading Italian scholar, Ranuccio Bianchi Bandinelli. Two long essays, "La pittura classica" (Classical Painting) and "La pittura ellenistica" (Hellenistic Painting), are especially useful. The former is a general history of the themes and styles of paintings from the different Greek and Roman periods; the latter is an attempt to reconstruct the stylistic progression of Hellenistic painting. Additional articles and reviews deal with more limited topics, such as the significance of the paintings from the Greek Tomb of the Diver at Paestum, discovered in 1968. Color and black-and-white photos follow the text. Before these plates is an alphabetically arranged table of Greek paintings known from literary sources to have been moved to Rome.

*Ancient Painting from the Earliest Times to the Period of Christian Art*, a lengthy handbook by Mary Hamilton Swindler that was published in 1929, is still the only comprehensive overview, in English, of all the periods of Greek and Roman painting. This intelligent survey begins with Paleolithic painting, covers Near Eastern and Greek Bronze-Age painting and all the later phases of Greek and Roman painting, and ends with painting from the Early Christian era. An outline of historical circumstances introduces the discussions of paintings from each civilization and period. Surviving paintings and copies and literary descriptions of lost works are considered in these discussions. Footnotes and a lengthy bibliography at the back enrich the author's treatment; numerous black-and-white and color illustrations, including reconstructions of lost Greek wall paintings, enable the reader to achieve a good sense of stylistic development.

Certainly one of the most masterful surveys of Greek wall painting is *Greek Painting*, by Martin Robertson. Using literary descriptions of lost masterpieces and echoes of the same works in vase-painting as his evidence, Robertson reconstructs the progression of style, mood, and thematic content of Greek wall painting. Special emphasis is given to the sixth and fifth centuries B.C., when Greek vase-painting was a high art form; vases from these centuries, therefore, yield an especially true sense of the quality of lost contemporary wall paintings. Robertson also introduces Minoan wall painting and Minoan and Mycenaean vase-painting. All the illustrations in this excellent introduction to Greek painting are in color, and there is a general bibliography at the back. Another useful introduction to both Greek and Etruscan painting is *Greek and Etruscan Painting*, by Tony Spiteris. This broad survey begins its discussion with the Greek Bronze Age, and then covers all the later periods of Greek art. A brief chapter reviews Etruscan tomb painting, whose technique and style shed some light on the methods of execution of lost Greek wall paintings. A dictionary, with entries that are indicated in the text by asterisks, appears along with other research aids at the back. All the textual illustrations are in color.

*Pittura greca: Da Polignoto ad Apelle* (Greek Painting: From Polygnotus to Apelles), by Paolo Moreno, can be consulted as a supplement to Robertson's handbook. Here recent finds of original classical paintings, such as those from the Tomb of the Diver at Paestum and the tombs at Vergina, are incorporated into a stylistic history of Greek wall painting from the fifth and fourth centuries B.C. Numerous black-and-white and color photographs accompany the textual discussion (see the bottoms of the pages for citations of illustrations), and a useful bibliography and several indexes appear at the back.

*Masterpieces of Greek Drawing and Painting*, by Ernst Pfuhl, contains a selection of 160 plates (some in color) from the 800 plates in his earlier German publication, *Malerei und Zeichnung der Griechen* (Painting and Drawing of the Greeks). Besides the plates, this English edition—translated by the great scholar J. D. Beazley—has extensive commentary that relates surviving works of vase-painting, wall painting, and mosaics to lost works by the great painters that are known through literary descriptions. After the textual commentary is a bibliography, updated by Beazley, and a "List of Artists of the Attic Vases Illustrated," by Beazley.

*The Greek Painters' Art*, by Irene Weir, covers the major categories of evidence regarding wall and floor decoration, that is, preserved paintings and mosaics, literary sources, and vases. In addition, this reference contains much useful information on observable paint traces on free-standing sculptures and reliefs, architectural sculptures, and architectural members. In many cases, these paint traces were much clearer in 1905 (when the book was published) than they are today, as the black-and-white photos make clear. The lengthy bibliography at the back is of interest for the researcher wishing to familiarize himself or herself with the nineteenth-century literature on ancient painting.

Additional handbooks explore further aspects of Greek painting. For example, the Metropolitan Museum of Art publication, *Greek Painting: The Development of Pictorial Representation from Archaic to Graeco-Roman*

*Times*, traces the "development of three-dimensional representation" in Greek art from the Bronze Age to the Greco-Roman era. An introduction by Gisela M. A. Richter, in which vases, paintings, and literary sources are used as evidence, outlines the general progression from two-dimensional to three-dimensional representation; a series of black-and-white photographs of vases and paintings in the Metropolitan Museum of Art, accompanied by commentary and captions, then illustrates specific steps in this progression. *Form and Color in Greek Painting*, by Vincent J. Bruno, focuses on two controversial topics: "the development of three-dimensional form by means of shading," and "the use of color, in particular the presumed restriction of color adopted by classical painters" (p. 17). In reconstructing the development of these two aspects of Greek painting, Bruno uses for evidence preserved paintings on tombstones and plastered wall surfaces, polychrome paintings on vases, and ancient literary sources. His illustrations, most of them in color, include accurate watercolor sketches made by the author from the monuments themselves. This reference includes a list of abbreviations, a bibliography of books and articles, and scholarly footnotes.

*Aegean Painting in the Bronze Age*, by Sara A. Immerwahr, is a comprehensive and up-to-date review of painting from the palaces and other structures of the Bronze-Age Greeks. The different phases of Minoan, Cycladic, and Mycenaean wall paintings, broken down into categories of thematic content, are the focus of the main chapters. Additional chapters deal with evidence for dating, techniques of execution, and painting on vases and *larnakes* (terra-cotta burial chests). Plans, reconstruction drawings, and color and black-and-white photos accompany the text. In addition, a catalog of examples, arranged by provenance, can be found after the last chapter and before the notes. After the notes is a lengthy bibliography; at the front of the volume is a list of bibliographic abbreviations.

*Roman Painting*, by Amedeo Maiuri, is perhaps the best introduction to the subject in English. This study, illustrated by excellent color plates, reviews Italian painting from its inception in South Italy in the fifth century B.C. to the destruction of Pompeii in 79 A.D. The author discerns two tendencies in Roman painting: a classicizing style in which earlier Greek prototypes were imitated, and "a new, bolder handling of line and color" in which "the artists sponsoring this movement treated the incidents and protagonists of the ancient legends on human, realistic lines" (p. 11). The main chapters in Maiuri's lucid consideration are entitled "Pre-Roman Painting in Southern Italy"; "Official Painting in Rome"; "The Mural Painting of Campania" (the region including Pompeii); "Pictures with Figure-Subjects"; "Nature in Pompeian Painting"; and "Scenes of Everyday Life." At the back are a bibliography and thematic index.

*Römische Wandmalerei vom Untergang Pompejis bis ans Ende des dritten Jahrhunderts* (Roman Wall Painting from the Destruction of Pompeii to the

End of the Third Century), by Fritz Wirth, investigates the period of Roman painting not covered in Maiuri's handbook, that is, the era of the Roman Empire from the late first century A.D. through the late third century A.D. The author discerns six different stylistic tendencies in this time span, each of which is discussed in a separate chapter. The consideration of each style begins with an introduction on the spiritual climate of the era; general observations on the style of all contemporary Roman art appear next, followed by a consideration of trends in wall painting. Footnotes and black-and-white illustrations accompany the text.

Three further English surveys of Roman painting, while lacking profundity in their textual discussions, have useful aspects. Two of these references—*Roman Painting*, by Gilbert Charles-Picard, and *Roman and Palaeo-Christian Painting*, by Gérald Gassiot-Talabot—have good selections of illustrations in color. In addition, some aspects of Charles-Picard's arguments, while not fully developed, are of interest; for example, this author suggests that Roman historical reliefs were influenced by conventions and examples of Greek and Roman paintings. The handbook by Gassiot-Talabot, like its companion volume by Spiteris in the Funk & Wagnalls' History of Painting series, includes a dictionary which has entries on Roman painters and on sites with Roman paintings. The third handbook, *Roman and Etruscan Painting*, by Arturo Stenico, contains concise summaries of the four Pompeian styles and the thematic categories of Roman painting.

A more detailed description of the four Pompeian styles or schemes of wall decoration can be found in chapter 2 of Ludwig Curtius's *Die Wandmalerei Pompejis: Eine Einführung in ihr Verständnis* (The Wall Painting of Pompeii: An Introduction to Its Appreciation). The other three chapters in Curtius's study are an introduction, which includes a summary of early Pompeian scholarship; a stylistic history of panel paintings, which points out difficulties in attempts at distinguishing contemporary stylistic traits from those derived from Greek prototypes; and a discussion of selected masterpieces, such as the frieze from the Villa of Mysteries. This reference has black-and-white and color illustrations, and notes at the end of each chapter. In *Die Wände Pompejis*, Schefold refers to this book as "Curtius." Another reference which provides a lengthy explanation of the four styles of Pompeian painting is *La pittura ellenistico-romana* (Hellenistic-Roman Painting), by G. E. Rizzo. This richly illustrated study also includes detailed descriptions and discussions of Roman copies of Greek originals; and attention is devoted to both nonmythological themes of Greek inspiration and Roman subjects. At the end of the text, before the plates, is a bibliography. This book is cited by Schefold as "Rizzo."

*Mosaics*, by H. P. L'Orange and P. J. Nordhagen, is an excellent introduction to Greek, Roman, Early Christian, and Early Byzantine mosaics. The authors emphasize changes in technique, placement, and thematic content of mosaics, and they demonstrate how mosaics were planned to add decorative appeal, functional clarity, and religious content to rooms and structures with different purposes. This reference has black-and-white and color illustrations and a general bibliography at the back. A useful and up-to-date survey of mosaics is *La mosaïque antique* (Ancient Mosaics), by one of the world's leading authorities on mosaics, Philippe Bruneau. One chapter of this concise consideration reviews general aspects of mosaics; here is included a useful characterization of the evidence, in the form of the mosaics themselves and the limited number of literary comments on them. Additional chapters outline the technical and thematic development of Greek Classical and Hellenistic and Roman Imperial mosaics, and our knowledge of the mosaicists and their clients. Unfortunately, this illustrated survey has no footnotes or bibliography.

The first type of mosaic with figural and ornamental designs to be produced by the Greeks was composed of smoothed pebbles. In *Untersuchungen zu den antiken Kieselmosaiken von den Anfängen bis zum Beginn der Tesseratechnik* (Investigations on Ancient Pebble Mosaics from Their Introduction to the Beginning of the Tessera Technique), Dieter Salzmann discusses and catalogs all known Greek examples of this technique, along with some prototypes from non-Greek cities such as Gordion in Phrygia. Salzmann arrives at a chronology of his examples through historically attested foundation and destruction dates of cities with pebble mosaics, through dates secured by evidence from excavations, and through stylistic comparisons with similar depictions from other media of art. His comprehensive illustrated catalog of examples, the first to be attempted for this type of mosaic, includes not only floors comprised entirely of pebbles, but also floors composed of a mixture of pebbles and unsquared stone tesserae. The latter mixed technique directly precedes the adoption of mosaics formed exclusively of squared tesserae.

Three illustrated articles describe major examples of different classes of Roman floor mosaics from the Roman Republic and the Empire. These articles, by Marion Elizabeth Blake, become progressively more limited in their geographic scope, because "it became evident that the mosaics of Rome and its immediate vicinity developed independently after the close of the second century." The articles are entitled: "The Pavements of the Roman Buildings of the Republic and Early Empire"; "Roman Mosaics of the Second Century in Italy"; and "Mosaics of the Late Empire in Rome and Vicinity." Thematic and other indexes appear at the end of each article. *Roman Wall and Vault Mosaics*, by Frank B. Sear, is a useful study of mosaics that were not positioned on floors. This reference has a descriptive catalog, with bibliographic citations and illustrations, that includes all known Italian and provincial wall and vault mosaics and their prototypes in other media from the third century B.C. through the fourth century A.D. It also contains several general chapters on the history of wall and vault mosaics, their thematic content, and their materials and techniques. In the second chapter, the author points out that since many Roman wall mosaics decorated fountains, themes related to water, such as Neptune and fish, are frequently recurring motifs.

*Römische Stuckreliefs* (Roman Stucco Reliefs), by Harald Mielsch, is the only scholarly survey of the stylistic development of Roman stucco reliefs from walls and ceilings, and of the dependency of these decorations on contemporary wall paintings, reliefs, and statues in the round. Besides containing general discussions along these lines, Mielsch's study features an illustrated and annotated catalog of examples of stucco reliefs from Rome, Latium, southern Etruria, and Campania. At the front of the volume is a list of the bibliographic abbreviations used in the catalog and the textual footnotes. Another useful feature is the index at the back ("Motive") which permits the researcher to look up mythological and nonmythological themes in the text and catalog.

## Bibliographic Entries for Handbooks

Bianchi Bandinelli, Ranuccio. *La pittura antica*. Edited by Filippo Coarelli and Luisa Franchi dell'Orto. Biblioteca di storia antica 11. Rome: Editori Riuniti, 1980.

Blake, Marion Elizabeth. "Mosaics of the Late Empire in Rome and Vicinity." *Memoirs of the American Academy in Rome* 17 (1940): 81–130.

——. "The Pavements of the Roman Buildings of the Republic and Early Empire." *Memoirs of the American Academy in Rome* 8 (1930): 7–159.

——. "Roman Mosaics of the Second Century in Italy." *Memoirs of the American Academy in Rome* 13 (1936): 68–214.

Bruneau, Philippe. *La mosaïque antique*. Lectures en Sorbonne. Paris: Presses de l'Université de Paris, Sorbonne, 1987.

Bruno, Vincent J. *Form and Color in Greek Painting*. New York: Norton, 1977.

Charles-Picard, Gilbert. *Roman Painting*. The Pallas Library of Art, no. 4. Greenwich, Conn.: New York Graphic Society, 1968.

Curtius, Ludwig. *Die Wandmalerei Pompejis: Eine Einführung in ihr Verständnis*. Cologne: E. A. Seemann, 1929. Reprint. Hildesheim: Georg Olms, 1960; bound with reprint of: Klinkert, Walter. "Bemerkungen zur Technik der Pompejanischen Wanddekoration." *Mitteilungen des Deutschen Archäologischen Instituts. Römische Abteilung* 64 (1957): 111–48.

Gassiot-Talabot, Gérald. *Roman and Palaeo-Christian Painting*. Translated by Anthony Rhodes. History of Painting. New York: Funk & Wagnalls, 1965.

Immerwahr, Sara A. *Aegean Painting in the Bronze Age*. University Park and London: Pennsylvania State Univ. Press, 1990.

Ling, Roger. *Roman Painting*. New York: Cambridge Univ. Press, 1991.

L'Orange, H. P., and P. J. Nordhagen. *Mosaics*. Translated by Ann E. Keep. Methuen's Handbooks of Archaeology. London: Methuen, 1966.

Maiuri, Amedeo. *Roman Painting*. Translated by Stuart Gilbert. The Great Centuries of Painting. Geneva: Albert Skira, 1953.

The Metropolitan Museum of Art. *Greek Painting: The Development of Pictorial Representation from Archaic to Graeco-Roman Times*. Introduction by Gisela M. A. Richter. New York: Metropolitan Museum of Art, 1944. Reprint. New York: The Museum, 1957.

Mielsch, Harald. *Römische Stuckreliefs*. Mitteilungen des Deutschen Archäologischen Instituts. Römische Abteilung. Ergängzungsheft 21. Heidelberg: F. H. Kerle, 1975.

Moreno, Paolo. *Pittura greca: Da Polignoto ad Apelle*. Milan: Arnoldo Mondadori, 1987.

Pfuhl, Ernst. *Malerei und Zeichnung der Griechen*. 3 vols. Munich: Bruckmann, 1923. Reprint. Rome: "L'Erma" di Bretschneider, 1969.

———. *Masterpieces of Greek Drawing and Painting*. Translated by J. D. Beazley. New York: Macmillan, 1955.

Rizzo, G. E. *La pittura ellenistico-romana*. Thesaurus Artium. Milan: Fratelli Treves, 1929.

Robertson, Martin. *Greek Painting*. The Great Centuries of Painting. Geneva: Albert Skira, 1959. Reprint. New York: Rizzoli International Publications, 1979.

Rumpf, Andreas. *Malerei und Zeichnung der klassischen Antike*. Handbuch der Archäologie im Rahmen des Handbuchs der Altertumswissenschaft 4. Munich: C. H. Beck, 1953.

Salzmann, Dieter. *Untersuchungen zu den antiken Kieselmosaiken von den Anfängen bis zum Beginn der Tesseratechnik*. Archäologische Forschungen 10. Berlin: Gebr. Mann, 1982.

Sear, Frank B. *Roman Wall and Vault Mosaics*. Mitteilungen des Deutschen Archäologischen Instituts. Römische Abteilung. Ergänzungsheft 23. Heidelberg: F. H. Kerle, 1977.

Spiteris, Tony. *Greek and Etruscan Painting*. Translated by Janet Sondheimer. History of Painting. New York: Funk & Wagnalls, 1965.

Stenico, Arturo. *Roman and Etruscan Painting*. Translated by Angus Malcolm. Compass History of Art. New York: Viking, 1963.

Swindler, Mary Hamilton. *Ancient Painting from the Earliest Times to the Period of Christian Art*. New Haven: Yale Univ. Press, 1929. Reprint. New York: AMS Press, 1979.

Weir, Irene. *The Greek Painters' Art*. Boston: Ginn, 1905.

Wirth, Fritz. *Römische Wandmalerei vom Untergang Pompejis bis ans Ende des dritten Jahrhunderts*. Berlin: Verlag für Kunstwissenschaft, 1934. Reprint. Darmstadt: Wissenschaftliche Buchgesellschaft, 1968.

# SUPPLEMENTARY SOURCES

The scholar who initially defined and proposed the chronology for the four Pompeian styles was August Mau. (For this author's account, in English, of the styles, see *Pompeii: Its Life and Art*, pp. 457–70.) Recent scholarship has challenged Mau's conclusions regarding the beginning of the Fourth Style. Attributions of new examples to this style and new information on these examples from excavations have led authorities such as Rolf Winkes to the belief that the Fourth Style, with its achievement of depth in the articulation of architectural members, did not begin in the reign of the Roman Emperor Nero, as Mau proposed, but had an early phase in the reign of Tiberius. According to Winkes, this early phase of the Fourth Style coexisted with the continuation of the flatter Third Pompeian Style. Winkes's new definition and dating of the outset of the Fourth Style is explained in *Roman Paintings and Mosaics,* an exhibition catalog for holdings in the Museum of Art at the Rhode Island School of Design. Many of these holdings are paintings from a villa at Fondo Bottaro near Pompeii which Winkes believes are early Fourth Style. Additional paintings and mosaics described in the catalog are painted portraits from the Fayoum oasis in Egypt and floor mosaics from Antioch-on-the-Orontes.

Very little work has been done in the realm of attributions of Roman panel paintings to specific Roman wall painters. Mabel M. Gabriel, in *Masters of Campanian Painting,* expresses the belief that the hands of individual masters can be distinguished if one studies these aspects of panel paintings: "personality and individual characteristics; composition; color and light; brush strokes and details" (p. 5). Using these criteria, Gabriel establishes corpora of works for four painters from Herculaneum and Pompeii. Her discussions of attributions cover the aspects mentioned, as well as the thematic content of the works. In chapter 4 of "Pompeii: The Casa dei Dioscuri and Its Painters," L. Richardson attempts to establish the bodies of work of seven figure painters who decorated walls from the House of the Dioscuri in Pompeii and other structures at Pompeii and at Herculaneum. Richardson justifies his attributions with numerous photographs—both general views and details—and with precise explanations of stylistic similarities between works assigned to the same artist. At the beginning of Richardson's chapter on attributions, the author presents a critical review of previous attempts at establishing Pompeian painters' oeuvres (including that of Gabriel). Schefold's *Die Wände Pompejis* makes references to Richardson's book with the abbreviation "Rich." Studies such as Gabriel's and Richardson's are useful because they should permit the researcher of copies of Greek originals to distinguish the details that are common stylistic traits in the works of the Roman copyist from those derived from Greek prototypes.

Painted copies of statues and animated figure types whose poses are derived from statues appear frequently on the wall decorations of rooms from Roman buildings. Until recently, these representations of statues, which often occur in the contexts of architectural and landscape settings, were believed to be fantasies on the part of Roman wall-painters. However, as Eric M. Moorman demonstrates in *La pittura parietale romana come fonte di conoscenza per scultura antica* (Roman Wall Painting as a Source of Knowledge for Ancient Sculpture), a sufficient number of examples of actual structures and gardens with statues has now been investigated to merit the tentative conclusion that the paintings with statuary do in fact replicate real environments. Furthermore, these seemingly accurate depictions of statues permit us to restore missing parts and lost painted details of incompletely preserved statuary replicas of the same figure types; they also supply copies of previously unknown statuary types. Moorman's fascinating study, besides containing discussion chapters that touch on the issues just delineated, has an illustrated catalog that presents painted representations of statues in alphabetical order according to provenance or current location; entries for examples from Pompeii are organized topographically, that is, with the same arrangement as the buildings in Schefold's *Die Wände Pompejis.*

One of the most difficult problems that confronts the scholar of ancient wall painting is determining the origin of the detailed and spatially accurate depiction of landscape. The first paintings in which landscape is a significant component date from the first century B.C., and come from Rome and the region that encompasses Pompeii, called Campania. Unfortunately, surviving evidence pertaining to Greek landscapes is very incomplete regarding the preceding third and second centuries B.C. Thus one can argue that the Roman examples were derived from lost Greek prototypes, or one can propose, with no evidence available to refute the view, that detailed landscapes were a Roman invention. In "Romano-Campanian Mythological Landscape Painting," Christopher M. Dawson adopts the second approach. He supports his belief regarding the originality of Romano-Campanian landscape painters through the comparison of Roman representations of myths in landscape settings with traditional Greek schemes for the same myths, in which the only landscape details are those essential for the story line. The author suggests that the Roman development of landscape as a background for episodes from mythology "led to the non-mythological landscapes of the later Second, the Third, and the Fourth Styles, which were almost certainly the creations of Romano-Campanian painters of that period" (p. 172). The third chapter of Dawson's study consists of an illustrated, descriptive catalog of Romano-Campanian mythological landscape paintings; in *Die Wände Pompejis,* Schefold refers to entries in this catalog with the abbreviated citation "Dawson."

One of the most popular forms of Roman mosaic decoration was that in which figures were executed with tesserae of black volcanic stone, or *selce,* and the background and interior details of the figures were composed of tesserae of white limestone or marble. This mosaic technique was used to create compositions of all types for floors of Roman rooms whose ceilings were flat or vaulted. The technique was in vogue during most of the Roman Empire, from circa 20 B.C. through the third century A.D., and forms the subject of an imaginative study by John R. Clarke entitled *Roman Black-and-White Figural Mosaics*. Clarke's study is divided into two parts which investigate two aspects of black-and-white figural mosaics: "the relationship of the composition of figural mosaics to their architectural contexts, and the style characteristics of mosaics in the various periods." Unlike previous scholars, who have dismissed mosaics of this class as inferior to Roman mosaics in the Greek polychrome technique, Clarke asserts that black-and-white mosaics had several important architectural functions, such as "spatial division and enclosure" and "traffic direction," and he demonstrates that they showed a high level of execution as well as often exhibiting a lively and expressive quality. Furthermore, the author outlines how this mode of mosaic decoration was responsive to changes in other artistic media such as the increase in construction of large vaulted spaces in the late Roman Empire. In short, according to Clarke, the evolution of black-and-white mosaics can be used as a source of evidence by those who insist on the originality of Roman art.

The black-and-white mosaic technique was not dominant everywhere in the Roman Empire, although its influence was universally felt. In *The Mosaics of Roman North Africa: Studies in Iconography and Patronage*, Katherine M. D. Dunbabin argues that mosaicists from this region "adopted the techniques and compositional methods of the Italian black-and-white mosaicists, while retaining the use of polychromy" (p. 10). This author demonstrates further that the large and descriptive polychrome compositions of north Africa were frequently used as a vehicle for expressing the "interests and activities, social, civic, and religious, of the society or the individual" (ibid.). *The Mosaics of Roman North Africa* begins with a useful introduction that explains the emergence of the African polychrome technique. A general chapter outlines our knowledge of African mosaic workshops, patrons, the mosaicists themselves, and the dating of the mosaics. Discussions of predominant themes in African mosaics—among them the hunt, the amphitheater, and the circus—follow. The last textual chapter investigates the influence of the African style on the mosaics of other regions such as Sicily. At the back of the volume, before the color and black-and-white photos, is an annotated catalog of African mosaics that are discussed in the text. An explanation of bibliographic abbreviations used in this catalog appears at the front of the volume and a lengthy bibliography including general books on mosaics and literature specifically on African mosaics can be found following the catalog.

## Bibliographic Entries for Supplementary Sources

Clarke, John R. *Roman Black-and-White Figural Mosaics*. New York: New York Univ. Press, for the College Art Assn. of America, 1979.

Dawson, Christopher M. "Romano-Campanian Mythological Landscape Painting." *Yale Classical Studies* 9 (1944): 1–233. Reprint. Rome: "L'Erma" di Bretschneider, 1965.

Dunbabin, Katherine M. D. *The Mosaics of Roman North Africa: Studies in Iconography and Patronage*. Oxford Monographs on Classical Archaeology. Oxford: Clarendon Press, 1978.

Gabriel, Mabel M. *Masters of Campanian Painting*. New York: H. Bittner, 1952.

Mau, August. *Pompeii: Its Life and Art*. 2d ed. Translated by Francis W. Kelsey. London and New York: Macmillian, 1902. Reprint. New Rochelle, N.Y.: Caratzas Brothers, 1982.

Moorman, Eric M. *La pittura parietale romana come fonte di conoscenza per scultura antica*. Scrinium: Monographs on History, Archaeology, and Art History, no. 2. Assen: Van Gorcum, 1988.

Richardson, L. "Pompeii: The Casa dei Dioscuri and Its Painters." *Memoirs of the American Academy in Rome* 23 (1955): 1–165.

Winkes, Rolf. *Roman Paintings and Mosaics*. Catalogue of the Classical Collection, Museum of Art, Rhode Island School of Design. Providence, R.I.: Museum of Art, Rhode Island School of Design, 1982.

## Additional Supplementary Sources

Andronikos, Manoles. *Vergina: The Royal Tombs and the Ancient City*. Athens: Ekdotike Athenon S.A., 1984.

Bastet, F. L., and Mariette de Vos. *Proposta per una classificazione del terzo stile pompeiano*. Translated by Arnold de Vos. Archeologische Studiën van het Nederlands Instituut te Rome 4. 'S-Gravenhage: Ministerie van Cultuur, 1979.

Blanckenhagen, Peter H. v., and Christine Alexander. *The Paintings from Boscotrecase*. Appendix by Georges Papadopulos. Mitteilungen des Deutschen Archäologischen Instituts. Römische Abteilung. Ergänzungsheft 6. Heidelberg: F. H. Kerle, 1962.

Bruneau, Philippe. *Mosaics on Delos*. Translated by Odile Didelot. Paris: Diffusion de Boccard, 1974.

Bruno, Vincent J. *Hellenistic Painting Techniques: The Evidence of the Delos Fragments*. Columbia Studies in the Classical Tradition, no. 11. Leiden: E. J. Brill, 1985.

Dorigo, Wladimiro. *Late Roman Painting*. Foreword by Sergio Bettini. Translated by James Cleugh and John Warrington. New York and Washington: Praeger, 1970.

Ehrhardt, Wolfgang. *Stilgeschichtliche Untersuchungen an römischen Wandmalereien von der späten Republik bis zur Zeit Neros*. Mainz am Rhein: P. von Zabern, 1987.

Engemann, Josef. *Architekturdarstellungen des frühen zweiten Stils: Illusionistische römische Wandmalerei der ersten Phase und ihre Vorbilder in der realen Architektur*. Mitteilungen des Deutschen Archäologischen Instituts. Römische Abteilung. Ergänzungsheft 12. Heidelberg: F. H. Kerle, 1967.

Hirsch, Ethel S. "Another Look at Minoan and Mycenaean Interrelationships in Floor Decoration." *American Journal of Archaeology* 84 (Oct. 1980): 453–62.

———. *Painted Decoration on the Floors of Bronze Age Structures on Crete and the Greek Mainland*. Studies in Mediterranean Archaeology, no. 53. Göteborg: Paul Åströms Förlag, 1977.

Joyce, Hetty. "Form, Function and Technique in the Pavements of Delos and Pompeii." *American Journal of Archaeology* 83 (1979): 253–63.

Kebric, Robert B. *The Paintings in the Cnidian Lesche at Delphi and their Historical Context*. Mnemosyne: Bibliotheca classica batava, Supplement 80. Leiden: E. J. Brill, 1983.

Laidlaw, Anne. *The First Style in Pompeii: Painting and Architecture*. Archaeologica 57. Rome: Giorgio Bretschneider, 1985.

Mansuelli, G. A., L. Laurenzi, and S. Lagona. *Arte romana: Pittura—Arti minori*. Guide allo studio della civiltà romana 7.3. Rome: Jouvence, 1979.

Marinatos, Nanno. *Art and Religion in Thera: Restructuring a Bronze Age Society*. Athens: D. & I. Mathioulakis, 1984.

Maxwell-Stuart, P. G. *Studies in Greek Colour Terminology 1: ΓΛΑΥΚΟΣ*. Mnemosyne: Bibliotheca classica batava, Supplement 65. Leiden: E. J. Brill, 1981.

———. *Studies in Greek Colour Terminology 2: ΧΑΡΟΠΟΣ*. Mnemosyne: Bibliotheca classica batava, Supplement 67. Leiden: E. J. Brill, 1981.

Morgan, Lyvia. *The Miniature Wall Paintings of Thera: A Study in Aegean Culture and Iconography*. Cambridge Classical Studies. Cambridge: Cambridge Univ. Press, 1988.

Napoli, Mario. *La Tomba del Tuffatore: La scoperta della grande pittura greca*. Bari: De Donato, 1970.

Ovadiah, Asher. *Geometric and Floral Patterns in Ancient Mosaics: A Study of Their Origin in the Mosaics from the Classical Period to the Age of Augustus*. Rome: "L'Erma" di Bretschneider, 1980.

Parlasca, Klaus. *Mumienporträts und verwandte Denkmäler*. Wiesbaden: Franz Steiner, 1966.

Parrish, David. "Annus-Aion in Roman Mosaics." In *Mosaïque romaine tardive: L'iconographie du temps, les programmes iconographiques des maisons africaines*, pp. 11–25. Ed. by Yvette Duval and published with cooperation of Université Paris XII, Val de Varne. Paris: distributed by Didier-Erudition, 1981.

Ragghianti, Carlo Ludovico. *The Painters of Pompeii*. Translated by Shirley Bridges. Milan: Edizioni del Milione, 1964.

Robinson, David M. *Mosaics, Vases, and Lamps of Olynthus Found in 1928 and 1931*. Vol. 5, *Excavations at Olynthus*. The Johns Hopkins University Studies in Archaeology, no. 18. Baltimore: Johns Hopkins Univ. Press; London: Humphrey Milford; Oxford: Oxford Univ. Press, 1933.

Ronczewski, Konstantin. *Gewölbeschmuck im römischen Altertum: Studien und Aufnahmen*. Berlin: Georg Reimer, 1903.

Schwinzer, Ellen. *Schwebende Gruppen in der pompejanischen Wandmalerei*. Beiträge zur Archäologie 11. Würzburg: Konrad Triltsch, 1979.

Wadsworth, Emily L. "Stucco Reliefs of the First and Second Centuries Still Extant in Rome." *Memoirs of the American Academy in Rome* 4 (1924): 9–102.

# AUTHOR-TITLE INDEX

Adam, Sheila, *The Technique of Greek Sculpture in the Archaic and Classical Periods*, 153, 155

"Addenda to *Apulian Red-figure Vase-painters of the Plain Style*," Alexander Cambitoglou and Arthur Dale Trendall, 177, 178

Addison, Julia deWolf, *Classic Myths in Art*, 138, 140

"Additions to Monuments Illustrating Old and Middle Comedy," John Richard Green, 118, 121

*Aegean Painting in the Bronze Age*, Sara A. Immerwahr, 253, 256

Aellen, Christian, Alexander Cambitoglou, and Jacques Chamay, *Le peintre de Darius et son milieu*, 180, 181

Agard, Walter Raymond, *Classical Myths in Sculpture*, 139, 140

Aichholzer, Peter, *Darstellungen römischer Sagen*, 95

Akurgal, Ekrem, *The Art of Greece*, 25, 26

Alexander, Christine, and Peter H. v. Blanckenhagen, *The Paintings from Boscotrecase*, 261

Alföldi, Maria R.-, *Antike Numismatik*, 214, 223, 235

*Alinari Photo Archive from the Archivi Alinari, Florence*, 132, 136

*Allgemeines Lexikon der bildenden Künstler von der Antike bis zur Gegenwart*, Ulrich Thieme and Felix Becker, 131, 137, 150, 151

Alram, Michael, *Die Münzprägung des Kaisers Maximinus I. Thrax*, 235

Alscher, Ludger, *Griechische Plastik*, 152

*Altattische Malerei*, Karl Kübler, 166, 167

*The Amasis Painter and His World: Vase-painting in Sixth-Century B.C.*, Dietrich von Bothmer, 165, 167

*Amazons in Greek Art*, Dietrich von Bothmer, 116

Amyx, Darrell A., *Corinthian Vase-Painting of the Archaic Period*, 27

# SUBJECT INDEX

*prepared by Janet Russell*

Frances Van Keuren holds a bachelor's degree in Greek and Latin, and a Ph.D. in Classical Archaeology. She has been teaching ancient art history for the last eighteen years, during which time she saw the need for a research guide such as this one. Her research has focused on mythology in classical and post classical art, ancient numismatics, and research methods. Her recently published book *The Frieze from the Hera I Temple at Foce del Sele*, which proposes a new reconstruction for the architectural sculptures from a Greek temple in southern Italy, won a James R. Wiseman Book Award for 1991 from the Archaeological Institute of America.